W9-CLG-947

THEOLOGY IN THE CATHOLIC COLLEGE

THEOLOGY IN THE CATHOLIC COLLEGE

edited by

Reginald Masterson, O.P.

The Priory Press • Dubuque, Iowa

Revisores Ordinis: J. J. McDonald, O.P., S.T.M.; B. J. Endres, O.P., S.T.Lr., S.T.D. *Imprimi potest*: J. E. Marr, O.P., S.T.M., Prior Provinicalis. *Nihil obstat*: J. J. McDonald, O.P., S. T. M., Censor Librorum. *Imprimatur*: ✠Leo Binz, Archiepiscopus Dubuquensis, die 6a Martii, 1961.

First Printing

Library of Congress Card No. 61-11123

Printed in the United States of America

ACKNOWLEDGMENTS

Because of the broad scope of this volume it is impossible to adequately thank all those who have contributed to it indirectly. Special mention must be made, however, of the officials of The Priory Press, who have encouraged and supported the project since its inception, and of the authors (some of whom are among the most active and productive Dominican scholars in the United States), whose efforts will no doubt be rewarded by the satisfaction of having contributed to the apostolate of college theology. Thanks also must be extended to the Reverend F. L. B. Cunningham, O.P., S.T.Lr., S.T.D., who supervised the publication and without whose assistance in preparing these articles this volume would not have been possible; and finally, to the 1961 ordination class of the Province of St. Albert the Great, whose enthusiasm for their future apostolate prompted the initiation of the entire project.

With the grace of God may it prove a valuable aid to them and to all who are engaged in the work of theology in the Catholic college.

Reginald Masterson, O.P.

St. Rose Priory, Dubuque, Iowa
Feast of St. Thomas Aquinas
March 7, 1961

CONTENTS

THEOLOGY IN THE CATHOLIC COLLEGE

INTRODUCTION

Some twenty-five years ago Catholic educators approached the late Father Walter Farrell, O.P., with the lament that too often the graduates of Catholic colleges, soon after their departure from their Catholic educational environment, ceased to be militant Catholics. Indeed, these Catholic college graduates were often surpassed in zeal for the apostolate by fellow Catholics who did not enjoy the advantage of such higher education. An analytic survey of the situation revealed that the difficulty was not so much with the graduates as with the method in which religious education had been imparted to them; their defect was not of their making but a lack of the Catholic vision of things, of wisdom.

The Catholic way to make a man wise is through the integration of all his learning by focusing it upon God, the First Truth. A Catholic educated in this way sees things in their proper perspective; he possesses a distinctively Catholic vision of reality. His activity, guided by such a vision, is marked by confidence, expertness, maturity. To promote the truly Catholic way of religious education, the Dominican Fathers began an apostolate to restore theology to its rightful academic role in the Catholic college. Since the initiation of this work the teaching of theology has become their largest single work in the United States. Members of the three American Provinces are now teaching in approximately seventy Catholic colleges. The publications of The Priory Press, a publishing house under the auspices of the Province of St. Albert, are being used in well over 100 colleges, and *The Thomist*, founded in 1939 by the Fathers of the Province of St. Joseph as a quarterly review of speculative philosophy and theology, is found in the libraries of 95 per cent of the Catholic colleges.

With an ever increasing number of Dominican priests engaging in the college theology apostolate, it became apparent that special teacher preparation must be given to them to guarantee successful participation in it. It was towards such preparation that a seminar was begun several years ago at the theology house of studies of the midwestern province (St. Rose Priory, Dubuque, Iowa). As the seminar developed, it became apparent that graduates of theological seminaries, however well trained in the sources of divine revelation, in the scientific character of the nature of theology, in its principles and in the development of the various treatises, only too often did not possess theology as an acquired wisdom, as the vision which would enable them to judge all human learning, as all human activity, in the light of theological principles. Were they to enter the college classroom with this deficiency, they would be adequate to expose the scientific aspect of theology and to emphasize its speculative character in the investigation of the meaning, order and interrelation of divine mysteries; but they would not be able to make these truths meaningful precisely as they related to the student's quest for eternal happiness or as normative of his moral behavior, nor could they effectively contribute to the academic unity and wholeness of the higher learning.

Why this problem? On the one hand, the long absence of theology from the academic scene had resulted in the devitalization of its integrating function. As sudden intense physical activity can have fatal effects on a body which has lost its physical energy, so likewise many precipitate and abortive attempts at the restoration of this function had had calamitous results that frightened away the handmaids of this Queen of the sciences. Theologians often withdrew from the task in fear of failure. On the other hand, the effects of this integrating function had disappeared from the curriculum of the college. Once freed from such subordination, other intellectual disciplines threw up the smokescreen of past abuses by the theologian to avoid any danger of subservience. As a result, the oft stated truth that theology has an integrating role to exercise with regard to other intellectual pursuits remains for most theologians as for most educators a speculative truth, accorded lip-service in theology texts and college catalogs, but apparently incapable of practical realization.

One of the main purposes of this volume is to point the direction for the actual restoration of this specific function of theology. It is an essay—in reality a series of essays, in the primitive meaning of the word—that has not been undertaken without fear, nor in ignorance of past mistakes. Necessarily it had to be a co-operative venture, for no single theologian could be expected to be sufficiently trained in all the other disciplines to be able to provide truly intelligible practical solutions to the manifold problems which confront the college theology teacher as he faces his noble and complex task. This project, then, has been the fruit of several years of reflection and collaboration. Having seen the necessity for such a work, an effort was made to determine the ideal outline of contents; when this was completed, there arose the even greater task of finding suitable authors to provide the required studies. In the fulfillment of the task the ideal was not completely realized, and not all the possible areas of investigation have been adequately treated. But after examination of the contributions received by an experienced group of college theology teachers, the careful judgment was reached that the scope actually realized was sufficiently comprehensive, the studies completed sufficiently penetrating, to justify publication.

It was inevitable that a group of articles written about such closely related aspects of a single subject would result in a material coincidence of problems treated. This overlapping was retained wherever it was felt essential to the integral presentation of the individual subject matter of a particular article. Moreover, one will note divergence of viewpoint among the authors. Rather than detracting from the presentation, it can be hoped that such divergency will serve as a reminder to the reader that the volume is not intended to be a definitive answer to the problems under investigation. It is impossible to furnish a general answer that will prove workable in every concrete situation. These studies, in short, are the present expression of the thought of those who are engaged actively in the apostolate of college theology and intended to serve as a guide to further investigation.

Of their nature they mark a beginning, not an end.

1

THEOLOGY IN THE CATHOLIC COLLEGE*

Walter Farrell, O.P., S.T.M.

A pioneer in the restoration of theology to its rightful place in the Catholic college, the late Father Walter Farrell, O.P., S.T.M., was a theological light for the Church in general; more particularly, his ideal of the Dominican intellectual apostolate remains as an abiding inspiration to his American brethren. Best known for his widely acclaimed four-volume A Companion to the Summa, *the following article might well be classified as the "keynote address" to all his theological creativity as well as to this series of studies.*

Every man guides the steps of his life by wisdom, or a counterfeit of it. For every man must act in the light of some supreme value, some last end.[1] Seeing his days, his years, all his works in the light of this goal to which all else is subordinated is to see with the eyes of some kind of wisdom.

This wisdom may be a counterfeit, leaving its victim stupid, though his comfort never be disturbed by the knowledge of his stupidity. His final goal, for example, can be mundane, and his vision, consequently, the vision of worldly wisdom. His goal can be one of hedonistic devotion to pleasure, giving him a vision of animal wisdom. Or it can be a diabolic wisdom that sees all things only in the light of

*This article is re-printed with permission from the *Catholic Educational Review*, XLVIII (1950), 289-298. The editor has taken the liberty of making such minor emendations as make Fr. Farrell's perennial wisdom applicable to the changed academic conditions of the '60s.

one's own pride. Theoretically, it would be possible for a man to view his life purely in terms of man's natural powers and to estimate these powers without error; he might, then, theoretically have the vision of the wisdom of the philosophically wise man who sees all of life in the light of nature's goals. But this is theoretical.[2] In fact, man lives in a supernatural order; in fact, man's nature has been wounded by sin; in fact, no man escapes error in his own thinking; in fact, man cannot find his fulfillment within the limits of nature.[3]

The only available wisdom remaining for the true guidance of the life of man is the divine wisdom, either as it is divinely infused in us, or as it can be acquired from the starting point of divinely revealed principles. The first is the divinely infused virtue of faith and its perfection through the infused gift of the Holy Ghost. This wisdom is the common possession of all those in the state of grace, whether they be nine years old or ninety; these are gifts that can be instantly lost by our perverse action. The second or acquired wisdom is the science of theology, proceeding to a body of conclusions from the divinely revealed principles of faith.

A discussion as to theology in colleges, then, is inescapably a discussion as to the plausibility of giving college men and women the only true adequate wisdom which can be acquired through the efforts of the human mind. Is there room in the colleges for the only wisdom a man can acquire? Shall Catholic colleges be concerned only with learning because secular colleges find it impossible to give wisdom? Is stupidity (the contrary of wisdom) an inevitable concomitant of learning? Must the colleges insist upon stupidity in their graduates? Understand, please, that I am not using epithets here; this is the technical and accurate word, stupidity, for the absence of wisdom.

With the question posed as frankly and honestly as this (you'll admit it is frank; I can prove it is rigidly honest), it becomes evident that there are two questions which never should have been asked in this matter, namely: can theology be taught in college? should theology be taught in college? However, these questions have been asked; indeed, they are the questions that have engaged most attention in recent years.

By way of puttng these questions to one side for the rest of our discussion, let me summarize their answers briefly.[4] *Can* theology be taught in college? Well, if the question means can you turn out professional theologians, the answer is, of course, negative. The same would be true of a college course in mathematics as far as producing mathematical wizards, or college chemistry as far as producing finished research chemists. But if the question is, can a human science be imparted to college students, can an intellectual habit, to some degree of perfection, be cultivated in the minds of men and women of college age—well, the answer must be affirmative. A negative answer can be given only under pain of condemning all students as morons and all professors as utterly incompetent in this field. It can be done, for it is a human thing, acquired by the human processes of the mind of man proceeding from principles to conclusions. Every normal student can acquire something of this intellectual habit by the normal process of working at it under the guidance of a professor with an ordinary possession of this science. The subnormal men and women should not be in college as students; nor, for that matter, as professors. On the factual side, the thing has been done, and is being done in many Catholic colleges today.

If it can be done, *should* we teach theology in college? St. Thomas insisted that the study of wisdom is, of all the pursuits of man, the more perfect, more sublime, more useful and more full of delight.[5] Nor is he arguing about a perfect grasp of wisdom, for he insists, "knowledge of the noblest things, however imperfect, confers the greatest perfection on the soul."[6] He maintains that "it is useful for the human mind to be exercised in these reasonings, however feeble they may be" in comparison with the objects of this knowledge.[7] I have argued elsewhere that this science of theology, this divinely human wisdom, is the principle of integration of the Catholic's knowledge and the source of the perspective of wisdom, both of which are the distinctive boasts of the Catholic college.[8] In strict justice, the Catholic student has a right to expect at least this from the Catholic college. Should we teach theology in college? Rather, how can we possibly justify the lack of wisdom in a college that is Catholic?

These two questions really shouldn't be asked. The answers are so completely obvious, while contrary arguments are simply evasions of the issue. There are no good reasons why the student's mind should not be matured by the science of the faith, as it is matured in every other line of intellectual endeavor in the college.

Teaching College Theology

With these two questions to one side, we can and should focus our attention on the really pertinent questions. How can you teach theology in college? What good will the imparting of this science do?

In approaching the question of how theology can be taught in college, it is essential that we distinguish the radical and absolutely essential method from the immediate, proximate methods which over-lie this solid foundation. The first cannot be departed from in the inculcation of any science. The distinction between the two is some-thing like the distinction to be made between the part played by the skeletal formation in determining the shape of a man and the part played by the disposition of the flesh on those bones. Without the bones, however careful you are of the flesh, all you have is a formless, shapeless heap. Without this radical method of teaching a science, the student, in the words of Thomas, is sent away "empty as a vacuum."[9]

Though it may be superfluous to outline this fundamental method for a group of college professors, yet, for the sake of completeness—and because in this subject matter it has been repeatedly overlooked—let me say it again. To impart a science, you must begin at the be-ginning with the evident principles; go from them, step by step, to conclusions; from these more particular principles you go on to still more detailed conclusions, and so on down the line. Beginning at the beginning, moving step by step, down through the middle to the end. Any other procedure defeats the end of teaching, which is properly the imparting of a science or an intellectual habit. If you begin in the middle, skip huge chunks of the intermediary processes, make your points by the thunder of your voice or the awful dignity of your presence, you may give the student some disparate information, an opinion, faith in your words—but you do not lead him from a knowledge of what he knows to a knowledge of what has formerly been unknown; you do not teach.

To attain the primary end of teaching, to impart a science, you must follow a perfect order, with complete integrity of essential material, and by the rational method of proceeding from principle to conclusion. This is the constant burden of St. Thomas' emphasis in *De Magistro,* for this, above all, is the thing that must be said to a teacher. "Knowledge of principles produces a science of conclusions in us."[10] "The proximate effective principle of science is not signs, but reason running from principles to conclusions."[11] The certitude of science comes entirely from certitude of the principles: then only are the conclusions known certainly when they are reduced to the principles: ". . . not by a man exteriorly teaching, unless insofar as he reduces the conclusions to principles, teaching us."[12]

The intellectual vision of the professor is the immediate principle of his teaching; but the teaching will consist rather in the transfusion of the science of the things seen than in the vision of them. The teacher is not a contemplative sharing his contemplation, but a man doing a chore in the active life by imparting the intellectual perfection which will enable others to see for themselves.[13] As a matter of fact, the teacher has a humble work, as humble as the housemaid's throwing up of a shade to let the light of the sun in; for what the teacher does is to remove the impediments to our seeing the light of truth. If he is at all successful, the sun will shine in our minds, we will see for ourselves the connection between principle and conclusion.[14]

Granted this inviolable method, the primary object of teaching—the imparting of an intellectual habit—is safeguarded. Any infringement on this method, either as regards order, integrity of essential matter or rational processes, will assure the student of an empty mind though he may have a crowded memory. The immediate or proximate methods overlying this fundamental one will be dictated by such considerations as the uses to which the acquired science is to be put: in the case of theology, obviously the science can be put to use for the work of the priest, for the lay apostolate, for personal sanctification, for the fuller flowering of domestic happiness, for the perfection of the social order—in a word to all the uses to which true wisdom is applicable. Other elements determining these proximate methods are the condition of the students, the time that can be filched for the course, and so on. The variety of these methods will be one of emphasis, of compression or of expansion, methods of inciting the students to the necessary work, checks on student labors, and so on.

Most of the objections to college theology flow from a concentration on these immediate, proximate methods to the obliteration of the radical and inviolable method which is essential to all teaching.[15] When the primary objective is clearly seen, namely, the imparting of an intellectual habit, it is hard to understand the truncations and mutilations that have been proposed—and by teachers—in the name of the immediate or proximate methods. It is hard, for example, to justify the selection of a few chunks from the material of this science as being eminently and sufficiently satisfying to the layman's needs: say the Incarnation, marriage, the sacraments, the Mass. Or, on the basis of the interests of freshmen, to begin towards the end, upsetting the order of the science, with human details of Christ's life. The parade of a professor's knowledge in untouchable lectures which the student endures passively is inexcusable in view of the primary objective of intellectual habit; for a habit of thinking, of course, demands exercise. Sheer boredom or laziness on the part of the faculty may settle for a "practical course" consisting, say, of a year on the life of Christ (devotionally treated, of course); another year on the liturgy, liturgical prayer, the Mass; marriage is always good for a year, with plenty of interesting detours and blind alleys to keep the class lively; to fill up the four years, if the religion course staggers through that far, there are always such possibilities as "life problems," "Catholic action" or "social Christianity."

In all this, we have pushed the prime objective, the imparting of a science, far out of sight. I have said elsewhere:

> This divine science . . . cannot be had unless God is its beginning, center and end; it cannot be distorted as to order or substantial con-

tent. It is not to be had through piecemeal or selective presentation of this or that mystery; it is a body of related, tightly interwoven conclusions. Concentration on its sources is not a communication of the divine wisdom;[16] nor is a presentation whose complete appeal is to the pictures of the imagination or the details of history. Certainly it cannot be had by concentration on man or humanity, not even the humanity of Christ. In the very beginning of his *Summa Theologiae,*[17] St. Thomas had warned us: "God is in very truth the object of this science. . . . Some, however, looking to what is treated of in science, and not to the aspect under which it is treated, have asserted the object of this science to be something other than God—that is, either things and signs; or the works of salvation; or the whole Christ, as the head and members. Of all these things, in truth, we treat in this science, but so far as they have reference to God."[18]

The Wisdom of Faith

What good will it do to teach theology in college? Some of its benefits should be clear from the considerations just given. However, to make its benefits clearer, let us look at them under some separate headings. 1) What good will the teaching of theology do from a purely academic point of view? 2) What good will it do to the student group? 3) What enduring benefits can be expected of it among the graduates of such a course?

In answer to the first question, it is clear that the intellectual maturity conferred by the acquisition of an intellectual habit—the acquisition of science—is an objective worthy of the endeavors of a college. For by this, teaching has lived up to its purpose, education is accomplished, and the student is thus equipped to further educate himself in this science; he has the equipment to think, to search, to learn. As St. Thomas would put it, he is now not in both an essential and an accidental potency to know truths of this order (e.g., infant and sight), but merely in the accidental potency; now all he needs is to have his attention drawn to the thing to be known (e.g., point a finger for more to see).[19] When the science in question is theology, the student is being given intellectual maturity in his faith to match the mental maturity he acquires in college in other lines; and is thus equipped to further educate himself, to use the intellctual tool of habit.

Taking the thing comparatively, this intellectual habit of theology will give more of perfection than any other study the student engages in; for this is the supreme humanly divine wisdom, and insofar as a man gives himself to the study of wisdom he already has a share of true happiness. It is more sublime, because through it a man especially approaches the likeness of God who made all things in his wisdom. Because likeness is a cause of love, the pursuit of wisdom particularly leads to the union of man to God through friendship.[20]

The penalty for not giving the student this science is, in this matter, to send him away intellectually empty. Without any name calling, but in the strictest use of the terms, this means to send the student away stupid; for stupidity is the absence of wisdom.

How about the student group? What effect will a theology course have on it? The obvious procedure in relation to this question is to have recourse to the actual student groups who have had this course for a couple of years, or to check with the college authorities as to their judgment of the student group as a result of this course. I do most earnestly invite you to make such an inquiry. Among the things you will discover is that this science rapidly becomes the leading topic of discussion among the students. Each class opens up new horizons which the mind cheerfully rushes to investigate, and students will cudgel each other by the hour on the interpretations, applications, significations of the newest things that are yet so very old. No, this is not an optimistic exaggeration. It is what should be expected. St. Thomas long ago insisted that the pursuit of wisdom was by far the most delightful of all the studies of man because there was no bitterness in its intimacy, no boredom in its findings, but only joy and gladness.[21]

This is what the mind of man was made for, of course it enters into it joyfully; this is the mystery on which the mind of man is nourished and grows, of course it reaches out for it hungrily. Coming from one who knew well the bitter labor of study, there is special weight to Thomas' claim that wisdom turns bitterness to sweetness and labor to rest;[22] a claim borne out by this modern student response to the science of theology. They find themselves, these students, plunged into discussion in all their social contacts; and why not, since this science will always have wider and deeper applications than any other. More profoundly, more quietly, sometimes with a certain reluctance, the student is forced into making wisdom's inevitable applications to personal life; and again, why not, since by this science we judge human things and human actions in the light of the divine.[23]

As for the graduates, the alumni and alumnae, well, granted a proper inculcation of this science, you have sent them out into life with the intellectual equipment, and the positive appetite, to educate themselves further in this science. They have wisdom, as the efforts of man achieve it from the starting point of divine truths. Since everyone must order his own acts and judge them,[24] you have put them in a position to live and act wisely. In concrete terms you have loosed on the world not only Catholics who are leaders, but Catholics who are leaders because of their Catholic wisdom; not merely good Catholics, but good thinking Catholics. The apostolic benefit conferred upon the millions of their contemporaries who stagger through life by the distorting light of false wisdoms is incalculable.

You see, the wisdom of faith and the wisdom of the gift of the Holy Ghost are gifts given for personal sanctification; they confer nothing at all *per se* by way of capacity to guide or enlighten others. If for this we are to depend entirely upon God, then we must hope and pray for the gifts freely given (*gratiae gratis datae*); on the other hand, the human acquisition of the divine wisdom of theology by the very manner of its achievement assures the ability to communicate it. We can be teachers of men because we have wisdom to give to them in the only way that men can be taught.

Perhaps the benefit to graduates is best seen in terms of the full implications of the absence of wisdom. For the completely accurate and technical term for the lack of wisdom is stupidity. That stupidity implies, and guarantees, a sluggishness of heart and obtuseness of faculties in sharp contrast to the clarity of wisdom's vision, particularly in the highest and most important steps in a man's life.[25] This stupidity assures an ineptness in perceiving the divine light that dissipates the imprisoning darkness of the world. Isidore had defined a stupid man as one whose soul is undisturbed by sorrow and ignominy and who is unmoved by injury; upon which St. Thomas elaborates by explaining that the utter depths of stupidity are reached when a man doesn't even know he is injured. This is stupidity at its finest, *simpliciter*,[26] when, for example, he doesn't even recognize, let alone resent, attacks on his dignity, his family, his love, his very humanity —the sort of attacks which are routine in American intellectual circles today.

On the other hand, this divinely wise man who possesses the science of theology has the full heritage of his faith's treasures, the keys to unlock still more treasure rooms, the light to flood his own days and to guide the steps of others. He is an intellectually mature Catholic. Shall he be allowed to grow up in a Catholic college? Or must he be kept at the infantile stage because there are so many important subjects in college that we have no time for this maturing? It is time, I think, that we gave up the comforting pretense that there is some choice in this matter and admit frankly that the canons of justice and honesty apply to us as well as to the rest of men.

Footnotes to Study 1

[1]St. Thomas, *Summa,* I-II, q. 1, a. 6.

[2]Largely theoretical; wholly inadequate.

[3]St. Thomas, *op. cit.,* II-II, q. 45, aa. 2, 4 and 5.

[4]For a fuller answer to these important questions, see my article, "Theology in Catholic Colleges," *Proceedings of the National Catholic Educational Association,* XLVIII (1946), 239-44.

[5]I *Con. Gent.,* Chap. 2.

[6]*Ibid.,* Chap. 5.

[7]*Ibid.,* Chap. 8.

[8]Cf. *art. cit.,* 242-243.

[9]*Quod. IV,* a. 18.

[10]*Q. D. de Ver.,* q. 11, a. 1, ad 2.

[11]*Ibid.,* ad 4.

[12]*Ibid.,* ad 13; cf. the body of the article.

[13]*Ibid.,* a. 4, ad 3.

[14]*Ibid.,* a. 3, Sed Contra 6.

[15]Cf., for example, "Religion for College Students," by Rev. W. H. Russell, *Proceedings of the National Catholic Educational Association,* XLVIII (1946), 215 ff.; "Towards a Theology for the Layman," by J. C. Murray, S.J., *Theological Studies,* V (1944), 43-75.

[16]Cf. St. Thomas, *Quod. IV,* a. 18.

[17]I, q. 1, a. 7.

[18]*Art. cit.,* 243.

[19]Cf. *Q. D. de Ver.,* q. 11, a. 1, ad 12.

[20]St. Thomas makes these points explicitly; cf. I *Con. Gent.,* Chap. 2.

[21]*Loc. cit.*

[22]*Summa,* II-II, q. 45, a. 3, ad 3.

[23]*Ibid.,* a. 3 and ad 1.

[24]*Ibid.,* ad 2.

[25]Cf. St. Thomas, *Summa,* II-II, q. 46, a. 1 and ad 1.

[26]*Ibid.,* ad 4.

2

THE ROLE OF CATHOLIC COLLEGE EDUCATION

Thomas C. Donlan, O.P.

Ever since the publication of his Theology and Education *Father Donlan has been a recognized authority in this field. A Doctor of Sacred Theology, he was professor of moral theology at the Dominican theological studium, St. Rose Priory, Dubuque, Iowa, for many years. Twice president of the Society of Catholic College Teachers of Sacred Doctrine, past vice-president of the Catholic Theological Society, at present he is vice-president of The Priory Press. He collaborated on the very successful College Texts in Theology series published by that firm.*

No cogent discussion of the role of Catholic college education can be carried on in isolation from the larger problems of which this is but a part. It will be necessary, therefore, to survey some fundamental notions about Catholic education generally as a preface to the determination of the role of Catholic college education.

In its widest sense, education comprises whatever tends to the improvement and perfecting of the human being. More precisely, education refers to all the efforts of elders that are directed to lead the young to a greater degree of personal participation in the general culture. It is clear that education thus understood is a vastly extensive process embracing the efforts of parents, schools, churches and government. It is also clear that the complexity of contemporary culture superimposed upon the complexities of the human beings who are to be educated must make the total educational process an extremely involved undertaking.

An understanding of any complex reality requires careful analysis, as an apprentice watchmaker must disassemble an intricate timepiece if he is to understand its workings. Yet analysis is only the first step, for this must be followed by synthesis for true understanding. The alternative is the contemplation of the chaos of unrelated multiplicity. The parts must be reassembled in proper order if the watch is to become a timepiece.

Let us begin, then, by a brief analysis of the general principles of Catholic education as a prelude to understanding the role of the college within that framework.

The General Principles of Catholic Education

Ultimately, all education is a practical undertaking. In practical affairs, the most important question concerns purpose: what is the goal of Catholic education? Briefly, the final goal of education is identical with the ultimate end of life itself. "It is therefore as important to make no mistake in education as it is to make no mistake in the pursuit of the last end, with which the whole work of education is intimately and necessarily connected. In fact, since education consists essentially in preparing man for what he must be and for what he must do here below in order to attain the sublime end for which he was created, it is clear that there can be no true education which is not wholly directed to man's last end, and that in the present order of providence, since God has revealed himself to us in the person of his only begotten Son, who alone is 'the way, the truth and the life,' there can be no ideally perfect education which is not Christian education."[1]

On the one hand, it is impossible to distinguish Catholic education from other Christan undertakings in terms of the absolutely ultimate end which is common to them all; on the other hand, it is possible to distinguish Catholic education from other systems which are directed to some different ultimate end. The absolutely ultimate end must, of its very nature, be unique, because there cannot be two ultimates in the same order. It follows from this that no Catholic educator should derive any comfort from seeing some remarkable resemblance between his system and any other that is not wholly ordained to a goal that can be known only by divine faith.

Always subordinate to the ultimate purpose of life itself, which is to see God as he is himself, education attains a proper and distinctive goal that is ultimate in its own sphere. "The proper and immediate end of Christian education is to co-operate with divine grace in forming the true and perfect Christian, that is, to form Christ himself in those regenerated by baptism."[2] This is the proper and immediate end of Christian education taken in the broader sense to include the activities of the Church, home, school, state and the effects of the social environment. No one of these agencies attains the goal in isolation from the rest, but by the discharge of its proper function each agency contributes toward the common end.

Each educational agency has its own proper end by which it is distinguished from other agencies. Thus the home enjoys a primacy of natural right in all that pertains to the education of the child, and this by reason of the basic title of parenthood. The Church, by virtue of her title of supernatural motherhood, enjoys a primacy of supernatural right in the education of her own subjects precisely as Christian. The state, by virtue of its direct relation to the temporal common good, enjoys a primacy of natural right in education for citizenship and civic responsibility precisely in view of good social order. Among the three basic societies into which the child is born, viz., the family, Church and state, there exist a due subordination and co-ordination of rights which must be determined in view of the absolutely ultimate end for which they all exist, the education of the whole man.[3]

Because the same identical person is subject in different ways to all three educational agencies, there is bound to be a certain amount of overlapping in their efforts. This gives rise to the possibility of confusion which can be avoided only by careful delineation of responsibility and by a co-operative discharge of duty on the part of each. Confusion in this very delicate area not only harms the common good but also invades, and sometimes curtails, the very basic rights of the child himself. It is regrettable that today these rights of the child are often neglected both in discussion and application of educational theory.

The school is not among the primary agencies of education. Indeed, its entire authority to teach is derived from that of the parents and the Church, and it is subject to the direction of the state in matters pertaining to good social order. A key to understanding the role of the school is found in the fact that the encyclical *On The Christian Education of Youth* does not begin to speak of the school until the final one-third of its entire length: "Since, however, the younger generations must be trained in the arts and sciences for the advantage and prosperity of civil society, and since the family of itself is unequal to this task, it was necessary to create that social institution, the school."[4]

Herein we find a most fundamental and fruitful distinction between *education* and *schooling*. These are not coextensive terms. Schooling is a part of that whole which is education. The proper and distinctive role of the school is to train the young ". . . in the arts and sciences for the advantage and prosperity of civil society." This is to say that the inculcation of the intellectual virtues is the primary and distinctive goal attained by schooling.

To maintain that the intellectual virtues are the primary and distinctive goal of schools is to state a principle of subordination, not a principle of exclusion.[5] In Christian thought there is no place for theories which deny the need for moral influence in schools or which maintain the objective superiority of intellectual formation over the life of grace. But neither does Christian thought prove congenial to confused thinking which would grant primacy to grace in every area of human effort. No one would defend the view that Catholic doctors should be better trained in the theology and technique of baptism than in the theory and practice of obstetrics. Yet every Christian agrees that salvation is more important than safe delivery. The hallmark of reason enlightened by faith is *orderly* progress toward the ultimate end through the attainment of intermediate goals. Like every other agency of Christian education, the school is subject to the moral law and must actively promote a Christian environment, but the primary and distinctive goal of the school is the training of the mind. This goal is primary simply because learning is the immediate result of teaching; it is distinctive because the school is designed precisely for academic instruction. All of education involves some kind of learning, generally fortuitous as to order. Schools are designed to teach the arts of learning and communication in academic order according to the norms of pedagogy, and from this beginning to exercise the mind in the arts and sciences.

Let us repeat: the school is not one of the primary agencies of education but an instrument set up by them, imperfect and incomplete. While its basic function *as school* can be determined philosophically, it may possess other functions attributed to it as an institution, and these can only be discovered by investigating the positive law which constitutes it. In the case of the Catholic school (elementary, secondary or university), it is the pope and bishops who, as divinely appointed teachers, must determine the further function and scope of the school as it is an institution of their making. Beyond any doubt, over and above their function as schools, Catholic schools should co-operate immediately and proximately in the common educational task of forming the whole man, for such is the mind of their institutors. Albert Cardinal Meyer, Archbishop of Chicago, seems accurately to express this other function of the school according to the mind of the popes and the American hierarchy when he writes:

> If in the welter of current opinions, we are to remain faithful to the education principles constantly set forth by our recent popes, it seems to me that our chief task is this: we must devise a balanced program aiming at intellectual excellence and intensive spiritual perfection, with all of it ordered toward the welfare of the individual student and then of the social order of his era. In other words we must seek to educate the complete person to virtue or excellence of all his faculties natural and supernatural, that he in turn may leaven the social order with the principles of Christ. This is the synthesis for which Pius XII has called, especially in our Catholic universities.[6]

Does this other function militate against or change the primary function of the school, the training in the arts and sciences? Not at all. Rather, the school co-operates precisely as an adjunct to the Church and family to assist in the formation of moral virtues in order that the intellectual virtues will be best utilized for the attainment of the student's supernatural goal. In the Christian school, study, like teaching, is undertaken out of the love of God, and the truth gained by it acts as an inspiration and guide to a deeper love of God and a more perfect observance of his commandments. In such a conception, moral, spiritual and intellectual developments powerfully assist one another. This does not mean, of course, that non-academic activities undertaken for the spiritual formation of the student or consequent on the primary function of the school are excluded; it does mean that they must be judiciously chosen lest they obstruct the fulfillment of the teacher's duty to teach and the student's duty to study. And it does mean that that anti-intellectual spirit which converts the school into an institution for "life-adjustment"—the spirit which animates "progressive education"—is alien to Catholic school tradition, whatever the undeniable merits of some of the particular proposals of the "progressive" program; and no less alien would be an anti-intellectual pietism which would convert the school into a retreat-house.

To sum up, we may re-cast these thoughts in a scholastic analogy. The school is an instrument of the family, the Church, the state. Like any instrument, it has its proper nature and power, its specific operation; but over and above this it participates in the higher power of the principal agent, communicated to it to attain an effect beyond its native capacity, although proper to the principal agent. As a moral being, the school's function *as school* determines its nature, its native powers, its proper activity; the proximate and immediate end of such a social institution is to inculcate intellectual virtue (analogously at different levels), its specific means are teaching and learning (study). As an instrument of the Church, the school's function as institution is incomparably higher, for it shares in the power and the apostolate of the Church herself (in virtue of the Church's institution) to form the will as well as train the intellect, to implement the Church's integral educational program, to educate the complete person. But like any instrument, it can only attain the effect of the principal agent through its own proper power and operation; only through attaining its proximate and immediate aim of intellectual education can the Christian school achieve that nobler aim for which Christ's Church has created it.[7]

Virtue and the Christian School

The Church insists that Catholics attend Catholic schools, and she makes great sacrifices to provide schools for her children. It is important to recognize that this is not simply provision for moral security, but that it is also an insistence upon academic superiority. The Church holds forth a high ideal of academic excellence which cannot be realized by an institution that relies upon spiritual advantages to supply for demonstrable academic deficiencies. The truth of these statements need not be supported by lengthy quotations from authoritative sources (although this could be done); their truth comes forth from the fundamental Christian view of total reality, and particularly of man's role in the divine plan.

The indispensable elements in any school are teachers and students, and both have specific and distinctive vocations in the Christian life. Each in his own measure and in his proper function must make the life of learning a repayment of divine love. If the Old Law forbade the offering of blighted and defective sacrifices, surely the demands of the Christian vocation of study or teaching cannot be met by incompetence or indolence.

The school, then, precisely as a Christian institution, necessarily confronts us with the problem of the interrelationship of the moral and intellectual virtues in the service of Christian perfection. And an understanding of this relationship between moral and intellectual virtue in Christian schooling requires, in turn, a clear concept of the relationship between the intellect and the will.

These two supreme faculties of human nature are extremely complex. They cannot be compared by some simple measurement, like a scale which would determine with finality which is the superior power. Intellect and will may be compared both absolutely in relation to their proper nature and objects, and relatively in terms of something extrinsic and accidental to their natures. Thus sight is absolutely superior to taste in terms of its superior object, but relatively it is better to taste something delicious than to see something ugly.

The object of the intellect is being, which is the simplest and least restricted of all for it is coextensive with reality without any qualification. The object of the will is the good, and goodness adds the note of desirability to being. Hence the object of the will is more qualified and more complex than the simple and universal reality of being. For a thing to be known, it need only be made the object of man's attention; for a thing to be willed, it must first be known as good and desirable for him who wants it. A confirmation of this is had in the fact that man's ultimate happiness consists essentially in a direct, intuitive knowledge of God as he is in himself; the will's part in man's beatitude, the enjoyment of God, comes as a consequence to the beatific vision.

In relation to some particular object, however, the will can enjoy superiority over the intellect in this life. The intellect draws all being to man's level, elevating and ennobling the things beneath him and drawing down the things above him. Thus knowledge of evil does not degrade a man; the Angelic Doctor had expert knowledge of the most shameful vices. Knowledge is always completed at man's own level. Love, on the other hand, terminates in the things that are loved, and not in the will itself. Hence in this life it is better to love God than simply to know him, and it is worse to love things beneath us than to know them.

All this must be viewed against the fact that the will can love only what the intellect knows, for the will is a blind faculty dependent upon the light of knowledge for what it can seek. There is a sense, then, in which it is better "to feel compunction than know how to define it," but it remains true that one must know something of compunction before he can desire to experience it.

Intellect and will, however, are not competitors. They are congenial powers operating in the person.[8] Their respective roles can be identified; they cannot be separated. The whole man is subject to education, but his mind is the special object of teaching in the schools. This is a matter of emphasis on the faculties of learning, it is not an exclusion of the powers of loving, nor of their education.

Man realizes both his human and divine potentialities through the cultivation of virtue, by which he assumes self-control over his natural and supernatural faculties. The moral virtues bespeak a change in man's very being, because they make him good and his operations good, true means to his last end. The intellectual virtues beget an improvement only in man's operations; by them he acquires promptness, ease and delight in his distinctively rational acts, but not necessarily the good use of these acts. The acquired virtues make man more human, and, in conjunction with infused virtues, they make him more divine.

Intellectual and moral virtues, then, are designed to exist harmoniously. This important fact has been well stated by Pierre H. Conway, O.P., in his *Principles of Education, A Thomistic Approach*:

> A complete "education" in the mind of Aristotle and St. Thomas will provide in a single framework not only for the intellectual virtues but also for the moral virtues without which the former cannot genuinely thrive. Thus Aristotle envisions the acquisition of the moral and the intellectual virtues as part of a continuing unified development: "Now in men rational principle and mind are the end toward which nature strives, so that the birth and natural discipline of the citizens ought to be ordered with a view to them. . . . Wherefore, the care of the body ought to precede that of the soul, and the training of the appetitive part should follow; nonetheless, our care of it must be for the sake of reason, and our care of the body for the sake of the soul" (*Politics,* Bk. VII, Chap. 15 [1334b 10]).
>
> This same interdependence of the moral and intellectual virtues involved in Aristotle's and St. Thomas' concept of education is emphasized when Aristotle begins to treat of the virtues in Book II of the *Ethics.* At this point St. Thomas states: ". . . in the first part [Aristotle] determines concerning the moral virtues. In the second, concerning the intellectual virtues, in Book VI. . . . And the reason for the order is because the moral virtues are more known and through them we are disposed to the intellectual virtues" (*In Decem Libros Ethicorum Aristotelis ad Nicomachum Expositio,* II, lect. 1, n. 245 [Spiazzi]).[9]

Hence the schools cannot be indifferent to moral training—no school can function in an atmosphere of moral anarchy. The Christian school, in fact, is far from indifferent to the values of grace and faith. The contrary is true:

> It is necessary not only that religious instruction be given to the young at certain fixed times but also that every other subject taught be permeated with Christian piety. If this is wanting, if this sacred atmosphere does not pervade and warm the hearts of masters and

> scholars alike, little good can be expected from any kind of learning, and considerable harm will often be the consequence.[10]

But the intellectual arts and virtues are the primary pattern of academic education, to be sure, for they are the natural results of teaching. Learning is the natural result of teaching and study. Learning is growth in the arts and virtues of the intellect. Knowledge is the immediate result of schooling, because it is the very first result and it precedes any other, even though some of the other results may be objectively more important. Thus the use one makes of sacred doctrine is more important than the learning of it, but the learning must come first. There just isn't any other way to proceed.

Learning is the distinctive result of schooling. This does not mean that all lessons, or even the most important lessons, are learned in school. It simply means that the school, and the school alone, is specifically designed for learning. Throughout life men learn things as they happen to come along; in school under the guidance of teachers men learn things precisely as they should occur according to the art of pedagogy. The school does much more than teach, and some of the other things are more important than the teaching, but teaching and learning distinguish the school from all other educational agencies.

That the school is a force in moral training cannot be denied. That it is not the ideal or principal cause in moral training is evident in the disordered behavior of those who lack other moral forces in their lives because of poor home conditions, lack of religious instruction and other causes. The school depends for its authority on the more basic social units. The school is the creature of the family, the state and the Church, and it cannot be expected to function as their substitute or replacement.

The atmosphere of even the best schools is not sufficiently personal, sympathetic or understanding to replace the moral force of a family. The best teacher and the most competent administration never approach the dignity and majesty of the Church as a moral force. The most progressive school, wholly dedicated to "learning to do by doing," can never approximate the educational effects gained from actual participation in civic life. Alma Mater commands pathetically weak allegiance in comparison with the ties of blood in the family, the bond of faith in the Church, or the devotion of patriotism to the homeland. All of this serves to indicate that the school is not an all-sufficient force in moral training. Indeed, whatever efficacy the school may enjoy in moral training is in proportion to its union with the family, the Church and the state, of which it is an extension, not a competitor.

Schools should create and maintain a thoroughly Christian atmosphere by means suitable to their purpose, but they should not be conceived or operated as centers of indoctrination or as hot-houses whose plants will perish in the chilly atmosphere of the world outside. They should be, in the words of Pius XI, training-grounds of Christian learning "in the arts and sciences for the advantage and prosperity of civil society." Sharing in the role and power of the Church, they will, of course, be a great deal more; but they must first be what they natively are before they can become effective instruments.

The Levels of Schooling

Man's growth is a gradual progress through illimitable stages. At what precise moment does the boy become a man? His growth in virtue is similar. There are stages in education, degrees of virtue, and schools must be accommodated to them.

In the beginning of schooling *at the elementary level,* there must be a strong emphasis upon moral discipline. The school must take care of the very young while it leads the children through the first steps of academic progression. The academic aspects of schooling should become more emphasized as the child grows older and begins to form habits of study.

Elementary education embraces a period of the child's life when experience is accumulated rapidly and when it first takes on a synthetic unity by being expressed in formulae. The child grasps a great deal of information at the early stages of schooling. Although he is generally unable to formulate experience for himself, he is quite able to memorize formulations which he is taught, and he is capable of understanding them when they are explained to him in terms of analogues which he already knows. Thus the child comes to know stories taken from history or from the Bible or from folklore. He learns rhymes, songs and numbers. As memory improves, he learns the art of correct speech and comes to a nascent ability to organize his thoughts in terms of words and sentences. He begins to acquire basic arithmetical skills. He learns new prayers in addition to those he was taught at home.

In the early grades, the child comes to learn the truths of faith formulated in the catechism. The questions and answers epitomize the sacred truths he has learned heretofore in stories, songs, pictures and prayers. These formulae should be memorized, because the child cannot be expected to formulate these truths for himself. In elementary education, that is the task of teachers.

Once the formulae of the catechism are memorized, they should be applied to the other knowledge he is acquiring. The idea that God is the Creator of heaven and earth and of all things should become a focal point for the child's varied experiences and knowledge of reality. The multiplicity of duties to which he is bound should be unified in the idea that God made him to know, love and serve him in this life so as to be happy with him forever in the next. Thus through the catechism the child is given the solid foundation of a true Christian attitude, and his knowledge of mundane things is enhanced by seeing them in their divine context.

Elementary education should lay the solid foundations of literacy. At the end of this period of schooling, the youngster should be able to read, write, spell, calculate and remember with facility. He should have a solid grounding in the catechism, with special emphasis upon the sacraments he has received and receives, the liturgical functions he shares, the duties he must discharge, and the prayers he should say.

Secondary schooling marks the beginning of advanced education. Upon the foundations laid in elementary school, the student should be instructed in academic disciplines; self-activity should be stressed and curiosity harnessed through experiment and controlled research, which will begin with simple problems definitely formulated by the teacher.

It is at this level that the student begins to acquire the liberal arts precisely as habits. Elementary schooling is characterized by information; secondary schooling brings consolidation, insight and true intellectual formation.

The student in the secondary school should be brought to see the relationship of principle to conclusion, of cause to effect. It is by such exercise, carried out along the lines of a well-ordered curriculum, that he grows in the liberal arts and the sciences.

In the college preparatory school (the secondary school of which we are here speaking), it is indispensable that the student learn something of the art of logic in a sense broad enough to include those other liberal arts that are necessary to understand anything well. Without this it is impossible to read intelligently or to listen intelligently. Very importantly, without a basic grasp of the art of logic it is not possible to learn anything scientifically.[11]

In the area of sacred doctrine, as in other subjects, the secondary school must lead the student to more advanced understanding. The impulse of new experience is a strong force shaping the adolescent's attitude toward religion. He begins to discover wider areas of difficulty in following the Christian code, and the curiosity necessary for all intellectual growth leads him to reappraise authoritarian teaching. His expanding social circle brings him into contact with those who do not share his beliefs, and he is confronted with questions which he finds difficult to answer.

Yet the adolescent's lack of experience and his insufficient mastery of intellectual tools required for true explanations of sacred doctrine conspire to preclude anything as lofty as a course in theology. What can be done is to present Christian doctrine not simply after the manner of convenience in memorization (as in the catechism), but rather according to the order of principles which give true intellectual order to divine truths. The secondary school should present Christian doctrine as an organic entity that provides an intelligible framework for a truly Christian attitude. A solid foundation in such a course, involving as it must a rather wide reading of Sacred Scripture, will be an ideal preparation for the college course in theology.

In short, the secondary school should produce the literate Christian who has facility in the arts of learning and communication, some knowledge of science together with some experience of scientific method, and the solid beginnings of an intellectually convinced Catholicism.

Coming to a consideration of *college education* we leave the domain of the many and enter the preserves of the few. College education is carried on in favor of a small minority, an elite, however great its numbers. Yet upon this small minority the Church spends her best educational effort. What should these colleges be? What should they produce? What may the Church expect from them?

From several viewpoints, particularly the historical, sociological and legalistic, Catholic colleges can be explained as a kind of Maginot Line in which young Christians take refuge and man the defenses against the forces of anti-Christianity in the diverse forms described by their texts and teachers. If this were the only reason for their existence, then the Catholic colleges have largely failed, for the simple reason that there are more Catholic collegians on non-Catholic campuses than in schools directed by the Church. A good fortress should at least accommodate the majority of the defenders.

This defensive concept runs into another and more serious difficulty both in the teaching of the gospels and in the essentially missionary nature of the Church. These seem to call more for the outlook of the blitzkreig than for the Maginot Line mentality.

Neither can the Catholic college be viewed as a spiritual finishing school for an elite. Precisely as an academic institution the college functions to train the young in the arts and sciences, and the majority of these are concerned with mundane realities and perfections of the temporal order. Progress in academic endeavor cannot be made unless the temporal order is taken seriously. While the Christian may not be "of the world," it is equally true that he must be "in the world," and this cannot be accomplished without a supernaturally grounded sense of values that accords due worth to temporal realities. Schooling envisages, among other things, the "advantage and prosperity of civil society." To achieve this, the college graduate must have competence in the arts and sciences, for if he does not, he will never have even the opportunity to shape worldly realities according to the principles of supernatural faith.

Finally, the Catholic college is not a school quantitatively superior to non-Catholic colleges simply because it offers courses in sacred doctrine which are lacking in other colleges. It may be possible to distinguish supermarkets in terms of those which sell bakery goods and those which do not, but such a standard cannot be applied to colleges. This is forcefully stated by Pope Pius XI:

> For the mere fact that a school gives some religious instruction (often extremely stinted), does not bring it into accord with the rights of the Church and of the Christian family, or make it a fit place for Catholic students. To be this, it is necessary that all the teaching and the whole organization of the school, and its teachers, syllabus and text-books in every branch, be regulated by the Christian spirit, under the maternal supervision of the Church; so that religion may be in very truth the foundation and crown of the youth's entire training; and this in every grade of school, not only the elementary, but the intermediate and the higher institutions of learning as well.[12]

The natural and unalterable exigencies of human living demand that all men must act according to some supreme standard, in the light of some supreme and ultimate goal. They must see all of their lives in the light of this goal. In other words, they must direct their lives according to some wisdom, to which all else is subordinated; they must ". . . put things in their right order and control them well."[13]

In view of the general end of Christian education, the curriculum of the Catholic college must make a positive academic contribution toward the acquisition of a specifically Christian wisdom. The Catholic college must assist the student to habituate himself to think, and to think as a Christian; to judge the realities of life, and to judge them by specifically Christian standards; to act, and to act in a specifically Christian manner. In fine, it is the task of the Catholic college to develop the student in Christian culture, to habituate him by academic means in Christian wisdom.

The Catholic college, then, does not exist to train people to repeat some Catholic formula about art, politics, history, economics, philosophy or anything else. Rather, the Catholic college exists to exemplify and to communicate academically that Christian culture which is the fruit of Christian wisdom.

Christian Culture

History shows clearly that Catholicism is a culture, a specific life-view marked by definite characteristics and based upon unchanging principles. This culture has flowered in differing degrees at different times. It is discernible in the apostolic and patristic periods; it smoldered through the Dark Ages to burst forth in the Middle Ages; it waxed and waned through the Renaissance, the Reformation, the era of industrialization; it continues in modern times. This culture is not simply an adherence to a religious creed, it is rather a basic approach to all of life.

There is a strong temptation for those living in a secularized society to consider Catholic culture as something anachronous. To relegate to museums the works of Ignatius of Antioch, Augustine, Anselm, Aquinas, Bonaventure, Fra Angelico, Dante, Bellarmine and the rest is to miss the point; it is to confuse the catch-word with the culture, for each of these in their creations of beauty and intelligence were simply reflecting Christian culture as it was developed in the genius of their own period.

It is not easy for contemporary Catholics to realize that millions of their own faith hold today substantially the same principles and views of life that John Chrysostom and Dante and Francis of Assisi held. In recognizing the sharp differences between today's world and that of our intellectual and spiritual forebears, it is a great mistake to conclude that this is due to a difference in principles. The shadows change, and greatly; the substance of faith and of principle remains always the same. Upon that foundation rests the essential unicity of Catholic culture.

Culture and schooling are not co-extensive terms, but they are definitely related. The Catholic college should be a seedbed of culture for the younger generation. It can only be so if elders make it such.

Culture is often communicated by a kind of infection rather than by injection; there is a sense in which it must be caught and cannot be taught. Yet the college must provide a kind of injection in the sense of a deliberate effort to teach the elements of Christian wisdom and to induce by teaching an understanding of Christian culture. And this must be done entirely under the guidance of Christian principles.

It is basic to Christian thought that grace perfects and does not destroy nature. Implicit here is a demand for competence and indeed excellence in the natural arts and sciences. If the college is to be a source of intellectual and cultural growth, then the very best human instrumentalities must be employed. It is only from a clear and profound understanding of the natural order that analogies with the supernatural can be culled. Divine science truly depends upon human understanding and effort. Piety can no more substitute for learning than butter can substitute for steel; they simply belong to different orders. The Catholic college must have uncompromisingly high academic standards.

In the academic order, the proper mode of divine truth is found in sacred theology. In its best development, theology is *scholastic*—a product of schoolmen, designed specifically for academic teaching, and completely at home in schools. Without theology as an integral element in the curriculum, a college can be called Catholic only by extrinsic denomination.

It is theology, in conjunction with the arts and sciences of the natural order, that completes and perfects the academic communication of Christian culture. If the curriculum is deficient through the lack of the only academic expression of Christian wisdom, how can it be an instrument for the formation of the Christian mentality and for the communication of Christian culture? To eliminate theology from the curriculum of the Catholic college is to secularize the sole distinctive cause of the academic communication of Christian culture. No effect should be expected to excel its cause.

The Catholic College and Our Times

It has been pointed out that the prevailing climate of America is secularistic, and that this attitude (or "culture") is the mortal enemy of supernatural faith.[14] The college graduate enters into a secularized society, a society functioning upon premises taken for granted rather than explicitly declared. These premises are completely opposed and even antagonistic to Catholic culture. This is a simple, objective fact which is quite independent of the sincerity of some of those who propose these secular principles.[15]

The Catholic college must make a positive contribution toward preparing its graduates to live effectively as Christians in the midst of this alien atmosphere. The graduate must be sufficiently competent to recognize the dimensions, the effects and the tactics of secularism. This means that he must be well exercised in the liberal arts without which nothing can be rightly understood. Further, the graduate must be equipped to make specifically Christian judgments, and for his level of education this requires that he possess the beginnings, at least, of the habit of theology. There are ignorances which are not permissible to the educated Christian, and Catholic college training must free him from them.

Moreover, the Catholic college must prepare its graduates to communicate their culture to the society in which they live, and it must convey to them the urgent necessity of doing this. Every Christian must strive to influence his environment in the measure of his capacity. The Catholic college graduate should have a special competency to influence those of his own educational level, and this basic ability should be developed through academic means in the colleges. At the intellectual level, at least, the Catholic college should be the major source of those who are able to communicate Christian culture to modern secularized society.

While it is true that the anti-supernatural and anti-religious nature of secularism must evoke the determined opposition of the Church and of Christians, it is a mistake to conclude that opposition on religious grounds will explain the entire conflict. Errors about God, logically pursued, must lead to errors about man, and mistaken notions of the supernatural to mistaken ideas about the natural order. Secularism is anti-rational. As such it is fittingly the object of apostolic concern among Christians specially trained along the lines of the intellectual virtues; these should be the graduates of Catholic colleges.

The Catholic layman has a special vocation to mediate between the milieu in which he lives and the spiritual realities which are the source and substance of his divine faith, hope and love. The Catholic college, functioning to impart to its students an intellectual grasp of Catholic culture, must necessarily affect the way in which its graduates fulfill this vocation. The results of Catholic college education will be diverse, and while they are not directly or immediately of the spiritual order of grace, they are all related to and influenced by the supernatural.

As an institution of learning, the Catholic college should instill in its students a respect for and a love of learning. If this element is lacking, no one can pursue the life of learning and make it a vocation. All knowledge begins with curiosity, which is a kind of appetition or love. Thus the student starts from love in order to learn, and he should love better for having known well. It may reasonably be expected that the Catholic college should foster zeal for learning based upon a realization of the obligations deriving from opportunity and an understanding of the sanctifying power of the loving pursuit of truth.

For the Christian, love of God is inseparable from love of neighbor. This is evidenced by the glorious history of material and physical help given to the unfortunate by Christians. But it is no less evident in the spiritual work of mercy which is the communication of truth. Men do not live by bread alone; their need for truth is as real. To satisfy another's need for bread, it is enough to give of what one has; to satisfy his need for truth, it is necessary to give of what one is.

It is to be expected that the Catholic college should be a community of Christian scholars, with all that implies. The liturgy should modify and flavor the entire atmosphere of the campus. Works of the apostolate which are germane to the intellectual life should be encouraged. But all of these must be colored by the distinctive characteristics of an institution of learning, of a community of Christians engaged in the intellectual life.

The indispensable virtues of the student are docility and studiousness. These are virtues demanding self-control and renunciation which motivate, control and channel self-activity. It must be remembered that they stand between two extremes. A supine acceptance of indoctrination has no more to do with virtue than it has to do with learning, and that is nothing at all. The college assumes a positive obligation to foster these virtues in its students because they are the indispensable prerequisite for learning in a Christian manner. Hence the spiritual direction offered by college chaplains must be attuned to the specialized vocation of students.

Learning is the one indispensable qualification of a teacher; without it, he simply cannot be a teacher. But the teacher's attitude reaches far deeper than the lessons he imparts in class. It is from the indefinable communication of zeal from master to pupil that the beginnings of scholarship are brought forth. When this is elevated and ennobled by divine charity so that it becomes truly a spiritual work of mercy, we approach close to the ideal relationship between the young Aquinas and his master, Albert the Great. This is a path toward the love of God that can be followed only by teachers and students. That this path is actually followed should be evident on any campus worthy of the name Catholic.

Conclusion

A short essay on a large subject cannot say very much. An introductory essay should limit rather than explore, should raise questions rather than answer them. This essay was written with these goals in view; the exploration and the answering are left to more specialized articles which follow.

No attempt has been made here to assess existing colleges or actual programs. Enough effort has been invested in that worthy cause. Here only some basic principles were set forth and some ideals delineated. The Catholic college occupies a position of crucial importance not only for Catholicism but for education as well. As Catholic, a college has the freedom, unique today in schools, to explore the totality of truth, both divine and human. This freedom begets a great responsibility to make sure that neither divine nor human truth is slighted, but that both are served as well as possible at the collegiate level. The college which fails as a school has no true claim to the name Catholic; if it fails to be thoroughly Catholic, it cannot rightfully claim to be a good school.

Footnotes to Study 2

[1]Pius XI, encyclical *On the Christian Education of Youth,* Dec. 31, 1929 (N.C.W.C. trans.), 4-5.

[2]Pius XI, *op. cit.,* 36.

[3]Cf. the pastoral letter of the American hierarchy, 1919, in *Our Bishops Speak,* 1919-1951, ed. by Raphael M. Huber, O.F.M. Conv. (Milwaukee: Bruce, 1952), 61 f.

[4]*Ibid.,* 29.

[5]The severe criticism given by Kevin J. O'Brien, C.SS.R., of the "intellectualist" position in his *The Proximate Aim of Education* (Milwaukee: Bruce, 1958) seems to indicate that he has not fully grasped this point nor understood sufficiently its implications. For a defense and explanation of the "intellectualist" point of view see Pierre H. Conway, O.P., *Principles of Education* (Washington: The Thomist Press, 1960), Vincent E. Smith, *The School Examined: Its Aim and Content* (Milwaukee: Bruce, 1960), Neil G. McCluskey, S.J., *The Catholic Viewpoint on Education* (Garden City: Doubleday, 1959), Leo R. Ward, C.S.C., *New Life in Catholic Schools* (St. Louis: Herder, 1958), and my *Theology and Education* (Dubuque: Wm. C. Brown Co., 1952), among others; Father O'Brien's "devotional" educational position is directly criticized by Richard Rousseau, S.J., in "What *Is* the Aim of Catholic Education?", *Catholic World,* CXC (1959), 24-30.

[6]"Education and Communication," *Proceedings of the National Catholic Educational Association,* LIX (1957), 32-49. In a later address the Cardinal repeated this passage and quoted his statement that the "education program of the Church expressed by the popes" is an *integral* one, embracing the "twin objectives of both doctrina et pietas"; cf. "The Role of the Seminary," *Proceedings of the National Catholic Educational Association,* LVII (1960), 74-81.

[7]A similar distinction (although expressed far better and in other words) constitutes one of the major points of Cardinal Newman's *Idea of a University;* cf. the fifth chapter, "Knowledge Its Own End." For a "reconciliation" of this view with the teachings of Pius XI in *Divini Illius Magisteri,* see the review by Urban Voll, O.P., of the new Longmans' edition of Newman's classic in *The Thomist,* XI (1948), 511-514.

[8]Cf. *Q. D. de Ver.,* q. 24, a. 4 and ad 10, a. 6 and ad 1 and ad 4.

[9]See Part Two, Chap. 1, IV, "Moral Virtue Indispensable to Intellectual," 51-55 (reference cited in footnote 5).

[10]Leo XIII, *Militantis Ecclesiae,* Aug. 1, 1897, quoted in Pius XI, *op. cit.,* 31.

[11]For a text prepared for this purpose, cf. Benedict Ashley, O.P., *The Arts of Learning and Communication* (Dubuque: The Priory Press, 1958).

[12]*Op. cit.,* 30 f.

[13]St. Thomas, I *Con. Gen.,* Chap. 1.

[14]Cf. the 1952 statement of the bishops of the United States, "Religion, Our Most Vital National Asset" (Washington: N.C.W.C., 1952), 5 f.

[15]For an interesting example, cf. Robert Lekachman, "An Unreligious View," *Religion and the Schools* (New York: The Fund for the Republic, 1959), 79 ff., and my reply, "A Scrutiny of 'The Unreligious View,'" *The Catholic Educator,* XXX (1959), 210-212.

Footnotes to Study 2

3

THE NATURE OF SACRED THEOLOGY

Reginald Masterson, O.P.

Professor of dogmatic theology at St. Rose Priory, Dubuque, Iowa, and for eight years Director of the Graduate Program in Theology at Saint Xavier College, Chicago, Father Masterson (who holds doctorates both in philosophy and in sacred theology) is well known to teachers of college theology through his frequent appearances on the programs of the national conventions of the SCCTSD; he is also president of the Dominican Educational Association. An associate editor of Cross and Crown, *he has recently edited* Seeking the Kingdom, *a volume of essays on the spiritual life.*

There has never been a time when man could say that he was man and nothing more. From the dawn of human existence man has been destined by the providence of God to share in his intimate Trinitarian life. This ordination to share in divine life, while not destroying human perfections, demanded that man could never rest in purely human goals, no matter how sublime. He must direct his thoughts, his words, his deeds to a supernatural goal. To Adam was given a magnificent share in divine perfection; to him also was given the fulness of revelation concerning his divine goal. When he brought the doom of sin on himself and his progeny, not only did Adam lose the fulness of this supernatural revelation, but he also left us with the heritage of an intellect morally incapable of readily arriving even at the purity of human truth.

Since original sin did not destroy man's supernatural destiny, it did not destroy his need for supernatural knowledge. Only through such knowledge could he ever attain the sublime goal of eternally sharing in the life of God. Precisely because such knowledge surpasses all purely human intellectual efforts, there was demanded another gift of revelation to serve as the guide in directing human life to its freely given divine goal. The inspired words of Sacred Scripture and Tradition are God's answer to that need. Realizing that the proper utilization of these newly revealed divine mysteries would require a knowledge of the truths proper to the human intellect, a merciful God did not limit his gift of revelation merely to the supernatural order, but extended it even to those basic natural truths which are the necessary preambles to the acceptance of faith.

Just as truly as the truths revealed by God to man are in themselves of an order which transcends all creation, so the assent which the mind must give to them is beyond human grasp. Subjective assent to truth must always be proportioned to the object of such assent. In the case of assent to revelation, this necessarily involves the assent flowing from a supernatural habit of intellect. This divinely given supernatural habit in the mind of man enabling him to assent to the mysteries revealed on the authority of God revealing is nothing other than the theological virtue of faith. This body of revealed doctrine, necessary to man because of his ordination to the supernatural life of God and his difficulty in clearly grasping the basic truths of the natural order without error, thus lies beyond the scope of even the most noble of human wisdom.

Divine faith, by which man assents to revelation, is an intellectual habit; it is a perfection of the human mind. Our intellect, however, was never made to be satisfied with mere assent either to natural or supernatural truths. The human intellect is naturally curious; it is made to inquire into the nature of the truths to which it assents. Since the mind cannot clearly penetrate the meaning of revealed supernatural mysteries, it seeks at least some reconciliation of the two orders of nature and supernature; it tries to discover what is implicitly contained in the supernatural principles revealed; it attempts to manifest insofar as possible the meaning of these truths;

it draws from these truths by the aid of reason the conclusions which are contained in them. Moreover, the human mind orders the truths of faith among themselves for greater intelligibility and to derive greater directive force from them in man's striving to attain God. Divine revelation, therefore, opens to the human intellect an infinite vista for human speculation and investigation. It is this disciplined human investigation of divinely revealed truths, made known in Sacred Scripture and Tradition, assented to by faith, which constitutes theology.

The Nature of Theology

The necessity for theology for mankind as a whole is clear. Hardly less evident is the need of colleges and collegians for something of the same divine discipline. And yet, despite the fact that in the past few years serious attention has been given to the problem of theology or sacred doctrine in the college curriculum, surprisingly little time has been devoted to the nature of theology. Those charged with facing the problem in a particular situation almost invariably become involved with the methodology and content of theology programs at the college level. Necessary as these latter considerations are, they are incapable of being given intelligent directives without the prior consideration of the nature of sacred theology itself. The most elementary knowledge of the general principles of human learning shows that the nature of the subject to be taught necessarily is the first factor in the determination of the methodology and content of the course to be given in that subject. While such a basic principle does not eliminate the necessity of accommodation of the subject to the student at the various educational levels, it nonetheless remains the primary norm in such adaptation.

This same principle should guide us in the problem of theology in the college curriculum: the nature of theology ought to serve as the guiding principle for the arrangement of such theology courses; for the determination of their order and content; for their adaptation to the college student; and for the specification of the relation of the theology courses to the rest of the college curriculum. The development of the corresponding intellectual habit is the ultimate reason for the study of any science. As the end serves to direct the selection and use of means in practical matters, so the acquisition of the intellectual habit, the end of study, will serve as a guide to the selection of matter and the methodology involved in the presentation of the matter. It is for this reason that St. Thomas gives consideration to the nature of theology in the very first question of his *Summa Theologiae;* it is the reason why a correct understanding of the nature of theology is an essential prerequisite for the comprehension of the remaining articles which are contained in this volume.

In investigating this important matter—of first practical importance for the college—we shall develop the following propositions:

1. Theology is a true science.
2. It is primarily a speculative science.
3. But it is no less really a practical science.
4. Moreover, it is a divine-human wisdom.
5. The proper object of this science-wisdom is God himself.
6. Its character as a scientific (discursive) wisdom points up the fact that theology has many diverse, if unified functions. Many of these are immediately operative in the college milieu.
7. It follows from these considerations that theology should be presented to college students in a liberal scientific mode.
8. Admirably adapted to this purpose is that system, so highly approved by the Church, known as Thomism.

Let us examine these several propositions—by no means self-evident, by no means unchallenged—in some detail.[1]

Theology as a Science

One of the problems which the modern student faces is the use of the term "science" as applied to theology. In its current acceptation this term is ordinarily limited to the experimental sciences. Science in the Aristotelian-Thomistic usage is not confined, however, to this narrow meaning of the term, but includes all those intellectual disciplines which offer certain knowledge through causes. It is according to this interpretation that theology is properly entitled to be classified as a science, because from revealed principles it draws conclusions which offer knowledge through causes, and it does this with a greater certitude than that provided by any purely human science.

The most serious difficulty raised against the classification of theology as a science is not the modern objection that it does not deal with observable physical phenomena, but rather that which objects to this classification on the grounds that the principles of theology, accepted on faith, are not clearly known by the theologian. One is not generally judged to have scientific knowledge concerning matters which he accepts merely on faith, even divine faith. But such reasoning fails to distinguish between the principles of the supernatural order—the object of the virtue of faith—and the virtue of faith itself by which man is enabled to assent to them. The principles revealed for our acceptance by faith are nothing other than the truths of the supernatural life of God, a sharing in his very knowledge. As such they provide us with the greatest certitude possible. The medium by which we assent to them is accidental to their truth and certainty. While faith renders their meaning imperfect in the mind of the theologian, it by no means prohibits them from being the first principles for scientific investigation by the theologian. The physiological principles according to which the Salk vaccine operates are no less true because the technician who administers it fails to understand why it acts in a particular way to prevent bacterial infection.

One hears a great deal these days about "seminary theology," "lay theology," "theology for sisters." The uninitiated is often led to believe that there exists a distinct theological science for each of the various classes of listeners who undertake the study of theology. Another error, with more serious consequences, is the theory that there exists a distinct theological science for each of the subjects which fall under theological consideration. Such wooly thinking has led to many unfortunate consequences in the adaptation of theology to the college level. The ultimate determination of the nature of any science necessarily comes from the formality under which the subject matter treated by it is considered. Though the eye may fall upon a variety of objects, it remains a single power of the body because it views them all precisely as they are colored objects; the secondary features of a colored object (its size, shape and depth) are attainable only through the primary aspect. Similarly, the science of theology is one, in no measure atomized by the multiplicity of the mysteries which are investigated by it. Theology treats in a systematic way divinely revealed truths and all else precisely under the aspect of revelation. To alter this formality is to alter the nature of theology.

Theology as Speculative Science

Failure to understand the nature of theology has led many to expect results from theology courses which this science is not directly ordained to engender in the student. There are many at the present time who confidently expect that those emerging from the college theology classroom should be fervent apostles of Catholic Action. This may happen; it may be the result of the course in theology; but, if so, it is an accidental by-product. Though it likewise participates in the nature of a practical science, theology is principally a speculative science. But even in this former function it is not directly ordained to action. There is such wide misunderstanding on this point that it seems necessary to set forth clearly these aspects of the theological science.

Virtues are distinguished into intellectual and moral virtues; the former perfect the mind of man, the latter his appetites. Intellectual virtues are further subdivided into speculative and practical virtues, insofar as they perfect the speculative or practical intellect of man. This is not to convey the idea that man has two intellects, one speculative, the other practical. For it is accidental to what is known whether it is directed to operation or not.[2] The distinction between the speculative and practical functions of the intellect is taken from the end of the act of knowledge. The intellect as speculative directs its knowledge to a consideration of the truth of what is known, while as practical it orders knowledge to operation. Thus truth is found both in the speculative and practical intellects, but in the latter case such truth is directed to operation.[3] Indeed, perfect speculative knowledge of truth is demanded before it can be perfectly practical. Correct speculative knowledge ought to precede practical knowledge. Implicit in this general principle is the truth that one can only have a profound understanding of morals when there is also a right understanding of the dogmatic truths upon which they are based. One can never have a right understanding of the work of faith and charity in Christian life unless such understanding is based upon a knowledge of God's own knowledge and love and their perfect realization in the Trinity.

While speculative and practical knowledge do not diversify the human intellect itself, it is nonetheless true that they imply specific differences in human sciences, for they imply diverse aspects of intelligibility from which such specification is drawn. Precisely as it constitutes a speculative object, a known truth is considered in its nature or the properties of its nature; known practically, it is viewed in relation to its actual existence or attainment. This diversity is not wholly extrinsic to the object as known but proceeds from the very intrinsic knowable aspect of the truth which is grasped—the speculative object being wholly abstract, the practical in relation to what is required to attain realization outside the mind.

While human sciences are divided into speculative and practical sciences by reason of their object, theology contains the perfections of both but in a higher manner, and without being essentially diversified by this distinction. As indicated before, the unity of a science is ultimately determined by the aspect of intelligibility under which it considers the object. This, in the case of theology, is divine revelation, a participation in the very knowledge of God himself. The superiority of this kind of intellectual illumination places it beyond the dividing factors of human intelligibility and enables the theologian to attain the object of his pursuit, God, both speculatively and practically with one and the same science.

Since the most proper subject of theology is none other than God himself and all other subjects in light of this primary one, theology is necessarily more speculative than practical. The theologian's concern with man and his return to God flows from his concern with the Deity itself. One must not conclude, however, that since the theological science contains in a higher way the perfections of both the speculative and practical sciences every theological conclusion contains both aspects equally. The human composite contains the perfections of animal and vegetative life, but this fact does not require that in every act of man both of these formalities be present. The precise manner in which the speculative and practical functions are exercised by the theological habit will be discussed later.

Theology as a Practical Science

What of theology as a *practical* science? Surely, many declare, this aspect of theology should be stressed to the average college student so as to produce a perfectly formed Christian inflamed with apostolic zeal. Unhappily, this attitude manifests a failure to understand the true nature of practical science as it applies to theology.

What is it that makes a science practical? As we have indicated, it is the order to operation which distinguishes practical knowledge from purely speculative knowledge. For although many things which are known lie within the competency of the knower to produce, they are not known for the purpose of production. The knowledge of nuclear fission is more often than not acquired for some purpose other than the fashioning of an atom bomb. The knowledge which is acquired of such operable objects, while *radically* practical, remains in the realm of speculative knowledge, of knowledge for the sake of knowledge. The essential distinction between speculative and practical knowledge is derived rather from the *mode* of the knowledge. In the case of truly practical knowledge, not only is the object operable, but knowledge of this operable object is actually directed to operation or production. When a known object possesses this modality of being ordered to operation, then such knowledge is essentially and formally practical. And since the specification of an intellectual virtue is taken from the formality of the object precisely as it is known, a practical science has for its object not merely the operable, but the operable *as such.*

One further, and very important distinction is necessary, that is, between the *essentially* practical science and the *actually* practical science.[4] "Practical" in this latter sense implies that the object which is known as operable as such is carried to the ultimate limit of practicality. Precisely in what does this ultimate limit consist? It consists in the practical knowledge's being determined by the end, not the end of the science or of knowledge, but the end of the scientist himself. Every truly practical science is practical because it is known as ordered to operation—from this point of view it is impossible to distinguish the essentially from the actually practical science. The perfectly or actually practical science, therefore, must be distinguished from the essentially practical science by reason of the end of the scientist himself. The one who possesses a perfectly practical science *actually wills to put it into execution.* One might object that the specification of the scientist by the object as an end actually to be attained is extrinsic to the nature of a practical science and hence does not constitute a basis for distinguishing between the essentially and actually practical sciences. To conclude thusly would be to deny that the end precisely as it exercises its causality as end adds nothing which is properly different, and one would reduce science which is practical by reason of its object to that which is practical by reason of its end.

What precise effects concerning the college theology program does this distinction regarding the essentially and actually practical sciences have? Very significant ones, indeed, and well worth enumerating:

> *First,* theology must be classified not as an actually practical science but as an essentially practical one. It is primarily concerned with imparting *essentially* practical knowledge, for it considers the operable (for example, an act of virtue), not as it actually specifies the action of the theologian, but as an object of practical knowledge. An act of charity thus considered does not exercise its proper causality as proceeding from the will and does not differ from other objects of knowledge; it acts as extrinsic formal cause of the act of knowledge. In perfectly practical knowledge, on the other hand, the end exercises its proper causality and moves the agent to action. Hence the theologian is not formally *as theologian* concerned with the ultimate end of man precisely as it actually motivates the life of the student; he is rather interested in communicating the truth about the nature of this goal as the end of human life.

This must be carefully understood in the same formal sense in which it is stated; to distinguish is not to falsify. Secondarily and *ex consequenti,* theology is an actually practical science in the sense that it must be ordered directly and explicitly by the one possessing it to his own good and the good of others. In the course of instructing the student about supernatural truths the theologian will present them not only in a scientific way but also as sapiential principles which guide all the activities of human life. To accomplish this the theologian necessarily employs practical exemplification, rhetoric and dialectics. When the priest-theologian employs these same truths as preacher, chaplain or spiritual director, he strives directly to be an instrument of God's grace in moving the will of the student to put them into actual practice. But this does not negate the basic fact, here insisted upon: theology is not a perfectly practical science but an essentially practical one, not preachment nor catechetics nor counseling nor charismatic experience, but discursive wisdom, and this primarily, intrinsically and *per se.*

Secondly, the theologian is nonetheless concerned with the ultimate end as *possible* of attainment by his student, though not immediately with the actual attainment of that end. This is likewise a consequence of the fact that theology, an essentially practical science, considers the end as an operable object of knowledge and not as actually exercising its causality precisely as end. It is clear that this approach does not make theology only radically and not essentially practical; since it considers many of the objects known by it precisely as operable (the virtues, for example), it preserves the mode of knowledge proper to an essentially practical science.

Thirdly, perfectly practical knowledge as it is defined involves the appetite or will of the scientist, whereas essentially practical knowledge does not. Let us repeat once more: the *primary* interest of the theologian as theologian is not with the actual motivation of the student to attain the ultimate end of human happiness, the beatitude of glory, but only with expounding it as within the reach of man elevated to the supernatural life.

The very nature of theological science thus demands that we part company with those kerygmatists who would make the immediate aim of the communication of theological science the stimulus to action.

Fourthly and most importantly, perfectly practical science does not remain within the intellect completely because it presupposes the impulse of the will and of rectified appetite. On the other hand, knowledge which is only essentially practical and which limits the consideration of the operable object to extrinsic formal causality remains within the intellect, and hence the truth which is known is not necessarily measured by rectified appetite. Unfortunately, a good theologian does not have to be a good man. Hence, though theology is an essentially practical science, *there is only speculative truth in it.* When the theologian treats of the ultimate end of man in moral theology, he considers it as falling within reach of the Christian soul, but he himself communicates only speculative truth about its attainability.

In fine, when we classify theology as a formally or essentially practical science, we do not intend to draw it into the realm of actually exercising final causality but limit it to the teaching of speculative truth.

Does this validate the charge that the study of theology is merely sterile intellectualism? To do so is to contradict the statement of the Vatican Council that "reason, enlightened by faith and through attentive, zealous and sober research, acquires with the help of God's grace a very fruitful understanding of the mysteries—either through analogies with natural knowledge or through the interconnection of the mysteries with one another or with the supreme end of man."[5] For the Angelic Doctor love was the basis of the pursuit of divine truth and likewise its end. It is possible for a Christian to undertake the ardent pursuit of theology from motives other than its being an avenue to greater love, but it is unlikely that he will long persist in such effort from mere natural motivation. "In the ardor of his faith," writes St. Thomas, "the Christian loves the truth which he believes. He turns it in his mind, he embraces it and seeks for all the reasons he can find which will support this meditation and this love."[6]

The Certitude of Theological Science

Not only is theology both speculative and practical, it stands at the summit of both these divisions of purely human sciences. Speculative knowledge seeks the truth for its own sake—the higher the order of truth the more valuable is the knowledge which it attains. No one would suggest that any human science attains a more worthwhile speculative knowledge than that of the truths revealed to us by God about his own divine life. Nor can one adequately claim superiority for the pursuit of human speculation on the basis that it affords greater certitude concerning truth, whereas the truths reached by the theologian leave many areas of doubt and dispute. Not only is theology superior to other speculative sciences by reason of its subject matter, God and all things in relation to God, but likewise from the point of view of the certitude involved in theological science.[7] This remains true even when the theologian uses principles taken from the inferior sciences of metaphysics and physics.

Certitude as it pertains to science involves the firm adherence of the mind to the conclusions drawn from the principles of the science. That a conclusion of a science be certain demands, in turn, that it truly flow from the principles of that science: hence the more certain the principles of the science, the greater the certitude of the conclusions. Since the theologian assents to the conclusions of his science upon their resolution to the principles of faith, the certitude by which he adheres to theological conclusions exceeds that of all natural certitude. The fact that this resolution may take place through the medium of a natural premise in no way militates against this reasoning. The theologian uses the principles of natural sciences ministerially, and in such a way that they participate in the certitude of the higher knowledge of faith. The adherence to supernatural truths is an imperfect state due to the imperfection of faith and may leave subjective doubt in the mind of the theologian; but insofar as he adheres to these truths on the authority of God revealing, the firmness of his adherence to them exceeds all natural certitude. Any doubt in the mind of the theologian does not arise from lack of certitude on the part of the divine truth itself, but rather from the weakness of the human intellect when confronted by a supernatural mystery. Such subjective doubt cannot be removed merely by more intensive consideration of the mystery, but only by a greater disposition of the will for the acceptation of divine revelation or by stronger motives of credibility. The teacher of moral theology frequently encounters difficulties of this kind in expounding Christian moral principles; he soon realizes—or should realize—that they arise rather from a weakness of faith than from failure to understand the reasoning involved in their presentation.

As to the supremacy of theology among practical sciences there exists no reasonable doubt: it provides the truths which direct man to his final goal, the enjoyment of the clear vision of the triune God.

The Wisdom of Theology

Theology, however, is not limited to a merely scientific function, namely, the drawing of conclusions from the revealed principles, but is indeed the highest acquired wisdom. In addition to *science,* there are two other speculative habits proper to man, namely, *understanding* (by which he is enabled to assent to the first speculative principles) and *wisdom.* Wisdom encompasses the work of both understanding and science. As regards the first principles of knowledge, wisdom goes beyond mere assent to their truths and seeks to manifest their meaning as well as to defend them; it likewise extends to the conclusions which are drawn from these principles. Saint Thomas writes:

> This doctrine [theology] is wisdom above all human wisdom, not merely in any one order but absolutely. For since it is the part of a wise man to arrange and to judge, and since lesser matters should be judged in the light of some higher principle, he is said to be wise in any one order who considers the highest principles in that order. . . . Therefore he who considers the absolutely highest cause of the whole universe, namely, God, is most of all called wise. Hence wisdom is said to be the knowledge of divine things. . . . But sacred doctrine essentially treats of God viewed as the highest cause—not only insofar as he can be known through creatures just as philosophers knew him—but also so far as he is known to himself

alone and revealed to others. Hence sacred doctrine is especially called wisdom.[8]

Theology is, however, an *acquired* wisdom; it is the fruit of human intellectual industry. While it begins with the revealed principles accepted by the simple assent of faith, it goes beyond the mere acceptance to an examination of these truths in the light of reason, investigating their credibility, manifesting their meaning and drawing conclusions. Theology is not to be identified with the wisdom which is enumerated among the gifts of the Holy Ghost. The gift of wisdom is gratuitously bestowed upon every Christian in a state of grace and enables the soul under the impulse of the Spirit of God to judge and inquire about divine things from a certain connaturality for them. "Its judgment is unique, proceeding from a special impulse, by which the mind is elevated to judge with promptitude, and by which the soul is united and subjected to God from a connaturality and experience of divine things."[9] The judgments which the theologian makes from the divine viewpoint proceed from the laborious effort of human reasoning. The acquired wisdom of theology presents no antithesis to the gift of wisdom, however; on the contrary, it can serve as a suitable disposition for one's acquired meditation, and this leads to the infused contemplation wherein the gift of wisdom fully operates.

The Proper Object of Theology

Granted that theology is an acquired wisdom whereby reason operates under the light of faith to defend, explain and draw conclusions from divinely revealed principles, there remains the question of the proper object or principal subject of this discipline. What is the precise formality under which the numerous revealed truths are unified in the theological treatment of them? The failure properly to determine this formality has led to many problems in the arrangement of a truly theological program for Catholic colleges. As each new development of theological dogma has evolved there has been a tendency to over-emphasize it. This involves the danger of subordinating the theological system through which the development has evolved to the dogma, rather than of integrating the new doctrine into the already existing synthesis. This pitfall is not proper to theological science; it endangers every science properly so called. The temptation is great in all fields, but college courses in theology have been peculiarly susceptible and only too frequently have succumbed. Thus we have had courses "liturgically oriented," centered around the doctrine of the Mystical Body, geared to the need for lay apostles, kerygmatically inspired. One would not seek to derogate from the value of these courses in the broader religious instruction of college students; but caution must be exercised to determine whether they are the proper method to inculcate the wisdom, properly theological, of which we have been treating.

The proper object of a science is that formality under which the object of the science is considered; it is that which is principally attained by the science and the aspect under which all other secondary objects are treated. As the faculties of the body are distinguished by their diverse formal object, so also the sciences and all habits are similarly diversified. The proper object of theology is nothing other than God himself precisely as he is in his supernatural life. Theology in all its functions is concerned with the principles revealed by faith, and the subject of these principles is constitutive of the formal object of the theological science. Angels, men and all creation pertain to theology only by reason of their relation to God. It is for this reason that any system of theology properly so called must begin with a consideration of the nature of God, his attributes and the Trinity of Persons within the Godhead. Christ, the sacraments, the Mystical Body—all become theologically meaningful in relation to the triune God. No one denies that the theological treatise on God and the Trinity constitutes a formidable tract for initiating the college student into sacred doctrine, but the practical difficulties involved do not outweigh the necessity of furnishing the student from the beginning with a knowledge of the formal object of this science. Initiating college theology with less difficult tracts may have its advantages from a pedagogical point of view; but it is theoretically indefensible and, experience shows, of dubious practical value.

The Functions of Theology

The determination of the proper object of theology brings another problem to the fore, on the surface a speculative one, but with vital practical ramifications. How can one explain the unicity of theological science while explaining the diversity of its functions? This is but the specific localization in theology of the universal problem of the one and the many which has perplexed philosophers over the centuries. The answer to this question likewise has serious implications for the college theology program because it will determine the methodology of presentation.

We have seen that this discursive wisdom "sees" all that comes within its purview under the one light, considers all its various and diverse subjects under the one formality. Hence it is one science, not many, not divisible into various species (as mathematics, for example, may be properly subdivided into arithmetic and geometry). But if theology in this sense has no parts, it is equally evident in other senses that it is a whole composed of parts. For it is concerned with myriad material objects and includes numerous separate treatises wherein these diverse objects are studied (those on God, the Trinity, creation, the angels, man, the various virtues, etc.); and yet together these different objects constitute but one total object (all of revelation), since all are considered according to their ordination to God, and they are ordered among themselves as of greater or lesser importance according as they more or less approach to God. Like the human body which is a whole composed of various integral parts of varying importance (feet, heart, head, etc.), so also is this human-divine wisdom an integral whole.

Theology is a unity amidst diversity (or of diverse elements) in a still more important way, in terms of a potestative whole. Conceived of in this manner, theology has a remarkable diversity of functions, to be sure; but it retains its unity, its wholeness, since each of these functions contains the whole nature of theology, even though no one of them contains its entire power. What is it that enables any nature or habit to be a potestative whole—that is to say, a single nature having a diversity of functions? The formal reason is the eminence of its nature, which combines the perfections of several other natures or powers. The classic example of the potestative whole is the nature of man, which combines human, sense and vegetable life in a single substance. While the human soul is the principle of every vital action of the human substance, no single action proceeding from the human person represents the total power of the nature. Each action of man proceeds from the principle of its activity by means of a specific faculty to attain an object proper to that faculty. Seeing is a sense activity but proceeds from the soul as its vital principle by means of the intermediary sense faculty.

In a comparable way, the habit of theology combines in itself its participation of the very knowledge of God with the power of human reason, and thus forms a single specific habit; but because of the combination of these two sources of knowledge, it exercises, as we have already indicated, a diversity of functions with regard to its object, God. Thus whether one defends the principles of faith, attempts to manifest their meaning, or orders them among themselves, the activity proceeds from the single habit of theology. But in each case the theologian uses a different function of the habit. Far from being unrelated, these diverse functions have a determined connection and subordination to one another. Just as the various functions of the human person must be exercised in an orderly way, so the diverse functions of theology demand proper subordination.

First of all, theology has various functions to perform with regard to its material object, the truths formally revealed and those virtually or implicitly contained in revelation. In explaining and defending the articles of faith, theology exercises its sapiential function, whereas in deducing conclusions from these truths it performs its scientific function. In every act of faith, however, three things are involved: 1) the fact of divine revelation; 2) the relation between this revelation and any particular mystery; and 3) the particular mystery revealed. Precisely as wisdom, theology both defends and explains these three facets of revelation. Apologetics is that branch of theology which explains the nature, possibility and suitability of divine revelation. The reasonableness of believing in divine revelation is likewise presented by this function of the theologian, along with the refutation of the objections raised against the fact of its existence.

Positive theology explains and defends the second aspect of every act of faith, namely, the relation between a particular truth and the body of revealed truth in general. To accomplish this sapiential function the theologian must know the fonts of revelation and the authentic sources of its interpretation. While this function demands that the theologian first ascertain the fonts of revelation, his proper office consists in explaining and defending what is most certainly revealed by the divine author in each of the sources. Depending upon the source being investigated, this work of positive theology is variously named "biblical" theology as it considers the proper interpretation of Sacred Scripture; "symbolic" theology as it considers divine tradition, the teachings of the Church, the councils and pontiffs; and "patristic" theology as it considers the doctrine of the Fathers and theologians.

In the task of explaining and defending the intrinsic meaning of the truths revealed (the third element of each act of faith), scholastic theology employs analogies to natural truths, makes known the relation of revealed truths to one another, and indicates the ordination of these truths to man's supernatural goal. In its scientific function scholastic theology determines the laws of theological deduction and then proceeds to deduce conclusions from the principles of faith.

Theology, like every scientific habit, is perfective of the human intellect. Because theology is both speculative and practical, it considers the truth about God both for its own sake as well as to provide the truths which must guide man in his attainment of the Godhead as his supreme goal. Hence in regard to the mind of man theology exercises a twofold role: one as it perfects the speculative intellect of man in the contemplation of divine truth in dogmatic theology; and the other in moral theology by providing the truths for regulating man's activity in reaching God.

Theology and the Other Human Sciences

The function of theology in regard to the other human sciences has perhaps been subjected to more discussion in recent years than any other function of the sacred science. With the reintroduction of theology into the undergraduate college curriculum there has arisen the vain hope that such a change would automatically integrate both the remainder of the subjects in the curriculum as well as the arts and sciences in the mind of the student; on the other hand the specter of a theological "imperialism" that would destroy the autonomy of all other intellectual disciplines has been raised up. These attitudes of hope and fear do have some foundation in reality, but a true picture of the interrelation of theology with the rest of human learning should dispel the distortions they convey.

In general, theology exercises three different functions with regard to the other human intellectual habits. First of all, it judges all human sciences, not only with reference to the principles of the science, but also in regard to their conclusions. This office pertains to theology because it judges all things in the light of the ultimate cause of all things, God as First Truth. In exercising this function the theologian acts both negatively and positively. Since the order of truth is one and there can be no contradiction between natural and supernatural truth, the theologian first judges whether or not the principles and conclusions of the human sciences are in conflict with revealed truths and theological conclusions.

Far from hampering the pursuit of human knowledge, such judgment greatly assists the scientist in his pursuit of truth by freeing him from the path of error; the judgment of the theologian gives to the scholar a clearer insight into the search for the knowledge of natural truth. The Catholic scholar does not resent the *magisterium* of the Church but realizes it is a safeguard that will both guide him in the ordered pursuit of his science and protect him from the pitfall of many deceits, especially from the error of the agnostic scientist who, in using the principles of his human science as the norm for judging the ultimate problems of his destiny, makes his science serve as a pseudo-wisdom.

Since theology itself is a human wisdom, acquired by human effort, it too is liable to error in its judgments. Evaluating the rectitude of the conclusions of human science is often a long and laborious task unless these conclusions are patently contrary to the revealed truth as proposed by the Church. The lack of such obvious opposition means that the theologian must reserve judgment until he has carefully re-examined by thorough investigation the apparent contradiction between scientific finding and his theological principles.

In this role of judging other sciences theology plays more than a merely negative role. It also has a positive role by declaring the consonance of certain natural discoveries with the principles of faith. When such concordance is declared there should be an immediate positive approach to determine what light faith can shed upon the newly discovered truth and, in turn, the significance of the truth to the theologian in his investigation of revelation. In exercising this role theology does not, therefore, go beyond the limit of its own competence. Indeed, it is the glory of the Thomistic synthesis that it restored to reason its proper province with its own method and rights in the investigation of truth.

The second function of theology which it exercises with respect to the inferior sciences is to order and direct them. It is this function which has been called into question in the current struggle to find a principle of unity or integration in Catholic education. Simply speaking, to integrate a curriculum means to posit a principle of order among the diversity of human arts and sciences. To answer the question, "What should be the principle of integration in a Catholic college?", one must first answer the question, "What is the proximate goal of Catholic college education?" A clear answer to this question has been given by one such institution:

> If we confine our consideration to that order of learning which pertains to the school, to the development of the intellectual virtues, it is not difficult to see what the principle of this order must be. The ambition of the school should be to take the student as far as he can go toward the development of the loftiest intellectual virtue, even as the doctor takes every measure in view of the ideal of perfect health, even when he knows he must be content with much less.
>
> But the highest intellectual virtue will be that which is closest to the life goal of the student . . . the development of perfect charity. Now the virtue of mind most closely connected with charity will have to be some sort of wisdom. As charity is ultimate in the will, so is wisdom in the mind.

> The goal of schooling, therefore, must be to bring the student as far as possible along the way toward wisdom. If we leave him at the level of intuition and common sense experience, he will never be equipped for the complexities and specialized thinking required in our developed culture. And if we leave him at the level of science he will be intellectually and personally disintegrated and a disintegrative force in society.
>
> What wisdom can the school teach? . . . it cannot teach that very highest wisdom which is most closely connected with charity, the infused wisdom of the Holy Spirit, without which all other knowledge can be a source of diabolic good as well as the highest good. This must be the constant thought that keeps the school humble. But it can teach the highest of acquired wisdoms, sacred theology. And to this it can and should closely link the highest natural wisdom, metaphysics.[10]

The problem of bringing unity out of the multiplicity of arts and sciences is, then, a question of subordination of the various parts to that which is ultimate in the order of human learning. As the family and state each have their own ends and their own means to attain them and yet are both subordinate to the Church, which orders them to a supernatural goal without destroying their respective autonomies, so each of the arts and sciences has its own proper sphere and principles, but ultimately all must be subordinated to the ultimate human wisdom which is sacred theology. In exercising its control over these other intellectual habits sacred theology is not despotic. It has rather a political dominion over them, respecting the rights of each. It thus plays an architectonic role with regard to the purely human sciences.

Not only must theology exercise an integrating role in the curriculum but also in the ordering of the learning of each student. To accomplish this task requires the college teacher of sacred doctrine to be conversant with the arts and sciences and employ them in the communication of his subject. This volume is directed to assist him in the accomplishment of that task. But the theologian must not be the sole faculty member with an integral view of human learning. Every teacher at the college level should have at the very minimum a liberal scientific knowledge of theology. Indeed, there is every reason to expect that the teacher in the Catholic college has an initiation into a truly scientific grasp of the truths of faith. Without this minimal knowledge of theology, such teachers will be unable to leave the Christian imprint on the intellectual virtues which they are striving to inculcate.

As Gilson has so clearly stated, the bridge between the knowledge of God and the human sciences is theology. In order for the teachers of the arts and sciences to build this bridge subjectvely, it is necessary that they have studied the knowledge of divine things in a scientific fashion. To attempt to refer human knowledge to God in a "pietistic" fashion can only have disastrous results.[11]

Far from disdaining the truths of the lower sciences, theology makes use of them in the task of defending and explaining revelation. While the object of theology, God himself, is supremely knowable, our knowledge of him through faith does not attain to a clear knowledge of him; this must await the eternal vision of heaven. Theology ". . . accepts its principles, not from other sciences, but immediately from God by revelation. Therefore it does not depend upon other sciences as upon the higher, but makes use of them as of the lesser and as handmaidens; even so the master sciences make use of the sciences that supply their materials, as political of military science. That it thus uses them is not due to its own defect or insufficiency, but to the defect of our intelligence, which is more easily led by what is known through natural reason (from which the other sciences proceed) to that which is above reason, such as are the teachings of this science."[12] When employed by theology in the defense and explanation of revelation, these lesser sciences participate ministerially, as we have said, in the theological function, and hence share a greater certitude than that proper to them within the scope of their own science.

The Liberal Scientific Knowledge of Theology

Few would argue that it is possible to teach theology to undergraduates at a perfect scientific level. Even were this the case, it would be improper to attempt it at the level of liberal education, for this does not aim at producing perfect scientists in any field. Is it then possible to adapt theological science to the undergraduate level of liberal scientific knowledge, and, if so, can this level of communication properly be termed "theology"?

The aim of a liberal scientific knowledge of theology is comparable to the aim of such knowledge in any given subject matter. Such an aim is to impart to the student, first of all, the nature of the subject to be taught; second, the divisions of the subject matter; third, the method of the science and its various parts; fourth, the manner of distinguishing valid from invalid procedure; and finally, the principal conclusions of the subject. The experience of qualified teachers indicates that this aim is capable of accomplishment in sacred doctrine or theology. A college student is capable of grasping the nature of this acquired wisdom and understanding the various functions with regard to its object and subject. Such students, especially those blessed with a background in Catholic secondary education, are able to learn the principles of the various theological tracts. Ability to understand how the main conclusions of the tracts flow from these principles is comparable to the college student's ability to reason in any of the other scientific subjects which he is pursuing: that is, the ability to follow and reproduce scientific arguments in each of the tracts. This level of teaching theology just as rightly deserves to be termed "theology" as does the teaching of chemistry at a liberal scientific level proper to undergraduate study to be termed "chemistry." There is, no doubt, a basis for not calling the end product of the college theology course "theology" among those who conceive of seminary courses and college courses in a univocal fashion, but this does not invalidate the affirmative response to the question involved. The difficulty of imparting a liberal scientific knowledge of theology without sufficient philosophical background on the part of the student is taken up in a later essay in this volume.[13]

One condition for the liberal scientific theology is that it must present theology as both a wisdom and a science. To accomplish this aim it is imperative that the order of the subject matter of theology be left intact. As we have indicated, this may present difficult pedagogical problems; but to sacrifice order for the sake of more facile presentation tends to minimize the sapiential character of theology, which views all things from a divine viewpoint. Moreover, this aim requires that all the functions of theology must be defined and their methodologies explained. While scholastic theology is not the sum of theology, emphasis at the undergraduate level must surely be placed upon this aspect of sacred doctrine rather than upon positive theology. The student is hardly in a position to launch into the sources of theology before he knows the principles and methods of the science. While one must not neglect the sources of revealed truths, the liberal scientific knowledge of theology proper to the undergraduate level should emphasize rather the meaning and relation of revealed truths and the principal conclusions drawn from them.

Thomistic Theology

There exists within the Church a plurality of theological systems. The human mind always tends to a system in the investigation of truth, and this tendency reaches its zenith when confronted with divine truth. Insofar as they respect the divine truth, the Church has approved and encouraged this theological plurality of such systems. The question arises with reference to college theology, "Which of these systems is most adaptable to the presentation of this science at an undergraduate level?" Père Chenu remarks that the Church should express her preference, because this falls within the scope of her authority to teach; he adds that her decision must also affect our judgment of the religious truth of a system.[14] Benedict XV, congratulating Fr. Pègues on the appearance of his French edition of the *Summa* in catechism form, remarked:

> The eminent commendations of Thomas Aquinas by the Holy See no longer permit a Catholic to doubt that he was divinely raised up that the Church might have a master whose doctrine should be followed in a special way at all times. The singular wisdom of the man seems suitable to be offered directly not only to the clergy but to all who wish to extend their study of religion, and to the people generally as well. For nature brings it about that the more clearly a person approaches to the light, the more fully is he illuminated.[15]

Father Ramírez concludes, from his study of the approbation given by the ordinary *magisterium* of the Church to the Thomistic synthesis, that "the Church concedes the highest theological authority to Thomas alone over the other ecclesiastical writers of all times. Therefore, his canonical authority in the field of theology is truly the greatest over each and every one of the Fathers and Doctors."[16] This does not mean, however, that all theological progress ceased with the death of the Angelic Doctor. It means only that in following his theological positions one can be certain of finding a faithful and truly Catholic understanding of revelation. As Lacordaire stated: "St. Thomas is not a boundary, but a beacon."

Not only is the Thomistic synthesis of theology to be preferred from the point of view of the authority of the *magisterium*, but pedagogically the system of the Angelic Doctor, both in method and in content, is unsurpassed in exposition of the truths of faith according to the true order of learning.[17] The originality of St. Thomas' genius can especially be appreciated in the order which he conceived for the *Summa Theologiae*. Prior to St. Thomas, most attempts at synthesis of doctrine assumed the chronological order of sacred history in the Bible. This greatly encumbered any effort to systematize and synthesize the great body of Christian doctrine, and demanded a work which would combine the logical and historical approaches to the matter of theology. In St. Thomas the Church was gifted with a man equal to the task. Reaching back beyond Christian and even Aristotelian conceptions, he chose a scheme advanced by Plato which united time and eternity, God and creatures, in one great theological synthesis. The Platonic notion of procession and regression allowed for unity in the *Summa* according to an intrinsic principle of organization—God, both in himself and as principle and term of all things. Hence in the first part of the *Summa*, St. Thomas treats of God considered in his divine essence and in the distinction of Persons. The procession of creatures follows, as the emanation from the first principle of being results in the production, distinction, conservation and government of creatures.

Chief among those creatures which God has made is man, created to his own image. Here we encounter another Platonic notion, that of God as exemplar and man as the image. In the second part of the *Summa*, St. Thomas begins with the *reditus* of creatures to their source. As he notes, "A gyration or circling about, as it were, is to be noted in the procession of creatures from their first principle, since all things return to their source, as to their end."[18] A general consideration of the ultimate end of man is followed by detailed inquiry into the means for its attainment. The circle would now seem to be complete, and the regression of creatures to their creator effected. But this is not so; as Fr. Chenu points out, the transition from Part II to Part III of the *Summa* is a "passage from the order of the necessary to the order of the historical."[19] Man has erred, and original sin has crippled, indeed rendered impossible, his return to the cause of his being. Hence, the third part of the *Summa* treats of Christ, who "showed unto us in his own person the way of truth, whereby we may attain to the bliss of eternal life by rising again."[20] Thus the Savior himself and his benefits to the human race complete the general outline of the *Summa.* The return of man to God has been accomplished through Christ, and the plan of theology so conceived encompasses all the matter of sacred doctrine in a unified whole, preserving a unity which has its source in God's own unity.

In thus organizing the treasure of Christian religion, St. Thomas has produced a literary work which pre-eminently deserves the title of "order of learning," for here he has expounded concisely the doctrines of our faith, organized them synthetically, and presented a product admirably suited for teaching this doctrine to others.

Pope Pius XII stated the fact admirably:

> It is that wisdom of Aquinas which collected the truths of human reason, illustrated them with brilliance, and most aptly and solidly unified them into a wonderful whole. It is the wisdom of Aquinas which is especially suited to declare and defend the dogmas of faith. And finally, it is his wisdom which was able to refute effectively the basic errors continually arising, and conquer them invincibly. Wherefore, dear sons, bring to St. Thomas a heart full of love and zeal. With all your powers strive to explore with your intellect his excellent doctrine.[21]

Footnotes to Study 3

[1]Those who may wish to investigate this important subject further should consult Franciscus Muniz, O.P., "De Diversis Muneribus S. Theologiae," *Angelicum,* XXIV (1947), 93-123 (most of this fine article, which forms the doctrinal basis for much of the present study, has been translated by John P. Reid, O.P.,

as *The Work of Theology* [Washington: The Thomist Press, 1953]). See also Edwin G. Kaiser, *Sacred Doctrine* (Westminster, Md.: The Newman Press, 1958); M.-D. Chenu, O.P., *Is Theology a Science?* (New York: Hawthorn Books, 1959); M.-J. Congar, O.P., "Théologie," *Dictionnaire de Théologie Catholique,* XV, 341-502 (especially 378-392, 447-502). Other references, including those to more basic sources, will be found in the works listed.

[2]*Summa,* I, q. 79, a. 11.

[3]*Ibid.,* ad 2.

[4]We have retained the distinction made by St. Thomas in *Q. D. de Ver.,* q. 3, a. 3, between *scientia practica actu* and *scientia practica habitu* and adopted his phraseology rather than that of modern authors who phrase this distinction in terms of *speculatively* and *practically* practical knowledge (cf. J. Maritain, *The Degrees of Knowledge* [New York: Charles Scribner's Sons, 1959], 311-16).

[5]Cf. Vatican Council Sess. III, *Dogmatic Constitution on the Catholic Faith,* Chap. 4, "Faith and Reason"; Denz. 1796.

[6]*Summa,* II-II, q. 2, a. 10.

[7]*Ibid.,* I, q. 1, a. 5.

[8]*Ibid.,* I, q. 1, a. 6.

[9]John of St. Thomas, *The Gifts of the Holy Ghost* (New York: Sheed & Ward, 1951), 124.

[10]*The Liberal Education of the Christian Person* (Chicago: St. Xavier College, 1953), 26-27.

[11]Étienne Gilson, *Christianity and Philosophy* (New York: Sheed & Ward, 1939), 119-120.

[12]*Summa,* I, q. 1, a. 5, ad 2; a. 8, ad 2.

[13]Cf. Study 6, "Theology and Philosophy."

[14]M.-D. Chenu, O.P., *Is Theology A Science?* (New York: Hawthorn Books, 1959), 112.

[15]Letter of Feb. 9, 1919, *AAS,* XI (1919), 71.

[16]Santiago Ramírez, O.P., "The Authority of St. Thomas," *The Thomist,* XV (1952), 46.

[17]Chenu, *op. cit.,* 112.

[18]*I Sent.,* d. 14, q. 2, a. 2.

[19]"Introduction to the Summa of St. Thomas," *Thomist Reader* (Washington: Thomist Press, 1958), 26.

[20]*Summa,* III, prologue.

[21]Pius XII to the students of the regular and secular clergy at Rome, June 24, 1939, *AAS,* XXXI (1939), 246.

4

THE OBJECTIVE OF COLLEGE THEOLOGY

Urban Voll, O.P.

A Lector and Licentiate in Sacred Theology and a candidate for the doctorate, Father Voll has had wide experience in the teaching of theology at the undergraduate level, both in men's and women's colleges. Now lecturing at the Xaverian Brothers College, Silver Springs, Md., he is an editor of The Thomist. *He is actively engaged as a lecturer in the "Theology for the Laity" series in Washington, D.C.*

Any discussion of aim is likely to prove a thorny task. Motivation usually lies buried so deeply in the personality that the basic reasons for our activity are more often simply assumed rather than explicitly explored. In the very assumption there lies peril. The man who plods along the valleys of life with scarcely a glance at the towering peaks rising before him risks missing his ultimate destination. While a human being should be making straight tracks towards the vision of heaven, he may be just wandering through the shifting sands of life, not redeeming the time. Yet another danger—that of being misunderstood—awaits the one who, if not so presumptuous as to play the guide, would nonetheless (rather as a persistent gadfly) question half-conscious and obscurely formulated objectives. The answers as they emerge from the dialogue may seem either unbearably platitudinous or unrealistically abstract.

Still the effort of discovering aim remains imperative, for it is of the human essence. Other animals may blindly trace the path of life marked out for them by their Maker; as mechanical specialists, they perform their single task very well. The human person, however, must exercise his own prudence under divine providence. Not only is the unexamined life, as Plato said, not worth living; the unanalyzed course of action may result in wasted effort. There is also that peril of perils, the awful possibility of ultimate frustration.

The uninformed might think that the importance of aim would be most fully realized and practised by those who live in what has been called "the house of intellect." The college campus is recognized as a place of human learning. This learning is sometimes supposed to be more than an amalgam of unassorted facts; the world legitimately expects that the academicians will give some direction, if not to the world beyond its walls (although that too is frequently hoped), at least to their own activity. Despite such high hopes, there is more aimlessness on the academic scene than professors care to admit. The pompous declarations of catalogs and the florid oratory of commencement addresses will not stand too close scrutiny. For instance, the accrediting agencies rightly demand a clear formulation of objectives; yet these same agencies are content with an evaluation of the means selected towards the achievement of those objectives, and remain very chary about judgments on the validity of the objectives themselves. If the question of aim is occasionally raised, there is an embarrassing pause followed by rapid retreat: "That, of course, is a matter of philosophy." Philosophy in this semantic context seems to signify personal opinion, even prejudice, which is beyond polite discussion. Another example of academic vagueness about aim might be taken from a current and somewhat predominant theory of education which consists in the formulation of objectives not in intention but as they are actually accomplished. This outright denial of the nature of finality means that we cannot know where we are going until we actually get there. As a concrete instance, in a large state university the department of philosophy (a place one might expect clarity on ultimates) changed its original, stated aim to a skeptical spirit towards all philosophies, when this result, according to student response to a questionnaire, was actually achieved.

Such confusion of purpose would seem less likely in Catholics, to whom a supernatural goal has been revealed. The Catholic educator, as a believer, accepts without question the advice of the Old Testament preacher to remember the last end, and is not likely to forget the command of the divine preacher of the New Testament to seek first the kingdom of God. In point of fact, Catholic educators, in official pronouncement, are likely to be extremely explicit about their ultimate motivation, which they usually assert is the greater glory of God, and secondly, as subordinate to it, the salvation of souls.

Granted this motivation (which must be present in every course in the curriculum of a Christian school), what is the special objective of the course in theology? If a place in the curriculum is to be assigned to it, the college administration, the Church and any other interested agencies have the right to expect that the end of theology is at least being sought. Thus, for any thorough analysis of the aim of theology in the college, the finality of theology itself must be considered.

While it may seem too obvious to deserve mention, there must be some agreement on the proposition that we teach *something* to someone. The proponents of student-centered curricula are fond of the slogan, "You teach students." True, but the transitive verb "to teach" has a double object, one direct, the thing taught (which St. Thomas calls "the object of the interior concept")[1] and the other indirect, in the dative case, which is the student to whom the knowledge is communicated ("the object of the audible word").[2] Thus learning must precede teaching; the teacher himself must first study, humbly contemplate the truth he is later to communicate. The nature and function of that learning has a primacy of authority as well as of place in the solution of the problem. Of course, those who emphasize the importance of the student are quite right in this respect; knowledge of a subject by no means implies, as every student knows, the ability to communicate. Thus to approach the problem of the aim of theology in the college one must ask questions about the nature and purpose of theology and the nature and purpose of a college student undertaking such a study.

The Historical Situation

Before entering what might be called the metaphysics of the problem, the historical situation must be reviewed. We are dealing here with something more than a sphere of abstract essences; we are rather confronted with an existential reality in all its concrete conditions of time and place, namely, twentieth century America. The American Catholic college of today cannot—indeed, should not—escape the ambient culture. God himself lives in eternity; the destiny to which he has called his children is likewise timeless, union with God himself. Yet the Word of God became flesh at a particular moment in human history in the hills of Palestine, and Christ's Church delivers his word and vicariously performs his action in second century Asia Minor, in medieval European monastery, and on the contemporary American campus. There will be helpful analogues from other times and other places, no doubt; nevertheless, today's college is a unique institution in a unique situation. Catholic colleges rightly trace their proud lineage to great universities in a glorious past, but a descendant is not by that fact the same as his ancestor.

Take, for one thing, the faculty of the modern college—clerical, religious and lay. If St. Paul manifests his early rabbinical training in his epistles, if St. Augustine remains to some extent the Platonist rhetorician in his preaching as a Christian bishop, it may well be that the professor in today's classroom, however devoutly Catholic in heart, is not always necessarily so in mind. Most of the teachers in Catholic colleges are either graduates of secular universities or of Catholic universities staffed by professors from secular universities. Teachings difficult to reconcile with Christian revelation may be imbibed uncritically in much the same way that young philosophers at the thirteenth century University of Paris accepted Arabian Aristotelianism. Until the advent of a vigorous, synthetic mind which can separate wheat from chaff, the ordinary student may rightly hesitate before the tables of secular learning. Shall he eat meats which may have been sacrificed to idols and thus risk poisoning his faith? Or shall he go away fasting into an obscurantist desert, out of contact with his fellow scholars from whom he can learn much, and, it may be added, to whom he can give much?

Another problem which the Catholic college at this time shares with every American college is the level of instruction. The students by age and previous training are beyond that level of secondary education which the European tradition calls college, and yet are certainly not sufficiently advanced to that caliber of graduate study represented by the university. The college "level" becomes doubly problematic by constant shifting. Observers of contemporary education see the old idea of the American college as a preparation for a professional elite (represented by pre-legal and pre-medical curricula) changing to a general, terminal education for the majority of the citizenry.

But the present and immediate concern is what the Catholic college has done in its relatively short history to make itself specifically Catholic in its course-offerings. The emphasis on curriculum is deliberate, for, whatever advantages there may be to atmosphere, it is not of the scholastic essence, but rather, in the philosophical use of the word, accidental. The crosses surmounting college spires, the habits of monks and nuns adding sober colors to the gaily attired crowds of American youth, wayside crucifixes on campus walks, statues and religious paintings embellishing academic halls, even the chapel with its worship of the Blessed Sacrament—all these may make the "outsider" vaguely uncomfortable and the Catholic at home, while providing occasions of grace, but they are not directly relevant to the act of teaching.

Besides the atmosphere, some have seen the value of the Catholic college as somewhat negative. In it nothing would be taught which would be explicitly opposed to Catholic doctrine. History and literature, to take obvious areas of possible conflict, would be free of any anti-Catholic bias. (As a matter of fact, critics have charged that in Catholic colleges Catholic mistakes are minimized and Catholic contributions overstated.) Science at first glance seemed to have as little bearing on religious questions as mathematics, for the material taught remained the same, whether the teacher was a pious nun or a blatant atheist. However, as the situation actually developed, it became apparent that the *weltanschauüng* of the teacher and the consequent interpretation given the matter—even by silence—might not be without importance. Though such contributions of atmosphere and negative orthodoxy might be genuine enough, they have seemed small when the Church's heavy contribution in both money and personnel is taken into consideration.

Besides, there were more direct and positive attempts to teach Catholic doctrine in the curriculum. Only yesterday, if conscience asked Catholic educators what they did to impart religious instruction, they would have pointed with legitimate pride to the heavier burden their students bore in courses of philosophy. These students were enabled to face their confused contemporaries with the magnificent tool—one might say, weapon—of Aristotelian logic, the solution to some modern epistemological difficulties, an appreciation of the place of the Greek and medieval philosophers in the history of thought, and perhaps even a smattering of metaphysics. Their courses in ethics were quite specific and detailed.

While such riches are not to be spurned, a doubt has been raised more recently by some Catholic philosophers—in what sense can philosophy be Christian and still remain really philosophical?[3] If philosophy is, as still proclaimed in introductory courses, the study of ultimate reality by reason alone, how can it be directly and specifically Catholic? The boundaries between faith and reason may not always be clearly marked, but surely there are boundaries. If the Vergil of philosophy could conduct the seeker of truth to the borders of paradise, he must still hand over his charge to the Beatrice of theology as the guide to the celestial spheres. Philosophy performs a most useful service as precursor, but the Baptist is no substitute for the Christ. Nor indeed had any Catholic philosopher ever said so, though some college curricula might have given that impression.

What then of the religion department, as it was called? It was universally inferior to the philosophy department, however that might have ranked with the other departments. Poorly equipped teachers, with few classes at awkward hours and easy-mark status, wondered just what they were supposed to be doing. They found themselves engaged on several fronts. First, there was a supplementation and continuation of previous training in Christian doctrine or the want thereof. Then there was apologetics, so necessary to the Church in the state of siege. This work had begun in philosophy with proofs for the existence of God, the spirituality and immortality of the soul, and perhaps the ethical necessity of religion, but it had to be continued, of course, in the religion-study of the divinity of Christ and his Church. Next, some inspiration towards Christian ideals was needed, and towards this end topics such as the life of Christ suggested themselves. Finally, there had to be some counselling in practical moral problems; this was usually accomplished in what amounted to an informal seminar called "Life-Problems."

What, then, were these teachers of religion actually trying to do? If their varied operations may now be evaluated in retrospect, it becomes obvious that all the functions were theological in character. To defend revelation against the attacks of the gentiles, to give, in St. Peter's words, "a reason for the hope that is in you" (I Pet. 3:15), is recognized as an important, albeit subsidiary work of theology.[4] To apply the principles of Christian morals to the concrete problems of life is the business of moral theology. As soon as any exegesis of the life of Christ or any part of the Bible (however elementary the explanation) attempts to go beyond philology, geography and chronology, it becomes explicative of revelation, and hence again theological.

Thus about twenty years ago the situation of the religion courses in America was such that a fruitful comparison might be made with the state of theology which St. Thomas discovered in the universities of his day. He complained about the multiplication of useless questions; that complaint might well strike a familiar chord in any teacher submitted to the question-box technique of the life-problem seminar. St. Thomas worried that beginners were confused by the want of a proper order of learning, since questions were treated "according as the explanation of books required." Père Chenu suggests that this would be a biblical order.[5] Religion teachers at first beguiled by the apparent simplicity of a Genesis to Apocalypse chronology soon discovered that frequent repetition of the same themes begot boredom and confusion.

In the last few years the members of the departments of religion began to speak of their courses as "theology." This was not mere fashionable status-seeking; they insisted that their course offerings should present at least the same level of excellence and challenge as the other courses. As every effort was bent in that direction, divergent proposals were considered. Beneath this question of better content lurked the problem of aim. The battle for the existence of theology was hardly won when the victors found themselves confronted with an internal question of essence, which in itself depended on the more fundamental definition of purpose. The first national convention of the Catholic College Teachers of Sacred Doctrine heard the various plans proposed by different groups in 1955,[6] but a year later the question of finality came up for discussion. Two points of departure were used, that of theology itself and the finality of the layman.[7]

Doctrine versus Student

Thus the historical situation arrives at the same impasse as the "metaphysical" problem of teaching. The nature and purpose of the doctrine to be taught must be sought; the pedagogical art must be employed to communicate this doctrine to a particular student. St. Thomas' distinction between the object of the interior word and the object of the audible word has already been mentioned.[8] Professor Gilbert Highet, in a deservedly popular little manual, *The Art of Teaching,* makes almost the same point. "First, and most necessary of all, he [the teacher] must know the subject. He must know *what* he teaches."[9] Later, in his history of great teachers, Mr. Highet singles out the Jesuits as an example of the second important element —adaptation for communication. "Now how could the few [important] men be converted, the emperor, the courtiers and the mandarins? Not as a Dominican priest with Pizarro had tried to convert the ruler of Peru, by giving him the Bible untranslated, but by approaching them through something they already admired."[10] Anyone can recognize the soundness of the two principles invoked here: first, only he who knows can teach; secondly, the teacher must lead the student from the known to the unknown.

Practice of the principles, as is so often the case, remains another matter. Apparently most of the errors in the art of teaching result from the application of one principle with a neglect of the other. Or, in other words, there is an excessive attachment to one object—either what is taught or the person taught—to the detriment of the other. Pizarro's Dominican was so bent on maintaining purity of doctrine that he forgot the Incas could not read Latin. The Jesuit missionaries were excellent at communication, but other missionaries complained to the Holy See that the Catholic faith was being compromised.[11] The Incas had to be converted by better teachers; the Church has at times to stem enthusiastic zeal when hard sayings are softened to make converts. The current controversies on public school education in our country are at root a variation on this ancient theme. The old-fashioned methods left a great deal to be desired in communication arts; the student-centered adjustment, on the other hand, has tended to eviscerate content.

Balance here is as important as it is to a tightrope walker, and perhaps as difficult to achieve. The balance can be maintained only by keeping the proper tension between the two magnetic attractions, the doctrine and the student. Certain teachers by the very inclination of temperament tend to be either scholars or shapers of men. Every college faculty has its examples of scholars who cannot communicate and leaders of youth who have little to communicate. Perhaps each could learn from the other to approach the ideal. The abstruse scholar must be reminded he is not addressing a vacuum or an academy of his peers, but a student; the molder of men must be more contemplative, a disciple to doctrine so that his influence has meaning beyond the communication of his own personality.

If it be granted, then, as a matter of common sense, that teaching has two ends—the purpose of the doctrine taught (*finis quod*) and the purpose of the student who is taught (*finis cui*)—do both these ends have equal importance, or does one merit subordination to the other? Virtue keeps the golden mean, rising like a peak between two extremes; yet virtue does lean towards one side. Courage, for instance, inclines towards audacity rather than to cowardice. If the professor of college theology would, as a newcomer on the academic scene, consult his colleagues of the other faculties, he might learn a few things. Likewise, he might not so easily alienate himself from the community of learning, where he may be suspected as an intruder, a preacher rather than a teacher, more of a chaplain and morale-builder—not to say propagandist—rather than a professor of a legitimate branch of knowledge.[12] For their part, the biologist, the mathematician have no intention of revising their respective sciences for undergraduate consumption. They naturally select, simplify and adjust in order to give a broad, liberal knowledge of the general content and methodology of their disciplines. But they would regard any imputation that the college biology or history or mathematics which they teach was essentially different from the science they had learned as close to insult, an accusation of tampering with their material. The teacher of theology has even graver reasons for unswerving fidelity to the message he is called to transmit, for that message is of divine origin. *College theology, then, is essentially theology as it is taught to a college student in certain existential conditions.*

In current talk about the role of theology in the college, the statement that the seminary course is not the model of the college course has been accepted as axiomatic; in fact, the phrase has become something of a shibboleth. What seems to be overlooked is the objective of the seminary itself, which is not the preparation of theologians but of priests. The seminary should not only teach theology as something liberal, to be sought for its own sake, but also as a preparation for a function, the sacred function of power over the eucharistic Body of Christ in the Mass, and derivatively over the members of the Mystical Body of Christ. The point which deserves emphasis is that both seminary and college—and indeed any educational agency—should take a long, careful look at the nature of theology itself before putting it into the service of some other end, even though that end is infinitely higher.[13]

In one of the pioneer efforts towards theology for the laity, the eminent Father J. C. Murray, S.J., bases his reshaping on the principle that theology does not exist for its own sake.[14] His preoccupation with the existential, historical situation prevents anything more than a superficial understanding of the essence of the science. In fact, in a later critique of scholastic theology, some doubt is cast on the validity and adequacy of Aristotle's concept of science.[15] Unquestionably valuable as Father Murray's efforts have been to discern the role of the laity in the Church, the sound metaphysical principle (which underlies this discussion on the art of teaching) that habits—such as science—are primarily specified by their object rather than by their subject must be strenuously maintained. The twofold object of teaching remains the focal poles of discussion. Moreover, several important factors militate against such subordination of the aim of the science to the aim of the student. For one thing, such an inversion of ends, if carried to a rigorously logical though absurd conclusion, would mean that, of two theological explanations, the one better adapted to the student needs would be adopted. Of course loyalty to truth demands that the more correct explanation would merit preference; in theology, particularly, the explanation which best expresses the mystery as revealed would have priority.

Furthermore, when the objective character of the science is attenuated for some other purpose—moving towards a student-centered science—the true and the good, because difficult to learn and practice, are likely to be pushed in the background for the interesting and the utilitarian. This in its turn could eventually lead to the forfeiture of the place of theology in the curriculum. Already proposals which involve "doing" as well as "learning" have been made. Such laboratory sessions would include liturgical participation, initiation into contemplative prayer, essays in apostolic aid activities (e.g., programs of witness and enterprises of effective sympathy for human beings in misery and so on).[16] One might wonder—how are such activities to be graded for report? But the promoters of such schemes have their own peculiar view of the college as a communicator of a "vital vision" rather than an institution for learning science.[17] Accrediting agencies, graduate schools and college administration, to say nothing of the rest of the faculty, might come to regard the department of theology as a ministry of propaganda and indoctrination, no matter how sympathetically they regarded such aims. The net result would be that theology, instead of occupying its rightful place with the other sciences, would inevitably be regarded as an extension of the chaplain's office. The chaplain in the armed services has at best a tenuous connection with the main purpose of the military; theology, in attempting more than its proper role, might be regulated to a morale-builder standing on the academic sidelines. Theology can demand a place in the academic community only on condition that it maintain its intellectual character, communicating a content and initiating the students in a methodology which are not duplicated by any other courses.

The Objective of Theology

Before speaking of the scientific aim of theology, however, it should be noted that what any teacher of sacred doctrine at any level intends to communicate is a certain content—divine revelation, and that in its totality. A sister preparing a little boy for his first communion, a seminary professor preparing a deacon for holy orders—both are communicating essentially the same content, although the degree of explicitness and emphasis are obviously quite different. This degree of explicitness is not a question of the gradual revelation evident in the Old Testament and in the preaching of Jesus; the revelation now complete is in process of explication. The inspired author of the epistle to the Hebrews mentions only two truths necessary for belief: that God is, and that he rewards those seeking him (Heb. 11:2). The current Act of Faith is a little more definite on the nature of God and the means of seeking him; four truths—the Blessed Trinity, the Incarnation, Redemption and Parousia—are named. Then an implicit formula, "these and all the truths thou hast revealed," is employed to cover any other revealed truths. The Apostles' Creed with its twelve articles goes into much greater detail on the mystery of Christ, though it takes but a breath from birth to death. The "Quicumque" adds many further explications on the intimate relations of the three divine Persons to each other and to the divine essence. Finally, catechisms, while graded for the different levels of elementary and secondary schools, still present in substance the same essential content.

Theology does no less, though in one sense it does a little more. Theology as taken here concerns the God of revelation, but the "ology" (*logia*) in its title implies an ordered discourse, a rational operation from principle to conclusion. There is something more here than simple faith. The believer accepts the content of revelation. God speaks; the man of faith listens and assents. But if the believer goes on to think, makes an attempt to discover the meaning of the revelation he has accepted, he is, whether he reflects upon it or not, theologizing. In this wide sense, every believer must be something of a theologian, as every man must be something of a philosopher. If the question, "Why theology?", is raised, the simplest answer would seem to be this: "Because it is inevitable!"[18] If the believer can and does reflect on the meaning of his faith, he can and ought to be taught to think correctly about those matters of ultimate concern which God has revealed. However low our opinion of the modern college student, few teachers would be so habitually pessimistic as to maintain without reservation that the young adult who puts in hours of laboratory research, reads the great classics in every field, grasps the elements of logic and mathematics is altogether incapable of thought. The older "religion" courses of the college were informally performing theological operations involving some explanation of revealed doctrines, their defense, an examination of revealed sources, and sometimes the use of logic or metaphysics and other instruments of human culture to penetrate the meaning of the divine message.

Speculation and Contemplation

It now seems generally conceded that the central themes of theology and something of its methodology ought to be taught in the Catholic college. While that position has apparently triumphed, some lingering doubts about the intrinsic finality of theology itself remain, especially in regard to the traditional idea that theology is primarily speculative. Perhaps the unfavorable connotations—"speculation" currently means something uncertain, such as the fluctuation of the stock market or the outcome of a horse race—might be avoided in putting it this way: theology is primarily contemplative. Even with such unfavorable connotations removed, some fear that pragmatic

Americans may not be charmed by anything which is sought for its own sake, especially when that is knowledge. However, recent interest in the contemplative life and renewed interest in liberal education and the humanities, which are pursued for what truth, goodness and beauty may be found in them—these may be the constellation presiding over a climate congenial to theological contemplation.

Students of Newman's classic, *The Idea of a University,* are aware of the noble efforts he made to establish truth as a good in itself. Knowledge is an aim, and truth itself is not really something man has so much as it is something which has him. Man is *not* the measure of things; the world outside is rather the measure of the human mind. It is a mark of intellectual health to be in touch with things external. To live in a world of fancy created by the mind, to ignore the reality outside, is, of course, in varying degrees an invitation to insanity. The scientist is objective; he sits down, first of all curiously, but also humbly, before the facts as they are, although he may later by reason of this contemplation be able to manipulate nature to his own purposes. The humanities make a good case for themselves in arguing that some things are worth knowing for themselves. Cannot an even better case be presented for divinity? The believer holds that the supernatural is as real as, in fact more real than, the world of nature; surely, then, he must consider that this supernatural sphere is worthy of intelligent interest—in fact, burning curiosity and serious study with the best instruments available.

Nevertheless, this has not been, nor is it now, the actual situation. The Jews, to whom God's initial revelation was made, seem to have been less interested in knowing God than in doing his will. Even much later the emphatically practical character of certain schools of Christian spirituality led some to think of the supreme revelation of God, his most intimate life in the Blessed Trinity, as a conundrum to be intellectually swallowed without attempt at digestion. In fact, when the intellectually curious attitude of the Grecian mind began to permeate the maturing Christian society, some were alarmed at the intrusion of such paganism, crying warnings against any league between the celestial Jerusalem and the too terrestrial Athens. There will probably always be some in the ranks of devoutly religious people who suspect any intellectual curiosity about the object of belief as undue and inordinate. The phrase from that expression of the *devotio moderna* which is the *Imitation of Christ*—"What doth it avail thee to dispute learnedly of the Holy Trinity, if by thy pride thou art displeasing to the Holy Trinity?" —will certainly be quoted. Passing over the fact that other schools of devotion almost opposite in spirituality have produced great saints, and accepting the question as it stands, is there really a necessary connection (which seems implied by many who quote it) between the abuse of knowledge by pride and knowledge itself?

As Chesterton somewhere remarks, what is implied as obvious beyond question is sometimes more important than what is actually said. The miles of typewriter ribbon and recording tape spun out on the argument between the purely speculative and the practical aims of theology go even deeper than ancient disputes on the primacy of intellect and will to the very personalities of the debaters. Manuals of applied psychology offer various categories of personalities: the physical, such as cerebral, visceral; the Freudian electra and oedipus complexes; the Adlerian introvert and extrovert types; and so forth. At least as meaningful as these classifications would be the ancient division according to what is proper to man, his reason. That ancient division into speculative and practical men is combined in the Platonic ideal of the philosopher-king, an ideal which is rarely achieved. This natural division is found in Christian thought as the contemplative and active forms of life, and embodied in the Mary-Martha antithesis. If there is any truth to this division (and there must be some for it to have survived so long in the works of great thinkers), then it might not be entirely improbable that those who argue so heatedly against the speculative in general and against the contemplative in religious matters are more or less unconsciously motivated by their Marthan solicitude about many things, and some intolerance towards those who occupy themselves with the one thing necessary.

When a religious order representing a school of spirituality adopts a particular emphasis, that emphasis will most likely make itself felt in the apostolate of that order as a corporate personality. This will also be true in academic matters. As a matter of fact, in a current discussion someone raised the question whether the particular spirituality of the teacher should enter into his teaching. Passing over the question of the propriety, it would seem somewhat likely that it actually *does*. If a religious teacher has been trained to make his meditation a spiritual exercise which must *always* culminate in some very practical resolution, it would seem unlikely that such a teacher would communicate any religious doctrine without explicitly drawing some practical conclusion. Since the thought precedes its communication, the attitude of mind which always looks for some norm for daily living is likely to be somewhat out of sympathy with a speculation it can only deem sterile, a contemplation it sees as fruitless. Thus, in speaking of the Christian kerygma, the practical Martha may just assume it is necessarily and always a challenging exhortation to activity. Some of the nuances of the divine love-letters (as St. Jerome suggests we think of the Scriptures, as loving communications of the secrets of hearts between friends) are surely going to be missed by such a person. The spirit of wondering adoration and affective love embodied in St. Paul's *O altitudo* will be passed over quickly to get to the practical, ethical, personal application.

Theology as Practical

This by no means should be taken as an attack on the practical. As we shall see very shortly, the practical is an important, even necessary part of the aim of theology itself. What is under attack here is the anti-speculative, anti-contemplative virus which lurks under many a proposal, not only for a student-centered curriculum, but for revisions in the content of theology itself, so that the Mystical Body of Christ or the economy of salvation or the life of Christ are the absolutely most important themes precisely because they are considered to have more practical impact. It is always a sad thing, a tragedy, when the speculative thinkers are exiled from the academic community, the one place they surely belong. It is a good thing when the contemplative is honored in the Christian community, for these souls are more directly occupied with the real and ultimate purpose of the Christian life. A professor in a Catholic college who is even by attitude anti-speculative and anti-contemplative is hardly going to be able to engender in his students a respect and love for what is in reality the higher function of the intellectual life.

But the most distressing thing is that theology itself is perverted and battered since it is primarily speculative. God, the principal object of theology by its very name, is non-operable. Human science may at times overlook the contemplation of nature and concern itself with harnessing its forces; the divine science cannot treat divinity as if he were an instrument to be manipulated.

Happily, however, there is no need for those who accept theology as more speculative to be anti-practical. Here there is no "nothing but," no "either/or" antithesis; theology represents a Kierkgaardian both/and. Theology is unique in being both speculative and practical, for its single object, God himself, is both a Truth to be known and a Good to be loved. As a matter of fact, if one were to consider only a quantitative consideration of the various treatises of theology, one might conclude that theology was more practical than speculative.

But, besides the fact that qualitative analysis comes closer to the essence and thus to the end of a thing, it would be giving an unjustified elasticity to the word "practical" to include the inspirational. For example, the treatise on the Blessed Trinity, while offering magnificent material for acts of adoration, humility, love, is in itself speculative. Even while admitting the full vigor of the Thomistic principle in the study of the life of Christ, "his every action is for our instruction," it would be a dangerous half-truth to present the gospels as only inspirational and merely as a pattern for the individual Christian life.

It is necessary, then, to be quite clear about the practical character of theology. If truth as such calls for contemplation, truth as goodness has the further aspect of desirability. The theologian has for his task not only the consideration of God as he is in himself (God as the Alpha, creator of all beings outside himself) but also God as the Omega, the end and purpose of all his restless striving. In that restless striving, in human activity, something new is added to theological contemplation—creativity. Certainly the heart and the flesh are in some way involved in contemplation, but the mind predominates. In the order of the practical, the mind is also involved, but the response to an end to be achieved through means is significantly entitled the "voluntary," from the will. If the major aim of theology is contemplation, it is not the integral aim of theology as it exists in the pilgrim still journeying towards his heavenly destination. Heaven is necessarily otherworldly, and any attempt to create a heaven on earth, even in theological contemplation, is false to itself, fantasy instead of reality, and doomed to frustration instead of fulfillment.

The Practical Aim of Theology

In insisting on the practical aim of theology, however, one must not identify the practical as if it were only exhortation or casuistry. Exhortation is not intellectual; persuasion and sermonizing undoubtedly have an honored place in the Christian works of mercy by which all are to be judged, but instruction, while in the same genus of a work of mercy, has its own specific difference. Even psychologically, overt selling in the classroom is not likely to achieve its purpose. The student who suspects that he is being "got at" through a sales-talk or commercial may arm himself with skeptical sales-resistance. On the other hand, instruction which leads to conviction is more likely to produce the desired action as flowing from the innate desirability of the object. Spiritual writers have remarked that genuine progress comes by way of steady meditation rather than by emotional spurts induced by revivalist technique. Moreover, exhortation instead of instruction, even in morals, and the consequent confusion of professor's lecturn with preacher's pulpit, has a pejorative effect on the theologian's status in the university community. There may be historical reasons why theology has been excluded from the secular campus and why it has been relegated to an inferior place on the Catholic campus, but one important reason for the present reluctance to admit theology to its rightful place seems to be a fear that the theologian will, by reason of his commitment in faith, be a doctrinaire zealot or an evangelist. If the theologian is going to be accepted, he will be expected to practice a calm objectivity, a serenity like that of St. Thomas.[19]

This quality of the intellectual is best achieved by the teaching of principles in morals. Examples, of course, there must be; applications there must be. Moral theology is by nature practical, and the perfection of the practical is in the concrete, singular action. However, the distinction between moral theology (which, as a science, deals with universal principles) and personal prudence (which deals with singulars) must be preserved. The theologian of all people should be the first to realize that he cannot perform the function of the Holy Spirit and his grace, and that he ought not to substitute dictation for counsel, and thus relieve the student of personal decision and responsibility. It is not without significance that that gift of the Spirit which is both intellectual and practical is not judgment or command but counsel. In short, even though the end of moral theology is practical, it is a practicality of the universal. It is a scientific study of the true as good. It remains an intellectual discipline.

The Aim of the Student

Here it is necessary to return to the very important problem of communication, lest the content of sacred doctrine be assumed to exist in a vacuum, a library or only in the mind of a don who thinks students an intolerable interruption to academic contemplation. Sacred doctrine, to use St. Thomas' initial phraseology, is obviously meant to be taught. Now that we have considered something of the intrinsic finality of the sacred realities taught, once the contemplative act which precedes the apostolic work of teaching is presupposed, the student himself should be focused in the teacher's vision.

The theologian, then, must descend from the rarefied atmosphere of Mount Olympus to the busy marketplace of the Agora. Or perhaps it would be more in the religious context to change the metaphor to a Moses descending from Mount Sinai to his and God's people on the plain below. The intention of the image here is not to suggest that the children of Israel may be busy worshipping a golden calf (though that may at times be the situation), but that they are indeed the children of the covenant.

By this is meant that the students must first of all be Catholics, that is, faithful, people with a personal commitment to God's word. Other auditors may be present, and it may be possible to present the material of sacred doctrine to them (although the method should then be apologetic, *contra Gentiles,* rather than expository). Unbelievers are in the minority in a class for Catholic theology, and certainly a separate approach for them is highly desirable. But their mention here serves to underline the absolute necessity of the student's assent to the principles of theology—the revelation of God, the teaching of his Church. This assent is no mere suspension of judgment, no poetic credulity given for the moment to appreciate the voyages of Ulysses or the journeys of Dante or Jules Verne. Entertainment by a teller of tales has its place, no doubt, but the confrontation of reality, even though it be an invisible reality, offers an infinitely higher and much more important challenge. The topography of the land of Oz and the constitution of the heavenly Jerusalem, however superficially similar, are really not in the same class.

Therefore the student of theology must have the infused faith which baptism gives; if he has not, he is no more in a position to study theology than the would-be student of geometry who cannot see the self-evident axioms with which his study must begin. Once it is admitted that the subject or material cause, the student, is a member of the faithful, it can easily be seen how the ultimate aim of theology itself and the student dovetail. St. Thomas tells us in his opening articles that another, sacred teaching is needed besides the philosophical disciplines *for human salvation.* The ritual for baptism has the priest engaged in an illuminating dialogue with the catechumen: "What do you ask of the Church of God? Faith. What does faith offer you? *Everlasting life.*"

Now obviously the faith which offers everlasting life is that which works through charity, living faith fruitful in good works, for the priest continues: "If, then, it is life that you wish to enter, keep the commandments. Love the Lord your God with your whole heart, and with your whole soul, and with your whole mind; and love your neighbor as you love yourself." Which brings up the important question—is the faith which is presupposed in the student necessarily a living faith, that is, must the student be in the state of grace? Wholeheartedly granting the desirability, we must admit that here we must be realist. One advocate of college theology presents an excellent analysis of actual students and breaks them down into an upper group of "supernaturalists," a lower group of "quasi-secularists," and a middle "average" group.[20] Perhaps it would not be completely foreign to the analysis to give the groups theological tags. The upper group would be those with living faith; they are described indeed as "doers of the word." Those in the lower group might with hesitation be said to have dead faith; they are found apathetic and antagonistic, with an almost violent desire to escape the moral consequences of belief. The reasons for hesitation in such classification go quite beyond the fact that the majority will be found in the middle group, which varies too much for any categorizing; actually, since God alone dwells in the mind, and we ourselves do not know whether we are deserving of praise or blame, we are not in a position to judge the state of soul of a student, any more than we are in a position to judge his predestination. However, we are certain of God's universal salvific will, of the universal efficacy of Christ's passion, and these imply in the moral order that charity, which includes the effective charity of this spiritual work of mercy—teaching—be extended not only to the actual friends of God but even to those who are only potentially so. Since the circumstances confine us to those who are, as St. Paul says, of "the household of the faith," there is at least some consolation in dealing with those whose potency to be members of Christ is at least actuated by some kind of faith and hope.

The Student as Christian

It has already been mentioned that the teacher of college theology has a great deal to learn from his colleagues who are expert in the other sciences. This openness of the theologian is not only useful as a means of forging an instrument by which the principles of revelation can in some manner be penetrated; there is also much to be learned about the nature of the student. However, it is precisely in this area of the *ultimate* end of the student that the theologian has nothing to learn from other human agencies, and, in fact, has everything to teach.

The theologian has to theologize, not only about theology, but about his act of teaching—a spiritual work of mercy—and about his student. The student, he must remind himself and any others who tend to forget it, is a creature of God, fallen through sin, redeemed by the blood of Jesus Christ, and destined for the beatific vision of the Blessed Trinity.

Here, however, the ultimateness of his view must not betray him into forgetting proximate ends, any more than the ultimateness of the end of Catholic education should make the Catholic administrator forget proximate and intermediate goals. This remark is to be taken as a judicious criticism of the evangelical approach in the classroom. While recalling the glorious supernatural destiny of the Christian, the teacher should also remember that this Christian is a student here and now, not a member of the Sunday congregation, much less a penitent seeking direction on his personal problems.

If there are some who seem to stress the ultimate end, there are others who seem to go to the other extreme to stress an aim which is too proximate. These latter are preoccupied with the role of the layman and his apostolate in the modern world. These considerations are by no means irrelevant; the discussion of the baptismal and confirmation characters in relation to Catholic Action is vital to the entire problem. But it is not the whole problem. Passing over the fact that some courses in college theology are offered to clerical and religious students, the danger in rearranging the entire concept of theology for the benefit of lay apostles is that it narrows and restricts the student. Apologetic themes and techniques are likely to assume proportions which are unrealistic. The soul of the apostolate, we are reminded, is the interior life, which is best nourished by doctrine and sound spiritual theology as normative. The circumstances of life as well as the inability of some will not permit every Catholic alumnus and alumna to be an apostle in the strictest sense. Some may be restricted in their apostolate to good example. Even those who are in a favorable position for the apostolate will be best prepared by the explication of the faith, for the apostolate which the college graduate as such should be prepared for is the intellectual apostolate. No doubt the rich veins of theological lore that are being mined on the lay priesthood and on terrestrial realities are of immense value and should receive special emphasis in the college. However, this emphasis on the part of the divine economy of salvation should not loom so large as to obscure other treasures of the divine message which are preludes to the vision of the Three Persons who, even now, we may hope, inhabit the soul of the student.

The Concern of the Teacher

"Even now" serves to underline the immediacy of the situation apropos of the student. Here is a Christian at a particular stage of development, not only physical and intellectual, but even supernatural, and with a particular present vocation, that of student. Other educators inform us that psychological and emotional maturity lag behind physical adulthood. With a tragic frequency, the human animal reaches complete growth, is capable of reproducing itself sexually without a corresponding intellectual maturity, either speculative or practical, which would give sufficient grounds for a hopeful prognosis of success in human life, particularly in its marital and parental aspects. Educators and counsellors are usually beset with such problems on the high-school level because of the incidence of puberty; less well recognized is the crisis which marks the transition from adolescence to full maturity which will occur in the last year of college or after graduation.

This is the general problem of the entire college administration and faculty; the supernatural dimension of the student is the concern not only of the chaplain but of the teacher of theology. The very special and direct concern of the teacher, however, is different from that of the chaplain. The vital element in the supernatural organism—sanctifying grace and charity—cannot be touched directly by any human agency; the chaplain, however, is the instrument of grace in his preaching and especially through the channels of the sacraments. Faith, the foundation on which the entire supernatural structure rests, is an intellectual affair having an object or content which is somewhat explicable and penetrable, and it is to this faith that theology addresses its appeal.

The faith of the college student is generally at a particular stage of development; it is no longer the simple, dependent, imaginative faith of the child, nor does it yet have the certitude, emotional balance and unromantic decisiveness of the adult's faith. In this transitional period, faith is likely to be at once idealistic and then again rationalist and suspicious.[21] Introspection and the problems of temptation and guilt harass the student in his personal life. Similarly, those who consider the aims of the student will do well to remember the many other disciplines which the student is learning. Obviously natural science raises many questions, but so also do sociology, history and literature.

If education is, as St. Thomas claimed, a self-active work of the student, the teacher is relegated to the humble role of presenting the material to the active intelligence of the student, who can be illumined and strengthened directly only by the Father of lights himself. In the instance of theology, moreover, the teacher may hope for divine assistance of an even higher order. Provided the student has faith living with love, the Holy Spirit may be expected to activate his gifts of understanding, knowledge, wisdom and counsel, to say nothing of all the support given the intelligence from the appetitive virtues and gifts.

The Summary

To sum up then, it may be said that the aim of the college student is immediately to begin the work of theologizing, to use his reason illumined by faith and assisted by all the natural intellectual virtues for a more fruitful understanding of God's word of salvation. This more fruitful understanding will be a tremendous help, not only in his terrestrial vocation, but as a means towards his supernatural and ultimate vocation in Christ Jesus. The teacher will assist him in this noble task, not only by presenting the data of revelation, but by using the insights into reality which the student is receiving in his other studies—science, the humanities and, particularly, philosophy. The teacher will be mindful of the differences in his students, not only in intellectual ability, but in cultural background (the "major" or area of concentration would need special care) and perhaps most important, in spiritual attitude. Nor should the particular, special vocation of the student be neglected. (For instance, the theological education of men will have to take into account masculine logic as well as the disinclination to practical implementation. The theological education of women must take into account feminine intuition and some impatience with truth for itself, when not seen as also good and beautiful.) The respective roles of fatherhood and motherhood cannot be rightfully ignored if all the ends of the student in due hierarchy are to receive their proper proportion.

In conclusion, two particular difficulties in an essay of this type should be pointed out, not to fend off rightful criticism, but to explain. First, the vagueness of generality is almost unavoidable in an exploration of aims, which, in one sense, are not real until they are realized. This is further complicated by the experimental nature and novelty of theology in the colleges. A biologist would perhaps have less agony in explaining his role in the college, but then he would not have to explain it, as the academic community accepts him as a founding father with clearly recognized status. Secondly, the consideration of so many aims—and some of them so idealistic as to seem almost impossible of realization—may give this discussion an air of impracticability. That too is inevitable. An ideal easily realized is hardly worth the trouble. All the prudence and art of the teacher is challenged to do what he can towards the ideal. In any event, he can, as the doctor of Christian truth, have confidence in divine help.

Footnotes to Study 4

[1]*Summa,* II-II, q. 181, a. 3.

[2]*Loc cit.* Cf. the good use made of this distinction by Charles F. Donovan, S.J., in "The Teacher's Twofold Allegiance," *Catholic Educational Review* LVIII (1960), 7.

[3]The name of Professor Étienne Gilson has been associated with the discussion. While there are numerous books and articles on this matter, I would suggest "Thomas Aquinas and Our Colleagues," in *A Gilson Reader,* ed. Anton C. Pegis (Garden City: Image Books, 1957), 278-297, precisely because it takes up the practical and difficult problem of philosophy in the Catholic college.

[4]Cf. *The Work of Theology* by Francisco P. Muniz, O.P. (Washington: The Thomist Press, 1953), 31-33.

[5]*Introduction à l'Étude de S. Thomas d'Aquin* (Montréal: Institut d'Études Médiévales, 1950).

[6]*Proceedings of the Society of Catholic College Teachers of Sacred Doctrine,* I (1955), *passim.*

[7]*Ibid.,* II (1956), 10-46. Gerald Van Ackeren, S.J., discussed the finality of the college course in the light of theology; Francis M. Keating, S.J., in the light of the layman.

[8]Cf. *Summa,* II-II, q. 181, a. 3.

[9]*The Art of Teaching* (New York: Vintage Books, 1956), 12.

[10]*Ibid.,* 197. Cf. also the passage on Jesuit insistence on the principle of adaptability on the preceding page. "Again and again and again they repeat that pupils differ, classes differ, ages differ, and that the teacher's duty is to teach not an abstraction, but the particular collection of boys he has in front of him."

[11]A brief statement of the Chinese rites controversy and the problem is given by Neill and Schmandt, *History of the Catholic Church* (Milwaukee: Bruce, 1957), 425 f.

[12]"Religion in the State University," by Gerard Sloyan, *Commonweal,* LXXI (1959), 7-10.

[13]Cf. the discussion on "The Responsibility of the Sacred Doctrine Teacher Precisely as Such for the Catholic Formation of the Student" by Joseph S. McCormack, O.P., *Proceedings of the Society of Catholic College Teachers of Sacred Doctrine,* II (1956), 65-69.

[14]"Towards a Theology for the Layman: The Problem of Its Finality," *Theological Studies,* V (1944), 47.

[15]*Ibid.,* 361-2.

[16]These suggestions were made by Gustave Weigel, S.J., in a paper, "The Meaning of Sacred Doctrine in the College," addressed to the Baltimore-Washington Region of the SCCTSD, November 1, 1955. They were repeated with approval by Francis M. Keating, S.J., in "The Finality of the College Course in Sacred Doctrine in the Light of the Finality of the Layman," *Proceedings of the Society of Catholic College Teachers of Sacred Doctrine,* II (1956), 35.

[17]*Loc. cit.* Cf. also Christopher F. Mooney, S.J., "College Theology and Liberal Education," *Thought,* XXXIV (1959), 134. Liberal education is described there as "transmitting a spiritual heritage through initiation into a culture, i.e., a set of values and needs" (p. 326). In the same issue, John L. McKenzie, S.J., in his "Theology in Jesuit Education" (pp. 347-56), presents a conflicting view. All these writers are agreed on one thing—the science of theology needs drastic revision to tailor it for the modern campus.

[18]Cf. M.-D. Chenu, O.P., *Is Theology a Science?* (New York: Hawthorn Books, 1959), 14-18, on "unwitting theologians."

[19]Cf. Gerard Sloyan, *art. cit.*

[20]Philip J. Hanley, O.P., "Collegiate Theology for Catholic Living," *From An Abundant Spring* (New York: P. J. Kenedy, 1952), 259-289.

[21]Cf. the suggestive remarks of A. Liégé, O.P. in his article, "Faith," in *The Virtues and the States of Life* (*Theology Library,* IV, ed. by A. M. Henry, O.P., trans. by Robert J. Olson and Genevieve T. Lennon; Chicago: Fides, 1957), 34-37.

5

AN UNDERGRADUATE THEOLOGY COURSE*

Thomas C. Donlan, O.P.

Ever since the publication of his Theology and Education *Father Donlan has been a recognized authority in this field. A Doctor of Sacred Theology, he was professor of moral theology at the Dominican theological studium, St. Rose Priory, Dubuque, Iowa, for many years. Twice president of the Society of Catholic College Teachers of Sacred Doctrine, past vice-president of the Catholic Theological Society, at present he is vice-president of The Priory Press. He collaborated on the very successful College Texts in Theology series published by that firm.*

The proper and immediate goal of every course of study is to habituate the mind of the student in some manner or other. In the case of the course in theology, the proper and immediate result envisioned is the *habitus* of theology. To see if such habituation is truly possible in undergraduate courses, the nature, subject, generation and growth of the habit must be examined.

The Habit of Theology

Like every other habit, theology pertains to the first species of quality. Here it must be distinguished from a disposition by reason of its permanence, its firmness and its origin from unchangeable principles of faith.[1] Theology proceeds from a group of first principles

*Much of this material has previously appeared in "Theology and Higher Education," *Proceedings of the Catholic Theological Society of America*, X (1955), 232-46, and my *Theology and Education* (Dubuque: Wm. C. Brown Co., 1953).

which are presupposed to it and which are held in virtue of another habit, namely, the infused virtue of faith. Thus, the *habitus* of theology is radicated in faith, but it is elaborated by diligent effort of reason. It is, therefore, formally an acquired habit.[2]

As we have seen, in its adequate conception, theology is not only a science which deduces conclusions which are virtually contained in the formally revealed principles of faith, it is eminently a wisdom which must defend and explain its proper principles.[3] As the supreme wisdom, theology must judge, order and use all other knowledge.

The various functions of the habit of theology—defensive, explicative, scientific and judicative—are related as members of a potential totality. This means that the essential perfection of the *habitus* is found in each of the functions, and that the force or power of the habit is exercised more perfectly in some rather than in others.

Theology is unique in this that it is knowledge simultaneously both practical and speculative, and its principal subject, therefore, is the intellect.[4] But, like every other acquired intellectual habit, theology is radicated also in the internal senses of memory, imagination and the cogitative power. This follows from the fact that the intellect in forming any habit must use phantasms which are produced by these sense faculties. Gradually the intellect acquires a certain capacity for considering these species. At the same time, and in virtue of the same exercise, these internal senses acquire a special *habilitas* whereby they readily provide the proper phantasms for the intellect. Thus the habit of theology resides principally and formally in the intellect, but materially and dispositively in these sense powers.[5]

It is the function of these internal senses to prepare the proper object of the intellect. Therefore, a man is remotely well disposed to acquire a habit when his body in general and these senses in particular operate well.[6] He is proximately well disposed when the sense memory is firmly retentive, when the imagination is free of extraneous images, and when the cogitative power promptly and easily produces the desired phantasms. To develop such facility in these sense faculties, many repeated acts are required. The amount of repetition required will depend upon the individual nature and the previous training of the student.

Is it possible that an intellectual habit could be formed by a single act? This is to ask if the potentiality of the mind could be perfectly overcome in a single demonstration, so that the mind would assent firmly to the conclusion in virtue of that one demonstration. Now if we suppose a firm and lively grasp of the principles of faith and if we also presuppose sufficient exercise to insure the proper remote and proximate disposition of the senses, then, absolutely speaking, it is *possible* to acquire the habit by a single act.[7]

Such a possibility seems rarely to be verified in practice. The acquisition of knowledge involves a transition from potency to act on the part of the intellect. Like most acts of generation, its full perfection is not ordinarily had immediately; rather, it is acquired successively.[8] Since habits resemble the acts by which they are acquired, the habits themselves are generally acquired by many successive acts instead of by a single demonstration.[9]

Whether a habit is generated by a single act or by many successive demonstrations and judgments, the nascent habit is imperfect. The first and more obvious imperfection of a new habit results from its lack of extension through the orbit of the material cause of the habit.[10] In view of the tremendous extent of the wisdom of theology through all its potential parts, and of the purview of each single part, the material limitation of the new habit is immediately evident, confined, as it must be, to one or a few judgments or conclusions.

The second and more significant imperfection of the new habit is the tenuous participation of the subject in the form or quality. Habits, like other qualities, admit of intensification and remission in proportion to the subject's participation in the form.[11] The imperfection of the intellect's participation in the new habit is evidenced by its lack of promptness, ease, clarity and joy in assenting to the new conclusions or judgments. The imperfect participation of the internal senses is noticeable in frequent failing of the memory, distractions in the imagination, sluggish presentation of phantasms by the cogitative power.[12]

"Anyone who has a science imperfectly so that he can lose it easily is better said to be disposed for the science than to have it."[13] The imperfect habit of theology described above is more of a disposition than a true habit. But it is the beginning of a true habit which, of its very nature, responds to exercise and tends toward the more perfect state of a true habit. No one ever acquired the habit without first having passed through the stage of disposition.

A permanent and naturally unchangeable disposition of the intellect is acquired only through a succession of acts proper to the habit. The beginning is found in a disposition. Gradually, through the exercise of repeated acts, the quality tends to the permanency, facility and satisfaction of a true habit.[14] Here we may remark on the importance of the order of discipline which brings to each single act the full force of all preceding acts, thus simultaneously consolidating gains and making advances. No other order of presentation can accomplish this.

How many acts are required, how much growth through exercise is necessary, before a student may be said to possess the habit of theology? Obviously, there is no mathematical or universal answer to this question. We encounter the problem of individual differences.[15] The presence of the habit must be judged in terms of the demonstrated capacity of the mind to perform acts proper to the habit, that is, to "theologize."[16] Now what characterizes acts that flow from a habit rather than from a disposition?

The first and less important sign of habituation is found in the range of theological material over which the student can elicit acts of defense, deduction and judgment. This is less important because it is a sign of quantitative perfection, and this is less formal in the judgment of a habit, which is essentially a quality. The more perfectly the habit is possessed quantitatively, the greater the variety and amount of properly theological material to which it will extend.[17] This, however, is not a case of simple addition, for the demonstrations and conclusions of theology are ordered, and one is derived from another. The ability to see and to show this order and dependence must be considered.

The second and more significant sign of the presence of a true habit is to be found in the degree of intensity characteristic of the participation of the subject in the quality. If the intellect can elicit properly theological acts clearly, easily and promptly, then the habit is present.[18] A prompt and correct judgment of reality in the light of divine revelation is a clear sign of the unshakable permanence of a true habit.[19]

The indications of an adequate *habilitas* in the internal senses where the habit of theology resides dispositively and materially are threefold:

1) The sense memory must have achieved a certain firmness so that theological concepts are familiar and easily evoked.[20]

2) The imagination must be free of distracting images which may diminish the efficiency of the habit or even impede and destroy its function.[21]

3) The cogitative power must be able promptly and easily to present the phantasms upon which the intellect works.[22]

These, then, are the qualities to be sought in the student of theology. All of them can be determined by examination and by exercise. Different students will attain different levels of perfection, as they do in any subject that is taught. The art of pedagogy, the order of the course, the zeal of the students will all play important roles in the end result. But there is no argument from the nature of habit, nor of the nature of the process of academic habituation, against the real possibility of bringing the student to a degree of perfection in the habit of theology.

A Course in Theology

It is not too difficult to demonstrate the need for courses in theology in the undergraduate curriculum. But the solution to that problem is not a denial that others exist. There is assistance available in the solution of the problems of constructing a course in theology for undergraduates in the prologue to the *Summa.* There St. Thomas states that the problem is threefold: the problem of content, the problem of order of presentation, the problem of method.

It is imperative to note that any adjustment made in the light of the finality of the student's vocation as a layman living in the world is purely accidental to the nature of theology. Essentially it is and must always remain a discursive wisdom about God and about other things in relation to God, based upon the principles of revelation and elaborated and developed by human reason in the light of that revelation.

At the very outset, it is necesary to make two fundamental distinctions. The first is between the content and the emphasis of the course. The second is between the essentials and the non-essentials.

Content refers to whatever can be comprised in theology. It is a broad concept embracing both essentials and accidentals, and includes the principles, processes and conclusions of theology without specifying their absolute or relative importance. The content of theology is found in the entire *corpus theologicum.*

Emphasis refers to the degree of explanation and demonstration accorded to different elements in the content. While content is intrinsic to theology and pertains to its essence, emphasis is extrinsic and pertains to its use. Thus emphasis will be the principal differentiating element in courses of theology designed to prepare men for the priesthood and in courses designed for laymen. A community of content will insure that both courses are truly theological; a distinction in emphasis will suit each to a particular need.

The essentials of theology are those principles, processes and conclusions that are indispensable for its existence as wisdom, i.e., as a true perfection or habituation of the intellect. If any of the essentials are omitted, the knowledge resulting from study is either belief or opinion, but it lacks the permanence and perfection of science and wisdom. Thus if the tract on the Trinity were omitted or essentially curtailed, a student could not acquire the habit of theology as a wisdom.

The non-essentials of theology comprise everything in the content except the essentials. Certain specialized tracts such as those on mystical phenomena and some aspects of positive theology are examples of those which are not essential to the constitution of the essence of theology.

In the light of these distinctions we may establish some conclusion regarding the content of theological courses for the undergraduate curriculum:

1. The proper and immediate goal of the course is scientific and sapiential knowledge of the truths of revelation, and of other truths in the light of revelation. Consequently, whatever is essential to the divinely human wisdom of theology must be

included in the course. If any essentials are omitted, the course is not truly theology.

2. The ultimate use of this theological wisdom is the personal sanctification of the students. Consequently, whatever is conducive to this end must receive special emphasis within the general framework of theology. Thus, for example, the grace of the sacraments and the proper dispositions for reception would be emphasized in the treatises on the sacraments.

3. The proper vocation which all Christian laymen share is to mediate between the spiritual and temporal orders, either through Catholic Action or through Catholic activity. Consequently, whatever is conducive to this end must receive special emphasis within the framework of theology. Thus, for example, the tracts on confirmation and the Mystical Body would be specially emphasized.

4. Certain parts of the content which are non-essential to theology itself will be specially useful in view of the layman's vocation and will always be included in the course for this reason. For example, certain details on the virtue of liberality as it governs alms-deeds, and some aspects of the virtue of observance and the virtue of respect which governs the relations of children to parents, must always be included.

5. Non-essentials which are specially necessary for the layman's vocation in view of contemporary conditions will be included and emphasized as long as circumstances warrant. For example, in our own day certain non-essential conclusions regarding interracial justice, war and peace, and the relationship of the individual to the common good, must be emphasized in the light of present day circumstances in which the students must work out their vocation. But it is conceivable that changes could occur that would allow these matters to be de-emphasized or even excluded in favor of others that would be more timely.

The Problem of Order

Once the content of the course has been decided, there remains the further problem of the order in which these elements are to be presented. Many suggestions have been offered on this count, but two are really fundamental, and, in a certain sense, are representative of all the rest: the content of theology may be taught either in the order of psychological appeal, or in the order of the doctrine itself, which is a real order of divine things.

When dealing with the problem of content, it becomes clear that there is a certain irreducible minimum without which theology cannot exist as a true wisdom. The same is not true regarding the order in which it is taught. Absolutely speaking, the intellectual habit of wisdom can be had no matter what order is followed. No particular order is so essential to theology that the divine wisdom could not be learned if some other were followed. But the order of presentation should be a positive assistance to learning, and from this aspect one order is better than another.

The most common order proposed by those who favor a presentation based on psychological appeal would group the various tracts around the Incarnation as their center and unifying principle. This solution to the problem of order should be considered carefully in terms of its probable results. In reality, this solution seems to propose more questions than it answers. Granted that presentation of the truths of the Incarnation could be given a greater appeal psychologically than, for instance, the tracts on the existence and nature of God, such a beginning would raise many questions that could not be answered theologically at that stage of the instruction. The Incarnation is understandable only in terms of divine goodness and of human needs. The divine goodness raises the question of goodness in itself and as an attribute of God. In turn, this poses the most fundamental question of the existence of God and of the divine nature. If such an order is followed, the teacher will be forced to give inadequate answers to many fundamental questions in order to clarify problems which cannot possibly be understood except in terms of other solutions that are prior, both in the order of doctrine and in the order of learning. Whatever advantages are alleged in favor of a departure from the order of the subject matter will be lost if they are had at the expense of clarity and ease of learning in relation to the entire body of theological wisdom.

Historically, it was proposed to seek the unity of theology in the *totus Christus* considered as the *objectum formale quod.* This theory was advanced by Robert Grosseteste and by Robert Kilwardby.[23] It was explicitly considered by St. Thomas and rejected. This involves a confusion of the material and formal aspects of theology. The *totus Christus* is indeed considered in theology, but under the more ultimate aspects of its relationship to God.[24]

Another difficulty arising from the proposal to change the essential formality of theology is the prodigious labor involved in such a task and the problem of discovering someone with sufficient genius to accomplish it. Because of the formal change involved, the new discipline would be analogous to theology, i.e., it would be more different than like what we now have. It is by no means immediately clear that whatever good effects might be expected from such a new discipline could not be had by the more simple method of modifying accidentally what is already to hand in traditional scholastic theology.

The order of doctrine is properly theological because it is based on the proper subject matter of theology. The purpose of this order of divine reality is to manifest the truth in regard to God himself, and in regard to other things insofar as he is their beginning and their end. This order is exemplified perfectly in the *Summa* of St. Thomas.

To follow this order in learning theology is a tremendous advantage in acquiring the divinely human wisdom. The clarity and intrinsic unity of this order is in itself a pedagogical device which is conducive to the acquisition and perfection of theological knowledge, because in it every advance into the unknown is made with complete dependence upon what is already known. Only rarely does one find in the *Summa* a reference to what is to follow. Thus the order of doctrine is in complete accord with the scientific nature of theological wisdom.

The order of doctrine leads the student to an appreciation of the unity of theology itself, and thereby preserves him from the harmful effects of the atomization of theology. In the order developed in the *Summa* there are no artificial distinctions into dogmatic, moral, ascetical and mystical theology. Rather is the entire body of theological knowledge unfolded as a sapiential wisdom of reality from the exalted aspect of divinity.

It is clear from the conclusions drawn regarding the content of undergraduate courses that the order followed must be flexible enough to admit the many non-essential conclusions that would not be emphasized in a seminary course. The order followed must be sufficiently lofty in view and flexible in scope to absorb, correlate and clarify whatever contributions are made to the body of theological knowledge. The order of doctrine exemplified in the *Summa* is suitable for this purpose, for it is like a vast intelligible frame of reference which can contain all the developments of theology and add a certain clarity to them by relating them to the whole deposit of divine wisdom.

There are three main reasons for adhering to the order of doctrine in presenting theology to undergraduates:

1) This order is most suitable for meeting the demands of science and wisdom, and these intellectual perfections are the immediate and proper goal of the course.

2) The order of doctrine is most suitable to that clarity of understanding which is so essential to the instruction of beginners. In this order the most fundamental truths are unfolded first. It does not presuppose answers, but rather concludes to them.

3) The order of doctrine is more conducive to personal sanctification, which is perfected in love begotten of knowledge. It cannot be maintained that any academic course is the immediate cause of sanctity, but it can be maintained that the disposition of the matter to be learned can promote sanctity within the limits of science by facilitating the learning of the doctrine, and by dispelling tedium, confusion and disgust.

In brief, an order of presentation that manifests the grandeur of divine truth and leads to an integrated view of God and of all else as related to God is a positive aid to contemplation. It is the contemplation of spiritual goodness and beauty that is the beginning of spiritual love.[25] This is an aid and support to charity, which is the bond of perfection and sanctification. A presentation following the order of subject matter is a positive aid in preparing undergraduates for their vocation as mediators between the spiritual and temporal orders. This order is a true framework for judging all things in terms of divine standards, and for viewing all things in terms of their mutual relations and of their ultimate relationship to God. This is truly the order of wisdom, and wisdom is the most perfect preparation for the lay apostolate that can come through human instruction.

The Problem of Method

The method of presenting theology to undergraduates presents formidable difficulties. This is not simply the problem of the methodology of learning in general, nor yet the problem of methodology from the purely pedagogical viewpoint. Rather the problem is special, and confined within the limits set by the nature of theology, on the one hand, and the capacities of undergraduates on the other.

In an effort to understand and explain this problem we can have recourse to a few passages from St. Thomas.

> The method of any investigation ought to be in harmony both with things and with us. For if it is not suited to the matter, things will not be understood; and if it is not suited to us, we shall not be able to apprehend the matter; for example, divine things are such by their very nature that they cannot be known except by the intellect. Consequently, if anyone wished to follow another method and to use imagination instead, he would not be able to understand anything of them as a result of his considerations, because truths of this kind are not thus to be known. But if, on the other hand, one wished to know divine things so as to see them in themselves, and to comprehend them with the same certitude with which sensible things or mathematical demonstrations are comprehended, this too would be impossible; even things which are in themselves understandable in this way cannot be perfectly grasped because of the weaknesses of our intellect.[26]

The use of a purely imaginative method of presentation is clearly unsuitable to the nature of theology. So, too, is a purely natural method of inquiry such as is employed in philosophy. The method of theology will not produce the same degree of evidence that is found in philosophy and the mathematical sciences, because the method of theology must share in the qualities of the principles from which it proceeds, and the principles of divine faith are not evident in themselves. On the other hand, the method of theology will be productive of greater certitude than the method of philosophy or of the mathematical sciences, because it will share in the divine certitude that is proper to faith.[27]

From the aspect of the nature of theology, St. Thomas teaches:

> . . . it is especially proper to this doctrine to argue from authority, inasmuch as its principles are obtained by revelation; and hence we must believe the authority of those to whom the revelation has been made. Nor does this take away from the dignity of this doctrine, for although the argument from authority based on human reason is the weakest, yet the argument from authority based on divine revelation is the strongest. . . . Sacred doctrine properly uses the authority of the canonical Scriptures as a necessary demonstration.[28]

Yet even authority is not sufficient for theology. The use of authority will determine only that a given thing is such or is not such, and its effect terminates at the imparting of information. In addition to authority, theology must use another method:

> Sacred doctrine also makes use of human reason, not, indeed to prove the faith (for thereby the merit of faith would come to an end), but to make clear other things that are set forth in this doctrine.[29]

This method of investigating divine truth by reason under the positive direction of faith is especially applicable in the schools where the teacher

> . . . intends not so much to dispel error, but rather to instruct his students so that they are led to an understanding of the truth; and then it is necessary to rely upon reasons which unearth the root of truth and which make [the students] understand how what is said is true; otherwise, if the teacher should resolve a question solely on the strength of authority, the student would indeed be certain that it is such, but he would acquire neither science nor understanding, and would go away empty-headed.[30]

The method of presenting theology to undergraduates, then, must retain its sapiential and authoritarian character and, at the same time, must be accommodated to the capacities of students at the undergraduate level.

In discussing the method of presenting theology to undergraduates, as in every other phase of the total problem, it must be borne in mind that the purpose of such courses does not demand the same degree of perfection or of penetration that is demanded of a seminary or a graduate course. A minimal degree of scientific apparatus will suffice to attain the beginnings of the theological habit in the student:

> The essence of a science consists in this, that from things known a knowledge of things previously unknown is derived, and since this can occur in relation to divine things, evidently there can be a science of divine things.[31]

The undergraduate course in theology is not intended to bring students to the ultimate perfection of the habit of theology, any more than undergraduate courses in mathematics or chemistry are intended to do so in those fields. Rather, it is intended to implant the beginnings of a true habit as a dynamic and vital perfection of the mind. Once radicated in the mind, this nascent habit should increase both intensively and extensively through use; it should stamp with permanence the student's convictions toward the realities of life as these are measured against a divine standard that is known and understood.

It becomes clear that the method of theology makes great demands upon those who teach undergraduate courses. The concepts necessary to theology must be sharpened by contrast, clarified by examples, and ultimately crystallized in definitions that are adequate for scientific reasoning and sapiential judgment. The teacher must force the exercise of the theological habit by confronting the students with problems. His method of teaching must always achieve the repetition of the acts of demonstration, defense and judgment that are proper to the divinely human wisdom. The acquisition and increase of the habit of theology, like any other intellectual virtue, are absolutely dependent upon the repetition of scientific and sapiential acts.

Conclusion

In the realities of today's collegiate environment, the teacher holds the position of paramount importance in bringing the students to a beginning of theological wisdom. The selection and wise use of suitable materials, the stimulation and direction of student activity, the manifestation of the relevance of theological truth to contemporay life—these are necessarily the duty of the teacher. This is a formidable task.

Historically, there is no precedent to guide the teacher of undergraduate theology. He is embarked upon a new path, and the traditional maps used in seminaries and graduate schools can only give general and approximate directions in the theological education of lay undergraduates. Very frankly, the college teacher of theology is required to exercise a unique pedagogical prudence.

Clearly, there is no book, no library, that can do the teacher's work for him. In theology as in other subjects, there will always be some few great teachers who accomplish their tasks by remarkably original and inventive means which prove highly effective. But they are the few, and their methods remain inimitable. If theology is to be a real possibility for the majority, reliance must be based upon ordinary competence exercised in an orderly and measured fashion that will make it possible to regulate the department of theology after the fashion of any other academic division of the college.

To achieve this, some sort of text which aims at the goals and applies the principles explained above becomes a practical necessity. An attempt to supply such a text is found in the series, College Texts in Theology, particularly the three volume *Theology: A Basic Synthesis for the College* (*God and His Creation; The Christian Life; Christ, and His Sacraments*), edited by Francis L. B. Cunningham, O.P.

These texts are not designed for self-education; they are tools prepared for use under the direction of the teacher—imperfect, no doubt, to be used with discrimination, requiring prudent adaptation to particular curricula and particular groups. But they supply adequate materials, and they present the essentials of wisdom in a properly theological order which will aid the teacher in his task. Used well by a competent teacher, these texts will make the foundation of a truly theological *habitus* truly possible under normally favorable academic circumstances. In present conditions they furnish an indispensable instrument for the undergraduate course in theology.

Footnotes to Study 5

[1]St. Thomas, *Summa,* I-II, q. 49, a. 2, ad 3.
[2]*Ibid.,* I, q. 1, a. 2.
[3]Cf. Study 3, "The Nature of Sacred Theology."
[4]St. Thomas, *Summa,* I-II, q. 50, a. 4, ad 3.
[5]*Ibid.,* q. 51, a. 3.
[6]*Ibid.,* I, q. 85, a. 5.
[7]*Ibid.,* q. 89, a. 5.

[8]*Ibid.*, I-II, q. 54, a. 4, ad 3.
[9]*Ibid.*, q. 52, a. 1.
[10]II *Con. Gen.*, Chap. 19.
[11]*Summa,* I-II, q. 49, a. 2, ad 3.
[12]*Ibid.*, q. 54, a. 1, ad 1.
[13]*Ibid.*, q. 53, a. 2, ad 1.
[14]*Ibid.*, I, q. 1, a. 7.
[15]*Ibid.*, I-II, q. 52, a. 1.
[16]*Ibid.*, I, q. 87, a. 2.
[17]*Ibid.*, I-II, q. 54, a. 4, ad 3.
[18]*Ibid.*, q. 52, a. 2.
[19]*Ibid.*, q. 53, a. 3.
[20]*Ibid.*, q. 51, a. 3.
[21]*Ibid.* q. 53, a. 3.
[22]*Ibid.*, I, q. 89, a. 5; I-II, q. 50, a. 3, ad 3.
[23]Cf. Robert Grosseteste, *Hexaemeron* (text cited by Phelan, *Mélange de Wulf,* 176); Robert Kilwardby, *De Natura Theologiae* (Munster: 1935), 17.
[24]St. Thomas, *Summa,* I, q. 1, a. 7.
[25]*Ibid.*, I-II, q. 27, a. 2.
[26]*In Boetti De Trinitate,* q. 4, lect. 2.
[27]*Loc. cit.*
[28]*Summa,* I, q. 1, a. 8, ad 2.
[29]*Loc. cit.*
[30]*Quod. IV,* q. 9, a. 18.
[31]*In Boetii De Trinitate,* q. 2, a. 2.

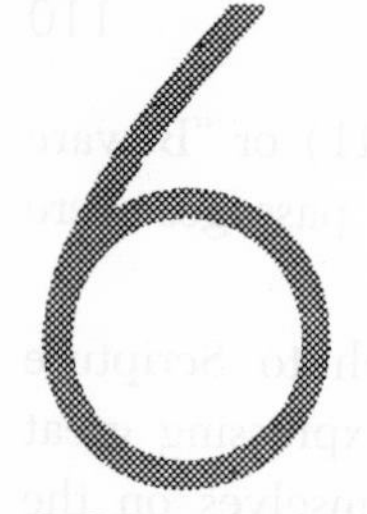

SCRIPTURE AND COLLEGE THEOLOGY

John F. McDonnell, O.P.

Well known to the Catholic laity of the Midwest for his long service as a lecturer for The Thomist Association, Father McDonnell did his graduate biblical studies at the Ecole Biblique, Jerusalem, and holds the Prolyta in Sacred Scripture from the Pontifical Biblical Commission, Vatican City. Since 1949 he has been professor of Old Testament exegesis at St. Rose Priory and Mount St. Bernard Seminary, Dubuque, Iowa, and is on the staff of the St. Xavier Graduate Program in Theology, Chicago.

The old-fashioned Bible box was used as a source of guidance in times of perplexity. Each neatly rolled cylinder that lay in it contained a Scripture text. When light or comfort was sought, a text was drawn from the box. Often the text was strikingly apt. That it should be to the point was a tribute not only to the resources of the Bible but also to the resourcefulness of those who stocked the box. The texts included were chosen from such glowing chapters as the ninetieth Psalm, the fortieth chapter of Isaias, the fourteenth chapter of John, and the eighth chapter of Romans.[1]

Naturally little help could have been drawn from the proliferating family trees which fill the first nine chapters of I Parolipomenon with over a thousand more or less unpronounceable names, nor the dietary laws in Leviticus (Lev. 11: ff.), even when the *cherogrillus* of the Douay becomes the *rock badger* of the Confraternity version. In the New Testament what knowledge or comfort could be gathered from St. Paul's description of his handwriting (Gal. 6:11) or "Beware of the dogs" (Phil. 3:2)? The limits of choice of the passages were set by their use as an oracle.

Wider but similar limits result when the approach to Scripture is through its use in theological proof. Certain texts expressing great Christian mysteries will by frequent use impress themselves on the memory. The text which gives the Incarnation its name: "And the Word was made flesh, and dwelt amongst us" (John 1:14), or St. Paul on the humility of the kenosis (Phil. 2:7), will be used again and again. Declarations of dogmatic or moral truth find authoritative statement in the Old Testament as well. The solemn opening of Genesis in which the origin of all things that are seen is traced to God (Gen. 1:1), or the statement of the oneness of God in the central prayer of Israel (Deut. 6:4), will not lack employment. The defense of the true meaning of debated passages and wide-ranging allusion in a domain well known to the theological author may add still a larger share of the Scripture to theological works.

However numerous they may be, these texts are still a small part of the whole and are seen in isolation.[2] They are divorced from their context. Acquaintance with them is not acquaintance with the Bible. Even mastery of them, were that possible in their scattered state, would not be mastery of the Bible. This is true because the Bible is no storehouse of quotations. It is a book. Its connection with theological teaching must be more than its availability as a magazine of apt expressions of doctrine. The mere piecemeal selection from the arsenal of a text as a weapon, now to repel a heretical assault on dogma, again to hold a moral position, fails to recognize what Scripture is. This failure to recognize the very nature of the material dealt with is in the highest degree unscientific. It may be as embarrassing as it is false.

A lawyer who stated that we have on the highest authority: "Skin for skin! All that a man has he will give for his life" (Job 2:4), found that a man may not dip into the Bible at random with impunity. An unkind newspaper not only pointed out that the words in Job are spoken by Satan, but suggested that the quotation indicated who was the highest authority for that lawyer.[3] Practically, his confusion shows the necessity of seeing any text in its context. The context too has its context, and the Bible in its entirety is the final literary context. It must be seen as a whole if it is to be used as an authority.

Scripture and Theology

It is precisely as an authority for that discipline that Sacred Scripture enters into relation with college theology. Theology must be taught in the Catholic college, at least on the level at which other courses are taught. In other courses, not only are conclusions taught, but the principles from which these conclusions are drawn, for the argumentation which leads to the conclusion is presented. For such a process in theology, Sacred Scripture, on whose foundation theology rests, is necessary. Although theology uses reason, it does not rest on it but on revelation. Argument from authority, therefore, especially befits theology, which derives its principles from revelation, and accordingly must accept the authority of those to whom revelation was made. In other fields of thought argument from authority, because implicated in human fallibility, is the weakest of all arguments. In theology, argument from authority is the most compelling, since the authority is that of divine revelation. Theology "makes use of canonical Scripture as being its own proper material and affording a necessary argument. . . . For our faith is based on the revelation made to the apostles and prophets who wrote the canonical books, and not on any revelation perhaps made to other teachers."[4]

On the other hand, it is not to be expected that the Bible, even extensively considered, can substitute for theology's orderly exposition of beliefs and practice. Clarity and (if nothing else) greater ease of access to teaching which is presented in the Scriptures "diffusely, under various modes of expression, and sometimes obscurely"[5] demand theological wisdom's clear and orderly presentation of the various truths of faith. This clearly ordered teaching must rest on Scripture and, if presented in scientific development, must be seen to rest on it. Accordingly, the college student, as anyone else applying himself to such a study of theology, must meet with the Bible itself as the source of the principles of his knowledge.

Obviously this contact is often lacking, even in the otherwise educated Catholic. Often a college education does nothing to refute Voltaire's sneer: "The Bible is a sacred book, for no one touches it."[6] The situation has bettered for English-speaking Catholics in recent years. The Bible newly translated in whole or in part, in various editions at every price level, is widely distributed among American Catholics. Unfortunately, distribution does not insure reading. The English Baptist preacher of the last century, Charles Spurgeon, is reported to have complained in a sermon, "The Bible is in every house, but in many the dust on it is so thick that you might write on it Damnation."[7] The transition from owning a Bible to reading it must be made if the college student is to acquire theology on his own level. The college course in Scripture must not only foster the reading of the Bible, but also the proper reading of it as a necessary argument in the discipline of theology.

The College Scripture Course

To bring about such reading is a major task of the college Scripture course. Here the principal difficulty is to achieve a consecutive reading of the Scripture. While no excessive difficulty arises in bringing the student to read sections here and there, this sort of reading brings him to the Bible only on the level of consultation for proof-texts or for lots. Sustained reading of the Bible as a whole, on the other hand, is only too often seriously hindered, especially for the Old Testament. Here the student is supported neither by habit nor tradition. Against reading the Old Testament, a combination of factors is at work. This is no new thing.

"Nothing in Pontus is so barbarous and sad as the fact that Marcion was born there . . . fouler than any Scythian . . . darker than the cloud . . . colder than its winter . . . more savage than the beasts of that barbarous region . . . a monster more credible to philosophers than Christians."[8] Even for Tertullian the invective is strong; but Marcion's primary offense was great. He had deformed the New Testament and had stricken the Old from the Bible. For him the Old Testament was the bad fruit of an evil tree, revealing a God of wrath opposed to the New Testament's God of Love.

Marcion lived in the second century. His heresy is long dead. While none today professes its name, there is still among many a distrust for the Old Testament, often unacknowledged and showing itself particularly in practice. They do not attack it, nor do they read it. It was no monster for philosophers but a Chinese Protestant minister who said: "Reading the Old Testament is like eating a large crab. There's a great deal of shell, but very little meat."[9]

The frankness of the statement is extreme, but the words are still symptomatic. Many a Catholic college student, who would almost by reflex action repudiate the stand, has his own lack of sympathy for much of the Bible. Since it is presented to him by the Church as God's word, he reverences it—but at a distance. At his arrival in college, his knowledge of Scripture, especially the Old Testament, may well have been small and largely second-hand at that. One might expect him to be acquainted with a few psalms, the stories of Old Testament events or heroes (usually learned not from the Bible itself but from a Bible history), some moving words of prophet or wise man, hit upon in the liturgy or caught as a text in a sermon. His knowledge of the New Testament is somewhat broader, but it lacks an Old Testament foundation. To this extent his understanding cannot be deep; much of St. Paul will be, in the words of St. Peter "things difficult to understand." (II Pet.: 3:16). Even the gospels will be seen more as simple biography than the working out of the great divine plan.

With something of this sort as the sum of his biblical learning, he may be little concerned with gathering more. He may, of course, be somewhat ashamed of his ignorance, especially as compared with the supposed knowledge of his Protestant friends.

The college course in theology will not correct such an attitude by exhortation to read the Bible, even where good will on the part of the student accompanies exhortation from the teacher. Mere direct acquaintance with the text is no guarantee of greater sympathy. It may again, especially in the Old Testament, increase uneasiness; for acquaintance brings new problems.

With it comes a new appreciation of the difficulty of thought and speech patterns, historically so far removed from those of the reader. The extraordinary variety of material capable of classification, seemingly only by forcing it into categories; the tedium of some passages; the coarseness, cruelty and low moral tone of others—at the same time as these fail to satisfy the mind's desire for unity, they combine to alienate good will. The picture may seem dark. Varying backgrounds of preparation may alter its tones. Yet even the best high school preparation will have given the student only a selective contact with Scripture which could not go much below the surface. The light to be introduced into the picture can come only from a proper approach to the Bible.

The Theological Approach

In a passage in his *Speech on the Arts of Uniformity,* Edmund Burke stressed the haphazard arrangement of many sorts of teaching in the Bible and thereby pointed unwittingly toward a solution of that and other biblical difficulties:

> Scripture is no one summary of doctrines regularly digested, in which a man could not mistake his way; it is a most venerable, but most multifarious, collection of an infinite variety of Cosmogony, Theology, Prophecy, Psalmody, Morality, Apologue, Allegory, Legislation, Ethics carried through different books, by different authors, at different ages for different ends and purposes.

This statement, peculiarly justified for the Old Testament, on its face is unexceptionable. We have already noted this heterogeneity as an obstacle to the reading and study of the Bible. Within the statement there is a clue to lead us to the knowledge that the variety is secondary and, to that extent, illusory. From Burke's words "theology" should leap to the eye, for it is not among its peers. The Bible does not present all of these matters separately from theology and on a par with it. Rather, each of these elements is treated for a theological end. The cosmogony of Genesis gives no scientific explanation to vie with modern theories: it asserts that all of the things man sees about him owe their origin to God; into the world God had created good, man introduced evil and spread it abroad. The cosmogony merely sets the stage for the drama of good and evil, and introduces a narrative of the origins of a people and the Law that is the condition of the covenant binding them to God, who has chosen them as his own, to play a great role in restoring the lost good.

This history is a history of salvation. At no place in all the history that follows is there a mere annalistic record of events, their mutual relations and connections with world history.

Even random examples show that the greatest claims to temporal fame may be omitted; the claim to renown of King Ezechias, the underground water system of Jerusalem, is dismissed in a somewhat apologetic aside. It has its importance, but it does not fit the theological intent of the one who formed the books of Kings: "And the rest of the acts of Ezechias and all his might, and how he made a conduit, and brought waters into the city, are they not written in the book of the words of the days of the kings of Juda?" (IV Kings 20:20). What was important was his relation to God, his religious reform, his zeal comparable to David's for purity of worship: "He did that which was good before the Lord according to all that David his father had done. He destroyed the high places, and broke the statues in pieces, and cut down the groves" (IV Kings 18:3-4). The ivory friezes which gave Achab's palace the name of "the House of Ivory" are dismissed in an aside, for their builder's claim to place and to lengthy treatment in the Old Testament was the wickedness of his treason against God: "And Achab the son of Amri did evil in the sight of the Lord above all that were before him. Nor was it enough for him to walk in the ways of Jeroboam the son of Nabat: but he also took to wife Jezabel daughter of Ethbaal king of the Sidonians. And he went and served Baal and adored him" (III Kings 16:30-31).

Didactic, lyric, prayerful or eschatologue, the psalmody of the Bible is religious song. Its apologue, parables and allegories clarify a religious message or attract the reader to investigate it. It teaches not ethics but moral theology. Right action is not commanded or urged that man should bring his life to agree with right reason, but because man is to imitate his God: "Be holy for I, the Lord your God, am holy" (Lev. 19:2).

This holiness was no mere separation from the profane. The moral character of the God of Israel demanded that his people be free from sin. To ritual cleanness, purity of conscience was added. In the New

Testament an even greater demand was to be made: "You are, therefore, to be perfect, even as your heavenly father is perfect" (Matt. 5:48).

This pervasive theological message is what should be sought in the Scriptures. For the specialist there is always a danger of becoming overly immersed in technique or the accessories of technique. He may not only be unable to see the woods for the trees, but miss even the trees in attention to the underbrush. In the interpretation of Scripture this results in preoccupation with critical method, philology, archeology or other aids in the search for theological truth to the detriment of the truth itself. Pope Pius XII pointed to this danger and the true end of the interpretation of Scripture when he said:

> With special zeal should they apply themselves, not exclusively to expounding these matters which belong to the historical, archeological, philological and other auxiliary sciences—as, to Our regret, is done in certain commentaries—but, having duly referred to these, insofar as they may aid the exegesis, they should set forth in particular the theological doctrine in faith and morals of the individual books or texts so that their exposition may not only aid the professors of theology in their explanations and proofs of the dogmas of faith, but may also be of assistance to priests in their presentation of Christian doctrine to the people; and, in fine, may help all the faithful to lead a life that is holy and worthy of a Christian.[10]

This theological doctrine sought in the Bible is there as a direct consequence of the very nature of Sacred Scripture. Its books are sacred and canonical, "not because, having been composed by human industry, they were subsequently approved by the Church's authority, nor even because they contain revelation without error; but because, having been written under the inspiration of the Holy Ghost, they have God for their author, and as such have been delivered to the Church."[11] Accordingly, they are more than Burke's "collection . . . carried through different books by different authors for different ends and purposes." They have a common message because they have a common author.

Granted that human authors from Moses to John the Evangelist worked at different times in a period of more than thirteen centuries, this does not induce the diversity one might expect. This is God's book as well as theirs. They were truly authors, but as God's instruments God was the principal cause of every one of their books. As in every exercise of instrumental causality, a greater impression is left on the effect by the principal cause than by the instrument. So each book of the Scripture is the word of God; each book conveys his message. Whatever likeness any of these books may have to extra-Biblical literature (as Tobias to the *Wisdom of Ahikar*), it is more unlike such literature, because it is a part of God's message to man in a way those books cannot be. Whatever diversity may exist within the Bible (as between the detailed legislation of Leviticus, the ardors of the Canticle of Canticles, the sublimity of the fourth gospel), its books have something essential in common. Differences may be multiplied, the result of the diversity of human authorship or the variety of goals; but this essential likeness remains. One may be richer in doctrine, more eloquent, more profound than another; but this note of perfection is in all. All have God as their author. The inspiration which effects such divine authorship is the formal, the perfecting element in Sacred Scripture. This makes the Scriptures what they are.

Biblical Theology

The college Scripture course must proceed with this recognition of what Scripture is. Any approach which fails to bear this constantly in mind cannot reach its essential meaning. Since by inspiration the Scripture is the written message of God to men about himself and the relation of this world and its creatures to him, the end of a formal approach—namely, one seeking the essential in the Scripture—must be that message. It is the primary and most important characteristic of a proper approach to the Scripture that it emphasizes the goal, a biblical theology.

This theology is more than a study of the religious ideas of the Scripture. Whether in the Old Testament or the New, it must be a study of these religious ideas under the light of faith. Ideally, many steps go into the study of the scriptural text. The precise text must first be determined, for we are concerned first of all with the author's words. The literary form of the passage must be investigated, since meaning is colored by forms of thought concretized in various types of literary expression. The intellectual and historical background of the Bible is not ours—indeed, it no longer exists and must be reconstructed—and so the situation in life from which the passage sprang must be rebuilt as far as possible. The meaning which the words had for those who first pronounced or sang or wrote them, and for those nameless toilers who combined and completed them, must be sought. In fine, we must try to put ourselves back in the frame of understanding of the ancient people of Israel, or the early Christian community who first read them or listened to them in instruction or liturgy.

This kind of study, carried on by the light of natural understanding using all the methods of literary and historical interpretation, may be profitable. There may be a like, though lesser, profit in the same type of study of the Koran or the sacred literature of the Brahmins. A study of this sort requires for profit only that the student have a sympathy for the text, derived from a certain minimum of religious feeling. A complete lack of religious engagement would make even such a study nearly impossible, and to demand it for objectivity would be tantamount to demanding color blindness for excellence in the art critic, or deafness for the fair criticism of music.[12]

But the ideal must go further. If no more than understanding, sympathy and method come into play, the investigation is not theological. The end product is a working out of the religion or a systematization of the doctrines of the Old Testament. Yet the Bible remains untouched in its true nature. Something more must be added. For believers, the study of the religion of the Old Testament must become a religious study of the Old Testament.

Theology is not only wisdom but the science of God, and of man and all other things in relation to God, worked out under the light of faith. Theology is not achieved simply because the field of investigation is a book about God. A science is determined, not by the matter studied—its material object—but by the light under which the study is made—its formal object. Biblical theology, the goal of Scripture study, is defined, then, by the fact that it seeks to know the books of the Bible as inspired by God and containing teaching given by God. The very existence and the fundamentals of the nature of inspiration are known only by faith.

It is faith which sets the limits of Scripture study, the area in which biblical theology may be found. It is faith which determines that all the books of our Bible, neither more nor fewer, are inspired. Thus it is under the light of faith that we reject apocryphal literature and include in our study the deuterocanonical books, which makes so marked a difference between what is received into our study of the Old Testament and what is accepted by Jews and Protestants. What falls largely into the field of intertestamental studies is for us still the study of the Old Testament. Taking this stand by faith, we preserve a true part of the riches of revelation and important links binding the Old Testament to the New.

If our approach is theological, no book of the Bible may be slighted. Each comes essentially with the same credentials. We cannot separate them from the field of biblical investigation by judgments on their literary style or poetic genius. For example, Wisdom may have been written by a very dull fellow compared to the supreme poet who gave us the searchings of Job into the problems of innocent suffering. Yet Wisdom too is the work of the Holy Spirit. In it there are answers to some of man's deepest religious problems, not found in the splendid eloquence of Job. There is more light on the just man's suffering in this life in Wisdom's promise of a reward in the next:

> This is he whom once we held as a laughing stock
> and as a type of mockery, fools that we were!
> His life we deemed madness,
> And his end dishonored.
> See how he is accounted among the sons of God;
> how his lot is with the saints!
> (Wis. 5: 3-6)

than in Job's noble confession of man's inability to sound the depths of God's mysterious ways:

> I know you can do all things,
> And that no purpose of yours can be hindered.
> I have dealt with great things that I do not understand;
> things too wonderful for me which I cannot know.
> (Job 42: 2-3)

It is only faith, the light under which the theological approach is made, which grants these diverse works equally the authority of inspiration. Only an approach in which faith is actually and continually a guiding light, and not one only in theory, will assure that the teaching of all the books will be sought.

Such an approach to the Old Testament may organize the acquired knowledge into categories traditional in systematic theology, or consider them in historic development. In either case it is evident that the Old Testament and its doctrines are incomplete in themselves. Whatever unity is discerned in its doctrines is relative for the Old Testament, is prolonged and completed in the New. The boundary of the Old Testament canon set at the second book of Machabees is not a doctrinal frontier, for the whole of the Old Testament looks forward in hope to a completeness not found within its own limits. Although our Lord went on to speak especially of moral matters in the Sermon on the Mount, after saying, "Do not think I have come to destroy the Law or the prophets. I have not come to destroy but to fulfill. For, amen I say to you, not one jot or tittle shall be lost from the Law till all things be accomplished" (Matt. 5: 17-19), the extension of the Law and the prophets included the Old Testament and its teaching, doctrinal and moral. The New Testament was not to abolish but to perfect the Old; to answer its questions and resolve its oppositions. Not so much as a dot or comma was to be lost until this purpose was complete. The many different glimpses of truth given in the words of the prophets and sages were to be completed in the truth given in God's Son (Heb. 1: 1-3).

In consequence the Christian finds a special value in the Old Testament, for, living under the new dispensation, he does not see himself as cut off from the old but as its heir. It is part of the patrimony on which he lives: "The whole of the Old Testament is the word of God, of *my* God, to his chosen people; a teaching which he gave gradually, which was progressively enlightened and completed, and which must be considered in its totality, a teaching which was given to the Israelites through the course of their history, but which they had to pass on to their children and to the children of their children until it reaches me who am their spiritual heir."[13]

The Unity of Scripture

The Christian, more truly than the Jew, is the spiritual heir of Israel. Without the New Testament, the Old is like an ancient fragment lacking parts which make it intelligible. The Old Testament is not static, it is in progress—and the New is the prolongation of that process. It is a completion because the Old Testament was only a preparation. The word of God is contained in both Testaments, but in each only partially. Together they contain the whole of the written message of God to man.

To be understood wholly, the Bible must be understood as a whole. It was an error of the days of ecclesiastical ignorance which turned the Latin noun *biblia* from the neuter plural, as it had been in the Greek, to a feminine singular. Yet it was a happy fault which gave us our English *bible* as a singular word and, in common usage, stressed the fact that God's word, united by the same inspiration, is in the eyes of faith more a single book than a library. Like any other book it can be fully understood only when read to the end. This unity means that there can, properly speaking, be no autonomous Old Testament theology, and therefore no theological approach which does not view the Old Testament in the light of the New.

This is not to deny that the theologian may confine his study to the Old Testament, or even to a book or collection of books within it. Since, as we have said, a science is specified by its light and method, the light may be directed and the method applied to a part only of the subject of the science. In this way one might have a theology of the Deutero-Isaias or of the prophets or of the Old Testament, as one might have a theology of St. John or the New Testament. Yet the theology of Isaias would not be independent of that of the prophets, nor that of the prophets independent of that of the Old Testament. So also the theology of Old or New Testament is not independent, completely separable from that of the other. They are interdependent elements of a pattern having its full meaning only when seen as a whole.

In the Old Testament the Pentateuch was the instruction of the Torah, for the Jews the sacred book above all others in their Bible. While it was the very foundation of their religion, it never comes to a conclusion. Its themes of promise, choice and covenant are carried on and repeated in the succeeding books, but do not find their realization in any of them. The very covenant which gives the Old Testament its name safeguards the promise which is never realized in any of its books. It has no fulfillment until Christ concludes the New Testament (or covenant), of which the covenants of the Law were figures. For the Law was a pedagogue leading to Christ (Gal. 3:24); but that pedagogue was like the Greek slave from whom St. Paul took the figure, not primarily a teacher, but one who led the way to education. This teaching was to come through faith in Christ. Without him that Law and all its sequels in the Old Testament cannot be understood.

St. Iranaeus remarked on the unity of the two Testaments, and the special lack of completeness of the Old, when he wrote:

> When the Law is read by the Jews at the present time, it is like a fable, because of all those things they have no explanation which relates to the Son of God as man. But when it is read by Christians, it is the treasure hid in the fields which is laid open and made plain by the cross of Christ, enriching the minds of men, declaring the wisdom of God, and making manifest his purpose towards men, shaping beforehand the kingdom of Christ, proclaiming the Good News of our heritage in the holy city, Jerusalem.[14]

These words, however, should not be thought to imply that either biblical theology, or Old Testament theology, is nothing more than Christology. Neither the expectation of Christ nor any other unifying subject other than God is adequate to theology. The development of God's kingdom, the unconditional submission to God's will, the Messianic hope and its fulfillment are all themes woven into and weaving together the theology of the Bible. God is the subject of theology.[15] The search for him in both Testaments is the source of their unity.

Theological Interpretation

This insistence on unity should not mislead us into blunting the edge of difference between the two. The Testaments are unified as beginnings and completion. They are not identical. The theological approach, while appreciating that the New Testament is the prolongation and perfection of the Old, and the Old, the prediction and preparation of the New, does not confuse their roles. It is not tempted to seek in the Old Testament the specific doctrines of the New. Neither the perfection of Christian doctrine nor the fulness of its morality should be demanded of the Old Testament. The theological investigation of the Old Testament under the light of its unity with the New may be led astray from the start by confusing completion with repetition. Not only an overly simple reading which, starting from a Christian viewpoint, makes no effort to accommodate to the ancient text, but some ancient and even "modern" interpretations foster this confusion by trying to introduce into ancient texts the problems and the solutions of problems belonging to the new dispensation. Here theological conclusions precede exegesis and do not flow from it.

The theological approach has the greatest respect for the literal sense of the text of the Old Testament, for it is that text which is inspired. Since that text gives the divine message in its original purity, the mind must be bared of preconceptions which would substitute its own thought for the meaning of the text. With that meaning found, it is to be placed in its total context.

Nor does this approach misprize historical development, since the inspired text represents God's revelation as given and added to in time. The historical development of doctrines through the course of the books of the Old Law is something given by faith, as well as by reason. Reason gives it as simply an evolving teaching; faith sees the development as a merciful cumulation of God's gift of knowledge. This diversity and growth is recognized in the inspired word in Hebrews: "God, who at sundry times and in diverse manners spoke in times past to the father, by the prophets, last of all in these days has spoken to us by his Son, whom he appointed heir of all things" (Heb. 1:1-2). To fail to recognize historical development and to do violence to the texts and so find the New Testament in the Old would amount to denying its newness. The Old Testament is rather a long process of gradually building foundations on which the New is raised. In it are found promises and hopes given to various men over a long course of centuries to be realized in the New.

The theological approach with its necessity for a wide view of both Testaments, its respect for the letter of the text with the consequent necessity of using all rational means for penetrating it, its recognition of historical development requiring the application of historical criticism, seems to have done nothing to surmount the obstacles that bar the student from Scripture reading and study. At least a random approach would require little of the reader if he got little in return. But this approach demands the addition of the light of faith, a deeper penetration and a more universal view of the Scriptures, and yet retains the same arduous human means. One thing is different: the means are now merely preliminary; when they have been used, the task is only partly done. In this case the gibe of Diderot might well seem justified: "I have only a small flickering light to guide me in a thick forest. Up comes a theologian and blows it out."

The situation is not nearly that dark. A great deal of light has been thrown on the obscurities which ordinarily repel the student. The difficulties of speech and thought, culturally and historically so alien, still demand the application of the resources of erudition. If the theological approach adds another dimension of faith without eliminating the need of these resources, it adds a powerful motive for their use. Since it seeks a meaning of the two Testaments as one, it seeks a religious knowledge important to each Christian. The Old Testament stories assume a new relevance with their relation to the new covenant of the Christian order which the student lives.

The situation is parallel for believing student and believing scholar. Père Roland de Vaux has said: "The elaboration of this biblical theology is the last goal of our studies and, if our work does not tend more or less closely to that goal, or does not help others to tend to it, many of us would not think it worthwhile to consecrate a lifetime to it."[16] Nor is it presumptuous that a student should see his goal as that of the scholar. If there is no intention of the goal, nothing will be put in motion; last in execution, it is still first in intention. If the full realization of this goal of a biblical theology still evades the scholar, it nonetheless beckons to the rawest neophyte.

With this goal before him, the student can see that the tedious, the coarse, the difficult passage is a building block in this theological edifice, important enough for the construction of theology to demand his application. Further, his recognition of the continuity of God's revelation from Testament to Testament also helps in removing that temptation (so widespread among a certain class of the imaginative pious) to allegorize the Scriptures.

The allegorizer abandons the literal sense of the texts to seek edification in figurative applications. Fostering this tendency is a view of the Scriptures, more especially of the Old Testament, as a collection of fragments. Each book, or even more restricted passage, stands lonely, unsupported by its fellows. Because the Bible is seen, at least practically, as a set of heterogeneous parts, each lacking relation to other parts, each part must justify itself. Food for the soul must be found in each single passage because the following passage is always new and contributes not at all to the reason for being of what went before. The recognition of the whole will prevent the student from thinking each of the parts must stand by itself. He should be willing to wait, for he can see that there will be meaning in plenty when the parts are joined into the whole.

Perhaps this insistence on the theological bearing of the sacred word of God seems like laboring the obvious; indeed it is—and should be—for those who are heirs of a powerful and fruitful tradition of theology, familiar with, and appreciative of theological commentaries on the Bible. But today even among Catholics the emphasis on seeing and seeking theological meanings in the Bible has largely, if not entirely, disappeared.

In the broad field of Scripture studies, in point of fact, there exists a great diversity of non-theological approaches to the *sacra pagina,* and not infrequently one or another of these is adopted in practice as the proper instrument (sometimes the exclusive instrument) for teaching Sacred Scripture, in the colleges as well as for the general public. The Protestant scholar, Herbert F. Hahn, lists several of these approaches: the critical approach; the anthropological approach; the religio-historical school; form criticism (which admittedly may end in theology, but only too often stops far short); the sociological approach; the findings of archeology.[17] He explicitly points out the insufficiency of these modern trends and methods to attain of themselves, without theology, the true meaning (to say nothing of the deeper meaning) of God's revelation.[18] This significant conclusion with its far-reaching implications is whole-heartedly concurred in by another Protestant scholar of no little reknown, H. H. Rowley.[19]

Surely Catholic scholars—presumably theologically trained and cognizant if not appreciative of papal directives in the matter—should reach the same conclusion, make it operative in their own researches, and implement it for their teaching of Sacred Scripture. But such is hardly the case. We may dismiss as ephemeral the attempt to place the primary emphasis in teaching college Scripture on literary forms, a concession to fashion which experience will prove to contain the seeds of its own dissolution. A more pertinent and permanent example would be a well-known introduction to the Old Testament for (apparently) a popular audience which gives only nine pages to a summary of the contents of the Pentateuch (in the form of outlines) and devotes some 56 pages to an apologetic of the Mosaic authorship of those books. It would be pedagogically naive to think that this materially assists the reader to grasp and understand the inspired word.

Even the great Bible of Jerusalem, a masterpiece of modern Catholic biblical scholarship, gives—unavoidably—the same impression of de-emphasizing "meaning" in favor of current critical trends. The one-volume edition (evidently designed for popular consumption) begins its introduction with a thorough and authoritative discussion of the Synoptic problem; only later (in the special introductions to the individual gospels) and then most briefly is the reader given any hint as to the "message" or revelation therein contained. What is primary in this kind of pedagogy? Rather a defense and qualification of the value of the literary traditions than an exposition of their meaning. And however valuable in itself, however necessary at certainly levels of biblical scholarship such a defense is, one may seriously question its usefulness as a pedagogical aid or an educational approach.

The Preparations

No claim is made that all difficulties are solved by choosing a proper point of view. The Bible remains a difficult book, no matter what we seek from it. Obviously the reading of Scripture requires some formal training to introduce the student. The complaint of St. Jerome long ago revealed the dangers of underestimating the requirements for knowing the Bible:

> You should understand that you cannot enter into the Scriptures without a forerunner to show the way. Not to mention grammarians, rhetoricians, philosophers, geometers, dialecticians, musicians . . . let me get to the lesser arts which are the work of the hand, not the mind. Farmers, masons, metal smiths and wood cutters . . . all know that they cannot be what they wish to be without a teacher. The art of the Scriptures is the only one that everyone everywhere claims for his own.[20]

If the course of introduction is not properly organized, it may swing shut the door which it intends to open. This it may do by so multiplying accidental or accessory materials intended to aid in Bible study that the student is overwhelmed by the magnitude of the task. Erudition should not be flaunted for its own sake. The resources of archeology and the many other disciplines which contribute to us our knowledge of the Bible should be introduced for use, and gradually. The theories of Herman Gunkel on the *Gattungen,* the significance of the Nuzi tablets for the understanding of Hebraic law, the contribution of the alphabetic cuneiform literature of Ugarit to our understanding of the psalms, the *procédé anthologique* and its influence on the Canticle of Canticles, Rudolf Bultman and the *Entmythologisierung* of the New Testament—these are not among the essentials of preparation for a reading of the Bible.

The very listing of these examples brings in another danger, that of the liberal sprinkling of foreign words in any technical work (and many not so technical) on Scripture. A kind of macaronic jargon sometimes results which is itself a danger to the beginner's courage. Much difficulty would be avoided by a firm adherence to the essential in introducing the Bible.

The extent to which the student may be prepared for reading the Scripture and be guided in his reading will obviously depend upon the time found for the Scripture course. What should be aimed at is the mark set by the nature of the problem and by ecclesiastical authority.

Since inspiration makes the Bible what it is, the course should first of all give an account of inspiration which, based on sound theology, recognizes the problems raised by the critical approach to the Scriptures. Basic to this is the insight of St. Thomas: "The principal author of Sacred Scripture is the Holy Spirit. . . ; man was the instrumental author."[21] What is required in commentary on this is more than illustrations of instrument. A true appreciation of inspiration will demand an adequate notion of instrumentality philosophically elaborated. The better the roles of principal cause and instrument are understood, the more clearly will appear the relationship of each to the effect in the concrete case. If the background is well understood philosophically, the student should be able to seek divine truth in the Scriptures without being disturbed by the variety of its presentation. A recognition that imperfect man has his part, although an instrumental one, should assist to reconcile the reader to traces of personal or national idiosyncrasy, or that arising from a particular historical state. Such a constantly recurring problem as the reconciliation of the creation account in Genesis with modern science finds a start toward its solution in the part played by the human author. No anceint Semite could be expected to write like Fred Hoyle, the Cambridge cosmogonist. On the other hand, the fact of divine authorship should account for mystery here and there in the Scriptures.

The canon of Scriptures may be treated in connection with inspiration, as it lists those books which are inspired. The involvement of the historical question of the canon in that of the ancient versions should allow all that need be said on the Septuagint or the *Vetus Itala* to be treated in that connection.

The rules of interpretation should not require extensive treatment. Emphasis should be placed on the Catholic rules of interpretation in relation to the Church's guardianship of the Bible.[22] The reason for the rules should be apparent from elsewhere in the theology course, since from his first introduction to theological sources the student should see the deposit of faith as intrusted to the Church. The most widely used of these criteria, that of the analogy of faith (Rom. 12:6), which tests interpretations against the standard of certain Catholic doctrine, should come into use naturally if he is learning any theology at all.

As for the rational rules of interpretation, the teacher should remember that although there are special applications to the special problems of the Bible, as an ancient as well as a divine book, these rules are used in all reading. The student should receive much in this regard from other courses in literature and literary criticism. The problems of literary forms and the investigation of sources are found for the classical literature of Greece and Rome as well as for the Bible. The student is far less likely to be disturbed by their appearance in biblical study if he has met them in the study of profane literature. Moreover, he is less likely to consider any reservations with regard to the validity of certain of their uses in the Bible as a matter of an overly conservative attitude based on a fearful faith, if he has seen the sharp reactions of some classical scholars against source theories, or the changing attitudes of literary critics to the study of forms.[23]

In any case, much of the task of rational investigation of the Bible must be done for the student by the expert. The human means of study of Scriptural meaning are myriad. It is evident that the student must himself supply all of these means. It is reported of Péguy that he regretted being unable to read the Old Testament in Hebrew; or, as he put it, "to understand the Bible in Jewish." "But," he added, "I have friends who understand it, and I understand their understanding." For those with less learned friends, translators, commentators, writers of introductions and notes, archaeologists, geographers and cartographers will supply for personal deficiencies. What they funish must be used, as it should have been composed, with the utmost scientific rigor and the calmest objectivity.

That aspect of introduction which presents individual books should, above all, be positive. Each book should be presented particularly with reference to its contribution to theological teaching. Far too often time is wasted here on secondary questions, to the neglect of the central truths of a book.

An example might be taken from the treatment of the book of Jonas. Here the question of whale or no whale is allowed to obscure the beautiful teaching on the mercy of God presented with a rather wry humor: even the most categoric of divine judgments condemning a most wicked city can be averted by penance. This teaching is the same and can be as easily found in the book with or without the whale.[24] Another sort of problem is created by presenting such data as the history and arguments for the documentary theory of the origin of the Pentateuch with such brevity and lack of nuance that the student is left with only a vague impression that the veracity of the books has been tarnished. "All I remember from one year in the Old Testament is that the Pentateuch was said to have been written by a number of different people designated by letters of the alphabet, and that this was supposed to have invalidated it somehow."[25] The writer was speaking of a famous Ivy League college for women, but the same sort of impression might be gathered elsewhere. Difficulties should be faced, but they should not be made the chief content of the introduction to individual books.

The Reading of the Bible

Above all, the Bible should be read. After these summary introductions, the Scriptures should be suggested for reading in accordance with the proper goal of Scripture reading. This is not primarily apologetic, much less is it done with apologies, as if at any time some error might be found. As has been seen at length, Scripture is read mainly for its theological content, the exploring of the sure grounds for doctrinal conclusions. Difficulties will certainly arise. Some of them, if not insoluble, at least will not be solved. Solutions of difficulties are not the object of Scripture reading; and if the introduction has been practical and the reader is well disposed, they will be accepted. A divine book is, by reasonable expectation, a difficult book. Certainly the answer to difficulties should be sought; but the search should respond to a felt need, the result of being puzzled in repeated reading by the same unexplained text.

The theological approach to Scripture demands a wide and frequent reading of the Bible. Many serious difficulties vanish when exposed to the light which one part of Scripture throws on another. As an example of the way in which the weight of the difficulty does not correspond to the degree of specialization needed to solve it, let us take the story of Esau and Jacob (Gen. 25:21-34; 27:1–33:16). A very minor problem is the almost incredible shagginess of Esau, a man so hairy that the hairy side of a kid skin might appear to be the skin on the back of his hands. The adequate solution of the problem—hardly of great moment—is found in a knowledge of Hebrew. The notion conveyed by the Hebrew word translated *hand* extends to the forearm, which may be hairy indeed. The question of the condoning of Rebecca's and Jacob's deceit is more frequently raised, and is also more important. A consideration of the surrounding context in the Bible—not merely the espisode as given, say, in Bishop Gilmour's Bible history—will show the misfortune which follows the deceivers. Rebecca's loss of both of her sons, and Jacob's flight from Esau to spend long years being tricked by another trickster, do not indicate the approval of a complacent author of Genesis. The larger question, and a more theological one—that of what the story is doing in the Bible at all—is answered by a reading of the Bible far beyond the bounds of Genesis. Exodus, the prophet Malachias, and the epistle to the Romans combine to show us here the foreshadowing of the doctrine of grace, the free choice of God which is not forced by any worth native to man. "As it is written: 'Jacob I have loved and Esau I have hated.' What shall we say then? Is there injustice with God? God forbid. For he saith to Moses: I will have mercy upon whom I will have mercy, and I will show mercy to whom I will show mercy. So then, it is not of him that willeth, nor of him that runneth, but of God that showeth mercy" (Rom. 9:13-16). Here the Bible is its own best interpreter.

The Value of the Approach

It may be objected that this approach as outlined will give only a superficial knowledge of the Scriptures. No college Scripture course can expect to turn out qualified exegetes. The field is too vast, the complications grow day by day.

But one need not be an expert to make his own investigation of Scripture valuable. "The slenderest knowledge that may be obtained of the highest things is more desirable than the most certain knowledge obtained of lesser things," says St. Thomas. There is insight as well as wit in Chesterton's, "Anything that is worth doing is worth doing badly." Moreover, there is room for all degrees of skill in reading the Bible; for there are messages plain as well as messages hidden. "The Bible," says St. Gregory, "is, if I may use the expression, like a stream with its deeps and shallows in which the lamb may wade and the elephant may swim."[26] A student convinced of the worth of the river may wade with the lambs, if he cannot swim with the elephants. With the latter's help, he may even venture deeply and not be out of his depth. If the approach has been assimilated, he *will* venture—and his knowledge should grow as his venturing is extended.

The chief relevance of Scripture to the college course in theology lies in its theological content, its authority for the principles of that doctrine. To arrive at these principles, Scripture must be read, and read with some initiation to the task. It must be read for its theological meaning, not merely for its literary interest, nor its apologetic questions, nor other subsidiary reasons. Because of the unity of the book and the coherence of its parts, it must be read extensively. Here, in spite of the philosophers, the comprehension increases with the extension. Read thus, it will verify what St. Paul wrote to Timothy: "All Scripture is inspired of God and useful to teach" (II Tim. 3:16).

And much else besides.

Footnotes to Study 6

[1]A description of such a drawing of biblical lots, together with the limitations of the practice, is given by George Arthur Buttrick in "The Study of the Bible," *The Interpreter's Bible*, I (New York: Abingdon Press, 1952), 167.

[2]Even St. Thomas' lavish use of the Scripture in objections as well as in direct proof or the Sed Contra leaves many pages of the Bible unmentioned. In the *Summa Theologiae* and the *Summa contra Gentes* entire books of the Bible remain unquoted. While it is not strange that no verse of the shortest books of the Old and New Testament, Abdias and Philemon, appears, I Paralipomenon, a book of some length, is represented by only two verses of its last 29 chapters. Of Genesis, 11 of 20 chapters, of Josue, 16 of 24, and even in the New Testament two of Mark's 16 chapters and six of the 28 of Acts

contribute not a single verse. At the same time, of the verses mentioned above, John 1:14 is used 40 times, Phil. 3:2, 33 times, Gen. 1:1, 33 times, and Deut. 6:4, 8 times. Even this restricted sampling shows how scattered and incomplete is a knowledge of Scripture derived from its theological use. St. Thomas' theology was, of course, based upon a wide personal knowledge of the Bible; he was *magister in sacra pagina* before he began to teach theology (cf. M.-D. Chenu, O.P., *Introduction à l'Étude de Saint Thomas d'Aquin* [Montréal: Institute d'Étues Médiévales, 1950], 207 ff.).

On the medieval use of the Bible in general see Beryl Smalley's *Study of the Bible in the Middle Ages*, 2nd ed. (New York: Philosophical Library, 1952) and C. Spicq, *Esquisse d'une Histoire de l'Exégèse Latine au Moyen Âge* (Paris: J. Vrin, 1944). For St. Thomas' use of Sacred Scripture see Chenu, *op. cit.*, 213-223, C. Spicq, "Saint Thomas d'Aquin Exégète," *Dictionnaire de Théologie Catholique*, XV, 694-738, J. Van der Ploeg, O.P., "The Place of Holy Scripture in the Theology of St. Thomas," *The Thomist*, X (1947), 398-422, as well as less recent articles by Gardeil, Vosté, Colunga, etc.

For a contrary view of the need of a course in Scripture itself cf. V. E. Smith, *The School Examined* (Milwaukee: Bruce, 1960), 281; he sees no reason for a special Scripture course, but would let the student's knowledge of the Scriptures depend on their pervasive use in all courses.

[3]The story is told in Stanley Cook, *An Introduction to the Bible* (Harmondsworth, Sussex: Penguin Books, 1950), 12.

[4]*Summa*, I, q. 1, a. 8, ad 3.

[5]*Ibid.*, II-II, q. 1, a. 9, ad 1.

[6]Quoted by Hilaire Duesberg, O.S.B., "Horoscope du Mouvment Biblique," *Nouvelle Revue Théologique*, LXXIX (1957), 6.

[7]Stanley Cook, *loc. cit.*

[8]Tertullian, *Adversus Marcionem*, Lib. I, cap. 1 (*Corpus Christianorum*, Series Latina, I [Turnhout, Belgium: Brepols, 1954], 442).

[9]Suzanne de Diétrich, *Le Renouveau Biblique* (Paris: Neuchâtel, Delachaux et Niestlé, 1949), 62. The whole section (pp. 56-60) on the unity of the Testaments shows that difficulty in fostering reading of the Bible comes chiefly from the O.T.

[10]Encyclical *Divino Afflante Spiritu*, September 30, 1943; cf. *Rome and the Study of the Scriptures* (St. Meinrad, Ind.: Grail, 1953), 92 (n. 24). Cf. *ibid.*, 104 (n. 54).

[11]Vatican Council, Sess. III, *Dogmatic Constitution on the Catholic Faith*, Chap. 4, "Concerning Revelation"; Denz. 1787.

[12]R. de Vaux, O.P., "À propos de la Théologie Biblique," *Zeitschrift für die Altestamentliche Wissenchaft*, LXVIII (1956), 225-27. My indebtedness to the distinguished French scholar will be obvious to anyone familiar with his work.

[13]de Vaux, *art. cit.*, 226.

[14]St. Irenaeus, *Adversus Haereses*, Lib. IV, cap. 26 (PG VII, 1053).

[15]*Summa*, I, q. 1, a. 7.

[16]de Vaux, *loc. cit.*

[17]*Old Testament in Modern Research* (Philadelphia: Muhlenberg Press: 1954).

[18]*Ibid.*, "Summary," 250-262.

[19]*The Changing Pattern of Old Testament Studies* (London: The Epworth Press, 1959).

[20]St. Jerome, *Epistola LIII, ad Paulinum* (PL XXII, 544).

[21]*Quod. VII*, q. 6, a. 1, ad 5.

[22]Pius X, apostolic letter *Quoniam in Re Biblica*, March 27, 1906; cf. *Rome and the Sacred Scriptures* (cited in footnote 10), 38 (n. 13).

[23]Among reactions to the history of traditions or source theories in biblical circles, it would be harder to find a sharper criticism than that of A. E. Housman, *D. Iunii Iuvenalis Saturae* (Cambridge: Cambridge U. Press, 1956), xxviii: " 'Nothing,' I hear it asked, 'about Nicaeus? Nothing about Epicarpius, nor Heiricius, nor the long-resounding name of Exuperantius?' No, nothing. The truth is, and the reader has discovered it by this time if he did not know it beforehand, that I have no inkling of *Ueberlieferungsgeschichte*. And to the sister science of *Quellenforschung* I am equally a stranger; I cannot assure you, as some other writer will assure you before long, that the satires of Juvenal are all copied from the satires of Turnus. It is a sad fate to be devoid of faculties which cause so much elation to their owners; but I cheer myself by reflecting how large a number of human beings are more fortunate than I. It seems indeed as if a capacity for these two lines of fiction had been bestowed by heaven, as a sort of consolation-prize, upon those who have no capacity for anything else."

For the limitations of form criticism, cf. also Helen Gardiner, *The Limits of Literary Criticism* (London: Oxford U. Press, 1957). These Riddell Memorial Lectures treat of literary criticism and Scripture from the point of view of the amateur of the Bible who is at the same time a professional in the field of literary criticism.

[24]On the whole question of Jonas see Alexander Jones, *Unless Some Man Show Me* (New York: Sheed and Ward, 1960), 48-68. This is in popular form, with much literary allusion—a reflection of A. Feuillet's articles in the Revue *Biblique* which are cited in the book.

[25]M.B.W., "Secular Education Some Years After," *Integrity,* I (1947), 36.

[26]St. Gregory the Great, *Moralia* (Expositio in Librum Job), "Epistola Missoria," cap. 4 (PL LXXV, 515).

7

COLLEGE THEOLOGY AND THE ARTS

Benedict M. Ashley, O.P.

A convert to Catholicism, Father Ashley studied at Chicago University and received his doctorate in political science from Notre Dame. After his ordination in 1948, he continued his graduate work at the Pontifical Faculty of Philosophy, River Forest, Ill., (Ph.D.), where he is presently professor of the history of philosophy. As a member of the Albertus Magnus Lyceum for Natural Science he has served as a consultant for the Saint Xavier Plan of Liberal Education and as a faculty member of that college.

In the patristic *De Doctrina Christiana* of St. Augustine, the medieval *Didascalion* of Hugh of St. Victor, the Renaissance *Ratio Studiorum* of the Jesuits, and the contemporary discourses of Pius XII we find a traditional conviction about theological education which can be summed up in two propositions: 1) the study of sacred theology must begin with the reading of the Sacred Scriptures; 2) the proper academic preparation for this sacred reading is the mastery of the liberal and fine arts.[1]

Current controversy about the teaching of college theology shows that all parties concerned are agreed on the first of these two propositions. All admit that the reading of Sacred Scripture is fundamental to the study of theology, not only for the seminarian or the professional, but also for the layman.[2] Therefore the problem to be considered is whether the layman who is to study such a scriptural course needs to be trained in the liberal and fine arts. As we consider this important point with respect to each of the arts in order, we may further inquire whether the presence of such a course in the curriculum will promote the growth of these arts in Catholic schools and American culture. Finally, we will seek to discover (at least implicitly) whether the traditional theory of the liberal and fine arts needs to be revised to suit this task and to take advantage of modern advances in knowledge and techniques.

Rhetoric and the Kerygma

The new emphasis on the use of Sacred Scripture in the teaching of religion has received warm papal encouragement.[3] "The word of God is living and efficient and keener than any two-edged sword" (Heb. 4:12), and it was given to man not merely to instruct him, but to transform him with a new life. The teacher of revealed truth may not choose his method of teaching merely according to human prudence or the natural art of pedagogy; he must imitate the divine Teacher who came "preaching the gospel of the kingdom of God, and saying, 'The time is fulfilled, and the kingdom of God is at hand. Repent and believe in the gospel'" (Mark 1:14).[4]

The "kerygmatic method" (from the Greek for "proclamation" or "preaching") is without question the one actually used by our Lord, by the apostles, the Fathers of the Church, St. Dominic and St. Francis, and by the great popes of our time. All addressed themselves not merely to intellects but to *men.* Only by preaching can the word of God take life in the human heart, and all other religious teaching must participate in this most sublime and Christlike method.[5]

Does this mean that Christian instruction is to be carried on without the aid of human art? The Fathers of the Church (some of whom, notably St. Augustine, were teachers of rhetoric) defended the human art of persuasion as an instrument of the kerygma, provided that it remained a handmaid of Christian wisdom.[6]

Their caution recalls the protests of Aristotle against the abuses of rhetoric which, he says, can arise from a wrong definition of the art. It is not merely the art of prose composition or elegant speech, since it searches not only for the right word but for the right *argument* which will bring practical conviction to the audience.[7] Nor does it consist merely in playing on the emotions of an audience, for it uses emotional appeal to remove obstacles to rational persuasion or to enforce rational decisions.[8] Finally, it is not an instrument which is indifferently available for moral and immoral purposes; it is designed to assist the man of true prudence in his guidance of others.[9]

It is obvious that a liberal art by which suitable means of rational persuasion are discovered is extremely useful to the teacher of Christian doctrine in presenting a living message to every audience in a manner suited to their needs. When the teaching of religion seems remote, abstract, unconnected with the pupil's life and interests, the cause is frequently a failure on the part of the teacher to obey the basic principles of rhetoric. The teacher may even succeed in being very interesting and amusing, or even dramatic and moving, and yet fail really to influence the lives of the students. It is only when the teacher knows how to show the practical value of the truths he teaches in terms of the student's own needs and desires that he can actually influence the student's behaviour.[10]

It is not only the teacher of theology who needs this art but also the student who in lay life will take part in Catholic Action. The layman does not have the office of apostolic preaching, but he shares in the apostolate. In his professional life he will frequently have to speak for the faith, not only publicly, but in private discussions.[11]

Furthermore, the layman must not only be able to use rhetoric but to appreciate its right use and to detect its abuse. Much of his spiritual progress will be fed on sermons and "spiritual reading," which present theological teaching in the rhetorical mode. He must understand how to appreciate and interpret such writing. Frequently the classics of spirituality are unintelligible to the modern educated Catholic because he lacks the flexibility required to appreciate the changes in rhetorical style which time inevitably brings. More seriously he may misunderstand and misapply the doctrine (of the *Imitation of Christ*, for example, or the *Ascent of Mount Carmel*), because he does not appreciate the mode in which they are written.

This decline in the appreciation of rhetoric and the inability of many modern audiences really to listen to serious oratory is not a growth in "sophistication," as some suppose, but the mark of an inarticulate and emotionally debilitated age, fed on advertising slogans and shock techniques. Poorly trained audiences make for poor orators. It is a mistake, I believe, to think that rhetoric is effective only when the audience does not itself understand that the art is being used. This may be true of the abuse of rhetoric, but good speaking calls for a liberal audience, an audience of freemen, intellectually alive and emotionally vigorous.[12]

We may conclude that the college teacher of theology needs the liberal art of rhetoric to make his teaching living and effective, while the student needs the same art for the lay apostolate and his own spiritual development.

On the other hand, theology not only profits from rhetoric, it also purifies and strengthens the art itself. First it supplies a rich treasury of rhetorical masterpieces on Christian themes. The teacher of rhetoric should seek the theologian's advice in finding examples of sermons and apologetic works which are classics of Christian persuasion. Not only should the theologian recommend such works, but he ought to co-operate in their interpretation. How fruitful for the student would be a discussion in which St. Augustine's *Confessions* and Cardinal Newman's *Apologia pro Vita Sua* were considered both by the teacher of rhetoric and the teacher of theology!

Theology cannot furnish guidance in the techniques of rhetoric, but it purifies rhetoric itself by showing its proper Christian purpose. The history of rhetoric demonstrates how easily this art becomes debased, and the present condition of advertising and political propaganda confirms this in an alarming manner.[13]

The student who has some understanding of the principles of rhetoric will read with admiration the lofty orations of Deuteronomy, the pungent proverbs of the wisdom literature, the torrential eloquence of the prophets, the marvelous range of our Lord's own sermons, and the contrasting styles of the writers of the epistles, especially St. Paul and St. John. He will then begin to see that human speech need not debase men to automatons moved by irrational drives or conditioned reflexes, but can be sacramental and life-giving. In the famous words of Bossuet:

> The body of Jesus Christ is no more really present in the adorable Sacrament than the truth of Jesus Christ in the preaching of the Gospel. The species which you see in the eucharistic mystery are signs; what is hidden under them is the very body of Jesus Christ. In sacred sermons, the words which you hear are signs; that thought that produces them and which they bear to you is the very truth of the Son of God.[14]

Poetics and Christian Humanism

The kerygmatic emphasis has been challenged on many grounds.[15] Certainly no one can deny that it is fundamental to the mission of the Church, and that in the pulpit, in the catechizing of converts, and in the teaching of Christian doctrine in the high school it is the best method.[16] Nevertheless, those who propose that it be used also in the teaching of college theology seem indeed to be proposing both what is difficult and insufficient.

The kerygmatic method in the academic atmosphere of the college classroom is very difficult, because under these circumstances preaching is more likely to arouse antipathy than produce conviction. It is insufficient, because college students who have had a reasonably adequate instruction in Christian doctrine in the lower schools are capable of a more theoretical understanding of revealed truth than can be conveyed by a practical appeal.

It is a mistake to think of the study of theology as simply a matter of *professional* training to prepare the seminarian and the lay apostle for their different social functions in the Church.[17] These functions pertain to the order of *means* and the active life of the Church. Theology is indeed a form of practical knowledge, but it is *principally* speculative, and pertains to the *end* and the contemplative life of the Church.

A great defect of Protestantism was its tendency to reduce Christian instruction to the sermon. In the Catholic Church, however, along with the kerygmatic movement, there has also come a development of the *liturgical* movement, in which the emphasis is not only on good living but also on good praying. The liturgy includes rhetoric but it passes on, up to the contemplation of the divine mysteries. The reading of Scripture does not consist only in sermons and moral direction but also in poetry and meditative prose which do not urge us immediately to any particular activity except that of contemplation and love. "I remember the deeds of the Lord; yes, I remember your wonders of old. And I meditate on your works; your exploits I ponder. O God, your way is holy; what great god is there like our God?" (Ps. 76: 12-14). Without this contemplative phase of Christian life it withers into pharisaical moralism or a naturalistic social activism.

According to the traditional conception,[18] the poet, dramatist or novelist is a teacher "who leads men toward what is virtuous by means of some fitting representation."[19] This formula very precisely distinguishes poetic writing (whether in verse or prose) from other kinds of writing. Like rhetoric it differs from pure exposition because rhetorical and poetical writing are addressed not only to the abstract intelligence but to the will and emotions, which are moved only by what is concrete. Hence as rhetoric is said "to persuade," so poetic writing is said "to lead" to virtue. Both *move* the audience. Poetic writing, however, differs from rhetoric, because rhetoric moves the audience to *action* by means of some practical argument, while poetic writing moves the audience to *rest* in the contemplation of some "fitting representation" of life. A representation is not an abstract proposition but an *image*, a concrete story of human life which strikes and delights man through his imagination by its vivid and moving quality (hence it is said to be "fitting," i.e., beautiful). How does this make the audience "virtuous"? Not merely by stating some abstract moral truth, since that does not of itself make anyone virtuous.[20] Nor by a preachment which immediately persuades the audience to moral action. Rather the moral effect of the poetic work is to be found first in the fact that it recreates us in a moderate manner which prepares us for virtuous activity, and secondly in the fact that a man who enjoys the contemplation of what is virtuous (e.g., the life of a tragic hero) is *disposed* to virtue, because we are disposed to imitate what we admire.

According to this conception poetic writing has a threefold function in human life. For the beginner on the road to wisdom it gives, in a transient form, a foretaste of the delights of contemplation which can be possessed permanently by the virtue of wisdom. Without this foretaste of beauty, as Plato so eloquently taught, we would never undertake the long journey. Secondly, and this is its most proper function, it gives a form of recreation which even the wise man needs, which does not take him wholly away from contemplation. Lastly, it is useful to the mentally and emotionally ill, because it again awakens in them normal emotional and imaginative responses. To these three we may add that it is fitting also as an expression of what is *ineffable,* a symbolization of the supernatural, and hence its special role in the Bible and the liturgy.[21]

Christian literature and art are, as it were, an expansion at a lower level of the contemplative truth found in the Bible and the liturgy, but it is not only in explicitly religious literature that theological truth is embodied. Every writer and artist, however secular his subject matter may be, is dealing with the mystery of human life which he has sensitively and attentively observed. If an artist is true to the demands of his art, he cannot help but show those facts that form the *praeambula fidei*: the innate longing of man for happiness in contrast to the actual misery of the human condition; the existence and providence of God manifested in creation and governance of the universe and of life; and the signs of grace in the world. Indeed, as a number of recent writers have pointed out, sometimes the unbelieving artist (provided he does not abuse his art) is a most striking witness to God and to man's need for God.[22]

It is not surprising, then, that many today are advocating what is often called a *humanistic* approach to the teaching of theology.[23] They believe that students would come to a much deeper appreciation of the spiritual riches of the Christian life if theological truths were presented to them in cultural terms, through the humane studies of literature, the arts and history.[24]

Three arguments are commonly proposed in its favor:

1) Such a presentation is suited to the level of the college student, who is still not equipped with the philosophical knowledge

needed for the abstract study of theology. Many Jesuit educators (who were the first to try to meet the problem of the higher education of *laymen*) found the answer to this difficulty in the idea of a Christian humanism. It would be folly to ignore the long practical experience from which they speak, and their record of proven success and papal approbation.[25]

2) It is more suited to the layman, who will not draw most of his spiritual sustenance in life from the reading of theological works but from the liturgy and literature.

3) It appeals to the *whole man,* not only to the intellect but to imagination, sensation and emotion as well. Hence it is particularly needed in our culture where there is a serious divorce of intelligence and sensibility.[26]

A recent writer has said that "in the renewed dialogue between literature and theology perhaps the latter stands to profit most. But, if this is the case, we must look upon such a situation as a temporary devitalization of theology."[27] We may at least agree that in the teaching of college theology literature will be found to be a very useful instrument to show students that theological problems are not concocted by theologians, but that they arise from the realities of life. If we first pose problems about particular moral matters (or, more generally, concerning the condition and destiny of man) in the concrete and penetrating terms of famous novels, we guarantee that these problems will be seen as genuine. The student who sees the problem of fidelity in marriage in the contrasting situations of *Anna Karenina, The Golden Bowl* and *The End of the Affair,* or of fortitude in *Antigone, Polyeucte* and *Lord Jim,* will not find theology remote.

On the other hand, theology does profit literature and the fine arts, not indeed by teaching them their own proper mode of expression, but by showing their ultimate significance in human life, and also by illuminating human life itself which they seek to depict. This role of guidance and illumination involves both the problem of censorship and the problem of inspiration.

There is no doubt that literature and fine arts are highly dangerous, as Plato long ago warned us. Since they teach us about human life (in the special way we have just analyzed), if they teach falsely they do a profound injury. This damage is done when the artist causes us to take pleasure in what is morally evil, or to be disgusted by what is morally good. St. Thomas Aquinas tells us that it is precisely characteristic of the representations of poetry that they make something appear lovable or hateful.[28] The theologian must, therefore, censor literature and art which is designed to make the morally evil seem good (the *ex professo* obscene), or the morally good seem evil. The problem with the more artistic sort of modern literature is not that it is obscene but rather that it portrays what is morally good as hypocritical, neurotic, boring. It is the vice of acedia or disgust that chiefly requires the healing knife of censorship.[29]

As a source of inspiration, theology can give real guidance to the artist in penetrating the reality of life. Some believe that no one has so deep an insight into reality as the poet. This is simply not true. Even great works of art sometimes show that the artist was completely blind to the deep supernatural dimension of human existence. It was theology that took Dante on his journey deeper and higher than other poets have even imagined they could travel. Furthermore, theology—keeping in mind the divine law, "Judge not that ye be not judged"—reminds the poet that in picturing life he ought not to fall into the neo-classic error of forcing life to conform to the conventions of art. Life is complex, obscure and does not come to judgment here below. The artist is obliged to simplify, clarify and complete life if his work is to be artistic, but he is forbidden to falsify life. Only a theological delicacy can enable the artist to find a way between the formlessness of bad romantic art and the false neatness of neo-classicism or pietism.

The inspiration which theology gives to the artist it must also share with the audience. No human work of art is perfect. All bear the defects of their sinful authors. The audience must be discriminating, but it should not self-righteously demand the impossible. A theologically trained reader, although he will not tolerate what is essentially bad, will nevertheless see the best in what is essentially good. By the light of theology a truly good reader can see in the work of art something more perfect than the artist has actually accomplished, as St. Thomas Aquinas saw in the philosophy of Aristotle something better than the pagan clearly knew.[30]

Fine Arts and Theology

Whereas the art of writing and the art of composing music are liberal arts (because they do not involve the actual manipulation of physical material), the arts of acting, singing or playing a musical instrument are not strictly liberal because they involve this physical craftsmanship. The other fine arts do not permit of a practical separation between arts of composing and executing, since in dancing, painting, sculpturing and architecture the artist ordinarily must actually engage in the physical production of the work. Nevertheless, from the viewpoint of the value of the product, all the fine arts have a liberal character, since a work of fine art is not for physical use but for spiritual contemplation and enjoyment.

Poetic literature by its power of narration (shared in some degree by dancing and acting) is able to represent human life and action, and it alone has the power to represent the thoughts which render human action deliberate and moral. On the other hand, since it appeals to the imagination but not to the external senses (except as to its sound, which really belongs to the art of music), it lacks something of the vividness of appeal of the other arts. Of the other arts music is most powerful in the representation of human emotion, and this it shares with dancing and acting. Painting, sculpture and architecture, because of their static condition, represent habitual character rather than emotion. Painting and sculpture do this through a representation of the human face and figure, or through "abstract" patterns suggestive of human states, while architecture provides an appropriate setting for human actions by similar abstract devices.[31]

Theology is concerned with these arts principally because of their use in the liturgy, which is both a practice of the virtue of religion and a witness to the faith which the theologian can use as a source of theological truth.

The college course in theology cannot give the student the experience of participating in the liturgy, but it must help him to see its importance and show him how to penetrate its intellectual meaning. A knowledge of the arts is useful in appreciating the mode of expression used by the liturgy, but only theology has the power to explain the truths which the liturgy signifies.

Two dangers have to be avoided. As the Protestant, Paul Tillich, has pointed out, liturgical symbols can become idols.[32] On the other hand, the Calvinist refusal to accept the liturgy is equivalent to a denial of the Incarnation and a return to the Old Testament. In order to find the middle course, theology is necessary both to indicate appropriate symbols in keeping with the Incarnation and to show their inner meaning which points beyond to God.

The theologian's interest in art, however, should not stop with the limits of sacred and liturgical art. He has also to encourage the development of an art whose purpose is Christian recreation, or to show how art produced by non-Christians can be purified for Christian use.

For the art of music this means that the theologian is interested in showing how music represents human emotions as they participate in or escape the governance of reason and faith. He will point out the extremes of romanticism, which glorifies infinite passion as if this were the true way for man to transcend himself, and of puritanism and excessive intellectualism, which reduce music to a mere geometrical pattern devoid of feeling. He will show how the liturgical chant sets a model of the Christian spirit of true detachment and mortification, yet at the same time of ardent love and supplication. And he will raise the problem of how, with this model before us, we can develop a Christian culture in which there can be a full-bodied secular music that still reflects this Christian norm.

As regards the visual arts the theologian will praise the dignity and beauty of the human body, and point out that this beauty was fully realized in our Lord and Our Lady, the New Adam and the New Eve. At the same time he will show why the Christian must observe the norms of modesty and decorum in the cult of the body. He will show how reverence for the body requires the proper use of clothing fitted to social function and to a right personal expression, and how this same sense of the importance of human life should be reflected in public and private architecture and instruments of daily use.

He will also point out the dignity of the arts themselves as intellectual virtues which give spiritual worth even to manual work, so that the true craftsman seeks to bestow even on humble instruments of use something of the beautiful and the contemplative.

The theologian must also discuss the problem of art in the modern world. Since the beginning of the eighteenth century the fine arts have gone through a series of crises culminating in the present flight from all representation in art. Romanticism (which denied the object of representation by making it a mere occasion for emotional effusions of the artist), realism and impressionism (which denied the object by treating it as a mere surface, a collection of phenomena), and abstractionism (which openly denies it)—all try to escape the object.

Some very eminent Catholic philosophers see in this the final emergence of the artistic *habitus* in its purest form.[33] Is it not rather the protest of the artist in being asked by our age to picture a world from which atheism has banished any divine meaning, and false science has banished any natural meaning?

If we believe many modern scientists, the world is merely a surface to be measured behind which there are no subsisting natures. Even human nature is only a series of mental states emerging from the chaos of the subconscious. The artist, deprived of any object and presented only with surfaces, is forced to turn his art into something non-representative, although this ultimately means submission to the irrational.

The theologian may see in this a disease to be healed or a demon to be cast out, but he cannot help but be genuinely sympathetic with the artist frustrated in his vocation by a culture which has made the world appear meaningless. He will help his students to see in modern art, not merely something absurd, but rather a search for meaning—an effort which is by no means always in vain, but which (along with the many signs of hope in our time) gives promise of a new age.

Grammar and Semantics

Traditionally, the name given to literary studies in the ancient *trivium* was not *poetics* (Aristotle's term) but *grammar*, a fact reflecting a basic confusion which has long plagued the liberal arts tradition. Indeed, it is still with us today in the work of the "New Critics," namely, the reduction of literary criticism to a study of the use of words and symbols.[34]

Grammar is best considered not as a distinct art in its own right but as a *common part* belonging to all the arts of discourse, since it deals with the external and conventional signs of thought, while the arts of discourse themselves deal with the thoughts signified. Aristotle treated grammar principally as a part of poetics,[35] probably because poetics was the first of these arts to be studied by the learner, and perhaps also because poetry exploits all the aspects of language more fully than do the other arts of discourse. In Hellenistic, Roman and Renaissance times the reduction of literary criticism to a study of style led to the identification of literature with the mere study of grammar and of "rhetoric," the latter term indicating a more advanced approach to the same problem.[36]

Yet the problem of language is of immense importance in the reading of the Bible. The layman confronts his Bible today without a knowledge of its original tongues, nor even with an understanding of the Vulgate Latin translation through which Scripture entered into the culture and liturgy of the West. Even in English translations problems of differing versions, their variations and their fidelity to the original—and the very flavor of the original which in greater or less degree they retain—disturb him.

St. Augustine in the *De Doctrina Christiana* stresses the tremendous importance of the concept of the *sign* in reading the Bible, in understanding the sacraments, even in understanding the incarnation of the divine Word.[37] In writing the Scriptures, God used as his instruments men who spoke not only with natural signs but also in human languages of their own invention. Every system of signs is imperfect; it can never exactly communicate human meanings, let alone divine meanings.

Yet when human language is used artistically it can be a marvelous bridge between one spirit and another, provided that in the listener there is a corresponding power of interpretation.

Thus the theologian hopes that the teachers of English and every language will prepare students to understand the problems of communication found in all aspects of life, and most crucially in the understanding of God's word. The student must see that grammar is not a mere question of "rules of good usage" but the forging of an instrument which has to be used with great imagination. The study of language should be a unified study of all those problems dealt with today under the heads of grammar, philology, linguistics, semantics, communications, cybernetics and philosophy of language.

The student who comes to a theology course unaware of the problems and techniques involved in interpreting any message will not be able to make much out of the Scriptures, ancient in origin and divine in content, or to understand how the doctrine of the Church can develop without addition or essential change.

The more theology comes to be a serious study in our schools the more this powerful stimulus to knowing languages will be felt in the language departments. It is obvious that the stimulus to study Hebrew will be greater for one who is interested in the Bible, but it is quite as true for the study of Greek and Latin with respect to theology. Not only is a vast part of Latin and Greek literature the work of Christian writers, chiefly engaged in expounding the Bible, but interest even in classical writers is indivisibly bound up with a concern for the tradition of Western culture, and in this the Bible—and theology—plays the central role. A well-informed interest in the Bible inevitably entails interest in classical civilization, while an interest in classical civilization becomes mere antiquarianism if it is not fed by the realization that this civilization still lives today in Christian institutions.

What of modern languages? Problems of the space-age have recently stimulated language study, even to the point where no further stimulus seems necessary. Yet how can this be more than temporary, unless there exists a deeper community life among men which requires that they talk not alone of technology and business but also about themselves and their souls? It is here that theology gives us insight into the fundamental reason for barriers in communication, and their only ultimate remedy.

In the eleventh chapter of Genesis the account of the Tower of Babel teaches us that the barriers which cut off men from communication with each other originated in man's pride. It is this which alienates him from God and isolates each people in its own stubbornness of mind.[38] In the second chapter of Acts we see that one of the first effects of the coming of the Paraclete was the gift of tongues, the speaking and interpreting of all languages. This miracle was the manifestation of the truth that only through the catholicity of the Church can men be united in a true communion of minds and hearts. This miracle summons the Christian linguist to use his art to achieve something of the same effect.

The search for a universal language has often been an effort of reformers who were materialists. They have sought some "minimal language" (Basic English, for example) which would be suited for business or technology. Such barbarian tongues are altogether too crude to be a fit vehicle of the subtleties of human thought or feeling.[39] A more spiritual approach to the problem must seek both to achieve universality and to retain the flexibility and characteristic genius of the national languages. Already we see indications of the solution toward which the Church seems headed. It will retain Latin as the sacred and catholic language at the heart of the liturgy and the universal theological life of the Church, and yet will freely incorporate the vernaculars into the liturgical rites.[40]

The goal of Christian education should be to make our people at least genuinely bilingual. To insist only on the vernacular is to neglect the unity of the Church, but to deny it an important place is to lose the variety and connaturality of speech. To be bilingual is to be freed from the identification of truth with the mode of its expression. To say that such a goal is impractical is to fall into that narrow notion of practicality which has already done so much harm in American education.

Dialectics and the Thinking Student

But the humanistic or cultural approach (which is narrowly so, and not fully "liberal scientific") to Christian doctrine at the college level is also open to a serious objection. One of the chief criticisms of Catholic education today is that it does not make the student think, but rather inculcates an attitude of passive acceptance. Some believe that this is due to an excessive attitude of reverence engendered in the classes in religion, which is then used by the student as an excuse for mental laziness in his other studies.[41]

This criticism, however, is not leveled only at Catholic education. Mortimer Adler's career in the United States has proved that educators were simply ignorant of the Socratic method of dialectics. Dewey revolutionized American education by insisting that learning begins with the recognition of problems, but the problems he emphasized were mostly practical problems. Adler went further and reminded us that the recognition of practical problems itself often presupposes that we have recognized and faced certain intellectual problems.

Hence many today are advocating that the teaching of theology in college must be a vigorous intellectual exploration in which the student is not merely "handed the doctrine" but brought face to face with theological problems which the teacher helps him to work out. Intellectual habits, like any natural habits, these educators point out, are only acquired by vigorous exercise.[42] There is much truth in their criticism that the kerygmatic approach is too narrowly practical and subjective, the humanistic approach too impressionistic. At some point the student must begin to face questions of objective truth about religion and strive to free himself from personal, subjective interests and from esthetic and imaginative appeals. The Catholic religion is personally helpful. The Catholic religion is culturally rich and attractive. But is it objectively true? A college education which does not get the student to face that question is highly dangerous. It cannot help but leave the student with the impression that, whereas in other fields of college study the question of objective truth is valiantly faced, it is assiduously avoided in the religious course, and covered over by subjective and esthetic appeals.

The notion of a dialectical approach to religious truth is, of course, very prevalent today in Protestant circles.[43] Yet, rather characteristically, dialectics tends for the modern Proestant to be a conflict of *attitudes* rather than of truths. Hence the term "dialogue," with its suggestion of a dramatic involvement of "I and thou." A dialogue or dialectic in this sense can hardly be the work of an academic course, since it is essentially personal and moral. The work of a college course must be dialectic in the Greek sense of a dispassionate inquiry which is necessary if a student is to learn to stand back from a question and see it clearly. This is the attitude we seek to create in courses in natural science or history.

Some will deny that such an attitude is permissible in religious matters, because such matters are of ultimate concern, and about such questions it is immoral to remain objective and aloof. Nevertheless, truth, even ultimate truth, demands of the searcher a submission to reality and a freedom from subjectivity. The serenity of St. Thomas Aquinas before ultimate questions is shocking to some, but it is a mark of the purity of his spirit.

The use of dialectics, however, is a delicate matter, since, as Socrates said, it is a kind of obstetrics, and the child might be still-born or injured for life. There is a threefold peril: (1) Poor students are likely to become bewildered by the conflict of opinions. If they despair they will sink into a worse passivity than ever. (2) Some superficial students will master the technique and vocabulary of debate and end in sophistry, which in religious matters often leads to spiritual mediocrity and cynicism. (3) Some who think more deeply may in their inexperience and vanity plunge too deeply and be seriously tempted against their faith.

For this reason dialectics must be used in a moral atmosphere of profound and humble faith and of sincere, hard-working intellectual inquiry. Prayer and serious study are necessary for those who ponder mysteries. At the same time the study of the art of dialectics itself is of great importance in exposing its possible abuses.

If the student understands the technique of inquiry, its tentative character which approaches the realm of certain knowledge but can never invade it, and the necessity of suspending judgment about speculative probabilities, then his fund of genuine certitude—whether of faith or of common sense or of science already acquired—will not be corrupted.

The "decay of dialogue," as Walter Ong calls it,[44] has been the disease of post-medieval education. The theologian will do much for all of education if he assists, at least by the example of his own teaching, in the restoration of dialectic. In contemporary theological writing we can find some perfect examples of the careful study and comparison of opposing opinions. In this the theologian will find an unexpected second in the science departments of his school, since (admittedly within rather narrow limits) the modern "scientific method" with its use of hypothetical reasoning is essentially dialectical.

In treating each main topic of theology the teacher should begin by an exploration of the problem and the study of various opinions. It is more important, of course, that the student should understand the problem than that he should be able to catalogue all the views. Then the student should be required to seek the principles and definitions appropriate to finding a solution to the problem. Each step of this process ought to be tested by the raising of serious difficulties. The mere interchange of opinions by a polite panel is not dialectics, nor is the aim of dialectics a consensus arrived at by a popular opinion poll.

The treatise on Mariology, for example, should begin with a serious discussion of the objections raised by Protestants to Catholic devotion to Mary. Difficulties about the historical development of Mariology should be discussed, and something seen of the controversy about the Immaculate Conception. Furthermore, questions should be raised about the actual devotional practices and attitudes of American Catholics. Only when the student sees that it is really a strange thing that a religion centered on the God-man should have given so much attention to a mere human being about whom we have only a few explicit lines in Sacred Scripture should the teacher begin to guide the students to the solution of this paradox. We must awaken the sense of wonder in our students if we are to see them really inflamed with a desire to understand the mysteries of faith better.

It is common today to hear it said that the Sacred Scriptures are not written with the Greek syllogistic mentality but with a special sort of Semitic mentality. Properly understood this is true and important, but some have pressed it to the point of denying that syllogistic reasoning has any place in reading the Scriptures. The Semitic mind is and was a human mind, and the laws of logic are universal. We do not, of course, find in the Sacred Scriptures the Greek mastery of dialectical art, but we do find a genuine dialectic, although it is not perfectly separated from the personal encounter of the "dialogue" taken in the modern sense. Indeed, the rabbinical mentality is highly dialectical.

The books of Job, Ecclesiastes, Jonas and many of the prophets show men struggling with the questions of life, confronted with problems of "to be or not to be." In the New Testament this exploration reaches its climax in our Lord's encounters with the blinded minds of his day. He is a greater Socrates bringing forth both the good thoughts of the apostles and exposing to the light the abortive and evil thoughts of the Pharisees and Herodians. Finally, in the epistles and the Apocalypse we see the Church already beginning the long intellectual work of penetrating and integrating the data of revelation.[45]

The theologian must not only help the student to think dialectically, but he must correct any tendency to abuse this art. Frequently today those who advocate dialectics go to the extreme of rejecting any limitations on the student's reading. They argue that unless a student confronts the great thinkers like Kant or Marx or Bergson he will not be prepared to meet difficulties against his faith which he is sure to meet in later life. Is it not better, they say, to read these authors under the guidance of a teacher than to meet them later and without help?

This is a delicate question; yet the college theologian is the person who must be prepared to meet it. He knows that the slogan, "truth has nothing to fear from discussion," is true only if we add the qualification, "provided that the discussion is between men of moral and intellectual virtue." The Church's law concerning forbidden books perhaps needs some revisions in view of current needs, but the principle on which it is based is unchanging. Men will not arrive at truth or be loyal to it if they keep all sorts of intellectual company, either in person or through reading, any more than they will keep good morals if they are indiscriminate about their friends. The weaknesses left in man by sin make him liable to false influences which must be guarded against. The fact that tyrants use this same argument to hide from men the truths that they need should not frighten us into an unlimited liberalism.

Granted the principle, the problem is to apply it. How can we guard the development of the student and at the same time prepare him to meet the temptations against which it is impossible to guard him? I personally would propose the following norm for discussion by teachers of theology better acquainted with actual conditions:

(1) Graduate students in universities should be advised to obtain dispensation from the Index and the general canons with regard to forbidden books for those materials that pertain to their field of specialization, but should be given some special theological direction even in the use of these. Ordinarily they should not read books of this sort outside the area of their specialization. The reason is that the reading proposed is necessary to their profession, and they are prepared to evaluate it critically—provided, however, that they also are acquainted with the relevant theological principles.

(2) Undergraduate students generally should not be advised to read any forbidden books, or to seek dispensation to do so, unless in the senior and junior year it may be necessary for them to study some such books in preparation for admission to graduate studies. The reason is that the undergraduate student who has not yet completed the college course in theology is not prepared to read critically works which the Church judges to be seriously dangerous for the average reader.

It is this last point which is perhaps most debatable. Is not the college junior or senior studying under the direction of a Catholic teacher much safer than the average reader? In my opinion the differences in maturity of the student and in the prudence and theological preparation of teachers are so considerable that we cannot be very confident of this.

The chief objection to this solution is that it leaves the student who does not go on to graduate school without direct acquaintance with the works of Kant, Hume, Marx and various novelists who are supposed to be known to all college graduates. To this I would reply that the average acquaintance of undergraduates with such works is too superficial to be of much real intellectual account. I see no reason why a Catholic who has only the Bachelor of Arts degree need be ashamed to admit that he never studied enough philosophy or literature to be prepared to judge such writers by personal acquaintance. But if this view seems strict to some, then they can attempt to obtain permission for juniors and seniors for some books of this type; then also they must take the responsibilities entailed.

The fact that undergraduate students are not reading these more dangerous and difficult books does not mean that they should not be required to read many things that are controversial and even shocking. The theologian, and other teachers as well, will not teach the student to think dialectically unless they subject him to constant controversy. But this should be kept within limits, the norms of which are those indicated by the Church when she forbids *ex professo* attacks on the faith and on the *praembula fidei*, as well as on basic moral principles. The teacher who thinks that this does not leave any room for serious debate is somewhat jaded.[46]

Science and Logic

Up to this point there is, I believe, a considerable agreement among college teachers of religion that the college program must be taught in such a way as to appeal to the student's personal needs (the rhetorical or kerygmatic approach), his imagination (the humanistic or poetic approach), and his reason (the dialectical approach). Some, however, contend that this is not sufficient. They argue that colleges which do not attempt to go beyond this level of development in most courses would be considered to have low standards.

In most subject matters which the student studies for a major part of his time, it is generally supposed that a student can acquire the *habit of science*, which graduate study will then perfect intensively and extensively. If this is possible in other subjects, why not in theology, to which a very considerable time is given each year of college?[47]

I think no one acquainted with the Thomistic notion of science is likely to deny the desirability of this goal. The only alternative to knowing theology as a science is to hold it as an *opinion* based on the student's human faith in his teacher. How can we claim that today the layman must be capable of applying theological principles to the solution of problems in his own profession with some degree of independent judgment, and at the same time leave him totally dependent for these principles on his trust in professional theologians? Surely he should have at least some degree of personal possession of the ability to think theologically, just as a doctor must be in some degree a scientist in order to apply the principles of science in his practice.

Hence it is that college science courses require some actual laboratory work, college history courses require some acquaintance with the methods of historical research, and college philosophy courses some acquaintance with logic and epistemology. Can we deny to the student of college theology a genuine introduction to the methodology of theology? Since it is this methodology which makes theology scientific, a course which aims at scientific knowledge should require of the student the art of logic in its full sense, the art of *scientific demonstration.*

Because the training of some teachers of theology has emphasized strongly the *positive* aspect of theology (the study of the sources of revelation), but somewhat neglected the speculative phase of theology, they are inclined to lay little stress on the logical structure of theology. It is in the proper balance of these methods, however, that St. Thomas Aquinas excelled, and it is for this reason in particular that he has been approved by the Church.[48]

The theologian who wishes to present theology according to its own interior character as a science and still more as a wisdom will constantly insist that the student seek the *proper reasons* of theological truth by tracing its roots in the articles of the Creed. As the student develops this capacity of relating one truth to another, he will begin to see in the Scriptures not merely a series of moving sermons, a beautiful story, or a fascinating development of religious insights, but a luminous manifestation of the Triune God from whom the whole universe flows and to whom it returns in the Incarnate Word, Head of the Church.

This power of mind can be developed only if the student is constantly exercised in defining, classifying, seeking proper principles and demonstrating. By this I do not mean merely memorizing the work of great theologians, although this has a very useful place, but in studying the ways in which theological doctrine has been built up. To do this the student must not merely know the forms of the syllogism and the rules of a good definition. Much more important is it to understand the theory of the logical structure of a science developed in Aristotle's *Posterior Analytics.* Scholastic manuals of logic seldom do justice to this aspect of logic, and the teacher of college theology should see that the course in logic given to his students treats this effectively. Today logic is experiencing a remarkable growth in the form of symbolic or mathematical logic, but it is not yet clear that this development will be of much assistance to the theologian.[49]

St. Thomas Aquinas in the very first question of his *Summa Theologiae* himself discusses the use of the liberal arts in theology. He shows (articles 9 and 10) how poetics and rhetoric are necessary in reading the Sacred Scriptures, but he also shows (article 8) that sacred theology must move beyond the level of the metaphorical and figurative presentation of revelation to an effort to penetrate that truth by analysis and demonstration. Sacred theology is a wisdom, but it is also a science which is able to carry on argument. Argument is necessary if revelation is to be defended against all opponents by dialectical methods, but it must also be demonstrative if it is to unfold the riches virtually contained in the organic unity of God's word.

The Mathematical Arts and Theology

Besides the liberal arts of the trivium which have just been considered, the ancients enumerated a quadrivium of mathematical arts: arithmetic, geometry, music and astronomy. At first sight we might think these utterly irrelevant to theology, but St. Augustine (taking a lead from Plato) was convinced to the contrary.[50]

Even if we discount the Platonic exaggeration of the value of mathematics for the ascent to wisdom, we cannot ignore this element in our tradition without still further deepening the chasm which today in the schools separates the humanities (with which theology is strangely classed) from the sciences.

Music has already been referred to it in its role as a fine art and need not be discussed further, except to note that its classification with the mathematical sciences is an indication of the important role which mathematical form plays in the fine arts.[51]

Arithmetic and geometry for the ancients comprised what we now call *pure mathematics*. It has a twofold connection with theology. First, the study of mathematics furnishes the student with the best possible example of the logical theory of a science. Legend has it that Plato put the motto over the door of the Academy, "Let no one who has not studied geometry enter here." We might put the same motto over the door of the college theology class, for the student who has not seen and understood how definition, axioms, demonstrations are used in the simple and clear materials of elementary mathematics will have a hard struggle to see them in theological materials.

The second connection of mathematics with theology is that in mathematics the student receives the clearest possible *analogates* for certain basic metaphysical concepts which are of utmost importance in theology. The notions of one, many, whole, parts, equality, relation, proportion, classification, etc., are most simply and exactly illustrated in mathematics.

The very notion of *analogy* itself—the basic methodological tool of the theologians—is derived from the mathematical notions of ratio and proportion.[52]

Astronomy (along with music) was for the ancients the example of *mathematical physics,* the use of mathematics applied to the study of physical nature, which today for many is the whole of science. Mathematical physics does not enter theology directly, but since it is an instrument of natural science taken in its fullest sense, it is connected with theology through natural science.[53] It is sufficient here to note that the theologian must make constant use of the findings of natural science in his work, since it is through the knowledge of the visible creation, which is the proper object of man's intelligence, that we must conceive something of the invisible order.[54]

We may conclude, then, that the liberal arts are powerful instruments for the study of theology. But does theology require these instruments of necessity, or only for greater facility in its difficult work? This question I leave to another essay in this volume.[55]

Some Practical Suggestions

From these considerations we may draw up a list of particular procedures which the college teacher of theology might follow in order to profit from the liberal arts known by his students and to stimulate the practice of these arts in their own proper departments.

1. At the begining of the theology course he should follow St. Thomas in showing the value of the liberal arts in the reading of Scripture and in theological reasoning.

2. He should not only talk about this but insist *throughout* the theology course on the use of these arts by the student. Thus in all Scripture reading he should point out the importance (and limitations) of *literary forms* in explaining the Scripture, and he should constantly dwell on the logical methodology by which definitions, divisions and demonstrations are arrived at. Papers written by students should be graded in particular on the basis of method.

3. He should make use of dialectic in preparing each principal question of the course, and insist on the students' learning

to ask questions, to discuss and to state their views in a clear and reasoned way. He should show them how this method is valuable in discussions with non-Catholics.

4. He should constantly make use of literary and artistic classics which express the natural or supernatural truths relevant to a particular treatise. For example:

1) In treating of the matter of Part I of the *Summa* on God and creation, he should refer to poetry, painting and sculpture which manifest the beauty and order of the universe and its present fallen state. He should discuss how the beauty of the world reflects the divine perfections, and how far short it falls. Thus he might point out the manifestation of God in the order of the universe to be found in the mosaics of Ravenna, the cathedral of Chartres, the frescos of Michaelangelo in the Sistine Chapel, and in the paintings of Rouault. What different aspects does each portray? Why are they incomplete? Why is it that the average Catholic church today shows us so little of any of these truths?

2) In treating of the matter of Part II of the *Summa* on man's moral life and the efforts to recover the image of God, the teacher has the vast riches of literature and music to draw from. In drama and novel all the vices and virtues can be found represented, while in lyric poetry and music will be seen exemplified the emotional strivings of man in his efforts to find inner harmony and peace.

3) In treating of the matter of Part III of the *Summa* the historical and incarnational theme is uppermost. Here the theologian should especially dwell on the history of human culture, and show how all the arts reflect man's spiritual progress. The Scriptures as the history of salvation should be seen as summing up the whole of cultural history, of which the central fact is the Incarnation. Then the development of Christian culture, centered in the liturgy and the sacraments, should be considered both in its successes and failures.

This should bring the student to the consideration of his own role. How can he use the liberal arts in a Christian way in order to study and recreate properly? How can he use them to worship better? How can he use them to carry on the apostolate? How can the Church in our present civilization work as a whole to carry on all these tasks successfully?

In his teaching the teacher of theology should not attempt himself to be an expert on all these matters, but he should show a sympathetic interest in them and a liberal acquaintance with them. He should encourage the students to apply theological principles to their other courses, and he should discuss with teachers of the liberal arts ways in which both in class and in the life of the school a vital connection can be established between theology and other subjects.

A final word of caution. The classics of liberal and fine art are (save for the Scriptures and the sacraments) human works, full of human imperfections. On the other hand, the judgment of the theologian (since he is not the *magisterium* of the Church itself) is also fallible. Hence his attitude to the actual practice of the liberal arts should not be that of the stern judge, but of the gardener who weeds and cultivates to improve the flowers. He should seek rather to find the goodness in literature and art than to underline defects, even if sometimes he is obliged to censor.

Footnotes to Study 7

[1]The teacher of college theology may study this tradition in the following: St. Augustine, *Christian Instruction* (the *De Doctrina*), trans. by John J. Gavigan, O.S.A., in *The Fathers of the Church,* Ludwig Schopp, ed. (New York: Cima Publ. Co., 1947). Hugh of St. Victor's great work is not yet (to my knowledge) available in translation (critical ed. of Latin text by C. H. Buttimer, Washington, D.C., 1939), but two similar medieval works can be consulted: Cassiodorus, *An Introduction to Divine and Human Readings,* trans. by L. W. Jones (New York: Columbia U. Press, 1946); and John of Salisbury, *The Metalogicon,* trans. by Daniel D. McGarry (Berkeley: U. of California Press, 1955). A work by George E. Ganss, S.J., *St. Ignatius' Idea of a Jesuit University,* includes a translation of the *Ratio* (Milwaukee: Marquette U. Press, 1954). Several significant papal statements may be found in *Pope Pius XII and Theological Studies* and *Pope Pius XII and Catholic Education,* both ed. by V. A. Yzermans (St. Meinrad, Ind.: Grail Publications, 1957).

[2]Clear evidence of this is found in the discussions of the Society of Catholic College Teachers of Sacred Doctrine, contained in their published *Proceedings of the Society of Catholic College Teachers of Sacred Doctrine* (cf. especially John F. McDonell, O.P., "Sacred Scripture Relevant to the College Course in Sacred

Doctrine," *ibid.*, III [1957], 76-81) and in their newsletter, *Magister* (for further references see the bibliography in the issue of January, 1959).

[3]"The same veneration [of Sacred Scripture] the bishops should endeavor daily to increase and perfect among the faithful committed to their care, encouraging all those initiatives by which men, filled with apostolic zeal, laudably strive to excite and foster among Catholics a greater knowledge of and love for the Sacred Books." Pius XII, *Divino Afflante Spiritu* (1943); cf. *Rome and the Study of Scripture* (St. Meinrad, Ind.: Grail Publ., 1946), 4th ed., 103. ". . . adult education must endeavor to put these wayward ones back into contact with a living tradition—especially that of the Church—through the at once simple and profound lessons of the Cathechism, Holy Scripture, and the Christian festivals." Pius XII, "Adult Education," March 19, 1953, cited in *Pius XII and Catholic Education,* 113.

[4]It is to be noticed that Christ not only taught his disciples (and hence their successors) *what* to teach but also *how* to teach it (Matt. 10:5-42). Their teaching is not to rest on human skill and preparation but on the divine wisdom itself, given by the Holy Spirit. Similarly the Church judges not only of what is to be taught in religious matters, but even the mode in which it is to be taught. This is evident from the encyclical *Humani Generis* of Pius XII, which is especially concerned with false theological *methods.*

[5]"Let [preachers] abstain from profane or abstruse arguments which exceed the common grasp of their hearers. Let them exercise the evangelical ministry not in the persuasive words of human wisdom, nor in profane vanities and the display and ornamentation of ambitious eloquence, but in the demonstration of the Spirit and of power, preaching not themselves but Christ crucified." *Constitutions of the Friars Preachers,* n. 753, paraphrasing I Cor.: 2:2 and 5.

[6]Cf. St. Augustine, *Christian Instruction,* Bk. IV, Chap. 2; St. John Chrysostom, *On the Priesthood,* trans. by Patrick Boyle, C.M. (Westminster, Md.: Newman Press, 1955), Book V, Chap. 2; St. Thomas Aquinas, *In S. Pauli Apostoli Epistolas,* I Cor., cap. 1, lect. 3; John XXIII, "The Priest: Preacher of the Word," in *The Pope Speaks,* V (1959), 275-279.

[7]*Rhetoric,* Bk. III, Chap. 1 (1404a 6 f.); Bk. I, Chap. 2 (1356a 1 f.).

[8]*Ibid.,* Bk. I, Chap. 1 (1354a 12 f.).

[9]*Ibid.* (1355a 20 f.).

[10]See the remarks of Pius XII on the art of speaking to small children in his discourse, "The Ideal Teacher," November 4, 1955, and to young people in "Counsel to Teaching Sisters," September 13, 1951, and his many observations on the role of example (which rhetoricians consider as "the argument from the character of the speaker"), as in "The Secret of Good Schools," January, 1954, and "The Ideal Teacher" just cited. These are all translated in *Pius XII and Education,* cited above, footnote 3.

[11]See John Courtney Murray, S.J., "Towards a Theology for the Layman," *Theological Studies,* V (1944), 43-75, 340-376. In these brilliant articles which have had wide influence on the manner in which college theology is being taught in this country, Father Murray analyzes in a very satisfactory way the different functions which theology must play in preparing the seminarian and the lay student for their different *social functions* in the Church. He does not, however, do justice (in my opinion) to the character of theology as a *wisdom* which is not a social *instrument* but a part of the very *goal* of the Church, as I will indicate further on.

[12]The ancient treatises on rhetoric frequently comment on the mutual dependence of rhetoric and a free citizenry, and the decline of rhetoric when the people sinks to slavery. See H. I. Marrou, *A History of Education in Antiquity* (New York: Sheed and Ward, 1956), 52-54 and 194-205. It is to be noted that Aristotle (*Rhetoric,* Bk. III, Chap 1 [1404b 18], says: "A writer must disguise

his art and give the impression of speaking naturally and not artificially. Naturalness is persuasive, artificiality is the contrary; for our hearers are prejudiced and think we have some design against them, as if we were mixing their wines for them," but he is speaking of style in this passage, not of the art as a whole.

[13]See Martin Mayer, *Madison Ave., U.S.A.* (New York: Harper, 1958), for some current "philosophies of advertising."

[14]*Carême des Carmelites,* 2ème dimanche: "Sur la Parole de Dieu."

[15]Cf., for example, Robert Henle, S.J., "Father Hofinger's Theological Courses for Sisters," *Catholic School Journal,* LVII (1957), 257-8. For a defense, see Johannes Hofinger, S.J., *The Art of Teaching Christian Doctrine* (Notre Dame, Ind.: U. of Notre Dame Press, 1957), and his article, "The Formation Our Catechists Need," in Gerard S. Sloyan, *Shaping the Christian Message* (New York: Macmillan, 1958), 221-242.

[16]I say "in the high school," because in the instruction of small children I believe the method is poetic rather than rhetorical.

[17]This seems to me the basic difficulty with the very persuasive argument of Father Murray (cf. *art. cit.,* footnote 11 above), which he rests on the opinion of Bilz that "theology does not exist for its own sake; rather, it stands in the service of religion and the Church. As a rule, one studies theology in order to employ in the service of the Church the knowledge one gains" (quoted *ibid.,* p. 47). Taking this as a basic principle, he considers the finality of the seminary course considered as *professional* training and contrasts it to a "theology for layman" which is "a professional course, as professional as the seminary course, but in its own peculiar way" (p. 74). I entirely agree that the social function of the priest and the layman are different and that it follows logically that the training *for these functions* must be different, but is it true that theology is principally learned to prepare either priest or layman for a social function? Bilz does not do justice to St. Thomas Aquinas' noble conception of theology as a *wisdom* which is first of all *speculative* in character (*Summa,* I, q. 1, a. 4 and a. 6). All Christians, whatever their special role in the Church, have a *common good* or *end* which consists in the contemplation of God as he is. It is the primary function of education to bring all to some participation in this vision, and theology is such a participation (but not the highest, which is found in the gift of wisdom). Hence theology belongs to the order of ends, not to the order of means. It has been a serious defect of most seminary courses in theology that they have failed to present theology first in this way, and then to show its special professional applications for the ministry. Are we now to make a similar mistake in the teaching of theology to lay people by turning it into a school for the lay apostolate? Rather let us teach in all higher schools a theology which is study of God for his own sake, and then add to this suitable application for the different social functions in the church. Education ought to bring the clergy and the laity together in a common delight in divine truth, not merely to divide them into different professions, each with its own limited perspective. See also the criticism of Father Murray's position in Gerald Van Ackeren, S.J., "The Finality of the College Course in Sacred Doctrine in the Light of the Finality of Theology," *Proceedings of the Society of Catholic College Teachers of Sacred Doctrine,* II (1956), 10-24.

[18]Of course many estheticians and literary critics, including Catholic writers, repudiate the idea that a work of art has *meaning,* or if it can be said to have meaning that this must be objectively true. See the summary of views by Lucius Garvin, "The Paradox of Aesthetic Meaning," in Susanne K. Langer, *Reflections on Art* (Baltimore: John Hopkins Press, 1957), 62-70.

[19]St. Thomas Aquinas, *Exposition of the Posterior Analytics* (trans. by Pierre Conway, O.P.; Quebec: M. Doyan, 1956), Bk. I, less. 1. Here *representatio* evidently translates the Aristotelian term *mimesis.*

[20]This is what modern critics mean when they insist that the meaning of a poetic work "cannot be paraphrased," i.e., the abstract statement of the truth contained in the poem does not convey this truth to the audience as effectively as does the concrete image presented by the poem.

[21]On the three functions of poetry and music see Aristotle, *Politics,* Bk. VIII. On the use of metaphor in Sacred Scripture and liturgy see St. Thomas Aquinas, *Summa,* I, q. 1, a. 9, I-II, q. 101, a. 2.

[22]See, for example, Amos N. Wilder (a Protestant), *Theology and Modern Literature* (Cambridge: Harvard U. Press, 1958).

[23]See Gustave Weigel, S.J., "The Meaning of Sacred Doctrine in the College," in Sloyan, *op. cit.,* 170-182. He says, in part: "College theology . . . must be productive of a penetrating humanistic understanding which produces an abiding and dynamic vision of the meaning of human life and work" (p. 179); ". . . we are conceiving it as humanistic contemplation, rather than scientific or mystical contemplation . . ." (p. 181). Perhaps the clearest explanation of what this term "humanistic" means is that of Father Van Ackeren, S.J. (*art. cit.,* footnote 17): "By strictly scientific knowledge theologians ordinarily mean the assimilation and understanding of the truths of revelation through the use of insights and conclusions of philosophy, especially of metaphysics. We have an example of this sort of knowledge in the *Summa Theologiae* of St. Thomas. Humanistic theological knowledge, however, means the assimilation and understanding of revealed truth through the insights and methods of the humanities. This mode of theological knowledge is exemplified in many of the writings of the Fathers of the Church, in some modern attempts at biblical theology, and most recently in the remarkable work of the German theologian, Father Michael Schmus, entitled *Katholische Dogmatik.* Both are true theological wisdom. But they are not distinct theologies. They represent rather different degrees of assimilation of human intellect to divine truth, different degrees of participation in the habit of sacred theology" (p. 18). The explanation is more explicit in the discussion which followed the delivery of this paper; in the pharaphrase of the editor, a humanistic approach to theology means "an understanding of the faith through analogies in the sensible rather than the intellectual order, by analogies which are more concrete and more easily recognized by persons without philosophical training. For example, in explaining the Second Person of the Trinity, he would use the analogy of Son rather than of Word. . . . Such an approach preserves the scientific character of theology insofar as it proceeds from principles known to conclusions. It is not strictly scientific since that would require analogies of an intellectual order and an understanding, as far as that is possible, of procedures accepted on faith. The humanistic approach, however, retains the formal object of this particular science, but it is scientific on a lower level of analogies" (pp. 39 f.). This seems to make "humanistic" equivalent to what Dominican writers sometimes call "liberal scientific." But see my later reservations as to this equivalence.

[24]See the interesting debate on whether the pagan or the Christian classics should form the basis of this cultural approach: Herbert A. Musurillo, S.J., "Dawson's Program: A Criticism," *Thought,* XXX (1955), 174-87; Christopher Dawson, "Reply to Father Musurillo," *ibid.,* XXXI (1956), 159-160.

[25]See the excellent work of Father Gnass cited in footnote 1 above.

[26]For a development of this point see the writings of Father Gerald Vann, O.P. (e.g., the recent *The Paradise Tree* [New York: Sheed and Ward, 1959]).

[27]Bernard G. Murchland, "Theology and Literature," *Commonweal,* LXXI (1959), 66.

[28]*Exposition of the Posterior Analytics,* Bk. I, less. 1. "Sometimes, however, our judgment inclines to one side of a question because of some representation, in the way that a certain food is made distasteful to a man if it is represented to

him under the likeness of something distasteful . . . and to this is ordered poetics."

[29]See Pius XII, "Christian Conscience as an Object in Education," in *Pius XII and Education;* "Statement of the American Hierarchy on Censorship," 1957 (*National Catholic Almanac,* 1958, 117-120); H. C. Gardiner, S.J., *The Catholic Viewpoint of Censorship* (Garden City, N. Y.: Hanover House, 1958); Walter Kerr, *Criticism and Censorship* (Milwaukee: Bruce, 1956).

[30]See the very stimulating articles of Father F. Lynch, S.J., "Theology and Imagination," *Thought,* XXIX (1954), 61-86, 529-54, XXX (1955), 18-36.

[31]For a more detailed discussion see my textbook, *The Arts of Learning and Communication* (Dubuque: The Priory Press, 1958), Part II, 231 ff.

[32]"The Religious Symbol," *Daedalus,* Summer, 1958, 1-21.

[33]See Jacques Maritain, *Creative Intuition in Art and Poetry* (New York: Noonday Press, Meridian Books, 1955) and Etienne Gilson, *Painting and Reality* (New York: Pantheon, 1957).

[34]See the trenchant discussion in the first chapter of Ronald Crane's *The Language of Criticism and the Structure of Poetics* (Toronto: U. of Toronto, 1953).

[35]*Poetics,* Chap. 20-22; but he also touches on grammatical questions in the *Rhetoric,* Bk. III, Chap. 2-4.

[36]See Ernst R. Curtius, *European Literature and the Latin Middle Ages* (New York: Pantheon, 1953), especially chapters 4, 5, 7 and 8.

[37]*Christian Instruction,* Bk. I, Chap. 2 and Bk. II, Chap. 1-6, 10-16.

[38]I am speaking here of the religious meaning of this account, not of the historical problem of the origin of languages.

[39]I am not forgetting that the *koiné* in which the New Testament is written was in some measure this sort of minimal language, but this is one of the aspects of the poverty and weakness through which God chose to manifest the power of the Gospel.

[40]"The use of the Latin language, customary in a considerable portion of the Church, is a manifest and beautiful sign of unity, as well as an effective antidote for any corruption of doctrinal truth. In spite of this, the use of the mother tongue in connection with several of the rites may be of much advantage to the people." Pius XII, *Mediator Dei,* Vatican Library trans. (Washington, D.C.: NCWC, 1947), n. 60.

[41]See, for example, the article of Justus George Lawler, "Obedience and Scholarship: An Obsession with Docility?", *Commonweal,* LXXI (1959), 15-19. The author well describes the abuse of the teacher's authority, yet I would wish to insist that the cure for false docility is true docility. The passive student is not truly docile, since docility means an *active* effort to follow the teacher's lead. The student who fails to follow the teacher's lead, whether by passivity or by following his own lead, cannot be taught. The notion that teaching is merely encouraging the student to discover truth for himself is simply a denial that teaching is possible, since it substitutes moral exhortation for teaching.

[42]A method of doing this which is frequently proposed (although I am not acquainted with a school in which it has been thoroughly applied) is that theology be taught by a "Great Books" system, i.e., by reading representative theological classics.

[43]For example of what this means in practice see H. R. Niebuhr, *Christ and Culture* (New York: Harpers Torchbooks, 1956).

[44]*Ramus: Method, and the Decay of Dialogue* (Cambridge: Harvard U. Press, 1958). I take it that Father Ong means by dialogue an intellectual dialectic, rather than a personal encounter in the sense explained in the text.

[45]This point is well made by Lucien Cerfaux, *Christ in the Theology of St. Paul* (New York: Herder and Herder, 1959), a study of the development of St. Paul's thought which shows how the great Apostle began to construct a theology profoundly true to the revelation given him, and yet using his own great intelligence and his rabbinical skills.

[46]See R. A. Burke, *What is the Index?* (Milwaukee: Bruce, 1952); J. J. Reed, S.J., "Permission to Read Prohibited Books," *Theological Studies,* XIX (1958), 586-95; "The Problem of Prohibited Books and the American Catholic Intellectual," summary of a special interest session by L. A. Arnoult, O.P., T. Heath, O.P., and Sr. M. Rose Eileen, C.S.C., *Proceedings of the Society of Catholic College Teachers of Sacred Doctrine,* VI (1960), 83-96; L. A. Arnoult, O.P., and J. J. Reed, S.J., "Problems of Prohibited Books: An Exploratory Discussion," *Proceedings of the Catholic Theological Society of America,* XV (1960), 137-154.

[47]This point of view was vigorously defended in this country by the late Walter Farrell, O.P., and has generally been followed by Dominican teachers of college theology. It has also been well stated by Father Gerald Van Ackeren, S.J., in "The Finality of the College Course in Sacred Doctrine in the Light of the Finality of Theology," with the qualification that he believes this pertains rather to the junior and senior year of college than to the lower years. Another excellent statement is that of Sister Jean Marrie, S.S.N.D., in the *Report of the Everett Curriculum Workshop,* 1956, 24-28.

[48]"If one considers all this well, he will easily see why the Church demands that future priests be instructed in philosophy 'according to the method, doctrine and principles of the Angelic Doctor,' since, as we well know from the experience of centuries, the method of Aquinas is singularly pre-eminent both for teaching students and for bringing truth to light; his doctrine is in harmony with divine revelation and is most effective both for safeguarding the foundations of the faith and for reaping, safely and usefully, the fruits of sound progress. . . ." Pius XII, *Humani Generis;* cf. *Pope Pius XII and Theological Studies,* 91.

[49]Some efforts have been made, for example, Salamucha's formalization of the Thomistic proof for the existence of God (recently improved by Augustine Wallace, O.P., in an unpublished dissertation, Dominican House of Studies, Washington, D.C.). Cf. C. M. Bochenski, O.P., "On Analogy," *The Thomist,* XI (1948), 424-447; and Ivo Thomas, O.P., "Logic and Theology," *Dominican Studies,* Oct., 1948.

[50]Cf. *Christian Instruction,* Bk. I, Chap. 37; *De Ordine* (translated by R. P. Russell as *Divine Providence and the Problem of Evil* in same volume), Chap. 15; *De Musica,* translated by R. C. Taliaferro in volume two of the same series, 153 ff. (especially Bk. VI).

[51]See my work previously referred to (footnote 31), *The Arts of Learning and Communication,* 247-256 and 339-352 for discussion of the role of mathematics in fine art.

52 See Santiago Ramírez, O.P., "De analogia secundum doctrinam aristotelico-thomisticam," *Ciencia Thomista,* XXIII (1921), 20-40, 195-214, 337-357; XXIV (1922), 17-38. I do not intend to deny that the concepts furnished by the philosophy of nature are also of utmost importance for theology, but they are more complex and less clear than those of mathematics.

[53]See my fuller treatment of this point, "Sacred Doctrine and Natural Science," *Proceedings of the Society of Catholic College Teachers of Sacred Doctrine,* III (1957), 24-28, and "The Role of the Philosophy of Nature in Catholic Liberal Education," *Proceedings of the American Catholic Philosophical Association,* XXX (1956), 62-84.

[54]See St. Thomas Aquinas, II *Con. Gen.,* Chap. 2-4. He notes in chapter four that the theologian is not concerned with the details of natural science, but he is very much concerned with the general view of the world which it presents.

[55]Cf. Study 10, "Philosophy and the Teaching of College Theology."

8

THEOLOGY AND THE NATURAL SCIENCES

W. A. Wallace, O.P.

Father Wallace brings a wealth of background to this problem. His introduction to science was through electrical engineering, which he studied at Manhattan College (B.E.E.) and Stevens Institute of Technology, before engaging in weapons research at the Naval Ordnance Laboratory during World War II. After the war, he resumed studies in physics at Catholic University (M.S.), then did advanced work in the philosophy and history of science at the University of Fribourg (Ph.D.). His theological degrees include the lectorate (Pontifical Faculty of Immaculate Conception College, Washington, D.C.) and, from the Swiss University of Fribourg, the doctorate. Now professor of natural philosophy and the philosophy of science at the Dominican House of Studies, Dover, Mass., he lectures weekly at the Massachusetts Institute of Technology on modern science as it relates to philosophy and theology.

Experience has shown that one of the trouble-spots that develop when sacred theology is used as an integrating factor in college education invariably turns up in the science department. Despite the lessons such experience should inculcate, it is also usually the case that college administrators are unable to cope with the situation, and that, by and large, scientists on the campus stand apart from their more amenable brethren, aloof and quite refractory to proposals of integration under the Queen of the sciences. Whatever the evil consequences of this reactionary stand, it does simplify the statement of the question, for an elaborate description of the state of affairs in various institutions need not be undertaken. The situation may be summarized instead by stating that, for all practical purposes, there is no integration of science and theology at the college level.

There are several possible explanations for this situation. One undoubtedly arises from the fact that the transition from a religion course to a systematic presentation of scientific theology at the college level is still in process, and, despite considerable progress over the past two decades, is viewed by many as an innovation in its experimental stages. In contrast with this, science courses are well established in the college curriculum and enjoy increasing prestige each day, as more and more emphasis is placed on science education as a necessary bulwark for national security. What is more, there is an immediate and obvious utility in studying science—a point that can hardly be overlooked by the average collegian. Add to this the fact that Catholic colleges, in particular, are under pressure to produce more and better scientists, and it is not difficult to understand why the science department can afford to be independent and somewhat critical of unrealistic integration schemes proposed by the theologian.

Apart from these extrinsic considerations, moreover, it is also true that attitudes of mind communicated in science courses are frequently hostile to theology, particularly when the latter is itself proposed as science. The equivocation involved in this use of the term is immediately sensed by the student, and science professors can hardly fail to exploit the fact that possession is nine points of the law. In the name of their science, theology professors will be claiming the highest possible certitude for their conclusions, while at the same time science professors will be insisting that the one thing essential to progress in science is a freedom to doubt which manifests itself in the right to call any statement whatsoever into question. The science student who is subjected to both views may succeed in compartmentalizing his knowledge for a time, but sooner or later the attitude of mind inculcated in one department will flow over into the other, and his questions are likely to prove irritating to professors of both departments.

Another factor to be reckoned with is the extensive knowledge of the physical universe now available to the scientist: not only is he flooded daily with new information, but his acquaintance with powerful methods for uncovering new truths gives him a confidence in science's ability ultimately to solve all problems. As opposed to this, it may appear to him that philosophers and theologians never find out anything new, that they always argue over the same questions, use naive methods of investigation, and seem incapable of arriving at any agreement even among themselves. The theologian, on the other hand, taking the supertemporal view, may justifiably question why there should be such emphasis on secular learning and technology in a Catholic institution, one whose avowed purpose must be to form the Christian person intellectually, i.e., to equip him with intellectual virtues (among them sacred theology, which holds a supreme position) by means of which he can grow to perfection in his early life.

Thus the argument can go back and forth, and while this is not an exhaustive list of conflicting attitudes, it should suffice to show that there are latent oppositions in the scientific and theological outlooks respectively. When these are voiced at a faculty level, it is not surprising that occasional friction (and even open hostility) develops between the science and theology departments.

The upshot of this faculty conflict, moreover, is that the college administrator is continually in a dilemma: how to reorganize curricula and integrate science with theology, when science professors are unsympathetic towards theology and even question its value as an integrating factor, and when theology professors have similar attitudes towards science and are not particularly interested in the problem of educating scientists who can compete, as scientists, with graduates of secular institutions. This poses a problem that is not easily solved; in fact, it is only fair to admit that no definitive resolution can be offered at the moment. What will be said here is largely tentative—more an appraisal of the situation than a solution—

but aimed at sketching a few objectives towards which ideal planning might be directed—granted that complete realization of any integrated program in this area still lies far in the future.

Sources of Tension

One cannot approach the problem of science-theology relationships without becoming acutely aware that in this field, as in few others, a considerable historical background continues to exert its influence on present discussions. Some of the great controversies of the past between scientists and theologians have never been completely resolved, and the specters of so-called martyrs of science are still on hand to distract those who would make an objective analysis of the issues for which they fought. Yet some progress has been made in unravelling the tangled skein of historical fact in this area. Certainly scholars are far removed from the type of thinking that would endorse Draper's conclusions in his *History of the Conflict between Religion and Science* (1875), where scientists are depicted as champions of the truth against intolerant superstition and the Church represented as destroying ancient science, precipitating the Dark Ages, and suppressing enlightenment until the revolution of the seventeenth century.

In the present day, moreover, there is no longer open war between science and theology. Indeed, there are very few prominent scientists who could properly be characterized as public opponents of religion. Instead, the conflict that was highlighted in the nineteenth century mind has given way to a period of irenicism; and where there used to be open hostility, there is now, in its place, a high wall of separation. But the disappearance of public conflict, while obviously most welcome, is not necessarily a sign that tension has disappeared. It is at least as likely that the parties to the conflict are no longer speaking the same language, that they have in fact lost interest in one another, that the one-time opponents look back on past struggles with rose-colored glasses, each content that he has secured the victory and not caring to delve further into embarrassing details.

The latent oppositions between scientists and theologians already mentioned are an indication of this continuing cold war, of conflict at a less public and more subtle level between the two disciplines.

But it is noteworthy that the tension does not spring from contemporary issues that are being debated—there being, as has been said, little live contact to provoke continuing public debate. Rather it comes from what may be termed traditional attitudes, attitudes generally accepted without question by the scientist as by the theologian, but figuring largely in their respective evaluations of any subject proposed for consideration.

That the theologian should be so influenced by tradition is not surprising; his very insistence on its importance, however, might make him appreciative of the fact that scientists also possess their traditions and that these too are not easily relinquished. One of these traditions, unfortunately, is that science and theology make strange bedfellows and that theology is to be viewed with suspicion as a likely source from which attack might come at any moment, as unreasonably and as unprovoked as it came against the progenitors of science in the days of the "martyrs." Other traditional views are analysable, like this, into historical and philosophical judgments which are communicated to the scientist indirectly in the course of his technical training, rarely examined with the care and attention given to the science itself, and passed on from teacher to teacher with surprising consistency and assurance.

The historical judgments center around a few celebrated personalities, of whom mere mention suffices to recall the incident and the impression it has created in the scientific mind. Giordano Bruno and Marco Antonio de Dominis, for instance, are two Renaissance thinkers who are regarded as having made notable contributions to science but whose revolutionary thinking did not meet with the approval of the Inquisition; the former consequently was burned at the stake as a heretic, while the latter languished to death in the prisons of Rome. Shortly afterwards, Galileo made the first clear break with Aristotelian tradition and placed modern science on solid footing, only narrowly to miss the same fate at the hands of the Inquisition—forced to repudiate his science in his old age in order to save his life. Nor is this record of persecution the unique possession of the Roman Church: the momentous thesis of Charles Darwin, which is commonly recognized by scientists as synthesizing all of the life sciences, met with the same stubborn opposition from Bishop Wilberforce and the Anglicans as did the Galilean reformation of the physical sciences in the Catholic countries.

Behind this historical opposition, the scientist senses more fundamental tensions resulting from philosophical positions taken by the founders of modern science, positions which in some cases diverge sharply from the traditional philosophy favored by theologians. For instance, the accent in modern science on measurement and controlled experimentation has undoubtedly given a positivist and empiriological cast to the thinking of the scientist. He conceives his science as being completely objective and public because it is based on verifiable experimental evidence; he is proud of the fact that all scientists agree on these matters, or if they do have differences of opinion, will shortly resolve them by appeal to experiment or measurement. He is consequently suspicious of qualitative and subjective evaluations, of insights that are not commonly shared, of explanations that are not empirically verifiable—and all of these he sees typified in the thought of theologians.

In a similar vein, the scientist has a practical bent which makes him more favorable to pragmatism than to the "sterile speculation" of theologians. He takes justifiable pride in the technological miracles of the atomic era, and whenever his theoretical world view is called into question he can always point to some recent device and say, "It works." His control over nature, and more recently over space, is truly fascinating. There is no stagnation, no eternal discussion of mooted questions; rather, scientific research is progressing with leaps and bounds, ever extending its horizons, moving into new areas which formerly were thought to be the exclusive domain of the philosopher. Small wonder that the scientist has unbounded confidence in the power of his new methods and views with suspicion any conservative orthodoxy that would impose limits on the domain and fruitfulness of his investigations.

Closely associated with this attitude is a methodological point of view in modern science that is not easily reconcilable with the dogmatic outlook found in theology. The history of science offers innumerable instances of progress being slowed or important discoveries being thwarted or rejected because of adherence to some axiom or principle that was generally regarded as certain or self-evident. This history has taught the scientist to be wary of committing himself to anything as *absolutely* certain; rather, he would prefer to speak in terms of probability, to question everything, to assign a hierarchy of probabilities to all his statements, but never to dogmatize on the basis of the past, never draw a conclusion that he would regard as unalterable or irrevocable. A competent physicist recently gave voice to the extremes to which this skepticism can go: "Although there are scientists who believe in God, I do not believe that they think of God in the same way as religious people do. If they are consistent with their science, I think that they say something like this to themselves: 'I am almost certain there is a God. The doubt is very small.' "[1]

Finally, there is general dissatisfaction in the scientific fraternity with any world view that is too anthropomorphic or homocentric—a view that is traditionally associated with the Judaeo-Christian heritage in theology. The transition from the closed world to the infinite universe has effected a revolution in the thinking of scientists even more startling than the Copernican revolution. Not only is man no longer seen as dwelling on a privileged body at the center of the universe; he himself is dwarfed to insignificance by the size of the galaxy in which his solar system is located, and this galaxy is only one of a billion others that populate the universe. On the temporal axis, all evidence points to a physical universe in existence for many billion years; man, on the other hand, is viewed as a late-comer on the cosmic scale, presumably evolved from matter by some accident of history by which the earth was formed in the vicinity of a sun with physicochemical conditions suitable for the generation of his particular form of life. Many scientists would say that terrestrial man is not the unique expression of human nature, while others would allow for the existence of supermen on other planets in the remote depths of space. An insignificant item in the spatio-temporal matrix of modern science, man is no longer looked upon as the lord of the universe. The theologian's concept that all the rest of creation is a mere scaffolding, that the universe is a stage for God to watch man's struggle for good and evil, is regarded by the scientist as outmoded and inadequate, if not slightly unreasonable.

On Understanding Science

In the face of these attitudes, the theologian who must deal with scientists or science students can resort to a variety of approaches. At one extreme, he can decide to remain completely aloof from controversy, to have nothing to do with attitudes of mind—and this either because they are not worthy of his serious consideration or because he himself feels that he has nothing to contribute by way of clarifying the issues and solving the problems that they present. This approach is not to be recommended: not only is it sure to alienate the science student from the outset, but theologically it is unsound. Scientific thought has become too much a part of contemporary culture to be neglected completely by the theologian. Moreover, the theologian's primary task is to place reason at the service of faith, and he cannot do this unless he understands well the contributions that have been made by science towards a fuller knowledge of man and the universe in which he lives.

Another approach, likewise an extreme position, consists in rubber-stamping with approval everything that appears in science textbooks or every statement that popularizing scientists have to make about their science. In the American college, this liberal approach is probably more prevalent than the overly conservative approach just mentioned, but it likewise has its dangers. A naive acceptance of everything proferred in the name of science can easily make the problem of critically evaluating the accepted data an impossible one. This is one area where the adage, *parvus error in initio magnus est in fine,* is particularly applicable: the theologian has to be sure of his ground from the outset before attempting a critique that could well be premature, ineffectual and ill-fated by the very terms of its undertaking.

Because of the importance of this consideration, it might be well to digress briefly on some history that is not unrelated to the present problem, that, namely, of the revival of scholasticism at the University of Louvain under the leadership of Cardinal Mercier at the turn of the century. There also it was realized that theology must confront itself with the facts of modern science and make a new synthesis of modern knowledge. The program that was projected for so doing was quite liberal—liberal enough, for example, to eliminate the "defects" of a historical system like Thomism, insofar as the latter was conceived as grounded in medieval science. The difficulties of a synthetic undertaking of this type were also recognized as enormous; in this spirit, it was conceded from the outset that no one man could bridge the gap caused by specialization through the centuries that had elapsed since the Middle Ages. Instead there was to be association between scientists and theologians, and, in the beginning at least, the theologian would have to accept scientific conclusions on the authority of the scientist. The proposed new scholasticism was intended to offer a practical solution, not a definitive one. The immediate aim was an incomplete, progressive, working synthesis, with which scholars would have to be content until something more perfect would become available.[2]

Looking back on the implementation of this program, one could say that science was taken uncritically on face value, and, for one reason or another, never really assimilated into a new synthesis. At the same time, there manifested itself a tendency to explain away conflict between science and philosophy through a type of conventionalism which refused to recognize any ontological value in scientific contributions and therefore permitted a facile reconciliation of difficulties by the simple expedient of rejecting the new scientific knowledge as valueless at the level of being. Theologians, moreover, were quite willing to sacrifice the natural philosophy of St. Thomas to the phenomenal approach of modern science and to draw the line of defense instead at metaphysics, understood in the Wolffian sense, which soon became identified with all of philosophy. A defensive apologetic was worked out on this basis, with its minimum objective being one of justifying the *praeambula fidei* at the ontological level, leaving the field of nature completely in the hands of the scientists.

The educational consequence of this solution was that philosophy and science became more and more separated in the curriculum and in the minds of the students—a situation that has reproduced itself in the American college, partly under the influence of the Louvain movement. Difficulties were solved by reiterating that "there is no conflict, because the disciplines are on different levels," and the end result was an implicit espousal of a type of double-truth doctrine. With regard to theology, science came to play largely a negative role, something to be taken into account, mainly for the purpose of eliminating erroneous interpretations.

This is not to censure the Louvain undertaking, for the circumstances of its foundation made almost inevitable the course it was to follow—to say nothing of the fact that if Cardinal Mercier had not taken the initiative when he did (whatever the limitation of his program) there might be little scholasticism left in the colleges to talk about today. But the fact remains that the thinking behind this approach was pragmatic, deferential to the Kantianism then ruling Europe, and geared to scientific thought at the turn of the century. In the intervening years, Kantianism has been repudiated, while natural philosophy has reasserted itself as an autonomous discipline independent of metaphysics. Science likewise has become more critical of itself, and progress has been made in evaluating scientific contributions logically through a renewed interest in Thomistic methodology. Thus the approach to science that appears now most feasible is one of intelligent interest and critical evaluation, making full use of advances in natural philosophy and methodology, while avoiding on one hand the extreme of bland indifference and on the other a too ready acceptance of everything proposed as true in the name of modern science.

Such an approach, of course, necessitates that Thomists again become "involved" in science, in its history and in its philosophy, that at least some become professionally competent in specific areas, and that all attain the level of competence proper to laymen of general education. This involvement on the part of those who have a technical formation in philosophy and theology can be expected to yield a twofold fruit. First, it should promote a less biased understanding of the history of science as it relates to theology (for the reported conflict is as much likely story as true history); secondly, it should reveal more of the positive content of science by showing the extent to which it has elements in common with other human methods of acquiring knowledge. The tensions sketched above that are experienced by scientists are traceable in reality to a double source: positively, they spring from an implicit realization by the scientist that he has a valid method of establishing and extending human knowledge—and of this he is deeply appreciative and perhaps over-confident; negatively, they spring from an inability to analyse some of his own implicit philosophical commitments or to appreciate the validity of other approaches that are less empiriological, but by that very fact better adapted to penetrate behind the appearances to the reality he is attempting to comprehend through his own investigations. His very preoccupation with the concrete problems of science, moreover, precludes that he should have the time and energy to acquire proficiency in more abstract methods of thought. The philosopher or theologian, on the other hand, having already acquired this facility, can put it to immediate use in evaluating the positive content of science in a way that is meaningful within a much larger context of knowledge.

Obviously it would be impossible to explain in detail here how such a program should be carried out, but a few examples may suffice to show how the present stress and strain can be alleviated, to the mutual benefit of both science and theology. The historical traditions lend themselves most readily to discussion, and these will be mentioned first. After that, a brief critique of scientific methodology will be attempted, in order to show how scientists actually make progress in acquiring knowledge and to indicate how their ways of knowing have more elements in common with traditional philosophical (and theological) procedures than would be suspected at first sight.

The Historical Record

That the Renaissance period is a fruitful source of misunderstanding for the Anglo-Saxon mind steeped in the traditions of modern science can be seen through even a casual examination of the cases of Giordano Bruno and Marco Antonio de Dominis. Both were apostate priests and renegades from religious orders, the former a

Dominican and the latter a Jesuit, and they came into conflict with the Inquisition over matters that were essentially philosophical and theological, having in fact nothing to do with experimental science.

Bruno, it is true, was a revolutionary thinker. Apart from this trait (actually found in a minority of scientists) he had no scientific background whatsoever. He had merely seized upon the Copernican controversy as an opportunity to air his Neoplatonic and mystical views about the infinite. Any Renaissance philosopher might have done the same, with a reasonable expectation of reaping the same consequences.

De Dominis, on the other hand, had made some contributions in optics, although these were not remarkably original, being already present in the medieval optical tradition. But such contributions pale to insignificance before the fact that he was an ambitious, unscrupulous character whose career had seen him go from professor at Padua to the bishopric of Segni, thence become Archbishop of Spalatro, from which office he apostatized to the Church of England. It was only when he attempted to return to Rome that he was apprehended and finally died in a prison of the Inquisition. As an impartial historian has written: "In view of the attempts occasionally made to regard de Dominis as a martyr of science, it is perhaps necessary to point out that there is no evidence that his scientific work led in any way to his condemnation by the Inquisition. His theory of the rainbow was certainly never considered heretical."[3]

The more publicized case of Galileo requires careful examination and study, but even a writer as unfavorably biased as Giorgio de Santillana will concede that science played an insignificant role in the entire proceedings. The popular image of Galileo as an indefatigable experimenter climbing the leaning tower of Pisa to put the theologians to rout with his measurements of falling bodies is an engaging one, but it does justice neither to Galileo nor to his adversaries. For one thing, Galileo's method had little in common with that ascribed to modern science; its most distinctive note was not its insistence on experiment but rather on the fact the book of nature is written *only* in the language of mathematics. Galileo's natural philosophy approached a type of strict mathematical realism in many respects similar to that of the Pythagoreans of twenty centuries previous. For him, experiments had no probative value. He performed experiments, it is true, but these were meant to appeal mainly to the popular mind—one who understood mathematics really had no need for them. The leaning tower experiments (if they actually were performed by Galileo, and most historians now regard them as legendary)[4] did not figure prominently in the Galilean controversy. Rather, it was the newly invented telescope, through which the casual passer-by, the man on the street, could see the mountains on the moon, that supplied the main evidence on which Galileo rested his case. The sarcasm, the wit, the brilliant invective with which the famous Italian stirred up a storm of argument are well known. Had he been less the showman, there could well have been no Inquisition, no trial, no embodiment of the so-called conflict between science and theology in this colorful symbol of Renaissance humanism.

In sober fact, it should be pointed out that Galileo never did prove that the earth went around the sun and not vice versa. Conclusive proof of the type now described in our astronomy textbooks had to wait two more centuries, for the experimental contributions of Foucault and Bessel. Thus, in a real sense, Galileo's "crime" had little to do with theology or revealed religion. It consisted rather in this, that he saw proof too easily, and then on the basis of insufficient evidence called into question a traditional interpretation of Sacred Scripture. Modern studies show his exegetical insights to be quite superior to those of Cardinal Bellarmine and the theologians of the Inquisition, but these do not remedy the faulty logic of his scientific arguments.[5] To say this is not to belittle Galileo's contributions to the new science of mechanics or the invaluable astronomical evidence that he uncovered—all this was most important, and certainly should have been more carefully evaluated by the theologians of his day. De Santillana's further inference has much to recommend it: "Had there been in Rome, at the time of the first crisis of 1616, a youthful Aquinas . . . instead of an aged Bellarmine," history might have been written differently.[6] But "there was no Aquinas," and all know the unfortunate stand taken by those who were in Rome to bring about what history will always regard as a tragic ending to a most unsatisfactory case.

A modern theologian, particularly one who is culturally so removed from Renaissance Italy as an American, can learn much from the history of Galileo's trial. There is an understandable tendency in this country to take a sanguine view of the decisions of the Inquisition, to forget that many of its censures were more political than doctrinal. Certainly the condemnation of 1616, repeated again in 1633, was a piece of philosophical and theological nonsense which speaks poorly for the state of theological science in Rome at the beginning of the seventeenth century. And a lesson is easily drawn to the effect that theologians of the twentieth century can ill afford to allow modern science to escape their comprehension, if they would not once again expose sacred doctrine to the derision of enlightened secularists.

The case of Charles Darwin does not hold the same interest for the Catholic apologete as does that of Galileo, but even here a study of the Darwin affair by competent historians shows more on the side of the theologians than has hitherto been granted. Bishop Wilberforce and the much spoken of Oxford meeting played a relatively insignificant role in the controversy; many of the Anglican clergy did in fact support Darwin, whose main battle was against the initial opposition of his fellow scientists. And the Catholic Church was never actually involved in this battle, nor has she formally attacked Darwin's theory as a whole, despite the fact that the question of evolution and its doctrinal ramifications daily receives more attention from her theologians.

Philosophical Views

To turn now to some of the philosophical commitments of the modern scientist, one finds again that the case against theology is not so clear-cut as first appears. That scientists implicitly subscribe to a philosophy is evident to anyone who has ever discussed philosophical issues with them. Generally, however, their formal training in this area is so meager that they are unable to identify the Cartesian or Kantian or Humean or Comtian strains in their own thought; even less are they aware of the more fundamental presuppositions on which these latter are based.

With regard to positivism, for example, it is true that all scientists can agree on the "facts," and to this extent their science is public and objective and empirically verifiable. But there is more to science than a mere cataloguing of facts, and as soon as one departs from this level to questions concerning theories and their interpretation, or the nature and extent of scientific laws, the agreement is not so wholehearted or universal. For instance, an examination of how discoveries are made or of the factors involved in the acceptance of new theories will show that scientists also have insights. These may make large amounts of data meaningful to them; they are not necessarily shared by their colleagues. Not infrequently there is considerable and prolonged argument over whether everything fits or not—and this merely at an *empiriological* level, to say nothing of what interpretation is to be given to the final result as an explanation of reality.[7]

Moreover, the objectively verifiable test is not the unique criterion for rejecting laws and theories. Every day in the laboratory scientists are disproving established conceptual schemes with one measurement or another and must decide which measurements to retain on the basis of common sense judgments. Again, some principles employed daily in science are actually incapable of empirical verification. The principle of mass-energy conservation, for example, is universally accepted; yet no one would pretend to be able to detect experimentally the creation of one hydrogen atom every thousand years in the average-sized laboratory—a phenomenon predicted by Hoyle in violation of the time-honored conservation principle. Likewise, the velocity of light *in vacuo* is universally regarded as the one *real* constant in the universe, desite the fact that everyone who has measured it so far has gotten a different value![8] The positivistic view of science has sound basis in fact, it is true, but it *can* be carried too far; the scientist also depends on insights, qualitative evaluations, beliefs, non-verifiable principles—for without these he cannot make progress in his science.[9]

With regard to the pragmatic character of modern science, a further point requires clarification. If scientists were to limit themselves strictly to technology and place *all* of the value of their contributions in the fact that something works, there would never be any argument with the philosopher or the theologian. The area of friction is precisely that in which the scientist, as pure scientist and not merely as research engineer, lays claim to *knowing* and not merely *doing*, when he claims to have made positive contributions to speculative knowledge of the physical universe. Not infrequently in this age of missile and thermonuclear technology it is difficult to distinguish between the two aspects of scientific research; indeed, it is somewhat ironic that scientists should occasionally have to argue with government officials that pure research is *also* important. But it is one thing to build a rocket that can escape from the earth's gravitational field; it is quite another to give a definitive answer to the question, "What is gravity?" In the latter case, the pragmatic test fails, just as it fails in solving the major speculative problems confronting the philosopher and theologian.

That science is progressive in a very unique sense is likewise debatable. There is no gainsaying the fact that more and more data are continually being accumulated, that theories successively undergo revision, and that something new is always being reported in scientific journals. But take away this elaboration *in extenso* of a basic technique for gathering information, and it will be found that all scientists say pretty much the same thing, that as a group they do not take kindly to notions that go against the main current of thought. Geniuses are few and far between in all walks of life, and the occasional one who appears is as likely to be rejected by the conservative scientist as he is by the conservative theologian. Why this is so is ultimately explicable in terms of the stability of the thought patterns associated with human intellectual activity; there is no reason why it should be placed at the door-step of the theologian as *his* fundamental failing and overlooked in the case of his neighbors in the intellectual community.

In similar vein, the scientist's freedom to doubt can be exaggerated out of all proportion when making out a case for the superiority of scientific methodology. A moment's reflexion will show that no scientist is as free to doubt as he may think he is: for instance, he cannot doubt about his own thought, or about his laboratory, or about the reality of the experiments he is conducting, or even about his measurements. He may reasonably doubt about the *accuracy* of his measurements, yes, but not that they *are* measurements of something—otherwise his whole undertaking becomes quite foolish and irrational. Moreover, to take up a career in science the beginner must surrender to its intellectual discipline and even accept authority in order to acquire professional status. The skeptical student who wanted all his doubts about induction settled before he took a laboratory course would not get very far in the pursuit of any science at the college or university level.

As to the new world picture painted by modern science in contrast with the homocentric view of the Judaeo-Christian theological heritage, this too depends greatly on the point of view of the individual scientist. Many eminent scientists have studied the new evidence and have not opted for any radical change in world view. The two founders of the modern era in science, Max Planck and Albert Einstein, saw no conflict between scientific investigation and religious belief. Others hold that the evidence available today to demonstrate the existence of a provident God who has all the characteristics of the God of revelation is more striking and more wonderful than ever. And whatever the merits of Pierre Teilhard de Chardin's *Phenomenon of Man* as a theological study, it does show that the evolutionary hypothesis is in no way refractory to integration within a Christian synthesis based on the phenomenological approach favored by science. For the rest, it might perhaps be noted that those who inveigh most vigorously against anthropomorphism are the very ones who have substituted, in place of traditional religion, a type of scientific humanism in which the accent remains on man, displaced slightly in the spatio-temporal co-ordinate system but nonetheless still the center and measure of all things.

These few observations on the history and method of science are in no way intended to belittle modern science or its place in the college curriculum. What they should do, however, is focus attention on the fact that scientific knowledge is not vastly different from other forms of human knowledge, that the scientist who feels so superior that he looks down his nose at the philosopher or theologian is as much to be pitied as the theologian who has no knowledge of the limitations of theological science. The day when any scientist can disdain knowledge of the history and philosophy of his science or of the relationship of his discipline to human culture in general is gone forever. And one of the precise aims of the Catholic college education, especially for the science student, should be that of locating science properly within the broader context of all intellectual endeavor, of showing its positive values but also its limitations, of bringing to an end the narrow specialization that produces the "technocrat" or "science fictionist" who is intolerant of anything not expressed in the jargon or conceptual schemes to which his science courses have made him accustomed.

One method of achieving this objective—and the one clearly indicated to the Catholic educator by papal authority—is first to locate modern science in the hierarchy of intellectual virtues proposed by St. Thomas Aquinas, and then to work out a feasible program for communicating these habits of mind to the student in proper pedagogical order. Such a program obviously cannot be elaborated here in its entirety; what will be attempted, however, is a brief appraisal of modern science according to the views of St. Thomas, and then a sketch of how it should be taught in the Catholic college, particularly in relation to the teaching of sacred theology.[10]

St. Thomas and Modern Science

The first encounter of any proportions between science and theology dates back to the University of Paris of the thirteenth century, when the influx of Aristotelian thought through the Arabs brought with it the scientific learning of the ancient world and provoked a hostile reaction from the theological faculty. The skirmish was sharp and the issue quickly decided, but the solution that was reached is still broadly applicable to present day problems. Largely through the work of two Dominicans, St. Albert the Great and St. Thomas Aquinas, the respective rights of faith and reason were vindicated and a harmonious balance established between sacred theology and natural science. In this rapprochement, science was neither rejected nor diverted in any way from its proper pursuits; rather, it was directly assimilated as a *necessary* foundation for the work of theology. And the Catholic Church, in officially adopting St. Thomas' philosophy as her own, has never ceased to insist that the only proper educational propadeutic to the study of sacred theology is a rigorous formation in the sciences that deal with the world of nature.

There are differences, of course, between the science that confronted the medieval theologian at the University of Paris and that taught now in our colleges. Some are so impressed by the dissimilarities that they fail even to discern the elements that the disciplines have in common—an obvious one, for instance, being their common goal. Medieval and modern science alike aim at a fuller understanding of nature, of the physical universe as it falls directly under man's observation. Much of the diversity, on the other hand, can be traced to the tremendous influence that mathematical physics exerts over all of modern science. Whatever else may be said about scientific method, it cannot be denied that the use of measurement and mathematical correlation has become the hallmark of the scientist in the present day. And granted that neither St. Thomas nor any other medieval could have foreseen the tremendous development that has taken place along these lines, he nonetheless did have the foresight to clarify the status of any natural science that uses mathematical reasoning in the elaboration of its subject matter. Thus his teaching on the role of mathematics in natural science is very much to the point today; indeed, it provides the basis for a Thomistic philosophy of science that can be extremely helpful in working out the pedagogical relationships that should obtain between modern science and sacred theology.

Robert Grosseteste and the Neoplatonists at Oxford University had been among the first to sense the importance of mathematical reasoning in physical science; they had actually worked out a theory of proof akin to the mathematical realism later adopted by Galileo in the early part of the seventeenth century. For them, mathematical structure was the fundamental entity lying beneath physical appearances; it was only necessary to discover this, and scientific explanation would then follow rigorously along mathematical lines. Possibly through Roger Bacon, the influence of this teaching was gradually felt at the University of Paris and provoked a decided reaction from the pen of St. Albert the Great. St. Albert's beginning was, in turn, taken up by his student, St. Thomas Aquinas. He elaborated more fully a theory of proof that accented the physical rather than the mathematical, but at the same time this proof allowed for a use of mathematics in obtaining such proof when investigating the world of nature.[11]

The help that mathematics can give to the natural scientist was conceived by the Angelic Doctor as being of two kinds: one which functions at the level of hypothesis to suggest *possible* physical explanations, the other which functions conjointly with physical reasoning to give *conclusive* explanation or proof.[12] An example of the first would be St. Thomas' evaluation of the Ptolemaic explanation of the motion of the heavens through eccentrics and epicycles. Viewed mathematically, St. Thomas noted, the observed appearances of the stars result "either from the motion of the object seen or from the motion of the observer. . . . It makes no difference which is moving."[13] But as a physical explanation, he showed considerable reserve towards the Ptolemaic hypotheses, noting that while they do account for the stellar appearances, "we must not say that they are thereby proved to be facts, because perhaps it would be possible to explain the apparent movements of the stars by some other method which men have not yet thought out."[14] His whole treatment of astronomical and meteorological problems, in fact, seems aimed at correcting a naive mathematicism among medieval Aristotelians, for he pointed out that Aristotle, in dealing with the heavenly spheres, had mistaken a suppositional theory for established fact.[15] He himself was at pains to elaborate the reasons why we cannot have certain judgments about the heavenly bodies;[16] yet, he observed, it is not stupid or necessarily precipitate to venture an explanation, for he held that a theory or supposition that does not conflict with the facts is far better than no explanation at all.[17]

In addition to this first or hypothetical use of mathematics in seeking a possible explanation, St. Thomas also conceived of mathematics as functioning directly in physical argument to furnish conclusive explanation or proof.[18] This too can best be illustrated by an example. In discussing the shape of the earth, he noted that the latter can be proved to be a sphere merely by an analysis of measurements made on its surface—essentially a mathematical proof.[19] But he regarded as more conclusive for the physicist a proof which arises not simply from a mathematical description of the earth's surface but which leads to a knowledge of the *physical causes* that make the earth to be a sphere. Thus he observed that "all gravitating bodies . . . approach the earth at the same angle, that is, at a right angle . . . and not in parallel lines."[20] This universal mode of gravitation "is what makes the earth to be spherical by nature," he said, because the spherical shape can alone satisfy the uniform tendency of all parts to a common center of gravity.[21] It should be noted in this proof that the physical cause which St. Thomas assigned need not make the earth to be a perfect sphere—"irregularities such as mountains and valleys arise," he conceded, although "not of notable dimensions compared with those of the earth," and he attributed them to "some other incidental cause."[22] Thus perfect mathematical shape, for Aquinas, does not exist in physical reality: it is only the human mind, abstracting from material irregularities such as mountains and valleys, that can conceive of the earth as a perfect sphere.[23] But the earth does have a natural or physical shape that is approximately spherical, and this shape can reveal to the inquiring mind the physical reason that makes the earth to have this shape in the first place.[24]

Space does not permit even a sketch of the historical consequences of this view of the use of mathematics in physical science as developed by St. Albert and St. Thomas. It is indisputable, however, that these men made clear, at a critical period of medieval thought, the distinction between hypothetical explanation and conclusive physical proof, while allowing for a legitimate use of mathematics in both types of reasoning. To this may be added the observation that some recently published texts can be used to argue to the existence of a Dominican school in optical science, beginning with encyclopedic collections of data by Thomas of Cantimbré, Vincent of Beauvais and St. Albert the Great, developing through the theoretical speculations of St. Thomas Aquinas, John of Paris and Peter of Alvernia, and culminating in the brilliant experimental researches and physicomathematical reasoning of Theodoric of Freiberg.[25] The historical import is not insignificant: within less than a century, this line of thought—quite independent of the Oxford school—furnished the first correct fundamental theory of the rainbow. And this more than 300 years before the publication of Descartes' *Discours de la Méthode* and *Les Météores,* where basically the same explanation of the rainbow is cited as one of the brilliant achievements of the new Cartesian methodology!

Of more immediate relevance to the problem at hand is the fact that the two different uses of mathematics in natural science pointed out by St. Thomas have their counterparts in similar characteristics of modern science, the very ones which are particularly important when considering its relation to sacred theology. For in modern science it is also possible to distinguish two different types of reasoning—not unconnected with St. Thomas' twofold use of mathematics, although not to be completely identified with it—and consequently two types of contributions that go to make up the body of scientific knowledge.

On the one hand, modern science contains a hard core of established truth about the universe based on observation, experiment and cogent reasoning—similar to the *conclusive* explanations or proofs cited by St. Thomas—and this knowledge is universally accepted and agreed upon in the scientific fraternity, forming the basis for all further investigation.[26] On the other hand, modern science consists of a much larger body of knowledge that is proposed merely as hypothetical explanation, as provisional truth about the universe—similar to the possible physical explanations recognized by St. Thomas as being at the level of hypothesis—and this is continually undergoing change, being from time to time subjected to even radical revision. The first element is quite stable, changing only slowly, and this by a process of gradual assimilation of new material. The second element shows all the signs of extensive and rapid progress, with new approaches and insights into the secrets of nature being continually suggested and subjected to experimental test, more frequently than not to be rejected, only to be replaced by more refined "guesses" suggestive of other approaches.

In relation to American collegiate education, it might be mentioned that this first element of modern scientific knowledge embraces much of the matter that is taught in core courses at the college level; the second element generally pertains to more advanced courses and to the study of techniques useful for scientific research. One might also say that the great prestige of science rests on the accomplishments contained in the first element, but that the most exciting part of scientific work (and this includes its teaching) is that connected with new techniques and recent discoveries contained in the second. And unfortunately, much of the misunderstanding about scientific method is traceable to a confusion between the ways in which contributions are made to these two areas respectively. It is difficult, to be sure, to draw a sharp line of demarcation and say definitively when any one discovery passes from the provisional stage to that of permanent contribution.

Science-Theology Integration

Since these two components of modern science also stand in markedly different relation to sacred theology, it will be convenient to consider them separately when discussing the integration of science with theology in collegiate education.

The first component more obviously than the second has something in common with the Thomistic notion of *scientia,* of science in the sense of true and certain knowledge through proper causes. Of capital importance in the teaching of sacred theology, this concept of science should be taught in as many contexts as are available in the college curriculum. And since the student's primary contact with reality is through the world of nature, it stands to reason that anything strictly scientific (in the sense of *scientia*) that he can grasp at this level is of particular value as a foundation on which to build his theological synthesis.

Yet even when considering the first component of scientific knowledge as strict science in the Thomistic sense, there are difficulties that stand in the way of direct integration with sacred theology. These difficulties spring from a twofold source. The first is that the fundamental content of modern science—the part, say, that would be communicated in core courses—is still too specialized to be of immediate use to the theologian; the certain knowledge that is implicit in modern science must first be integrated at a more generalized level, at the level of a general science of nature or of natural philosophy, if it is to be of service in theology. The second is that the teaching of scientific methodology (if taught at all in the college curriculum) is usually restricted to the methods used to acquire *new* knowledge. As a consequence, there is no emphasis on the logic required to examine the permanence of a contribuiton, to test whether an addition to the scientific corpus can be regarded as true and certain or whether it will remain subject to further revision. Since this reflexive habit of mind figures importantly in the study of sacred theology, anyone who would relate the findings of modern science to theological science must begin by finding out the Thomistic canons that govern demonstrative reasoning, so that he may ascertain whether or not the methodology he regards as scientific is also truly scientific in the Thomistic sense of the term.[27]

To remedy these two difficulties, at least two courses, traditionally regarded as courses in philosophy, should be offered to science students at the earliest opportunity. These two courses are logic and natural philosophy, both of which are already present in the curricula of most Catholic colleges. The needs of the integration being proposed, however, may well require a revision of such courses as they are currently taught in some colleges. For instance, a philosophy of nature taught as a branch of metaphysics would be useless for making contact with the specialized natural sciences, while one taught according to the content of V. E. Smith's *General Science of Nature* would be well suited to this purpose.[28] Similarly, a logic course that emphasized formal logic to the exclusion of demonstrative methodology would have obvious limitations, while one that covered the essential content of Aristotle's *Posterior Analytics,* or even the broader content of the entire *Organon* as sketched in Fr. B. M. Ashley's *Arts of Learning and Communication*,[29] would fill the lacunae created by an over-specialized program. Such courses, it should be noted, need presuppose no training in science. They can be taught in the freshman year, either as a propadeutic to specialized work in the sciences or concomitantly with introductory special courses where these are necessary as an early basis for more advanced work.

The pedagogical value of an early course in the philosophy of nature is that it supplies the science student with a philosophical analysis of concepts with which he is working throughout his entire science career. At the same time it gives him an opportunity to examine these in a pre-scientific manner, without becoming committed to a closed system involving metrical suppositions. This procedure is particularly helpful for relating the notions of matter, nature, motion, infinity, space, time and the continuum to the world of everyday experience, as well as for showing the possibility of a non-mathematical treatment of these concepts that is scientific in a generalized understanding of the term. Such usage thus introduces him to natural philosophy as a general science of nature and prepares him for a twofold development: one in the direction of specialization, making fullest use of mathematical and empiriological techniques in specific areas of scientific investigation; the other in the direction of still further generalization, such as he meets in the science of sacred theology, where the entire domain of human endeavor is re-examined in the light of divine revelation. The key concept, of course, is that of motion: it is movement in all its myriad forms that he examines closely in physics, chemistry, biology and psychology; viewed in a more general way, it is the analysis of motion that supplies the demonstration for the existence of the First Unmoved Mover, the one which puts much of sacred theology on a rational basis.

The study of demonstrative logic cannot be separated from this conceptual development of generalized science, for it is precisely the function of this logic to ascertain the characteristic features of such science and to relate it to other forms of reasoning which are less rigorous but frequently encountered in the specialized sciences and in human discourse generally. The utility of such a course is obvious to the theologian: it is only in the measure that the student understands the methodological ideals therein established that he has any chance of appreciating how sacred theology can be in any way scientific. But it is of equal, if not greater importance to his later work in science as this relates to theology that he become fairly expert in discerning a dialectical or hypothetical argument from one that concludes apodictically. For it is this facility in the particular area of his specialty that will enable him to distinguish his scientific knowledge into its two components: the true and the certain, constituting the first element discussed above; and the tentative and exploratory, which has been referred to as the second element.

With regard to this second component of scientific knowledge, its pedagogical utility is not immediately obvious to the theologian. Some would even regard it as a liability, at least insofar as the attitude of mind motivating its acquisition (sometimes known as the research mentality) would countenance hypotheses of all descriptions, including those opposed to revealed truth. At the level of *certain* truth, a Catholic scientist is at no disadvantage compared to his non-Catholic colleague; he knows that reason cannot disprove demonstratively anything that is divinely revealed, that the content of divine revelation is itself eminently reasonable. But because he has a source of certain knowledge, through his faith, that remains unavailable to the nonbeliever, there is an *apparent* limitation on the hypotheses he may propose. This limitation, it should be made clear, is not real. It does not restrict him in his search for truth, all it eliminates are false possibilities. But since these are not recognizable as false by the scientific fraternity at large, he is apparently limited in his choice of alternative explanations. The question of the eternity of the world as it relates to various cosmological and cosmogonical theories is a case in point. St. Thomas recognized that the eternal motion concept contained in the Aristotelian theory of the physical universe was unacceptable to the Christian because it is divinely revealed that the world had a beginning in time; thus he wasted no time in showing that the eternity of the world could not be demonstrated by reason alone.[30] The modern Catholic cosmologist is faced with the same difficulty in Hoyle's theory of the steady-state universe or

Gamow's theory of the non-static pulsating or hyperbolic universe. St. Thomas' position was simplified by the fact that those who were inclined to accept Aristotle's authority in cosmological matters would also subscribe to the Stagyrite's methodological canons for ascertaining when something was or was not definitively proved. Among his colleagues the modern cosmologist will find scientific disagreement even on questions of hypothesis, coupled with even stronger philosophical disagreement on questions of truth and certainty. His task thereby becomes proportionately more difficult.

There is yet another factor to be taken into account. The integration of science with theology is not to be viewed as a unilateral agreement in which theology uses science to serve its purposes and then discards it as soon as difficulty is encountered. There are pressing problems besetting the modern mind that arise from modern science, and some of these problems can receive solution in sacred theology even though they remain insoluble at the level of pure reason. Thus it becomes the theologian's task (and that of the teacher of sacred theology) to face up to such difficulties and complement the theoretical speculations of scientists with a theological analysis of problems to which solutions are available. Anyone acquainted with the *Summa Theologiae* of St. Thomas will recognize that its order and the magnificent sweep of its argumentation still set an ideal pattern for education in theology, even at the college level. But this does not mean that the objections proposed by St. Thomas or the specifically medieval problems to which he addressed himself should continue to be made problems for the modern student. "Sufficient for the day is the evil thereof"; the modern difficulties are the ones that automatically stimulate the interest of the student and also give him the exercise he needs to develop a theological *habitus* that will be most useful in later life.

It is in this area that the second component of scientific knowledge will find its greatest play. Here, indeed, the integration of science with theology could result in maximum fruit to both disciplines as well as to the student. Problems that should receive consideration abound in all the major tracts of sacred theology. The treatment of God and his creatures, for instance, cannot offer a proper rational foundation for the study of the Holy Trinity unless the student sees that the proofs for the existence of God have not been invalidated by the progress of modern thought. This means not only that the teacher understand the canons of proof used by the scienist for establishing the existence of entities not apparent to the senses, but that he answer the objections to the traditional proofs for God's existence taken from Newton's first law of motion or from Einstein's special theory of relativity.[31] Likewise the question of the temporal origin of the universe should receive consideration in the context of recent cosmological theories. While studying the production of creatures and the account of formation of the universe in Genesis, a full treatment of evolution—its factual and hypothetical status, as well as its theological implications—should be given. And when discussing man and his relation to the universe in which he lives, it would not be amiss to take up, from the viewpoint of divine providence, the biological and sociological problems caused by the so-called population explosion.

In similar fashion, moral theology can be enriched from contact with science. The modern approach to the mind-body problem makes available much information that was not available to St. Thomas when treating of the emotions and the voluntariety of human acts in the *Summa*. Similarly, an appraisal of psychoanalytic theories in the light of traditional doctrine invites treatment, at least at an elementary level. There are interesting problems connected with the transmission of original sin arising from the possibility of human life in other parts of the universe. And then specifically moral cases, such as can be solved through the application of general principles but which require in addition some background in science, await analysis for science students. Questions about the morality of eugenics, of the influence of new types of drugs on man's superior faculties, of the moral impact of technology on human society are all live ones; they can serve to illustrate principles that could otherwise be lost on the class through repetition of hackneyed examples. Again, since many science students will ultimately be engaged in government work or in weapons research, it becomes advisable now to devote considerably more space than did St. Thomas to the morality of warfare, even to take up the ethical problems associated with the development and use of nuclear energy. The hue and cry today is that scientists are assuming the leadership of the country and are unprepared to do so because of their naive ethical and political notions. One of the aims of Catholic education should be to assure that Catholic scientists will not be deficient in this regard.

Then there are topics in sacramental theology and in the tract *de novissimis* that should not be neglected. More than one science student has wondered how to reconcile his notion of the molecular structure of bread with the real presence of the body of Christ in the Eucharist. The treatment of the properties of glorified bodies, of compenetrability and impassibility, can be highlighted through reference to modern scientific views of matter. The questions of the ultimate destiny of the material universe, of the location of heaven and hell, of fire in purgatory, etc., are ones to which answers should not be given merely in terms of medieval physics. The great progress in physical science during the past three centuries should stimulate further speculation about these theological problems. And, in so doing, it automatically makes available an integrating device that unites apparently disparate subjects in the curriculum and places them in proper relation one to the other.

Curriculum Suggestions

Obviously this is only a sketch of some of the possibilities for science-theology integration. Yet the question immediately arises how any or all of this matter is to be worked into an already over-crowded college curriculum. Theology and philosophy courses for science students are usually pared to a minimum number of class hours, making it difficult to stress even the basic notions without seeking to cover additional matter. Thus the question of curriculum planning is one that deserves careful consideration if any integrated program is to reach the stage of practical realization, even in a limited way. The problem is further complicated by the fact that, in these matters, it is difficult to generalize: each college has its peculiar problems and limited means at its disposal with which to solve them. Still there is a great spirit of adventure now abroad in the educational community; hardly an institution is to be found that is not willing to conduct *some* experimentation, at least with a select group of students in an honors program. For those who are progressing in this direction, the following remarks may prove helpful, at least to suggest possibilities worth considering in the early stages of curriculum planning.

Despite individual differences, it should further be noted that there are general similarities among the science programs offered for general education in liberal arts colleges and among those designed to produce scientists in colleges offering degrees in science or engineering. A broad distinction may thus be drawn between the two types of program, and the problem of integration approached slightly differently in each.

In the liberal education program, natural science has primary value as discipline in objective thinking; in a secondary way, it should also give the student a cultural appreciation for classical contributions in the history of ideas. Such a program permits considerable freedom in the selection and ordering of the subject matter, there being no fixed syllabus and experimentation being the accepted mode in this part of the curriculum. In the Catholic college, full play can therefore be given to the ordination of matter towards a theological synthesis, provided that the autonomy of the sciences taught be safeguarded in the process.

One such program, already in full operation at St. Xavier College in Chicago, offers a two-year science sequence that is partly preparatory for, and partly concomitant with the college course in sacred theology.[32] The sequence is itself integrated with philosophy of nature, being divided into four semesters; the first of these is devoted to the general science of nature, the second to the principles and methods of physical science, the third to the principles and methods of biology, and the fourth to the principles and methods of psychology. Its primary objective is to provide the student with a general understanding of the world of nature, scientific in the modern and Thomistic sense alike, integrating the various branches of natural science and giving positive impetus to theological study. As secondary objectives, it proposes to give the student cultural appreciation for classical contributions in the history of science and at the same time furnish a broad base for specialization in some branch of science, should this be elected.

In view of these objectives, the general program is not merely an abridgment of technical courses usually given at lower collegiate levels with accent on technique and problem solving. Nor is it a Great Books course where the student is introduced solely to classical contributions in a particular field, without systematic integration. Rather, the whole of natural science is viewed as a *single* intellectual habit to be developed in the student. This habit consists in knowing the world of nature first in terms of the most generalized principles that furnish the explanations of all its varied phenomena, and then in terms of more specialized principles that apply only to particular areas of investigation. Following the basic division of St. Thomas, the concept of natural motion (or change) is stressed as the unifying factor that distinguishes this science from the other intellectual disciplines.

The Xavier program is so arranged that the student progresses towards the acquisition of the scientific habit by an orderly movement through the subject matter, with the accent on strict logical reasoning and critical analysis of the facts presented—the logic in this case being combined directly with the science. The first semester focuses attention on the basic problems of nature first raised by the Greeks, which was then rigorously examined in the long Aristotelian tradition, and which finally culminated in the development of modern science in the seventeenth century. This approach permits a thorough philosophical analysis of motion and all that it implies, not the least important by-product of which is the proof for the existence of God as the First Unmoved Mover, preparing the way at an early stage for theological wisdom with an acceptable scientific basis.

Succeeding semesters then build systematically on this foundation. Since motion is the unifying concept throughout the entire program, the general divisions are mapped out on the basis of the various kinds of observable motion that can be studied. The simplest motion examined in detail is gravitational motion, and this is studied thoroughly for the information that it yields first about the structure of the universe (Galileo and the Inquisition!), then about the structure of matter when taken into account with more complex motions, such as chemical reactions. Then an even more complex motion, biological growth, is taken under consideration and studied from the viewpoint of the definition and origin of life (Darwin and evolution!); finally, the most complex change known to man—psychological growth—is examined in relation to the problems of knowledge and volition. Through this progression, more and more highly organized bodies are being studied successively, from the atom all the way to man, with materials being supplied that are immediately relevant to a theological synthesis. Again, at each level the study is far from superficial, for the major topics in physics, chemistry, biology and psychology are studied, supplemented by demonstrations and laboratory experiments together with readings from classical contributions in the history of science.

This basic program, it may be noted, is followed at St. Xavier's even by students enrolled in the science department, on the theory that a broad preparation of this kind is most useful for later specialization. To meet the course requirements for a concentration in chemistry, for example, a student might be taking a freshman course in inorganic chemistry concurrently with the basic science sequence; the respective curricula are arranged to eliminate duplication, and the contrasting approaches (philosophical and technical) are found to be quite stimulating to the student.

In Catholic colleges heavily committed to a science or engineering program patterned after that found in many secular institutions, such a sweeping revision of the introductory courses might not be immediately feasible. Yet it should be pointed out that science education at the college level is moving rapidly in the direction of liberalizing and humanizing curricula during the formative years. The Massachusetts Institute of Technology, for example, requires of all students a two-year core course in the humanities, and allows up to forty per cent of the credits accumulated during the four years to be taken in this department. The Catholic college can afford to be equally liberal in this regard. Not having to be so eclectic in its offering, it can probably achieve more with the credit-hours available.

In a technical program, most of the specialized science courses can and should remain intact and basically unaltered, there being no reason why subjects at this level of specialization should conflict with the generalized thought of philosophy or theology.[33] This means that science-theology integration will be handled for the most part in introductory courses or in those designated specifically as philosophy and theology. The division of time between philosophy and theology can perhaps be somewhat arbitrary, since the theologian is continually using philosophy in the elaboration of his subject matter. But in view of the special difficulty of integrating science directly with sacred theology, it is recommended, as has been stated above, that this be effected through special courses in the philosophy of nature and in logic, or alternatively, through one substantial course in the philosophy of science which accents the Thomistic approach to nature and motion and the methodology of scientific proof.

Faculty Communication

The curriculum problem is admittedly a difficult one, but no less difficult is the problem of securing professors who are trained to implement effectively an integrated program of the type proposed. Much of the tension between science and theology departments mentioned earlier arises from the fact that the individual professor, while competent in the field of his specialty, is himself lacking in the integral view of science-theology relationships and consequently distorts the whole through over-emphasis on one or other of the parts. If the professor is deficient in this regard, it is extremely difficult to see how he can communicate an integral view to the student, however interested and dedicated he might be in furthering the cause of Catholic education, or however well-planned the program in which he teaches.

The ideal situation would be one in which theologians all had formal training in science and science professors all had formal training in theology—an ideal, it may be observed, that is theoretically realizable in colleges staffed by priests but rarely achieved in practice. In defect of its realization, however, the situation need not be regarded as hopeless. It should be possible, for instance, for the science professor in a Catholic college to acquire at least a cultured layman's knowledge of Thomism; particularly he should learn how sacred theology is science, yet differing in many respects from the special science in which he is trained. And similarly the theology professor can be expected to learn enough modern science to be able to use examples and incorporate relevant matter in his courses. Once this is done, the two can work further on the thorny problem of how to separate fact from hypothesis in particular areas of theological interest in contemporary science. In this matter, the science professor may well prove more adept, and consequently should assume responsibility for separating fact from theory in his courses wherever revealed truth is seemingly contradicted. In his own field, likewise, he should attempt to influence his colleagues (and particularly textbook writers) to keep fact distinct from interpretation in those few matters where anti-Catholic bias might be in evidence.

Thus through a process of continued education and association, faculty problems can be solved and tensions ultimately relieved. As a minimum requirement, however, there *must* be discussion and communication between departments—even stimulated, where need be, by the college administration. How such discussion is carried on—whether informally or through faculty seminars or in combined sessions with honors students or even in vacation workshop sessions—really matters very little. No matter how effected, however, it will be advisable to have some ground rules for communication. The following four such rules, part of a series worked out and proposed by Fr. Nogar to a group of scientists for discussing the problem of evolution,[34] may prove useful over a wider range of contexts.

> (1) Discussion must be conceived as an enlightened co-operative intellectual effort aimed at problem solving and not as a vindication of rights. In other words, there must be mutual respect and a spirit of co-operation, with each party saying what he really thinks, and not softening the blows because he thinks the other is basically unable to bear them.

(2) There must be a realistic confrontation of issues—the facile and sanguine statement that "if science remains within its own confines and theology stays in its own realm there will be no difficulties" defeats the end of liberal discussion and actually solves nothing.

(3) Communication must be at the level, not of the competence of the specialist, but of the competence of the generally educated person. Dialogue is *between* sciences or disciplines, not within them. Each participant must therefore make an intelligent adjustment in order to communicate, to use precise but non-technical language that accurately conveys his thought.

(4) It follows as a corollary that the theologian has an obligation to develop the mentality of the scientist, and the scientist too must develop the mentality of the theologian. The idea of "staying out of the other's field" is valuable for coming to perfection *within* a discipline; it is lethal when discussing issues of mutual importance and significance *between* disciplines.

Conclusion

With these thoughts it is possible to return to the note sounded at the begining of this chapter: to stress that science-theology integration in college education is a field in which little has been done to date and in which immediate and significant results are not to be expected from any program undertaken at the moment. Complete integration in this area will obviously require long years of tedious and patient work. Best results will probably come from a not too ambitious program in the beginning, working first to integrate science with theology through the agency of a course in the philosophy of nature or the philosophy of science, proposed as a type of generalized or fundamental science of nature, and coupled with a basic course in Thomistic methodology. Later detailed work can then extend to subjects taught in individual courses, with an attempt to dovetail and interrelate matters on specific points, depending on the interests of the student and the capabilities of the professor.

It should not be thought, finally, that the previous lack of attention or even that the initial difficulty experienced in this area need be a bad omen for the future. The lack of attention is easily explained by the fact that other more pressing problems of organization *within* departments have thus far absorbed the time and interests of administrators. Again, the very presence of interdepartmental strife in Catholic college education is yet another sign of its coming of age. And when the particular conflict is between the scientists and the theologians, it certainly is not something new from the viewpoint of history. What *is* new is the attempt to remove the sources of conflict at a most significant point, the point of common origin in the formation of Catholic scientist and Catholic theologian alike. Should this be done, it might well be one of the great contributions of the Church's enlightened program for college education in the United States.

Footnotes to Study 8

[1]R. P. Feynman, "The Relation of Science and Religion," in E. Hutchings, Jr., ed., *Frontiers in Science* (New York: Basic Books, 1958), 309-310.

[2]For a sketch of the Louvain program as it was originally projected, see M. De Wulf, *Scholasticism Old and New,* trans. by P. Coffey (New York: 1907), *passim.*

[3]R. E. Ockenden, "Marco Antonio de Dominis and His Explanation of the Rainbow," *Isis,* XXVI (1936), 40.

[4]See, for example, L. Cooper, *Aristotle, Galileo and the Tower of Pisa* (Ithaca: Cornell U. Press, 1935), 13-57.

[5]As Fr. J. Brodrick, S.J., states: "It is a curious and paradoxical circumstance . . . that as a piece of scriptural exegesis Galileo's theological letters are much superior to Bellarmine's, while as an essay on scientific method Bellarmine's letter is far sounder and more modern in its views than Galileo's." *The Life and Work of Blessed Robert Francis Cardinal Bellarmine, S.J.* (New York: P. J. Kenedy and Sons, 1928), II, 360.

[6]G. De Santillana, *The Crime of Galileo* (Chicago: U. of Chicago Press, 1955), ix.

[7]For a fuller clarification of this point and some others mentioned here, see an article by P. Black entitled "The War of Science on Religion" in the *Bulletin* of the Philosophy of Science Group of the Newman Association of Great Britain, No. 36 (October, 1959), reprinted in the *Bulletin of the Albertus Magnus Guild,* VIII (March, 1960).

[8]See the provocative series of essays by G. Webster, *Wonders of Science: Mysteries That Point to God* (New York: Sheed and Ward, 1956), particularly 37-38.

[9]An amusing debunking of scientists that points out some of their hidden beliefs is A. Standen's *Science is a Sacred Cow* (New York: E. P. Dutton and Co., Inc., 1950).

[10]A fuller justification of the position adopted here is given in an excellent article by Fr. B. M. Ashley, O.P., "The Role of the Philosophy of Nature in Catholic Liberal Education," *Proceedings of the American Catholic Philosophical Association,* XXX (1956), 62-85.

[11]Cf. J. A. Weisheipl, O.P., "Albertus Magnus and the Oxford Platonists", *Proceedings of the American Catholic Philosophical Association,* XXXII (1958), 124-139.

[12]See St. Thomas' *Commentaria in Octo Libros Physicorum Aristotelis,* II, lect. 3, n. 9; also the *Summa,* I, q. 32, a. 1, ad 2.

[13]*Commentaria in Libros Aristotelis De Caelo,* II, lect. 11, n. 2 and lect. 12, n. 4; cf. J. A. Weisheipl, O.P., *The Development of Physical Theory in the Middle Ages* (London: Sheed and Ward, 1959), 27-62.

[14]*Commentaria in Libros Aristotelis De Caelo,* II, lect. 17, n. 2.

[15]*Loc. cit.*

[16]*Ibid.,* lect. 4, n. 3.

[17]*Ibid.,* lect. 7, nn. 4 and 5; also *Commentaria in Libros Aristotelis Meteorologicorum,* I, lect. 11, n. 1.

[18]*Commentaria in Aristotelis Libros Posteriorum Analyticorum,* I, lect. 25, nn. 5 and 6.

[19]*Commentaria in Libros Aristotelis De Caelo,* II, lect. 28, n. 4.

[20]*Ibid.,* n. 1.

[21]*Loc. cit.*

[22]*Loc. cit.*

[23]*Commentaria in Octo Libros Physicorum Aristotelis,* II, lect. 3, nn. 4 to 6.

[24]*Commentaria in Libros Aristotelis De Caelo,* I, lect. 3, n. 6; *Summa,* I, q. 1, a. 1, ad 2.

[25]Full documentation is given in my study, *The Scientific Methodology of Theodoric of Freiberg: A Case History of the Relationship between Science and Philosophy* (Fribourg: Universitätsverlâg, 1959), 132-249.

[26]Those who are inclined to doubt that there is any such truth in modern science should consider carefully the words of W. Heisenberg: "With respect to the finality of the results, we must remind the reader that in the realm of the exact sciences there have always been *final solutions* for certain limited domains of experience. Thus, for instance, the questions posed by Newton's concept of mechanics found an answer *valid for all time* in Newton's law and its mathematical consequences. . . . In the exact sciences the word 'final' obviously means that there are always self-contained, mathematically representable systems of concepts and laws applicable to certain realms of experience, in which realms *they are always valid for the entire cosmos and cannot be changed or improved.*" *Das Nasturbild der heutigen Physik* (Hamburg: 1955), trans. by A. J. Pomerans as *The Physicist's Conception of Nature* (London: Hutchinson and Co., 1958), 26-27. (Italics mine.)

[27]An application of Thomistic methodology to some topics in modern science will be found in my article, "Some Demonstrations in the Science of Nature," *The Thomist Reader* (1957), 90-118.

[28]Dr. Smith's text is published by Bruce (Milwaukee: 1958).

[29]Published by The Priory Press (Dubuque: 1958).

[30]Cf. *Summa,* I, q. 46, aa. 1-3.

[31]See, for example, my article entitled "Newtonian Antinomies Against the *Prima Via,*" *The Thomist,* XIX (1956), 151-192.

[32]For details of this program, see articles by Sr. M. Muriel, R.S.M., "The Role of Natural Science in the Saint Xavier Plan," *The Catholic Educational Review,* LVI (1958), 397-404; Sr. M. Olivia, R.S.M., "Challenge Accepted," *Transactions of the Illinois State Academy of Science,* L (1957), 227-232.

[33]St. Thomas points out in II *Con. Gen.*, Chap. 4, that most of the details of natural science need not concern the theologian; only those details which have special relation to matters of faith properly pertain to theological science.

[34]R. J. Nogar, O.P., "Towards an Improved Dialogue between Science and Theology," *Bulletin of the Albertus Magnus Guild,* VII (February, 1960).

9

THEOLOGY AND THE SOCIAL SCIENCES

Daniel Roach, O.P.
C. H. Geraets, O.P.

Father Geraets (a Lector of Sacred Theology) and Father Roach are both members of the faculty of Dominican College, Racine, Wisconsin. They have collaborated on a volume of social philosophy to serve as a college text which will be published in the fall by The Priory Press. Father Roach is pursuing graduate studies in this subject at Loyola University, Chicago.

In imitation of her Master, Holy Mother Church has ever shown herself solicitous for the social happiness of men. In the very midst of the social ills of earth (and often because of them) she has maintained her triple mission of teaching, governing and sanctifying. But during the last century, the teaching mission, especially as it is concerned with the increasing ills of society, has taken on a new prominence and urgency. The "five great encyclicals," for example, are all social documents.

Although the Church herself has spoken out on behalf of the general social truths that govern human group relations, nonetheless she looks in a special way to her school system to formulate these teachings in a scientific way and to impress them on the minds of her children. For the school is the home of the arts and sciences. "Since . . . the younger generation must be trained in the arts and sciences for the advantage and prosperity of civil society, and since the family of itself is unequal to this task, it was necessary to create that social institution, the school."[1] At the college level, a sapiential understanding, defense and explanation of the faith is studied as theology; at the college level also the study of social science develops a reasoned understanding of man's relentless quest of social happiness.

Yet for a school to call itself Catholic it must do more than merely teach theology along with the natural arts and sciences. For "the mere fact that a school gives some religious instruction (often extremely stinted) does not bring it into accord with the rights of the Church and of the Christian family, or make it a fit place for Catholic students. To be this, it is necessary that *all* the *teaching* and the whole organization of the school, and its teachers, *syllabus* and textbooks *in every branch,* be regulated by the Christian spirit, under the direction and maternal supervision of the Church; so that religion may be in very truth the foundation and crown of the youth's entire training; and this in every grade of school, not only the elementary, but the intermediate and the *higher institutions* of learning as well."[2] Hence it is above all else necessary that the Catholic college, to be worthy of the name *Catholic,* consider well the proper relationship between theology and every art and science in the curriculum. It is a mere beginning, a *removens prohibens,* that nothing contrary to the faith be taught in any other field of study; far more demanding is the positive ordination of all natural knowledge to the truths of the faith. In other words, theology is the primary if not the exclusive integrating course in the Catholic curriculum.

If the proper relationship between the philosophic arts and sciences and theology is not presented in the classroom, especially at the college level, there is little chance of the students' discovering it on their own. And if they do not establish the intellectual relationship between social science and theology in their own minds, there is little chance of a working connection in their practical lives. Yet "the true Christian, product of Christian education, is the supernatural man who thinks, judges and acts constantly and consistently in accordance with right reason illumined by the supernatural light of the example and teaching of Christ."[3]

Hence the problem of subordinating social science to, and coordinating social science with theology is not an artificial make-believe. Neither is it easily resolved, for it means as always the brick-and-mortar work of maintaining the legitimate autonomy of reason and faith, while ordering the one to the other. But during the last hundred years an unseemly complication has become evident. Up until a century ago, there had always been general agreement among Catholic scholars on the nature and division of the social sciences. But since that time the social sciences have expanded as disciplines distinct from moral philosophy. And to a large extent Catholic colleges and universities have accepted this rupture, though it began and prospers in an atmosphere quite alien to reason as illumined by faith.

Since little profit can be gained from an intellectual discussion unless there is agreement at the outset about what is being discussed, it is necessary to begin this study with a review of the nature and division of the social sciences. Once the "whatness" and its elements are clear, then it will be possible to take up firmly the proper task at hand, namely, consideration of the relationship between the social sciences and theology. Then the sapiential functions of theology—using, ordering and judging all the philosophic arts and sciences—will be employed to analyze this kinship under two aspects: the contribution of social science to theology, and the contribution of theology to social science.

Nature and Division of the Social Sciences

The difficulty is a double trouble. Not only is there disagreement among Catholics about the unity or disunity of social science and moral philosophy, but even worse, the traditional notion and division of moral philosophy itself has been largely ignored or lost. Therefore, this part of our study will be divided into two major sections. The first will consider leading opinions about the twofold disagreement. The second will examine these in view of the traditional Aristotelian-Thomistic teaching on the nature and division of the social sciences.

With respect to the first problem, the relation of social science and moral philosophy, it should be noted that Catholic writers during the past three decades have generally accepted sociology and other such disciplines as new and distinctive sciences with formal objects or methodologies different from those of moral philosophy.[4] Though these opinions differ markedly, they may be grouped into two general classes:

1) The social sciences are normative (valuative, practical) sciences as is moral philosophy; but they differ from moral philosophy in method. Moral philosophy is obviously *philosophical* in method, dealing with certain and universal moral principles arrived at by way of philosophical analysis, while the social sciences are only probable, descriptive, dealing with empirical phenomena, proximate causes, etc.

2) The social sciences are not normative but completely free of value judgments. They are not about what ought to be; they are about what is. They are strictly empirical in their method and merely seek to build up a theory based on suitable hypotheses verified empirically.

The latter opinion offers one practical advantage: it parallels the general position of non-Catholic social scientists, who by and large believe that a normative science is a contradiction in terms, since value judgments necessarily are subjective, while science is, at least in aim, rigidly objective. The former view, however, continues to appeal to those Catholics (and they are probably many) who are interested in social study mainly because they want to carry the Catholic social movement into the market place.

Among the opinions on the nature and division of moral philosophy, the first three concern the nature of moral philosophy and the latter two its internal division.

1) Many Catholic teachers today handle moral philosophy as though it were a speculative discipline, a kind of "applied metaphysics." This conception is totally foreign to the view of St. Thomas.[5]

2) There is a twofold divorce of moral philosophy from the concrete, factual world of social life. On the one hand, its principles are derived as metaphysical abstractions with little or no empirical verification. And what is even more detrimental to ethics as a practical science is that the extension of these principles to concrete circumstances is often pitifully attempted.

The reason? Such extension again depends upon factual data and investigations.[6]

3) Theological problems and solutions often creep into ethics. The natural and supernatural are mixed, and moral theology is thereby confused with moral philosphy. Some, such as Maritain and his followers, do this by design since they hold that an adequate moral philosophy depends on truths of faith.[7]

4) Moral philosophy is either taught as a single science or arbitrarily divided into general and special ethics. The traditional division into three specifically distinct sciences—monastics, domestics and politics—is either totally ignored or mentioned only in passing.

5) The architectonic nature of politics (the ethics of civil society) as the principal moral science and practical wisdom has been almost irretrievably lost. Theological fears about the dignity of the individual, the rights of families and the freedom of the Church confronted with totalitarianism and socialism have perhaps been largely responsible. But conceiving ethics solely from an individualistic point of view has destroyed the balanced view of St. Thomas.[8]

Critique of Preceding Opinions

With respect to the opinions on the first problem, the relation between social science and moral philosophy, it may be pointed out, first of all, that the opinions seem essentially eclectic; they represent an attempt to accept uncritically the social sciences as developed by non-Catholics much influenced by positivism. Catholic philosophy is constructed on different ground, and its fundamental principles are opposed to many dogmas of modern positivistic science. This is why Catholics have to teach these courses as divorced from moral philosophy, leaving almost all basic normative questions and judgments to ethics or religion courses. While it is true that much useful and necessary information is imparted to the students in this manner, the seeds of compromise between moral values and social considerations have been sown, often to bear the fruit of skepticism in later life. Further, a scientific approach to the matter at hand demands that eclecticism be abandoned in favor of a profound critique based on philosophic principles. Only then can that which is worthwhile be sifted from positivistic errors; only then can the proper relation of social science to moral philosophy be determined.[9]

Secondly, it is not necessary to propose a detailed solution to the serious difficulties raised by these opinions. The unity of social science and moral philosophy can easily be vindicated by the Aristotelian-Thomistic principles of distinguishing sciences, not by mere differences in methodology, but by formal objects or subjects and first principles.

Those who hold that the social sciences are normative, but are divided by certitude and methods from moral philosophy, are actually making a material division within one science, not a specific distinction. Some of them attempt to show that social science has a different formal object from that of ethics, but this could be true only if there were a difference in degree of abstraction. Moral philosophy and social science do not differ in degree of abstraction, since both are in the first degree.[10] What is more, great confusion sets in when the principle of specification proper to speculative knowledge (i.e., the degree of abstraction) is extended to the classification of practical sciences, to which it is inappropriate.

It is likewise necessary to exclude the notion that social science is distinguished formally from moral science because it is empirical, deals with mere phenomena, or proximate causes, or that it is not certain. St. Thomas explicitly held that moral philosophy is characterized by these same traits.[11] In moral philosophy the general principles are universal, certain and necessary, but the science as a whole deals with truths which are speculatively uncertain, contingent and even singular.[12] For example, domestics deals not only with proving that monogamy is the best form of family, but also with discussing the particular forms the monogamous family takes in different periods of history and under various kinds of government and culture. It also gets down to the harassed family in twentieth century U.S.A., and even to a particular family and its troubles.

The modern social scientist uses statistics, questionnaires, surveys, typologies, case studies, etc., to obtain a more objective view of particular facts. This frees his science from subjective elements which, of course, threaten all sciences, but especially those sciences that study human behavior. These special methods of obtaining facts often make a modern social science text look very different from the usual scholastic manual of moral philosophy. Differences in method, however, are not essential: they do not specify. Moral philosophy is empirical in its beginning since it starts from general facts which can be objectively ascertained without the need of special fact-finding methods, e.g., that men need to eat and sleep, that men talk and reason, etc. As it descends to particular premises, the methods invented by modern investigators become more useful and necessary if solid objectivity is to be maintained. But moral philosophy does not fade into another science as investigative methods enter in.

Concerning the opinions on the nature and division of moral philosophy, much has already been said about the nature and division of moral philosophy according to Aristotle and St. Thomas. Therefore, it will be enough to consider briefly the remaining difficulties before proceeding to the reciprocal relationships between theology and social science.

The first two opinions look upon moral philosophy as a speculative science that does not get to concrete facts and practical detail. Yet if the social or moral sciences were speculative, they should have a speculative object. But all agree that they deal in human behavior. Now the science that considers human behavior speculatively is psychology (a part of the science of nature). Some would say that psychology treats of the individual, while social science treats of society. But this is not entirely true, since psychology studies man and all his properties, including his social nature, just as biology treats not only the individual bee and goose but hives and gaggles as well.[13]

It is clear to all that the modern social sciences are not merely psychology. Speculative sciences, like psychology, are sciences in the strict sense. In human behavior there is something *necessary* and *universal*, namely, what belongs to man by nature, and it is this that psychology captures. Much of human behavior, however, is not fixed by nature, but is the result of man's free choice and of historical developments, custom and chance. This is the precise aspect of human behavior that the social sciences are concerned with, human cultures and their institutions. These are not universal and necessary but contingent, and hence they cannot be the object of speculative science. On the other hand, they are the proper matter of the practical sciences, since these sciences have as their object the contingent that can be produced by human choice.[14]

The confusion of moral philosophy with moral theology must likewise be rejected if the true nature of the social sciences is to be grasped. Though the theory of Jacques Maritain subalternating moral philosophy to moral theology has become popular, it destroys the true relationship between faith and reason. For to hold that moral philosophy must accept certain premises on human faith from theology is to destroy its rightful dignity and autonomy as a natural science.[15] It is like saying that grace destroys nature. Father Ramírez, O.P., long ago showed by arguments which have never been refuted that such a conception reduces moral philosophy to theology.

Maritain is certainly correct in saying that in man's present condition moral philosophy is not a sufficient and adequate guide to action, since man in fact must attain a supernatural end or he will miss even his natural end. But although it is not an adequate guide absolutely speaking, it is adequate to direct human action insofar as this action must be submitted to the natural law. And that is all that is claimed for moral philosophy.

Despite the modern tendency to reduce moral philosophy to a single science or divide it into general and special ethics, the threefold division of Aristotle and St. Thomas into monastics, domestics and politics remains unshaken today. The sciences of individual life, of the family and of societies wider than the family cannot be reduced to a single science *because each has its own proper problems and proper control.* The first guides the individual in the management of his own life. The second guides the father in the management of the family which is his natural responsibility. The last guides the governors of a perfect society over which they have been placed by the consent of the governed.

Nor is general ethics a distinct science in its own right, but only that part common to all three of the moral sciences which are then artificially grouped as special ethics. Since all the moral sciences treat of human acts, but differ as to the complete attainment of the proper end of individual, family and society, and as to the special acts which are means to this completion, it is convenient to deal at the outset with the nature of human acts in general, and it is usual to place this at the beginning of individual ethics (Aristotle, *Nicomachean Ethics,* Bk. I-III, St. Thomas Aquinas, *Summa,* I-II). This treatise is more theoretical than the rest of ethics, and it deals with principles borrowed from psychology. But it does not consider them merely theoretically, but from the very outset views them only as they will be helpful in guiding practical judgment. Thus it begins with a study of the *end* of human acts, not merely as the final cause of human nature, but as the principle of moral decision, as that which man *ought* to seek.

Of the three moral or prudential sciences, politics is first in dignity, broadest in scope, and most important in application. Traditionally the practical sciences were called "architectonic" to emphasize their distinction and connection. All three are specifically distinct, but monastics and domestics are ordered to politics as the incomplete to that which is complete and perfect in the study of man's pursuit of happiness. Only that science which considers man as he pursues happiness in some perfect society has the final and complete view of human perfection. Therefore, politics is rightly understood as practical wisdom, "first philosophy" among the practical sciences. As a consequence it judges, orders and uses the lesser prudential sciences from its more lofty station. On the other hand, a good understanding of monastics and domestics is basic to an adequate appreciation of politics, since the common good of a nation is the completion and perfection of the same human happiness that man seeks as an individual and as a member of a family.

Surely political society does not exist to suppress individual rights, familial privileges or ecclesiastical jurisdiction. On the contrary, individuals, domestic units and lesser communities band together to form a larger society, a perfect society which has for its common good complete and perfect happiness. Within this great society there are many lesser social groups that have their proper functions, adding to the perfections of man's beatitude. Such societies as racial and cultural groups, classes, political parties, local and regional communities, economic and educational organizations, all have a part to play in man's life as a political animal. However, their contribution to happiness is studied as part of political science, the science of the civil society, since all is ordered to the same essential goal, *perfect* human happiness. Therefore they do not constitute specifically distinct social sciences. Heinrich Rommen has stated this well:

> Politics is and remains a part of the moral universe. For it is inexcusable to view politics merely as the technique or art of achieving and retaining social power for some selfish end through the skillful exploitation of human weaknesses, by deceit or by terrorist methods. Politics is rather the great architectonic art by which men build the institutions and protective forms of their individual and communal life for a more perfect realization of the good life. Its main function is to establish an order and unity of co-operation among free persons and free associations of persons in such a way that these, while they freely pursue their individual and group interests, are nevertheless so co-ordinated that they realize at the same time the common good under the rule of law.[16]

It comes down to this: the social sciences are nothing but moral philosophy. This is true even though at present social scientists tend to study only part of the field, while they neglect its more general and certain theoretical principles. For these they attempt to substitute hypotheses and to pursue a speculative method modeled after that of physics or psychology. Underlying this is the positivistic and deterministic denial of human freedom, or at the very least a denial that human freedom can be considered a fact of the scientific order.

These sciences are practical (although they borrow a theoretical knowledge of human nature from psychology) because they are concerned with studying the means to achieve individual, familial and public happiness. As practical sciences they do not remain in a cloud of generalities but descend to particular circumstances, especially to here-and-now American society, but also to other societies in the past and present which give additional experience for judging what to do today. Their method is empirical (as must be the method of every human science) for both the general and the special principles. Because they deal with contingent historical facts as well as universal ones, however, they must develop special methods of uncovering these hard-to-come-by facts, and they must frequently be content with rough generalizations and probabilities.

The multiplicity of names given today to the social sciences can be reduced to three specifically distinct disciplines or their parts. And yet, despite the formal distinctions between the practical sciences, there remains a very close dependence and relationship among them. For that which is essentially imperfect in an ordered whole is necessarily directed to that which is perfect in the same genus. Hence in the sciences concerned with human happiness, monastics is essentially ordered to domestics, and it, in turn, reaches its perfection only in and through politics. That is why among the prudential sciences politics is called practical wisdom; and that is why the moral sciences are architectonic in nature. Only through the breadth of political wisdom do the lesser practical sciences of domestics and monastics attain their final order and completion. This is their perfection.

In addition to these three social sciences three auxiliary disciplines may be added: 1) *history*, which is not a distinct science, but a part of the fact-gathering needed by moral sciences, especially by politics, the science of civil society; 2) *economics*, considered not as a moral science but as a technology (art) giving a general direction to the other technologies, used as a special instrument of the social sciences; 3) *rhetoric* (propaganda, etc.) which is the proper liberal art of the social sciences, since rule over human beings is a rational rule normally conducted by persuasion, rather than by force.[17]

Theology

Theology is a "discursive wisdom exercised under the light of divine revelation on every truth revealed by God either immediately and formally or mediately and virtually."[18] As a discursive wisdom theology has a fourfold potestative function; it can be considered: 1) in relation to its object; 2) in relation to its subject; 3) in its own internal ordination (*in ordine ad se ipsam*); or 4) in relation to the other sciences.[19] As far as the first two functions are concerned, moral philosophy is the natural counterpart of moral theology, because the social sciences deal with much the same matter as moral theology, but from a natural point of view. In working out the third function of determining its own nature, division, properties and method, moral theology is greatly aided by a ready knowledge of the nature, division and method of social science. But it is the fourth sapiential function of *using, ordering* and *judging* the other sciences that enables the moral theologian to determine more accurately the nature and method of his own discipline as well as to understand, explain and defend revealed moral truths. When the social sciences are scientifically organized and integrated according to their own proper principles and "lights," then, and only then, does theology find in them its friend and handmaid. The Aristotelian-Thomistic presentation of social science is such an integrated organization.

The mutual relationship of theology and social science will be treated under two titles, "The Contribution of the Social Sciences to Theology," and "The Contribution of Theology to the Social Sciences." In the first title there will be two parts, according as the moral theologian *uses* social science to explore the nature and method of moral theology, and secondly, as he uses it to unfold the object of his study, revealed moral truths. Under the second title the double role of *judging* and *ordering* social science will be considered.

The Social Sciences and Theology

Moral theology uses social science in regard to its own internal ordination, first of all. This is evident when we consider its nature and distinction. As wisdom, theology, of course, can look to no higher science to determine its nature, division, properties and method. Hence it must perform this basic task itself, using whatever tools are at hand. The first tendency would be to look up to God for guidance, since theology is radicated in faith; but God has not revealed a *science* of theology, he revealed the truths of salvation to be held by the simple assent of faith. Therefore, the theologian must look down to the natural order for his necessary instruments. And so the moral theologian looks to moral philosophy for whatever aid it can give him in structuring his own endeavor.

The first thing to be avoided is a blending or confusion of moral theology and social science into one course, "Christian Ethics." Each of these disciplines has its formally distinct light, first principles and proper subject matter. Therefore, moral theology must respect the rightful autonomy of social science to proceed according to its own way. There is no room for theological imperialism in any curriculum, but there is still less room for animosity or open war between theology and social science. Even as nature must be quick and ready to serve grace, so too social science must be quick and ready to serve theology.

Sometimes for reasons of practical expediency Catholic colleges teach only moral theology and omit moral philosophy as a separate subject. This can be done to relieve a crowded schedule, since in fact the moral theologian must incorporate most of moral philosophy into his science. But the procedure is far from ideal, since it leaves the student without an understanding of how to establish the conclusions of moral philosophy in their own right.[20] This understanding is important for apologetic reasons, since Catholics living in a secularist society must be able to defend their moral judgments by natural law arguments, without reference to the faith.

Thus ideally a college curriculum would contain for all students both moral theology and the three moral sciences, along with history, rhetoric and economics. If compression is a must, the best policy is probably to omit individual ethics, leaving its matter to the moral theology course, but to retain a course in social ethics. The reason for this is given by St. Thomas himself, when he says in the *Summa Theologiae* that he will omit discussion of the political states of life because these are ordered to the temporal good which is only indirectly the concern of the theologian.[21]

But the social sciences also have an important contribution to make to theological methodology. Moral theology, like moral philosophy, must descend to particulars if it is truly to serve its function as a practical wisdom. But revelation does not supply us with a knowledge of the circumstances in which man must live. Therefore, the moral theologian must reach down to the natural order for the concrete application of these principles to the details of secular life. This is the special importance of the social sciences, that they help the layman especially to bridge the gap between Christian ideals and current situations. Because many have not seen how to close this gap, they have concluded that the general principles are irrelevant and have succumbed to a sort of "situation ethics."

The theologian, then, must make use of the method and content of social science if he is going to make his moral theology course more practical.

In the area of general moral principles the theologian should make use of the modern techniques and data of psychology and of physical and cultural anthropology. In the first part of the second part of the *Summa Theologiae,* St. Thomas gives a marvelous analysis of the nature of human moral behavior and of its psychological principles. He did not merely draw his analysis from an abstract definition of man. Greek, Roman and Christian moralists had studied man acutely; they had observed all types and characters and their behavior in a variety of social situations. The practical work of rhetoricians in seeking to influence audiences, of historians in pondering on the course of human events, of politicians in breeding their successes and failures, of poets in drawing life-like representations of human nature, of spiritual guides in directing consciences, of secular and monastic legislators in designing social reform—all of these entered into the materials St. Thomas used. In the habit of those days, he presented conclusions without documentation of the modern type, but if St. Thomas had explicitly listed the sources of his observations, present day scholars would be astounded at their tremendous bulk.

Needless to say, since his time the methods of gathering and analyzing data have been highly elaborated. First of all the method of history was refined, with its analysis of sources, their comparison and synthesis. Then developed the archaeological techniques of digging up the past, reconstructing it and dating it, and the anthropological techniques of studying existing primitive cultures. The methods of culture and social geography have expanded beyond foreseeing. Sociological techniques, the use of case studies, intensive descriptions of typical communities, statistical findings, sociograms, etc., have developed and are still unfolding. All of these are aimed at doing in an extensive and precise way what was formerly done by the gross observation and reflection of men of affairs, travelers or politicians. These less formal methods have not become useless or obsolete. Indeed, the refined methods must themselves be controlled by ordinary experience if they are to be really significant and full of genuine insight.[22]

The theologian must make use of all he can to confirm and refine his general analysis of human behavior. Such works as Talcott Parsons and E. A. Shils, *Toward a General Theory of Action* (Cambridge, Mass.: Harvard U. Press, 1951), or Robert K. Merton, *Social Theory and Social Structure* (Glencoe, Ill.: The Free Press, 1949), or David Bidney, *Theoretical Anthropology* (New York: Columbia U. Press, 1953), will enable him to show that the traditional analysis is essentially sound, but that it requires certain refinements and precautions.[23]

Though the moral theologian must descend to concrete detail and practical problems, he should not make the mistake of thinking that Christian prudence can be taught in class by merely studying what it is about. It must be learned by Christian living. Thus the theologian as classroom teacher is principally concerned with helping the student to grasp the broad and basic principles of Christian morality, and showing him how to apply them to particular problems. The course must never become mere casuistry. Yet the broad principles must always be seen as having relevancy to actual Christian decision. For this reason the moral theologian and the social scientist must be persons of some genuine social experience, and not mere theoreticians. On the other hand, *he* should not fall into the errors of empiricism and pragmatism so common among American sociologists who sometimes act as if mere "fact gathering" and "problem solving" without theoretical foundation are the goals of their science.

The moral theologian should not expect his students to solve world problems, for they lack mature experience. He should realize Aristotle's warning that teaching ethics to the young cannot be perfect; it is only a beginning.[24] But he should also remember that if it is taught well, it is a right beginning.

In the second place, moral theology uses social science to understand, defend and explain the object of its study, revealed moral truths. The theologian must use all means available to handle supernatural truths as best he can and render them applicable to modern life. In doing this he must call on sociologists, social scientists and political theoreticians to continue their researches, and he must keep them on a sound basis of general moral theory. Only when modern social science is reintegrated with moral philosophy can monastics, domestics and politics serve their noblest function as "handmaids" of theology.

In the field of individual ethics (*monastics*), perhaps the most significant advances have been in a deepened understanding of human psychology. Recent biological and psychoanalytical understanding of man has brought to the fore the limitations of human responsibility and the subconscious factors that underlie human decisions. The step-by-step development to human maturity and the various psychotic and neurotic states which hinder this development are better known today than ever before.[25]

The moral theologian is gradually incorporating this material into his own outline, and correcting some of the scientific interpretations in the light of his deeper understanding of man, but it is important for him to realize that "depth psychology" is not really a study of the depths of human nature, but rather of its outer surface. The real depth of human nature is the spiritual core, his intellect and will, in which grace first does its work. From this core of spiritual health life must spread out to heal the libidinal surface of man. How false is the Freudian picture which interprets rationality as the mask, and animality as the core of human nature!

In the field of family ethics (*domestics*), the moral theologian must also make use of the modern knowledge of sexual life, of the male and female personalities, and especially of child development and education.[26] He must rid himself of certain anti-feminist and puritanical predilections of the past. Traditional manuals in familial ethics have always stressed the subordination of wife to husband. The new "freedoms" of women are frequently considered only negatively as threatening a mother's total dedication to her family. On the other hand, modern texts in the sociology of domestic life tend to equate wife and husband in authority and dignity within the family. They place excessive emphasis on "emancipation" without regard for household unity. A more balanced view would maintain the proper subjection of wife to husband and still preserve her dignity, freedom and queenly role within the family as well as in civil society.

He must also recognize that the family, although rooted in nature, has many determinations which are of a cultural and historical character. They vary from place to place and time to time, and they admit of great improvement.[27] Furthermore, he must see that the family is dependent on economic and social circumstances. Since the Industrial Revolution, domestic life in most Western countries has been pared of all but the absolutely essential functions. The number of children is often deliberately restricted. Intellectual formation in the arts and sciences is delegated to the school. Cultural life is centered outside the family, in community or regional circles. Most families no longer are economic units of productivity, though they remain economic units in consumption. All this the moral theologian must reflect when he preaches and writes about marriage and family problems.

A negative or romantic approach to the family must be displaced by a positive Christian realism based on modern social studies. At many periods in history the unity and stability of married life has been shaken, but few ages have known so rapid, so complete and so devastating a disintegration as has been taking place in Western nations since 1900. As the matrimonial bond relaxes and the importance of family life diminishes in society, there is a corresponding growth in the difficulties of governing domestic life. "Emancipation" has wreaked havoc, leaving the husband without a wife, the children without a mother, and the home without a heart. The rising problems of juvenile delinquency highlight the general breakdown of parental authority, especially of the authority of the father. To have practical effect, moral theology needs to use all these data on the pathology of married life today.

For the field of *politics* the theologian finds many uses, but he is not furnished with as much traditional guidance as in the other two moral sciences. This is largely due to the failure to appreciate politics as the architectonic social science which alone considers man's total pursuit of complete human happiness. The theologian must realize that the operational essence of every nation is made up of two interacting elements, social structure and public power. The social structure or organism is extremely heterogeneous and complex. Public power, on the other hand, is often streamlined and concentrated in the hands of a monarch or of a power elite. The well-being of each nation is determined by the proper relationship of these material and formal elements as ordered to the common good.

Recent social encyclicals have marked the general problems of the social organism or ordered element in society. First of all, the theologian must remember that the multiplicity of "social sciences" which today consider the various groups within the social organism are merely material divisions of one part of politics. These groups begin their range from the most natural societies—families and civil communities (local and regional). The intellectual, moral, medical, economic and recreational pursuits of citizens also form bases for distinct associations, "ordines," to promote and defend their proper ends, which are aspects of the one great common good. Along with and intermingled with these are classes, racial and cultural groups, plus a host of completely voluntary societies.

Then the theologian must strive to understand the legitimate integrity and autonomy of these diverse social groups. Social authority by nature belongs not only to government but to other social groups. In other words, society is by nature *pluralistic.*[28] Each of the *ordines* in society, which are organized along occupational lines, has its proper rights and duties which the theologian must trace in a general way while referring to sociology for a detailed analysis of the here-and-now. The restoration and promotion of these corporative orders in their distinct functions is the chief task of social reform today. It is also necessary to show against communism and equalitarianism that the class structure of society is natural, that co-operation between classes is necessary, and that the proper dignity of all men of every race and cultural group must be preserved.

Equally difficult problems concern the ordering element in society. This is the supreme social authority. Despite its diversity in function and complexity in structure, it forms an organized whole and is rightfully called the political organism. Here again such modern courses as "political theory," "government" or "public administration" are merely material divisions of the other part of politics. While it is a grave error to mistake the study of governments as the whole study of society, it would be equally a blunder to ignore it. Here again the moral theologian has been given great help and guidance by recent papal documents.

These documents have shown, first of all, that government is natural and good, that there are various legitimate forms of government, that the role of society is not merely military or economic but chiefly intellectual and moral. Secondly, they have shown that the totalitarian, socialistic, statist and theocratic doctrines of society are false. By distinguishing the principal and subsidiary functions of the state, governments are prevented from becoming omnipotent or omni-competent. Finally, the encyclicals have clarified and given direction to the problems of peace and international organization.

In all this the theologian cannot be content merely to discuss abstract principles. Neither can he properly enter the arena of politics itself. Rather, he must show the student how to apply Christian prudence concretely to solve these problems in lay social life.[29] Finally, he must understand well the fact that the political and social organisms provide him with the analogues he needs to unfold the nature of the Church.

The moral theologian must also show his appreciation of the art of economics and the other useful arts in solving social problems. He must know the importance of rhetoric and other arts of communication in promoting social debate and leadership. He must likewise show the student that, although in the twentieth century the members of Christ's body are faced with unique and special circumstances, they can be assisted in facing their world by a knowledge of the history of the past. Seeing history with supernatural eyes, he sees it as a promise of future triumph.

Theology and the Social Sciences

Once the nature of social science has been surely established and its usefulness to moral theology considered, one must turn to theology's contribution to social science. This is the work of *ordering* and *judging*. The social scientist needs this help, since the study of human conduct and history in the light of unaided reason ultimately leads to mysteries insoluble. To this pursuit theology will bring a guiding hand to put a stop to errors (as in the encyclicals on socialism, pacificism, marriage, etc.), and an ordering direction to indicate the deeper sense of human life and the wonderful resources to be found in grace and in the sacraments. Therefore, this section will have four major divisions according as theology orders and judges monastics, domestics and politics from a supernatural point of view and as it orders history in a special way.

Aristotle showed that the natural goal of man is the contemplation of God as he is knowable through nature. He also showed that by nature all men are born to assist each other in living a life according to reason. Because he is a complex creature of body and soul, the human being finds this effort difficult. Within himself he sees the struggle of soul and spirit. Within himself he suffers limitations in his prudence.[30] Yet, since the human mind can discover that by nature men ought to love God above all things, and nature is not vain, men for the most part ought to attain to this goal. This they cannot do by their unaided effort, but only by the special providence of God.[31] Hence the paradox of Job and all who have pondered on the human condition—providence should have brought most men to happiness, but the more that history is studied the more one sees man's abysmal failure.

Moral philosophy concludes that man's essential happiness is spiritual. In fact he has not reached it, and he seems to be incapable of reaching it. To this conclusion, moral theology has a profound response in man's creation in grace, the fall of man, and his elevation through redemption. Man had abandoned God, but God has not abandoned him. Man must return to the source from which he came, not merely in a natural way, but in a supernatural way. This answer must not be adulterated into empty gnostic symbolism. The fall is not merely the idea that man is a limited creature, nor is his superb redemption simply an awakening of his own condition.[32] The golden age of innocence, the disobedience and redemptive suffering are historic facts. They originated not in nature, nor in any metaphysical requirement of nature, but in the generosity of God conferring supernatural destiny.

The moral theologian dealing with the individual must especially show that charity is the source of Catholic morality. It liberates the human person from enslavement to taboo and inhibition, and it makes him free to follow the law of his true nature and supernature which are essentially ordered to God and neighbor.

St. Thomas in the *Summa Theologiae* does not end his treatment of morals with the general consideration of virtues and vices (I-II). Nor does he end it with the virtues and vices in particular (II-II), nor even with the states of life and the duties of various individuals within a functional society. He pushes on from this extension to the concrete historical consideration of the perfect life of the perfect man. Jesus Christ is the historical exemplar and personification of the virtuous life. Then St. Thomas indicates how in the history of the Church (treatises on the sacraments and the last end) the model of Jesus Christ must be reflected in all varieties of times and places. The moral theologian must evince a sense of history, and develop it even further than St. Thomas was able to do.

Since morality is "what a good man does," the moral theologian must seek ever more concrete criteria of personal and social morality in the study of truly good men and truly good institutions. These are to be found in their perfection solely in the Church. Only a sociologist who has considered the lives of the saints, or who has witnessed a zealous religious community or a fervent parish can have a deep appreciation of what human nature is at its best. The sociologist who takes his norm from the primitive, from the ignorant peasant, from the corrupted urban dweller, or from the harlot is like a physician who attempts a cure without ever having known a healthy man.

Theology and Domestics

Families, no less than individuals and societies, have frequently fallen into slavery, idolatry or the stultifying pursuit of the pleasures of the flesh as the goal of life. Even the most spiritual of pagan minds fell short of an accurate notion of God, creation, the soul and the moral law. Everywhere men have been bent on war, conquest, material gain, rather than on the development of virtue in their families and the direction of those families to the worship of God. This is the mystery of human life, and it does not receive any explanation in the human order, except the illusory promises of future bliss "after the revolution" or some similar "reform."[33] If only the children of men could be brought up in a really human way through virtuous family living!

Taking account of original sin on the one hand and the sacramental holiness of marriage on the other, the theologian must seek to restore the dignity of the woman and the child, the true authority of the father, and the rights of parents over children. In all this, the theologian needs to stress the sacramental mystery of marriage—that just as there is only one Christ and one Church found in an indissoluble union so there must be only one man and one woman permanently united. At the same time he must maintain the great superiority of consecrated virginity and celibacy, for persons who live these dedications more freely and completely contemplate the things of God. The theologian has to purify modern knowledge of its deep confusions about the ends and means of family life and about their dignity.

Theology and Politics

Man's political activity is indeed an enigma. For when it is said that man by nature is a social animal, this most properly means that he is the political animal of civil society. Here and here alone can "homo humanus" hope to find the fulness of earthly happiness. Yet, historically speaking, it is in civil society that man's rightful freedoms have been most frequently denied by totalitarianism. Nor is this tendency in political thought defunct today—Fascism, Nazism and Communism are its eloquent witnesses. Somehow the human person seems natively aware that something of the divine has been conferred on the state. To achieve harmonious balance between the state's rightful sovereignty and the rights and privileges of individuals and families is all but impossible when left to natural genius alone.

Today's theologian must expand the treatise on the states of life to deal with the theological involvements of government. He will still be unconcerned with the particular structures of government, but he must deal with Church-state relations, and with the various duties of rulers as these relate to the common good of the Church.[34]

The theologian is able to take social philosophy (which like economics is sometimes called a "dismal science") and show that the world of human society is tragic, but not meaningless. For he can show that in the Church is realized the perfect model of the social order. The Church should inspire the merely human social orders, although it may not be copied mechanically. The social experience of the Church is rich indeed, and modern sociology will learn a lesson by the study of ecclesiastical institutions in their coming and their going.[35] Here the good and the bad are seen intensified (*corruptio optimi pessima*). Hence, "religious sociology" denotes: 1) a study of religion as the most important single social institution (Dawson, Toynbee); 2) a study of ecclesiastical institutions as most instructive examples and models; 3) a study of existing social conditions in the Church (parish sociology, mission sociology, etc.), so as to assist her in her practical decisions.[36]

Theology and History

The historian has difficulty in making sense out of history; the pieces never quite fit and the story is never quite finished. But the theologian can perceive it in the light of sacred history. The theologian, then, should take what the student has learned in history classes and put it into relief against the background of sacred history, not only the Old Testament from Adam to Christ, but the New Testament, which shows the outline of history from the First to the Second Coming. This relating of history known naturally to history known supernaturally does not distort human history but gives it its fullest meaning.

In particular, the theologian will prevent the historian from falling into errors due to the introduction of false philosophies of history (evolution, dialectical materialism, etc.), and will keep him humble in the conviction that the pattern of human history cannot be humanly woven but only guessed at from the human point of view. The true pattern belongs to supernatural destiny.[37]

Conclusion

Thus the burden of theology as it bears on social science is light and fitting; social science realizes its highest goal in serving the faith. Negatively, theology will keep the social scientist from erroneous conceptions of human nature; positively, it will show him the practical ideal of human personality and society, to which he can contribute on the natural plane by his observations and analyses. In all this, the theologian has a heavy and continuing task; but he should set his face to its accomplishment.

Footnotes to Study 9

[1]Pope Pius XI, encyclical *Divini Illius Magistri* (On the Christian Education of Youth), rev. trans. (New York: The America Press, 1936), 24.

[2]*Ibid.*, 25-26. (Italics added.)

[3]*Ibid.*, 31.

[4]For a survey of current views among Catholics, see Sister Miriam Lynch, O.S.U., "Communication between Philosophers and Sociologists," *American Catholic Sociological Review*, XIX (1958), 290-309; Herbert Johnston, "The Social and Moral Sciences," *Catholic Educational Review*, XVIII (1957), 452-463, reprinted and enlarged in Leo R. Ward, *Ethics and the Social Sciences* (Notre Dame: U. of Notre Dame Press, 1959), which also contains other material by a variety of authors on the same topic; and Paul Hanly Furfey, *The Scope and Method of Sociology: A Metasociological Treatise* (New York: Harper, 1953). For a survey of current views among non-Catholics see Howard Becker and Alvin Boskoff, ed., *Modern Sociological Theory in Continuity and Change* (New York: Dryden Press, 1957).

[5]"The philosophy of morality is *in itself*, a speculative, intellectual habit; it belongs to the speculative intellect; it seeks universal truths. On the other hand, by reason of its ultimate purpose, which is to help man live a good life, it can be viewed as a practical science. It is, therefore, both speculative and practical; *speculative in itself, practical in its purpose* and application." Henri Renard, S.J., *The Philosophy of Morality* (Milwaukee: Bruce, 1953), 6. St. Thomas (*In Decem Libros Ethicorum Aristotelis ad Nicomachum Expositio*, I, lect. 1 and 2, nn. 1-31 [Spiazzi ed.]) clearly classes ethics as a science of the practical intellect along with art, and repeats this explicitly in the proemium of the commentary on the *Politics* (Spiazzi ed., nn. 1 ff.). Similarly the well-known seminary text of Joseph Gredt, O.S.B., *Elementa Philosophiae Aristotelico-Thomisticae,* 7th ed., (Freiburg: Herder and Co., 1937), I, 85; Thomas J. Higgins, S.J., *Man as Man, the Science and Art of Ethics,* rev. ed. (Milwaukee: Bruce, 1958), 9: "Ethics is a *philosophic* science, first, because it treats of the ultimate principles of conduct. To be a part of philosophy, or even a science at all, ethics must rest on metaphysics, the science of being-in-general. This is the ultimate science of self-evident principles which tests and validates the principles and postulates of all sciences. Without a grounding in metaphysics no science is properly anchored in reality and may prove to be a delusion. Once ethics, by means of metaphysics, shows that it is rooted in the bedrock of reality, then it becomes the metaphysics of the human and social sciences." Vernon Bourke, *Ethics* (New York:

Macmillan, 1951), 15, also accepts this notion: "Hence the existence of God, the immortality of the soul, and the freedom of man are to be used in Thomistic ethics. The ethician need not try to prove them; he takes them over from metaphysics." Thus these two last authors make ethics strictly subalternate to metaphysics by reason of the principles which it borrows, a conclusion which cannot be reconciled with St. Thomas' insistence that ethics can be learned *before* metaphysics. Cf. *In Decem Libros Aristotelis ad Nicomachum Expositio,* VI, lect. 7, n. 1211 (Spiazzi), *proemium* to the *Commentaria in Librum De Causis,* etc.

[6]Thus Bourke, *op. cit.,* 13 f., assures us that the method of ethics rests on metaphysics and not on empirical methods, such as are used by social scientists. Higgins, *op. cit.,* 7, describes the method of ethics (and of all of philosophy) as "deduction from analytic concepts."

[7]See Bourke, *op. cit.,* 8-13, who states the arguments pro and con, but who seems to favor Maritain's solution. There are many who follow Maritain's position implicitly by ordering ethics according to the theological plan of the second part of St. Thomas' *Summa.*

[8]None of the texts referred to recognizes the architectonic character of politics. There is a new text in manuscript form (*Social Ethics: An Introduction to the Social Sciences,* by the authors of this article) which attempts a thorough going return to the true nature of politics as prudential wisdom.

[9]For the positivistic origins of the modern "social sciences" see Simon Deploige, *The Conflict between Ethics and Sociology,* trans. by C. C. Miltner (St. Louis: Herder, 1936).

[10]The view proposed by some (see Jacques Maritain, *Degrees of Knowledge,* trans. by Gerald B. Phelan [New York: Charles Scribner's Sons, 1959], 178, note 1) that there are several levels in the first degree of abstraction is untenable. Maritain cites John of St. Thomas, *Cursus Philosophicus,* I, Log. ii, q. 27, a. 1, to show that medicine differs from the philosophy of nature in abstraction. What this passage proves is that practical knowledge is only scientific *secundum quid,* according to what is theoretical in it, and these theoretical principles are in the first degree of abstraction; but according to what is strictly practical in it, practical knowledge deals with the singular contingent which is *not abstract at all,* but an *experimentum* known by the particular reason (*vis cogitativa*). In this respect it is not scientific, nor classifiable as a science, but prudential or technical and hence to be classified not as a science according to degrees of abstraction but as a prudence or an art according to the end to be achieved.

[11]*In Decem Libros Ethicorum Aristotelis ad Nichomachum Expositio,* I, lect. 3, nn., 32-41 (Spiazzi).

[12]"Unde et solum *scientiae practicae* sunt circa contingentia, scilicet in particulari. *Scientiae* autem *speculativae* non sunt circa contingentia nisi secundum rationes universales." *Ibid.,* VI, lect. 3, n. 1152. See also VI, lect. 1, n. 1123, where he clearly states that by *particularia* and *contingentia* here he means the singular as it is known by the intellect, not of itself, but through a reflection on sensation. How then can ethics be a science? St. Thomas give the answer (*In Boethii De Trinitate,* q. 5, a. 1, ad 4) that a practical discipline can have a theoretical part which is scientific in its *mode,* but that nevertheless the discipline is properly classified as practical. Similarly, a moral discipline is a habit of the practical intellect, because its object is the *operabile,* a contingent singular actually to be produced by man, but it is a science *secundum quid,* i.e., according to that part of its knowledge which contains universal definitions and necessary demonstrations. Because some authors treat only this theoretical part of ethics, they consider it to be speculative science, but this is incorrect since that which is universal and necessary in moral matters can be reduced to *psychology,* since its necessity is that of human nature. It is only when these universal moral truths are viewed as applicable to the guidance of particular actions that they can be separated from psychology, and then this new discipline would be incomplete unless it considered not only the universal principles

but also their practical application, just as a study of medicine would be incomplete unless it considered the treatment of particular cases. This is why for St. Thomas *ethics* and *prudence* are not too distinct intellectual virtues from the side of *cognition*, but distinct only in that prudence also requires a right appetite. "Est autem considerandum, quod sicut supra dictum est, prudentia non est in ratione solum, sed habet aliquid in appetitu. Omnia ergo de quibus fit mentio, in tantum sunt species prudentiae, inquantum *non in ratione sola consistunt*, sed habent aliquid in appetitu. Inquantum enim sunt in sola ratione, dicuntur quaedam scientiae practicae, sc. ethica, economica, et politica" (*In Decem Libros Ethicorum Aristotelis ad Nicomachum Expositio*, VI, lect. 7, n. 1200). Some hesitate to say that *prudence* is in some respect scientific, because they say prudence is of the singular, but St. Thomas (*Summa*, II-II, q. 47, a. 3) shows that prudence is not only of the singular but also of the universal moral principles which it applies. From all this one can conclude that the three species of prudence (ethics, economics, politics) are virtues of the practical intellect, which are also sciences *secundum quid* according to their consideration of the universal and necessary moral principles, but which are perfect *cognitively* only when they consider the application of these principles to the singular, and that they are also *moral* virtues perfect only by reason of right appetite. The man who knows only the theoretical part of ethics has the *habit* of ethics, but imperfectly. The man who knows also the practical part of ethics, but who lacks moral rectitude, has ethics more perfectly as to cognition, but cannot be said to be prudent. The man who has both the cognition and the right appetite has the complete *virtue* of prudence, of which the cognitive aspect is rightly called *ethics*. Finally it should be pointed out that the appetite influences cognition insofar as it affects the ultimate practical judgment, so that one who knows ethics but who does not have a rectified appetite will not use this knowledge as the determinant of his actual practical decisions. Hence ethics is found complete and perfect only in the prudent man who is also the morally good man. Consequently Aristotle holds (*Nicomachean Ethics*, Bk. VI, Chap. 8, [1142a 11 f.] and I [1095a 2 f.]) that the young man does not learn ethics well both because he lacks experience (cognitive aspect) and moral virtue (appetitive aspect).

[13]Two popular textbooks have this to say: "It is to the extent that men are thus interdependent that they form the object of study of the science of sociology. Other sciences study men as individuals. The biological sciences study man as a living organism. . . . The psychological sciences study the neural and mental operations of man, both in their normal and abnormal states." Nicholas S. Timasheff and Paul W. Facey, S.J., *Sociology* (Milwaukee: Bruce, 1949). "*Psychology*. This science deals mainly with the individual without any particular reference to social life." E. J. Ross, *Fundamental Sociology* (Milwaukee: Bruce, 1939). The author is then forced to grant that *social psychology* must be a social science.

[14]This seems to be the omission in the discussion of Herbert Johnston, "A Pattern for Relating Ethics and the Social Sciences," cited in footnote 1 above. His distinction of four types of knowledge: (1) purely speculative, (2) speculative knowledge of a practical object, (3) remotely practical knowledge, (4) purely practical knowledge, seems solid and workable. In view of this distinction he wishes to place the social sciences taken in themselves as examples of (2), while taken with ethics they are examples of (3). This solution has two difficulties: (a) These divisions of knowledge do not necessarily *specify distinct intellectual virtues*, since as has been shown above (footnote 9), any practical discipline must include knowledge of both types (2) and (3), which Johnston himself concedes, and to be perfect must also include (4). (b) The social sciences can be speculative knowledge of an operable object only if they are reduced to *psychology*, since universal and necessary knowledge about human action is impossible unless it be considered under its universal and necessary aspects, i.e., as it is fixed by nature. This would eliminate most of the problems actually

studied by social sciences, namely, all the *historical* aspects of human behavior. It is true that social scientists claim to study these historical laws of social behavior other than psychological and biological laws, but it is this very claim which reveals their *deterministic* bias, since it is an implicit denial of free will. Hence to concede this position and to attempt to reconcile it with a Thomistic classification of the sciences is to introduce a contradiction into Thomism.

[15]Jacques Maritain, "Reflections on Moral Philosophy," *Science and Wisdom*, trans. by Bernard Wall (New York: Charles Scribner's Sons, 1940), 137-241. J. M. Ramírez, O.P., *"De Philosophia Morali Christiana," Divus Thomas* (Freiburg), XIV (1936), 87-122, 181-204. This is not to deny, however, that ethics can take into account empirical facts that are supernatural in origin. Thus Aristotle considers the enslaved condition of mankind which is a result of original sin, and the moral philosopher may note the extraordinary natural virtue of a saint; but these facts remain mysterious to moral philosophy. Furthermore, these facts are known from experience and not received on faith, even human faith, from the theologian.

[16]Heinrich A. Rommen, *The Natural Law*, trans. by Thomas Hanley, O.S.B. (St. Louis: B. Herder, 1947), 265-266.

[17]History cannot be a science of the natural order because one cannot know the proper causes of singular events except by divine revelation of the divine decrees. Hence Aristotle and St. Thomas always consider it as the material of science, not as science itself. Nevertheless, it is clear from Aristotle's effort to collect constitutional histories (of which the *Constitution of Athens* alone remains) that he considers history as most necessary to moral science. See also *Rhetoric*, Bk. I (1360a 30): "It is useful, in framing laws, not only to study the past history of one's own country, in order to understand which constitution is desirable for it now, but also to have a knowledge of the constitutions of other nations, and so learn for what kinds of nation the various kinds of constitution are suited. From this we can see that books of travel are useful aids to legislators, since from these we may learn the laws and customs of different races. The political speaker will also find the researches of historians useful. But all this is the business of political science and not of rhetoric." As to rhetoric itself: "It thus appears that rhetoric is an offshoot of dialectic and also of ethical studies. Ethical studies may fairly be called political; and for this reason rhetoric masquerades as political science, and the professors of it as political experts. . . ." *Rhetoric*, Bk. I (1356a 25). Cf. *Ethics*, X (1181a 12 f.). As for economics see *Politics*, I (1256a f.). Aristotle uses the term *economics* for the moral science or *prudence* of managing the members of a household, but also holds that there is an art (servile and useful in character, since its object is an external, useful work) of obtaining the material wealth needed for the household, yet distinct from the particular arts of actual production: *Politics*, I, Chap. 3, 1256a. This is not limited to the household, but extends to all the state, 1256b 38. It is this art which has today usurped the name "Economics." Probably a better name for it would be "the art of the arts."

[18]Francisco P. Muniz, O.P., *The Work of Theology*, trans. by John P. Reid, O.P. (Washington: The Thomist Press, 1953), 28.

[19]Cf. *ibid.*, 29-38.

[20]For a good defense of the importance of ethics in the curriculum see D. A. Dillon and John A. Oesterle, "Moral Philosophy in the Catholic College," *The Thomist*, XVI (1953), 449-471.

[21]II-II, q. 184, *Prooem.*

[22]On the current methods of sociology see Becker and Boskoff, *op. cit.*, Part II, 35-304.

[23]See also the article by Bidney, "The Philosophical Presuppositions of Cultural Relativism and Cultural Absolutism" in Ward, *op. cit.*, 51-76.

[24] *Nichomachean Ethics,* Bk. VI, Chap. 8 (1142a 11 f.); also Bk. I (1095a 2 f.).

[25] See J. Vanderveldt and R. Odenwald, *Psychiatry and Catholicism* (New York: McGraw, 1952).

[26] See John L. Thomas, S.J., *The American Catholic Family* (Englewood Cliffs, N. J.: Prentice-Hall, 1956), and Alphonse H. Clemens, *Marriage and the Family* (Englewood Cliffs, N. J.: Prentice-Hall, 1956), and the bibliographical references in each.

[27] See Carle C. Zimmerman, *Family and Civilization* (New York: Harper and Brothers, 1947).

[28] See B. M. Ashley, O.P., "Social Pluralism in American Life Today," *Proceedings of the American Catholic Philosophical Association,* XXXIII (1959), 109-116.

[29] J. Messner, *Social Ethics,* trans. by J. J. Doherty (St. Louis: Herder, 1957); *Ethics and Facts* (St. Louis: Herder, 1952).

[30] See *Nicomachean Ethics,* Bk. X, Chap. 7-9; *Politics,* Bk. VII, Chap. 13-15.

[31] Cf. St. Thomas Aquinas, II *Con. Gen.,* Chap. 25-49.

[32] The writings of Paul Tillich and others of similar tendency are widely influential and are leading at the present time to a "reinterpretation" or "demythologizing" of supernatural mysteries as mere metaphysical opinions.

[33] See Aristotle's puzzlement over the enslaved condition of man, *Politics,* Bk. I, Chap. 5-6, and St. Thomas, IV *Con. Gen.* Chap. 52.

[34] St. Thomas Aquinas' *De Regimine Principum* (doubts concerning the authenticity of any part of this work have arisen recently: see I. T. Eschmann, O.P., "St. Thomas Aquinas on the Two Powers," *Medieval Studies,* XX [1958], 177-205) would seem from its order and method to be such a theological treatment of government. The author uses the material of the Aristotelian *Politics,* but he proceeds in theological order from God as the ultimate end to a treatment of political forms, and he consistently uses arguments from theological sources.

[35] Cf. Don Luigi Sturzo, *Church and State* (New York: Longmans, Green and Company, Inc., 1939), *The True Life, Sociology of the Supernatural* (Paterson, N. J.: St. Anthony Guild Press, 1943). M. J. Williams, *Catholic Social Thought* (New York: Ronald Press, 1950).

[36] The most significant attempt in the United States to date seems to be the work of J. H. Fichter, S.J.: *Southern Parish* (Chicago: U. of Chicago Press, 1951); *Social Relations in the Urban Parish* (Chicago: U. of Chicago Press, 1954); *Parochial School* (Notre Dame, Ind.: U. of Notre Dame Press, 1958). His point of view, however (see his *Sociology* [Chicago: U. of Chicago Press, 1957]), is that sociology must be a purely theoretical, "value-free," science.

[37] Cf. Jacques Maritain, *On the Philosophy of History* (New York: Charles Scribner's Sons, 1957); Martin C. D'Arcy, S.J., *Meaning and Matter of History* (New York: Farrar, Straus, 1959); Christopher Dawson, *Dynamics of World History,* ed. by J. J. Mulloy (New York: Sheed and Ward, 1957).

PHILOSOPHY AND COLLEGE THEOLOGY

Benedict M. Ashley, O.P.

A convert to Catholicism, Father Ashley studied at Chicago University and received his doctorate in political science from Notre Dame. After his ordination in 1948, he continued his graduate work at the Pontifical Faculty of Philosophy, River Forest, Ill. (Ph.D.), where he is presently professor of the history of philosophy. As a member of the Albertus Magnus Lyceum for Natural Science he has served as a consultant for the Saint Xavier Plan of Liberal Education and as a faculty member of that college.

It is at least proof of serious concern that at the present moment there are so many disputed problems concerning the relations between theology and philosophy in the curriculum of the Catholic college. I will discuss some of these issues under three main headings:

1. *Is it possible to teach theology to students who are not already prepared by philosophical studies?* Father George Klubertanz, S.J., argues that to attempt this is to deceive ourselves by applying an honorific title to something which is only advanced catechetical instruction, and to deceive the student by leading him to think he understands when he is only mouthing words.[1] Father Gerald Van Ackeren, S.J., on the other hand, argues that it is possible to teach a theology which is genuinely but not perfectly a science to students who are not philosophically trained.[2] Professor Étienne Gilson tells us that it is possible to teach theology to the college student, but not possible to teach the young metaphysics without leading them into the mere verbalism which Father Klubertanz fears in theological teaching.[3]

2. *What sort of philosophical training would it be useful for the student of college theology to have, and how should it be used?* Many writers emphasize the importance of logic, or of the liberal arts, or of the humanities.[4] Others say that for students in the contemporary world the main problem is the relation of modern science to theology, and hence urge that the student be acquainted with natural and social sciences before attempting theology. Otherwise, they argue, the teacher of college theology will appear to be a mere medievalist. Hence these writers emphasize the importance of the philosophy of nature or the philosophy of science.[5] Still others insist on the importance of a separate course in ethics or in social philosophy.[6]

Finally, a great many emphasize that without metaphysics a scientific theology is impossible.[7] Here, however, some insist that the mere study of Thomistic metaphysics is inadequate as a preparation for theology, since Catholic theology is too wide and profound to be tied down to a single philosophical school of thought. Would it not be better to awaken the students' minds to philosophical and theological problems by a discussion of a number of the important thinkers of Western culture and of the contemporary world?[8] Many others, and from somewhat different points of view, argue that the very distinction between philosophy and theology is a merely formal one, which has little practical importance in the actual existential situation of modern man. Hence what is needed is a presentation of the Catholic outlook on life in its totality.[9]

3. *What influence should the course in theology have on the student's intellectual life as a whole and on the rest of the college? Should theology or philosophy integrate the student's education?* On this point many argue that theology should be the supreme integrating principle of the college.[10] Others contest it. Some argue that there cannot be a single principle of integration;[11] some believe that in the college only philosophy can be a proximate principle of integration, while theology is only remotely concerned.[12] Still others express fear that theology may assume an *imperialism* in the college, seeking to destroy the proper autonomy of philosophy and other secular disciplines.[13] Finally, there are those who plead for a conception of education which gives to every discipline a value of its

own as a pure search for truth, and urge that we discourage the tendency in Catholic schools to orient all studies to apologetic purposes. The search for truth of any sort is *ipso facto* religious.[14]

Each of these opinions deserves serious consideration, and none of the problems can be solved without both careful scientific investigation and practical experimentation. It is the duty of theologians, philosophers and educators to undertake such research and experimentation. For too long Catholic schools in the United States have taught philosophy and religion as a mere set of courses based on whatever textbooks were conveniently available and with a staff whose qualifications for the most part were graduation from a seminary. In the press of the practical difficulties of setting up a Catholic educational system, too little serious study has been given to settling the theoretical problems involved.

But what are we to do in the meantime, while we are waiting for these researches and experimentations, or for the St. Thomas Aquinas of our age to arise to propound the "modern Catholic synthesis"? In my opinion, our colleges must follow a *conservative* policy, *applying the best knowledge which we have at present.* This is by no means the same as a policy of conformism or maintaining the *status quo.* It will require some quite drastic reforms and some courageous swimming upstream against the current of American habits of thought in education. Our shame is that at present our Catholic schools are not basing their programs on *what we now know solidly,* but on all sorts of accidental considerations and ephemeral personal opinions. A strange medley of shallow novelties and tired traditions of fifty or one hundred years' standing takes the place of the *philosophia perennis* and Thomistic theology.

It would seem that we should rather root our program of theology and philosophy in the principles already approved by the popes, and in the explicit teachings of the Thomistic tradition which they have approved.[15] This is the only solid, practical basis for a present college program. If we do this, we still will not be relieved of the further obligation to continue research and experimentation in order to develop and improve our tradition, but we will at least not have foolishly neglected the means already at hand.

Philosophy and Theology

It might be thought the first question could be answered on the basis of experience; in fact, if we ask experienced teachers we get divergent answers. The result obviously depends a good deal on the ability of the teachers, although all agree that a knowledge of philosophy (provided that it be truly scientific) is highly useful.

A more solid way of approaching the question is to consider the nature of theology itself. St. Thomas Aquinas establishes the existence of theology by beginning with the revealed truth that the human beings whom God has entrusted with his revelation must be capable of teaching and defending it effectively.[16] He then shows what kind of a discipline it must be to achieve this purpose, and in elaborating this he finds it very convenient to compare it analogously with metaphysics, which is human wisdom.[17] This comparison reveals striking analogies and even more important differences.

If we ask whether natural theology or metaphysics presupposes that the student already know the lower sciences or philosophies, St. Thomas Aquinas' opinion is quite explicit in his texts, although it has been vigorously disputed by some.[18] They have been reluctant to accept St. Thomas' affirmative answer to this question for two reasons: first, some, influenced by the Scotist and Suarezian tradition, believe that metaphysics is presupposed to all the other sciences because it treats of *ens in commune;* second, it is the fear of others that the admission that the study of metaphysics presupposes a knowledge of natural science (or of any other special science) impairs its dignity and renders its conclusions subject to the fluctuating opinions of modern experimental or positive science.[19]

St. Thomas Aquinas, however, holds that, since no science proves the *existence* of its subject, metaphysics presupposes that the learner know with certitude that *ens in commune,* the subject of metaphysics, does exist.[20] It is not sufficient to know that it is merely possible, since no science is about the merely possible, nor could we know that this subject is possible except by showing that it actually is.[21] Now *ens in commune* must be known to us either directly by sense experience or by argument from sense experience, since all our knowledge originates in the senses.[22] However, the only being of which we have sense experience is that of material things, and thus if our supreme human science were based directly on experience it would be the science of material things as such, and this is the philosophy of nature (natural science).[23] According to Aristotle and St. Thomas, however, natural science discovers that there is a being (the first mover) who is not necessarily material, and it establishes this fact scientifically. Hence it becomes clear that there is a subject to be studied which really exists and which is distinct from the subject of natural science known to us from experience—namely, *being as such,* i.e., being separated from matter and motion.[24]

Those who deny this conclusion of St. Thomas for the whole of metaphysics or for some part of it attempt to show that it is possible for the student to see, directly from experience, that being is not necessarily material.[25] It may be granted that this is possible, since undoubtedly some awareness is contained confusedly and implicitly in common sense knowledge that we have spiritual faculties and that the world is the work of supreme intelligence. However, this knowledge and any discipline erected on it cannot be science, but only *opinion,* since there is no way to know the existence of the first mover or of the immateriality of the human soul in a scientific fashion except by the proofs established in natural science. This opinion may be *certain,* either because it is confirmed by divine faith (but then the student is not studying metaphysics but theology), or because of the certitude of human faith in the teacher, or because of common sense. But these last two certitudes are *extrinsic* in character, and the common teaching of Scholastics holds them to be an insufficient foundation for science.[26]

This conclusion is confirmed by a look at the recent textbooks which attempt to show the beginner in metaphysics that metaphysics has an object other than *ens mobile.* An examination of these explanations will show that they are in effect nothing but persuasions of a common sense sort which implicitly contain the proof of the existence of the first mover.[27]

Thus metaphysics cannot be learned by the beginner who has not already got as far as the proof of the first mover in natural philosophy. This in turn is not possible unless he knows logic, since it is generally admitted that without logic no science of the human order can be a genuine intellectual habit but must remain in the state of a disposition. The reason is that strictly scientific knowledge requires not only that we can demonstrate a conclusion, but also that we know this to be a strict demonstration, which is shown only by logic.[28]

Finally, St. Thomas holds that both a knowledge of mathematics and of politics is prerequisite to the study of metaphysics, but this point will be discussed further on.

Does this mean that metaphysics is subalternated to the special sciences? Far from concluding this, St. Thomas constantly vindicates the dignity and independence of metaphysics as a true wisdom. What we have shown about the prerequisites of metaphysics does indeed show that human wisdom is a rather humble thing,[29] but it does not disprove that it is a true wisdom, for two reasons:

> 1) Metaphysics depends on the lower sciences in a merely *material* way, not formally as occurs in subalternation, just as our intellect depends on the senses (but only materially) or as faith depends upon reason (but only materially). Metaphysics depends on natural science for a certain *fact*—namely, the existence of non-material being—but it understands this fact by its own proper light, since it resolves all that it knows not merely to facts of experience but to the intelligibility of being.[30]
>
> Thus the natural scientist can tell the metaphysician that there is a non-material being, just as sense can tell intellect that something exists, but it is only the metaphysician who sees why it is impossible that the first mover should not be, as it is intellect that tells us why sense knowledge reveals the natures of things.
>
> 2) The second reason why metaphysics is superior to the lower sciences is that it defends their principles. It does this even for logic. Because metaphysics resolves not to experience but to the intelligibility of being, it is able to show us why experience and knowledge based on it are valid.[31]

Thus the purely human wisdom of metaphysics is a genuine wisdom which rules over the other sciences, but it is materially dependent on them for the scientific establishment of the facts which it presupposes.

If we now compare metaphysics to sacred theology we will at once notice one point of similarity. Sacred theology also presupposes certain facts already established by an inferior type of knowledge. The principles of sacred theology come from supernatural faith, and supernatural faith presupposes the *praeambula fidei* or *motives of credibility* as a necessary condition. Just as we cannot know intellectually without the material provided us by our senses, and we cannot know metaphysically without the material provided by the special sciences, so we cannot believe with divine faith without a material but *sine qua non* condition, namely, the motives of credibility.[32]

But here the analogy ceases. In order to have perfect and firm supernatural faith it is by no means necessary to have scientific knowledge of the motives of credibility, but only a genuine, albeit perhaps merely common sense, certitude.[33] Nevertheless, given the supernatural virtue of faith, the theology erected upon it is a true science. Metaphysics erected on common sense remains only *opinion*, because it rests on opinion, even when that opinion may be certain because of something extrinsic;[34] but theology erected on faith (to which only common sense credibility need be presupposed) is a true intellectual habit. This is because supernatural faith gives a certitude far superior even to the most perfect natural habits.[35]

Hence from these facts a necessary conclusion: it is entirely possible for a student to acquire the intellectual habit of theology based on his knowledge of revealed truth possessed by faith, without any prerequisite scientific knowledge.

Two serious objections to this, however, come up. Does not theological reasoning sometimes require the use of a premise taken from philosophy? Furthermore, does not the *science* of theology at least require that the student know logic? How can he recognize a demonstration in theology, any more than in metaphysics, without a knowledge of logic? From these objections it would seem that any knowledge which a student ignorant of philosphy might have of theology could only be a science in the imperfect state, i.e., a mere disposition, not a true habit.[36]

The answer to both of these objections rests on the same principle. Thomist theologians generally hold that when a premise from philosophy or natural knowledge of any sort is used in theology it is used either in a *material* way (in order to apply revealed truth to some natural situation, as frequently in moral theology) or if formally, then the natural knowledge is *elevated* to a theological level. This elevation results from the fact that the theologian accepts the natural truth only after checking it by its conformity and harmony with revealed truth.[37] Thus a theologian can safely use St. Thomas' metaphysics in theology, because the Church has theologically certified it to be in harmony with revealed truth.[38]

What is true of the premises used in theological reasoning is also true of the *logical rules* used in the method of theology. The method of theology is not borrowed from merely human logic but is derived by the theologian from the revealed data itself. This is evidenced by the fact that God in the Scriptures not only inspired the content but the *mode* of teaching,[39] and that our divine Lord not only entrusted revelation to the Church but gave her fundamental instructions on how it should be taught and defended.[40] Furthermore, as was just mentioned, the Church acting in the light of revelation has approved certain methods to be used in declaring and defending the faith and disapproved others.[41] Thus even when the theologian uses the form of the Aristotelian syllogism he does so not because he is necessarily convinced of the validity of such reasoning on the basis of the science of logic, but because the Church approves this method of reasoning as right.

In order not to fall into exaggerations on this point, however, it is well to consider the various modes in which sacred theology may be known.[42] In its simply perfect state it is known only to the blessed in heaven, who alone see its principles with *evidence*. In this life even the greatest theologians possess it in an imperfect state, because they know it as a subalternate science, since they receive its principles on *faith* and not from evidence. Nevertheless, in this imperfect state the character of theology as a true science, as a genuine habit, is preserved, since the principles are known with infallible certitude and not merely by opinion.[43]

It is possible, however, to have a knowledge of theology which is imperfect as regards its character as a *discursive* habit. This would be found in the person who knows the principles of theology by supernatural faith and some of the conclusions of theology by *human opinion*. Such a person has a disposition to theology but not a habit.

Finally, we have the person who has supernatural faith, who has been *catechized* in those things which are necessary to salvation, but who knows little or nothing of the truths elaborated by theological science.

Within the three levels of (1) catechism, (2) knowledge of some theological conclusions, and (3) habit of theology as it is possible in this life, there are, of course, many degrees as regards extension and accuracy of knowledge. For example, a student in the second state might actually have much more theological information than one in the third, and yet lack the habit possessed by the latter. In order to have the habit of theology, as for any intellectual habit, it suffices for a student to have really understood a single theological demonstration.

We may, in particular, distinguish among those who have the theological habit; some possess it in the manner of an expert; others possess it in the manner of a liberally educated person. The expert has not only the habit (with the intrinsic facility which every habit provides) but also the extrinsic facility in its use which comes from his possession of various auxiliary habits which remove possible obstacles to its use. Philosophy is one of these auxiliaries. The liberally educated person has the habit with its intrinsic facility, and hence he is able to follow a theological demonstration presented by an expert and to appreciate (at least in favorable cases) its scientific cogency. But he is not necessarily able to extend the science to new conclusions whose solution would require auxiliary knowledge.[44] Such a person, for example, could read the *Summa Theologiae* or a papal encyclical with genuine understanding, not only of the conclusions, but of the reasoning. Yet he would not be able himself to engage in theological researches.

It is at this level of the difference between the expert and non-expert, both of whom have the habit of theology, that the role of philosophy necessarily enters. A theologian today who was not a good Thomistic philosopher would not be abreast of the present state of theological science and would not be able to carry on either his teaching or his research with the needed facility, just as he is not able to do this if he lacks a knowledge of history or of languages. For the non-professional, however, it suffices if he accept the conclusions of these auxiliary disciplines on human faith in the experts, since the results of these disciplines do not enter into the intrinsic structure of theology but only contribute to its greater manifestation.

Thus it is rather beside the point to argue that, since the seminary course in theology requires philosophy as a prerequisite, this must be the case for the non-professional course.[45] Equally is it pointless to say that the seminary course cannot inculcate the habit of theology, merely because an undergraduate course does not supply the student with all the auxiliaries of theology which are studied by the graduate student.[46]

By these facts the lofty character of theology is shown in its independence of natural disciplines, but this lofty character should not be exaggerated so that it appears that only a few can acquire the habit. On the contrary, on this point an optimistic position is more reasonable. The faith is given as a gift to most Catholics at the beginning of life, and they are sufficiently instructed in the articles of faith by catechetical methods during their study in the elementary grades. In order that their faith should reach maturity on its intellectual side, it is well that a great part of all Catholics be sufficiently educated, not only to see the faith in its bare essentials, but also to understand it as a unified whole.

To see the faith in this unified and mature way it is necessary that the faithful in large numbers should receive *theological* instruction, beginning as soon as their knowledge of the articles of faith is complete, namely, at the beginning of high school at the latest. Undoubtedly this more unified picture will remain only a *disposition* and not a true habit until the student's mind is sufficiently mature to be able to follow a line of demonstrative reasoning. We know that even high school freshmen can do this in simple materials (those of mathematics); there is no reason to doubt that with good instruction many will be able to do this even with theological materials at the college level, and hence to acquire a genuine habit of theology. But, of course, certainly graduate study is needed to form an expert in theology.

We should not omit to observe with Gilson that the certitude of faith greatly facilitates the acquiring of this habit.[47] Quite an opposite viewpoint–that faith in a human teacher is an obstacle to real learning—is advanced in some current discussions.[48] It is not an obstacle but a great help, in point of fact, since the teacher can then direct the mind with the most efficient attention to what is relevant. How much more is this the case in the study of theology, where the student's *sensus Catholicus* enables him to see and to grasp what is relevant! This is true also of the moral dispositions so important to learning,[49] since the student's hope and charity are immense helps in going forward in theological understanding even in adolescence, just as in other subjects moral defects are a great hindrance.

Some, of course, object that the student's faith makes him passive to the conclusions of theology, and hence he accepts verbally what is said, without understanding it. But this result is not due to faith but to indifference to faith. Often enough it is the consequence of keeping the student at a catechetical level of instruction when he is ready for something better, so that he gradually acquires a habit of inattention to an old routine.

Philosophical Training for Theology

The practical conclusion from what we have seen up to this point is that *in the college sufficient time should be given for all students to acquire a liberal knowledge of theology.* That does not mean, of course, that all students will really pass from disposition to true habit. That depends largely on their own efforts, since in no college course are we able to guarantee by some system of examinations that this transition is achieved. But it does mean that the course should be designed to show the student something of the demonstrative structure of theology, and that the student should be exercised in actual theological reasoning.

Since this intellectual habit of sacred wisdom is incomparably more important for the Christian's intellectual and practical life than anything else he might study, the college should give ample time to it.[50] However, this does not mean all the time of the college. The liberal knowledge of which we have been speaking can be acquired in a relatively limited amount of time. Once room for it has been given in the curriculum, the remaining time should be devoted to those studies which will best facilitate the learning of theology by giving the student a good liberal education in the natural order. Finally, the vocational needs of the student must be met.

In arranging the curriculum various practical considerations may necessitate that one or the other of these three objectives must be somewhat sacrificed to the others. In this case it is clear that the vocational need must be met, not because it is most important in itself, but because it is of immediate practical necessity. However, a Catholic school in particular must see to it that the vocational requirements are kept to the strict minimum of practicality and necessity. It has a duty to show the student that, although he has an obligation to make a living and to serve a social function, this is of itself of far less importance than his personal spiritual and intellectual formation. Granted that this minimum attention to vocation has been given, ample time must be given to theology.

What then about liberal studies of the natural order? Since they facilitate the study of theology (as we will show next), and since they contribute to the natural perfection of the student, they should be well provided for; but if a sacrifice is needed, then they should be sacrificed to the degree necessary to give sufficient time to theology. If after these requirements are met some time remains, then the student should be encouraged to devote it to more ample theological studies in preference to other studies.

If I were asked personally to estimate the amount of time in a college curriculum to be devoted to these respective aspects of education I would say, 25 per cent to theology, 50 per cent to other liberal studies, 25 per cent to vocational studies. The norm used in this estimate is that colleges commonly consider that about 25 per cent of the time in college is required for a "major subject," i.e., to have some real initiation to a particular intellectual habit.

Our problem now is to consider what the content of the liberal education should be which prepares for the study of theology. We are at once confronted with the question: should this be philosophy, or other subjects as well?

What is philosophy? If we are to take this term in its strictest sense it means *metaphysics,* and perhaps this usage would be the best, since the ancients called metaphysics "first philosophy," "philosophy simply speaking," and when moderns speak of philosophy they usually mean either metaphysics or some substitute for it.

St. Thomas, however, would not include under metaphysics all types of knowledge usually called philosophical, since he did not consider logic, the philosophy of nature or ethics to be part of metaphysics.[51] Philosophy in the wider sense included for him *all* intellectual disciplines which had a genuinely scientific character. Hence "philosophy" in this sense would include all subjects studied in college in a serious academic manner, even "domestic science" and "physical education" when these are taught in a genuinely theoretic way (which is no doubt possible).

Many Thomists today have abandoned this twofold use of the term "philosophy" to mean either metaphysics (when strictly taken) or all sciences (when widely taken). They wish to introduce a distinction between some sciences which are philosophy in the wide sense (such as logic, philosophy of nature, ethics) and other sciences which are non-philosophical (such as experimental natural science, mathematics and social science).[52] In my opinion the validity of this more complex division has never been proven, so that the simpler and traditional view of St. Thomas remains valid and very convenient.

What are these special sciences which constitute philosophy in a wide sense? They are: (1) the liberal arts, which include logic, literature and linguistic studies, to which may be annexed music and the fine arts;[53] (2) natural science, which includes the philosophy of nature, physics, chemistry, biology and psychology—all of which form a single discipline, according to St. Thomas, except for the mathematicized forms of natural science, which form an auxiliary discipline to natural science; (3) social sciences, of which there are three: individual ethics, ethics or sociology of the family, and politics or general sociology, with history (which is not a science in its own right) as a part of all three of these; (4) the useful arts, which are founded on the natural sciences and directed by the social sciences. This last class of studies, however, belongs to vocational, rather than to liberal education.

Of these which are most useful to the study of theology? The best way to answer this question is to consider two principles already mentioned above: first, theology is not strictly dependent on any of these and should be studied from an early age; second, the natural disciplines are ordered to metaphysics, and require to be learned in a definite sequence before metaphysics. From these principles we have obviously to conclude that the natural disciplines should be studied in their correct order, beginning from the lowest, and that the student should progress as far in this *cursus* as possible, but that the study of theology need not be delayed until all have been completed. Rather, as each natural study is completed, its assistance can be brought to bear on the study of theology, which is progressing by its own intrinsic dynamism simultaneously with these studies.

For example, the teacher of Christian doctrine in high school need not hesitate to employ theological reasoning with his pupils when he finds them able to follow such reasoning, whether they have yet studied logic or not. When they do study logic he ought to take advantage of this auxiliary *ad majorem manifestationem* of Christian doctrine.

Consequently, the most important help to the study of theology will be a knowledge of the liberal arts, and especially of logic.[54] These arts will facilitate the student's reading of the Scriptures and other sources, a reading which requires a knowledge of the types of discourse, literary forms, etc. They will greatly help in understanding the methodology of theology, its use of definitions, classifications and demonstrations. It would seem, however, that the *essentials* of these arts should be learned in high school, so that they will be available at the very beginning of college theology.[55] During the first semester of the freshman year of college these arts may be reviewed. During the second semester the college theology course should begin with an introduction which would be based on the first question of the *Summa Theologiae* and which would be devoted to a discussion of the nature of sacred theology, its method and sources, and its general order. This introduction should not be a mere abstract consideration of the nature of theology, but should be devoted to giving the student actual exercise in applying the liberal arts to the reading of the Scriptures and other sources, and to the formation of theological reasoning on familiar materials. For example, the teacher might take the first article of the Creed, "I believe in God the Father, creator of heaven and earth," and show how this article is established from Sacred Scripture and Tradition, and then show how theological conclusions may be drawn from it (e.g., that the power to create cannot be given to the angels or any creature). In this way the student will see the special character of theological reasoning, its distinction from a catechetical approach, and be ready to make use of the liberal arts through the theology course.

According to St. Thomas, in the order of natural learning the study of natural science comes after the liberal arts. The proper object of the human intelligence is the essence of material things, and the first questions that arise in our mind concern this visible world. The liberal arts were discovered and have their use first of all as tools by which natural science is made possible. Unfortunately today, however, natural science, although marvelously advanced in its details, has lost its unity and solid philosophical foundation. Mathematical physics has come to be the model of natural science, whereas in fact it is a discipline auxiliary to natural science properly so called; for natural science does not rest on mathematics but on the study of material things as they have a nature or internal principle of change and stability.[56] In order for natural science to play its role in theology, it must be placed on its proper foundation, the so called "philosophy of nature," which is not a distinct discipline but merely the foundational part of natural science.

If the study of natural science is begun with an exploration of the basic principles of material things—the nature of change, the four causes, place, time, action and the proof that the material world depends on a first mover—the findings of modern natural science will take on genuine meaning. The student will see that the natural world in all its richness of detail manifests the Creator. Without this foundation natural science is a mere collection of facts held together by mathematical hypotheses, a collection which is of technological use but which does not enlighten the human mind. It would seem that the study of natural science, beginning with a semester of "philosophy of nature" (roughly the content of Aristotle's *Physics*) and including a second semester in which these principles are shown in application to the physical world as it is now known to science, should occupy the college student's freshman year. In the sophomore year the first semester should be devoted to the matter contained in the First Part of the *Summa*. In this way the student will come to the theological study of the Creator and his creation equipped with some understanding of the natural proof of the existence of God, with such concepts as matter, form and the categories, and with the modern picture of the physical universe.

Those who believe that metaphysics should be taught before theology usually argue that without metaphysical principles the First Part of the *Summa* is unintelligible. A recent writer has shown that it is possible to use sensible examples or instances of these metaphysical concepts in teaching theology.[57] One can go even further and make use of these concepts in scientific form but at the level of the philosophy of nature rather than of metaphysics. The metaphysical concept receives its positive content from these more restricted physical concepts, which are the best known analogates.[58] Thus the concepts of act and potency, essence and existence, relation, nature, person, etc., are first known to us in their restricted physical meaning. Since the student cannot understand them in their transcendental meaning until he has first grasped them in their physical meaning, the alternative is either to delay theology until both the philosophy of nature and metaphysics have been studied, or to be content with this less perfect aid to the student's understanding.

The study of biology and psychology should be taken up in the sophomore year. The division between "rational" and "experimental" psychology should be dropped as non-Thomistic.[59] In this way psychology will come in the second semester of the sophomore year and will follow on and complete the theological treatise on man at the end of the First Part of the *Summa.*

According to St. Thomas, the study of the social sciences should follow on the study of natural science, because moral problems presuppose an understanding of human nature as God has made it, with its intrinsic finality which provides the fundamental principle of moral science.

In a four year college course in which the first two years were devoted to natural science, the social sciences would come in the junior year, after psychology at the end of the sophomore year. It would then be necessary to study Parts II and III of the *Summa* in the senior year, if the theological treatment of morals is to follow its philosophical treatment. But it may seem preferable to study the social sciences simultaneously with Part II of the *Summa.* In this case it will be found that *materially* speaking there will be much overlapping between the two.

Consequently it seems preferable to me to treat individual ethics in a very schematic fashion, showing the foundations of natural ethics and its methodology and order as distinct from moral theology, but leaving the details of individual ethics as well as the ethics of the family to the moral theology course. Then the rest of the time devoted to the social sciences should be devoted to *politics* in St. Thomas Aquinas' sense (*sociology* in the modern sense), since this is not treated by the theologian in detail. In such a course the social doctrine of the papal encyclicals should be treated insofar as it is ethical in character, but strictly theological topics such as the relation of Church and state should be left to the theology course.

The Third Part of the *Summa* provides us with the more concrete and historical aspect of theology by showing us the pattern of Christ's life as the supreme historical event, and by showing us the formation and organization of the Church and the general course of its history.

Hence for this part of the *Summa* (as well as for the discussion of primitive man in Part I, and of the Old Law in Part II)[60] a knowledge of history on the part of the student is of great importance, and at least a year's course (other than the course in sociology) should be devoted to history and required of all students.

It should perhaps be given in the sophomore year preceding the course in sociology, which should be built upon the facts which it provides.

As for metaphysics—philosophy in the strict sense—it should not be omitted, in spite of the difficulties which we have mentioned. Just as the course in sacred theology is only an introduction to the pursuit of divine wisdom, so metaphysics or natural theology can only be an introduction to human wisdom. Because of the great difficulty of the subject, such a course ought not to attempt a detailed consideration of methaphysical problems. Rather, it should give the student an outline of the chief metaphysical problems, and then exemplify the methodology of metaphysics by the study of two or three important questions. I would suggest that these problems should include the epistemological problem and the theological problem. Under the epistemological problem the student should be given a survey of the history of the main schools of philosophy and a defense of Thomistic critical realism and the division of the sciences. Under the theological problem he should consider how our knowledge of natural things is ordered to the knowledge of God. The problem of "Christian philosophy," however, should not be treated in a metaphysics course but in the course in sacred theology, since it is a theological and not a philosophical problem.[61]

These suggestions can be tabulated in the following manner:

FRESHMAN YEAR

1st Semester: Logic (unless, as is preferable, this has already been studied in high school)
Natural Science 1: cosmology or philosophy of nature

2nd Semester: Natural Science 2: the physical sciences
Theology 1: introduction (*Summa*, I, q. 1); exercise in uses of sources and method of theology

SOPHOMORE YEAR

1st Semester: Natural Science 3: biology.
Social Science 1: survey of history
Theology 2: *Summa*, Part I, God, creation, man, the fall

2nd Semester: Natural Science 4: psychology
Social Science 2: survey of history concluded

JUNIOR YEAR

1st Semester: Social Science 3: the nature and division of the moral sciences
Theology 3: *Summa,* Part II

2nd Semester: Social Science 4: politics (sociology)
Theology 4: *Summa,* Part II, concluded

SENIOR YEAR

1st Semester: Introduction to metaphysics
Theology 5: *Summa,* Part III

2nd Semester: Introduction to metaphysics concluded
Theology 6: *Summa,* Part III, concluded

Theology's Influence on Philosophy

After considering how the study of philosophy can be of use to the study of theology, we need also to consider what sort of influence theology should have on the courses in philosophy. Since, according to the conception of philosophy held by St. Thomas, this term covers all secular studies, this amounts to asking what influence theology should have on the rest of the curriculum.

The first and most obvious point is that it is primarily for theological reasons that the study of philosophy in the college should be under the guidance of the thought of St. Thomas Aquinas. Today there is a considerable and probably growing unrest with the Thomistic dominance in Catholic schools. The influences of analytic, phenomenological and existentialist philosophies are felt in various degrees, even in Catholic colleges. Of course, this is, in a sense, a good thing, since the popularity of such movements helps us to see certain defects in our presentation of philosophy. No doubt it is an inadequate understanding of the Thomistic synthesis which permits such philosophers to claim with some plausibility that they are dealing with genuine problems which we have overlooked.

Nevertheless, Leo XIII chose a definite philosophy for Catholic schools, not in order to hamper them, but in order to give them an immense advantage over secular schools. All study of philosophy must begin under some teacher. The notion that a beginner can excogitate his own system *de novo* is naive. No less unrealistic is the notion that the beginner can best enter into philosophical thinking by a survey of all systems of thought. Such surveys close the door to real philosophizing rather than open it. The only way really to understand what philosophy is, is by beginning with a single teacher and following him into the heart of the subject.

But it is immensely important to pick a good teacher, the best who appears. For this reason Leo XIII pointed out to Catholics a teacher whose thought is at the same time a marvelous synthesis of the main strands of Western thought and in harmony with the higher light of faith. The student who begins with him will make a straight beginning, and the way lies open for him to follow truth as far as his own abilities and energies permit.

But we must show students that they study Thomistic philosophy, not as the last word in philosophy, but as a sound beginning. Furthermore, we should show them that if this is to be a beginning, they must not merely scratch the surface of Thomism by memorizing a few tags and conclusions, but that they must really attempt to grasp his "method, doctrine and principles."[62] It is a matter of experience that those who go this far with St. Thomas are never content later to neglect his help.

It is important to recall too that the popes in recommending St. Thomas urged the return to the sources and to the pure tradition of Thomism. Most of the complaints against Thomism today arise from a failure to follow this advice. An eclectic "Thomism" taught in an un-Thomistic order (or no order at all) from inferior manuals has produced a real allergy to Thomism in many students.

In the United States, in particular, it is necessary frankly to face the fact that the teaching of the *philosophy* of St. Thomas has suffered from two rather painful distortions. First, Thomism of a very eclectic type, colored either by Suarezianism and various obsolescent theological controversies, or by the preoccupation of the neo-scholastics with the refutation of idealism, dominated the scene. Second, under the influence of the special views of Jacques Maritain and Étienne Gilson on the nature of "Christian philosophy," Thomism began to be presented in a quasi-theological fashion.

The only remedy for this is to return to the order and method of philosophy actually found in the works of St. Thomas Aquinas for the instruction of the beginner. At the graduate level he can pass his own judgment on the neo-scholastic and Gilsonian "reconstructions of Thomism."

It is of particular importance in view of this latter system of "Christian philosophy" that in our teaching we avoid the introduction of theological problems or principles into the philosophy courses. I have argued above that it is permissible under certain circumstances to omit certain branches of philosophy and allow the corresponding parts of the theology course to carry the burden of dealing with these problems from the higher point of view. The reverse is not the case. Philosophy courses should not become theology courses. If ethics is to be taught as a philosophical course, then the order, method and argumentation should be purely philosophical and not theological. The "Christian ethics" of Maritain is theology and not philosophy, and by the same token the Gilsonian presentation of metaphysics which begins with the revealed doctrine of God as he who is, is theology and not philosophy.[63]

Thomistic theology is the surest guarantor of the genuine distinction of philosophy from theology. Those who fear a "theological imperialism" in which the theology course undertakes to answer all problems have only to fear those who depart from traditional Thomism. To be sure, theology answers the most important problems of life better than philosophy, and (as I have been arguing) if the student cannot have time for both theology and philosophy then it is far better that he have theology alone. But it would be better that he have both, because sound theology does not pretend to replace philosophy.

The same is true of the control of metaphysics over the other departments of study. Metaphysics as a wisdom defends and orders all other natural disciplines, but it cannot substitute for them. Indeed, it is even less capable of this than is theology, because of its material dependence on the lower sciences.

The Thomistic tradition has generally agreed on the following distinctions which should guide us in this matter:

1. Sacred theology has a *negative* control over metaphysics and all natural disciplines, correcting them if they contradict revealed truth. It also has a *positive* control in that it approves certain natural truths as consonant with the truths of faith. It is in this way that theology approves of Thomistic philosophy. But this control, whether negative or positive, is wholly *extrinsic* to philosophy, that is, revealed truth does not in any way enter into the demonstrations of philosophy.

2. Sacred theology integrates all human learning by this extrinsic control and by making use of the results of natural learning as a help to understanding revealed truth, in the manner we have explained. By this service to theology, metaphysics and all the natural disciplines take on a dignity and value far above their intrinsic worth.

3. In the sphere of natural learning, metaphysics has a similar rule over the other disciplines. It corrects them, it guides them, and it elevates them. Through metaphysics the results of the other sciences take on a greater dignity in that they contribute to our natural knowledge of God. But metaphysics does *not* supply the proper principles of the other sciences. This is one of the reasons that the tendency of some to place metaphysics *first* in the order of learning is a dangerous one, since it leads to the notion that the other disciplines are founded on metaphysics.[64]

Thus the role of sacred theology over all knowledge, and of metaphysics over natural knowledge, is a true Queenship, but it is a rule over free citizens and not slaves. Each of the natural disciplines retains its own principles and its own mode of procedure, *and theology protects this independence.*

A school which "seeks first the kingdom of God" by giving theology its full rights and showing itself willing to sacrifice human learning to divine when this is necessary will be rewarded by having "all these things added" to it, in the form of the restoration of the proper dignity and autonomy of the natural disciplines.

How can this be realized concretely and not as a pious incantation? The theologian should take time in the theology class to show the student the proper value and role of the different sciences as they come up.

I have indicated above how this will occur. In the introduction to theology he should show the value of the liberal arts for all studies, including sacred science. In Part I of the *Summa* he should show the immense help that natural science and metaphysics furnish to the knowledge of the faith. In Part II of the *Summa* he should show the importance of the social sciences for Christian life, and in Part III he should show how a knowledge of social institutions and their historical development is needed for an adequate Christian philosophy of history.

Furthermore, the theologian should be invited by other departments to take part in certain of their own classes and activities, to show the students the relevance of these studies to the Christian vocation and the Church's interest in the growth and proper independence of each of these fields. Here the theologian should follow the wonderful example of Pius XII.

In all these matters the professor of theology should scrupulously maintain his own role. He should not claim to be a universal expert, nor should he pontificate on matters where theological science leaves questions open.

Perhaps it is not unfair to point out that if a trained theologian is asked to play this role there will be much less danger of "imperialism" than if the chaplain or even a zealous Catholic lay person is left to "express the Catholic point of view." The charge of imperialism has arisen because it was assumed that *the* Catholic view on every subject is self-evident to the priest or the Catholic actionist. Theologians asked to give an opinion *ex officio* will be found to be amazingly cautious about interfering with the proper autonomy of the different natural disciplines.

This does not mean, however, that the theologian should merely be requested to act in his *negative* office. He should not be asked, "Is it heresy for me to say. . . ?" Rather, he should also be asked,

"What light does the faith cast on our problems? What further significance for the faith is to be found in our discoveries?"

In this role the theologian and the course in theology will be found not to hamper the other sciences but to give them a deeper life.

St. Augustine said that he found no real interest in any book that did not speak of Jesus. The Christian must ultimately say the same thing of all studies. If he cannot see how they will help him to God, he cannot be really engaged in them. His Christian sense tells him that such studies are vanities.

The answer is not to throw away all studies but theology, but rather to call on theology to show that in every study (whether the Holy Name is written there or not) something is said of him who is the source of all being and all truth. It does this, not by substituting itself for other studies, but by awakening them to more vigorous life by its correction and its counsel, and by transforming their fruits by a kind of transubstantiation in which supernatural truth is perceived under the veil of natural truth and natural truth itself suffers no injury.

Footnotes to Study 10

[1]"The Nature and Function of Courses in Philosophy and Their Curricular Implications to Liberal Education," *NCEA College Newsletter*, Oct., 1956, 12-13.

[2]"Reflections on the Relation between Philosophy and Theology," *Theological Studies*, XIV (1953), 527-550. See also the same author's "The Finality of the College Course in Sacred Doctrine," *Proceedings of the Society of Catholic College Teachers of Sacred Doctrine*, II (1956), 10-24.

[3]Cf. Étienne Gilson, "Thomas Aquinas and Our Colleagues," in *A Gilson Reader*, ed. by Anton C. Pegis (Garden City: Doubleday Image Books, 1957), 278-297. This view has been practically implemented in the curriculum of Barat College, Lake Forest, Ill., as explained by Richard J. Westley, *Forest Leaves*, March 9, 1955: "Hence if we choose to teach you metaphysics, psychology, ethics, epistemology, logic and cosmology under this higher formal *ratio* of theology, who is to say that you are deprived of philosophy? We would agree that you are deprived of philosophy outside the context of the Christian life, but Thomas never conceived that men would some day tear these sections which they deemed philosophical from his *Summa*. He never entertained the idea that these sections, once torn from their context, would be studied apart. To do so is to erect a philosophy which is false—since it is not Thomas'; and it is to erect a doctrine (teaching) which cannot survive, since it has no roots."

For a discussion of whether St. Thomas thought metaphysics could only be studied at an advanced age see George Klubertanz, S.J., "St. Thomas on Learning Metaphysics," *Gregorianum*, XXV (1954), 3-18.

[4]See James V. Mullaney, "The General Principles of Integration in the Curriculum," *Proceedings of the Society of Catholic College Teachers of Sacred Doctrine,* III (1957), 9-18, and "The Liberal Arts in the Aristotelian-Thomist Scheme of Knowledge," *The Thomist,* XVII (1957), 481-505 for the notion of the humanities.

[5]See my articles, "Sacred Doctrine and Natural Science" in *Proceedings of the Society of Catholic College Teachers of Sacred Doctrine,* III (1957), 24-28; and "The Role of the Philosophy of Nature in Catholic Liberal Education," *Proceedings of the American Catholic Philosophical Association,* XXX (1956), 62-84.

[6]See David A. Dillon and John A. Oesterle, "Moral Philosophy in the Catholic College," *The Thomist,* XVI (1953), 449-471.

[7]Sister Mary Emil, I.H.M., *Report of the Everett Curriculum Workshop,* NCEA, 1956. This report defends the autonomy of philosophy in education in direct opposition to such views as those of Professor Gilson, which would replace ethics and metaphysics courses by a study of the *Summa Theologiae.*

[8]This view is often proposed, but there is little evidence that it has been thoroughly tried in any American Catholic school. The "General Program of Liberal Education" at the University of Notre Dame announces in its brochure that in its "theology tutorial," "materials for the systematic study of the sacred sciences consist predominantly of selections from the works of St. Augustine, St. Thomas, and some representative modern writers, as well as from conciliar and papal pronouncements." The basic reading list includes works of Tertullian, Clement of Alexandria, St. Athanasius, St. Cyril of Jerusalem, St. Augustine, St. Benedict, Boethius, St. Anselm, St. Bernard, Hugh of St. Victor, St. Bonaventure, Dante, Thomas à Kempis, St. Ignatius Loyola, St. Teresa of Avila, St. John of the Cross, St. Robert Bellarmine, St. Francis de Sales, Pascal, Newman, Leo III, St. Thérèse of Lisieux, Chesterton, Pius XI, Dawson, Tawney, Sturzo, Pius XII, Maritain, Gilson.

[9]I will not attempt to document this position, which is an attitude frequently met with in conversation but not very likely to be expressed in print by educators who have departments of philosophy and theology to reckon with.

[10]Cf., for example, Edward G. Kaiser, C.PP.S., "The Nature and Function of Courses in Sacred Theology and their Curricular Implications in Liberal Education," *NCEA College Newsletter,* Oct., 1956, 16 f. See also Thomas C. Donlan, O.P., *Theology and Education* (Dubuque: Wm. C. Brown, 1952), *passim.*

[11]James V. Mullaney distinguishes a threefold integration: in a liberal arts curriculum considered simply as *arts,* history is the methodological principle of integration; in a liberal arts curriculum considered simply as *liberal,* metaphysics is the hierarchical principle of integration; in a liberal arts curriculum as a whole, sacred doctrine is the *normative* principle of integration. Cf. "The General Principles of Integration of the Curriculum," *Proceedings of the Catholic College Teachers of Sacred Doctrine,* III (1957), 18 f.

[12]Father George Klubertanz, S.J., in "The Nature and Function of Courses in Philosophy" (cited in footnote 1), lists several possible principles of integration: integration by science; integration by logic or semantics; "subjective integration" around "the desires and aspirations of the subject himself and around man as an object" through general liberal education; integration through religion and religious knowledge; integration by theology; and integration by metaphysics (pp. 12 f.). He concludes that "metaphysics first provides an all encompassing framework, a structure for a mental universe within which every being has, at least in general, a proper place and function." But he fails to explain how metaphysics can embrace the supernatural level of being or order theological knowledge to other types of knowledge. Whatever is said here of metaphysics is also true of theology in a supereminent degree.

For a similar insistence that there are multiple centers of integration, but that metaphysics integrates these centers of integration, see James Collins, "Thomism in the Colleges," *America,* XCIX (1958), 50-54.

[13]George Klubertanz, S.J., "The Teaching of Thomistic Metaphysics," *Gregorianum,* XXXV (1954), 187-205. He strangely attributes this danger of "theological imperialism" to Dominican authors, although it is precisely the Dominicans who most strongly maintain the distinction between theology and philosophy. In fact, the accused would entirely agree with Father Klubertanz' distinction, according to which the governance of theology, although it has both a negative and positive aspect, is wholly *extrinsic,* so that theology can never substitute for philosophy. (See his *Introduction to the Philosophy of Being* [New York: Appleton-Century-Crofts: 1955], 110-12.) Does he not rather have in mind Gilson's "Christian Philosophy," which is really a part of theology (see his *Elements of Christian Philosophy* [Garden City: Doubleday, 1959], Chap. 2), or Maritain's moral philosophy subordinated to moral theology? Maritain was the originator of the epithet "theological imperialism," but it seems to me that it is the exaggerated view of "Christian philosophy" which he and Gilson have proposed which threatens the proper independence of philosophy, and it is for this very reason that Dominican theologians such as Mandonnet and Ramírez have so strongly opposed it.

[14]Gustave A. Weigel, S.J., made this point very strongly in a lecture delivered April 22, 1957, to the Educational Conference of the Religious Sisters of Mercy, Milwaukee, Wisconsin (printed as a brochure), but clearly overstated the case. Certainly each subject should be taught according to its own methods and principles, but this does not mean that the Catholic teacher should not show the relevancy of each subject to the understanding and defense of the faith. Indeed, this is the duty of every Catholic teacher, since the highest dignity of any study is that it is capable of serving the faith. All truth is indeed valuable for its own sake, but lesser truths take on more value when they become instruments of greater truths.

[15]In the article cited in footnote 12, James Collins criticizes the "exaggerated positions" with respect to Thomistic philosophy in the college. His remarks are very just, since it is quite true that we cannot find in St. Thomas a ready-made curriculum which will save us the trouble of meeting the concrete circumstances of our time. Nevertheless, the popes have constantly urged Catholic educators to base their educational plans on the principles, methods and principal conclusions of St. Thomas Aquinas. And among these principles is the division of the sciences and the order of learning (see Pius XI, encyclical *Studiorum Ducem,* in which St. Thomas' teaching on these matters is summarized and given special commendation). Our Catholic schools have not made a very consistent use of this division or order, first, because of the eclectic influences on Thomism, which have imposed divisions and orders foreign to the interior structure of St. Thomas' thought, and second, because of certain unfortunate attempts to revise this division in order to give autonomy to the so called empiriological sciences, with the result that philoospHy has been isolated from modern problems.

[16]*Summa,* I, q. 1, a. 1, and the commentary of Cajetan.

[17]*Ibid.,* a. 6. Compare with the *In Libros Metaphysicorum Expositio,* I. Also see *In Boethii De Trinitate,* q. 5, a. 2, a. 4; q. 6, a. 1 (translated by Armand Maurer, C.S.B., as *The Division of the Sciences* [Toronto: Pontifical Institute of Medieval Studies, 1953]).

[18]Cf. In *Libros Metaphysicorum Expositio,* VI, lect. 1, n. 1170 (Cathala-Spiazzi), III, lect. 6, n. 398 and XI, lect. 7, n. 2267. That this is not merely St. Thomas' paraphrase of Aristotle but also his own opinion is clear from *In Boethii De Trinitate,* q. 5, a. 1.

Father Klubertanz in "The Teaching of Thomistic Metaphysics" (cf. footnote 13) interprets these texts as follows: "What St. Thomas' argument says is this: since all human knowledge begins with sensible things, we must first study act and potency, and so on, in sensible things. But this study can be carried on metaphysically from the very beginning, for the first philosopher is concerned even with sensible things inasmuch as they are beings" (p. 197). He is further convinced by an article of Joseph Owens, C.SS.R. ("The Conclusion of the Prima Via", *Modern Schoolman,* XXX [1953], 109-21) that a physical proof of the existence of the prime mover would not be valid, that Aristotle's proof in particular is invalid because based on erroneous scientific theories about the eternity of motion, and that St. Thomas' proofs are purely metaphysical. However, the above texts show that St. Thomas himself requires *physics* and not merely sense experience to precede metaphysics, and that at least one reason for this requirement is because physics proves the existence of a prime mover. St. Thomas himself answers the difficulty raised by these authors about the treatment of an immaterial mover in physics in spite of the fact that the subject of physics extends only to material beings: "Natural science does not treat of the first mover as its subject or as part of its subject, but as the end to which natural science leads. . . . so it falls under the consideration of natural science, not in itself, but in so far as it is a mover" (*In Boethii De Trinitate,* q. 5, a. 2, ad 3). Finally, St. Thomas certainly considered the physical proof as given by Aristotle valid since he explicitly defends it; see I *Con. Gen.,* Chap. 13, where he answers the very objections raised by Father Klubertanz. St. Thomas, of course, might have been mistaken in all of this, but to attribute some other opinion to him is to ignore the evidence of the texts. In view of the texts already quoted, the several places in which St. Thomas insists that physics should be taught before metaphysics are confirmatory, even if they do not all explicitly refer to the need of the proof of the first mover. See *Expositio super Auctorem de Causis,* Proemium, VI, lect. 7, n. 1209 (Pirotta); *Summa,* II-II, q. 9, a. 2; *Expositio super Isaiam,* cap. 3; I *Con. Gen.,* Chap. 4; *In Libros Metaphysicorum Expositio,* I, lect. 2, n. 46 (Cathala-Spiazzi).

For the view that metaphysics begins with sense experience but without the intermediary analysis of natural philosophy see Robert J. Henle, S.J., *Method in Metaphysics* (Milwaukee: Marquette U. Press, 1950). These authors have the laudable aim of rejecting a merely conceptual approach to metaphysics and desire to ground metaphysics on sense experience, a purpose which is certainly authentically Thomistic and Aristotelian. At the same time, however, they distrust the power of natural philosophy and feel that the dignity of metaphysics is lessened if natural philosophy is considered its prerequisite. They fail to realize that a merely material (not a formal) dependence of metaphysics on natural philosophy does not weaken it, any more than the material dependence of intellection on sense knowledge or of faith on reason weakens the superior lights. Is there here perhaps a lingering influence of Suarez and Scotus, who doubted the physical proofs of the existence of the prime mover? The difficulties that confront their position can be seen from the controversy between Klubertanz and Owens on how metaphysics begins. See Joseph Owens, C.SS.R., "The Intelligibility of Being," *Gregorianum,* XXXVI (1955), 193, with Father Klubertanz' comment, *ibid.,* 194-5. Both follow the view of Gilson that metaphysics must begin with the establishment of a *separatio* between existence and essence. From this Father Owens argues that metaphysics must begin with the proof of the existence of God as he who is. Father Klubertanz seems to concede this, but believes that the existence of God can be treated twice, first in an introductory metaphysics which emphasizes the existence of God as the cause of experienced being and secondly in a natural theology which must follow some philosophy of nature treating of intellection and volition. As a matter of fact, the *separatio* of which St. Thomas speaks is not between existence and essence but between *being* and *materiality.*

[19]On the influence of Scotus and Suarez which led to placing metaphysics first in the philosophical curriculum see F. Van Steenburghen, "Réflexions sur la Systématisation Philosophique," *Revue Néoscolastique de Philosophie,* XLI (1938), 185-216. For the reasons that make some Thomists fearful of philosophy of nature as a prerequisite to metaphysics see George P. Klubertanz, S.J., "Being and God according to Contemporary Scholastics," *Modern Schoolman,* XXXI (1954), 1-17. This argument rests on two assumptions, neither of which is in agreement with St. Thomas' thought: (1) That the philosophy of nature is an "abstract" science of essence. For St. Thomas natural philosophy does not abstract from the existence of changeable things. Rather, it seeks to explain this existence insofar as it is the result of change and the cause of change. No science but mathematics is properly called abstract. (2) That the philosophy of nature treats only of physical entities. According to St. Thomas its *subject* is the physical, but it treats also of non-physical entities insofar as these are the causes or *principles* of its subject. That is why both the human soul and the first mover can be considered by the philosophy of nature. The predicates affirmed of spiritual entities are not physical terms. Rather, we affirm that spiritual beings are causes of physical effects. When we say that the first mover exists we do not attempt to say what mode of existence it has, but only that it is the agent of real physical effects. This is why Aristotle takes such pains in the third book of the *Physics* to show that an agent as agent is not necessarily changeable. The root of all these difficulties is a failure to distinguish between the *subject* of a science and the principles and causes of the subject.

[20]See Melvin A. Glutz, C.P., "The Formal Subject of Metaphysics," *The Thomist,* XIX (1956), 59-74, with its biographical references to the current controversy. Also William H. Kane, O.P., "The Subject of Metaphysics," *The Thomist,* XVIII (1955), 503-521. These authors believe that the source of the controversy on this point has been the failure to observe the *logic* which Aristotle follows in constructing his metaphysics, so that some of them attempt to *begin* metaphysics with the separation of existence and essence or with the act of existence or with the existence of God or with the transcendental concept of being. These are all attained in the course of metaphysical analysis, but metaphysics must *begin* more humbly.

[21]To know that an essence which we conceive is something which could actually exist, it is necessary to be sure that it does not contain contradictory notes. But because of the potentiality of the human intellect, none of our concepts of essences are wholly *explicit.* Further reflection can always make more explicit the notes which are confusedly contained in them. Hence even in mathematics where what is conceived is most simple we are not sure that a given conception is not self-contradictory unless we know that it has been constructed in the imagination. This is why the controversy over whether a non-Euclidean geometry is consistent can never be settled merely by reference to the axioms and definitions, for these can never comprehensively and explicitly describe the geometric continuum, but must ultimately be referred to imaginary constructions or to physical reality. The formalistic program of Hilbert is impossible to carry out. Hence the sad results in the late Middle Ages of the discussions about the *potentia absoluta* of God, which reduced questions to a discussion about metaphysical impossibilities; these questions were usually impossible to settle even in the negative sense, and could never be settled in the positive sense.

[22]This is a common point of agreement among Thomists, and those who are anxious to stress the experiential basis of metaphysics emphasize it very strongly. Yet there are two tendencies that weaken this common position: (1) Some seek to find an *a priori* element in intellection, or wish to found philosophy on our experience of the activity of the intellect. (2) Some propose a theory of "Christian philosophy" which insists that at least *de facto* true metaphysical insight is attained only with the assistance of faith.

[23]Those Thomists who believe that all problems of existence must be treated by a science distinct from the philosophy of nature (because the latter deals only with problems of essence) do not seem to notice that St. Thomas held that natural philosophy would deal with all problems of existence if only physical existants were known to exist (see references in note 18 above). In order even to raise problems about existence which transcend the physical order, we must first know that the first principle of existence of all things is not itself a physical existant. Then it becomes clear that existence as common to physical and non-physical existants must be treated by another science distinct from the philosophy of nature. Thus it is only by drastically limiting the scope of the philosophy of nature that some authors are able to find any problems for metaphysics to study. In fact they assume from the outset that there must be a science of metaphysics which studies metaphysical problems. St. Thomas, on the other hand, makes no such assumption. He begins with the obvious fact that if any science is possible it must be concerned with the physical world as we experience it. In the course of developing this physical science, he shows that it leads to the proof that a non-physical cause of the world exists, and that hence there are metaphysical problems to be dealt with. Only in this way can positivism be fairly answered.

[24]Frequently it is objected that St. Thomas does not go through this process of establishing the subject of metaphysics in the *De Ente et Essentia,* in *De Potentia* or in the treatment of the *quinque viae* in the *Summa Theologiae.* Is it not unreasonable to expect St. Thomas, whose style is the model of economy, to trace out the whole *via inventionis* in every treatise on a special subject? The proper method is to seek in an author's work for his most explicit justification of his premises, even if he sometimes uses them as so sufficiently acceptable to his readers for the purpose immediately at hand in a particular work as to need no further defense or explanation.

[25]George Klubertanz, S.J., "A Comment on 'The Intelligibility of Being,'" *Gregorianum,* XXXVI (1955), 195. He admits the need of some psychological knowledge for the treatment of the divine intellect because of St. Thomas' explicit assertion *Commentaria in Libros de Anima,* I, lect. 1. However, one concludes from Father Klubertanz' own words in *The Philosophy of Human Nature* (New York: Appleton-Century-Crofts, 1951), Appendix K, 399, that for him the philosophy of nature is subalternated to metaphysics, since it depends upon it for its principles, and this is subalternation in the strictest sense. This is formally denied by St. Thomas, *In Boethii De Trinitate,* q. 5, a. 1, ad 6 and ad 9.

For St. Thomas natural philosophy does not require metaphysics to establish any of its principles, while conversely metaphysics, although it presupposes natural philosophy as a material condition, is also formally independent of the philosophy of nature. It might be further remarked that in the sense that the philosophy of nature takes something from metaphysics (namely, the common axioms of all reasoning), so does every science, including mathematics, and these axioms are presuppositions but not principles of demonstration.

[26]John of St. Thomas, *Cursus Theologicus* (Solesmne ed.), Tom. 1, Disp. 2, qq. 2-3.

[27]Father Klubertanz, in showing how metaphysics is to be established, writes: "In the formation, therefore, of the complex intelligibility of 'being as being,' we make two judgments: (1) 'This (sensible) thing is,' and (2) 'Even for this sensible thing *to be* is not the same as for it to be a particular sensible or material thing with a definite essence.' This judgment does not imply that we know that an immaterial being exists or that we think such a being is possible" (*Introduction to the Philosophy of Being* [cited in footnote 13], 43). On the other hand, Father Owens tells us in "The Intelligibility of Being" (cited in footnote 18), 191: "The being of sensible things was, of course, grasped from the beginning in the judgment that those things exist, and it was grasped

as an act. But that it is related to the natures of those things as the act of a potency really different from itself is established only after the existence of God has been proven, and so only through the knowledge of nature which is essentially being." We may grant with Father Klubertanz that we know (from the fact of change) that even in a sensible thing its existence is not its essence. It does not follow that a new science other than the philosophy of nature is required to study this existence, as St. Thomas explicitly states (see *supra*, footnote 18). K. draws this conclusion because he thinks the philosophy of nature is only about essences, which is certainly not St. Thomas' view, for whom this is not true of any science (although it might be asserted of mathematics with proper qualifications). On the other hand, Father Owens goes much too far in holding that we must prove the existence of God as pure act before we can establish the real distinction of essence and existence in creatures. St. Thomas in the *Summa,* I, q. 50, a. 2, ad 3, gives a proof of the real distinction based on the composition of matter and form.

[28]See St. Thomas Aquinas, *Exposition of the Posterior Analytics of Aristotle*, trans. by Pierre Conway, O.P. (Quebec: M. Doyon, 1956), I, less. 1.

[29]In comparison with sacred theology, metaphysics (1) requires the lower sciences for the materials on which it reflects; (2) is only a speculative wisdom, leaving practical wisdom to politics, while sacred theology is both speculative and practical wisdom; (3) is less certain *quoad nos* than mathematics, while sacred theology participates in the certitude of divine faith.

[30]*In Boethii De Trinitate,* q. 6, a. 1, ad 3.

[31]*Commentaria in Libros Metaphysicorum,* IV, lect. 17, n. 736 (Cathala-Spiazzi).

[32]I *Con. Gen.,* Chap. 6. Cf. R. Garrigou-Lagrange, O.P., *De Revelatione* (Paris: Lethielleux, 1926), 265-288.

[33]*Ibid.,* 278; Vatican Council, *Dogmatic Constitution on the Catholic Faith,* Chap. 3, "Concerning Faith," can. 6; Denz. 1815.

[34]Opinion is often defined as "probable knowledge." However, if we contrast "science" with "opinion" and define the former as "certain and evident knowledge through the proper cause," then knowledge which is not through the proper cause and which is nevertheless certain remains to be classified. Thus we may be certain of the facts of history by reliable witnesses, and we may be certain through signs, remote causes, the concurrences of several lines of circumstantial evidence, the solid agreement of experts, etc. It would be more satisfactory to say that opinion is knowledge which lacks sufficient intrinsic evidence for certitude, but which may be either probable or certain from extrinsic grounds. Thus "common sense" contains both certain and probable elements. See Garrigou-Lagrange, *Le Sens Commun* (Paris: Descleé de Brouwer, 1936).

[35]*Summa,* II-II, q. 4, a. 8.

[36]Father Weigel's view is that theology as a science belongs to the work of a graduate faculty of theology in a university. From this must be distinguished a *theological college* or seminary which develops priests for their work, and *college theology,* which is part of humanistic training for the layman. Cf. "The Meaning of Sacred Doctrine in College," in *Shaping the Christian Message,* Gerard S. Sloyan, ed. (New York: Macmillan Co., 1958), 175. Of the former he says, "Never for a moment does the Church suppose all her priests will be genuine theologians. That requires a special charism, a particular disposition. Yet the Church demands that all her priests complete seminary training. Why? Because one of the by-products of exposure to theological work is the ability to express the Gospel clearly. The Church uses the former seminarian as her messenger. And his principal teaching function is catechetical work. The Church has found that if he is given some theological training, even though he is no theologian, he will become a better messenger. The Church is

not at all blind. She realizes very well that the majority of seminarians have not the slightest inkling of what scientific theology is. But that makes no difference. In pursuing the course of study which has for its by-product an ability to explain Christian doctrine better, the seminarian attains the purpose of the Church. For the Church's purpose in maintaining seminaries is to attain their by-product. Those who want to be scientific theologians find the faculty of theology open to them where it is waiting to be done. Hence in the form of a seminary we have a theological college. The main consideration to which these men are exposed is theological lore. The fact that strictly scientific method is not used does not change the fact that theology is somehow being pursued. With reason we refer to such an institution as a theological college rather than a theological faculty" (pp. 177 f.). I might note that the popes have repeatedly urged that the *Summa Theologiae,* which is a textbook of theology using a "strictly scientific method," be the basis of seminary instruction. Surely it is little wonder that our clergy are considered anti-intellectual if we are content to teach theology to them in the manner described by Fr. Weigel. John Courtney Murray, S.J., in his "Towards a Theology for the Layman," *Theological Studies,* V (1944), 43-75, 340-376, presented a much loftier notion of "clerical theology"; see his description, p. 62.

[37]See R. Garrigou-Lagrante, *De Deo Uno* (Paris: Descleé de Brouwer, 1938), 57-61.

[38]Cf. S. M. Ramírez, O.P., "The Authority of St. Thomas," *The Thomist,* XV (1952), 1-109, for a catena of papal statements.

[39]Thus the apostolic preaching found in the Acts of the Apostles and the theological explanations and argumentation of the epistles clearly receive their basic pattern and method from that of our Lord himself as found in the gospels. The Fathers of the Church, although they made use of Greek logic, did so only as they found it in conformity with their study of the Scriptures, and the Scholastic theologians in adopting Platonic and Aristotelian methodologies strove to do the same. At no time has the Church adopted a *method* of reasoning about divine things, either to defend them or to expound them, other than the method of Christ himself. Her use of methods borrowed from secular thought has been purely instrumental, and in each case she has purified them. The methodology of St. Thomas in theology is not *merely* Aristotelian logic. Rather it is a unique method proper to the study of supernatural revelation which, however, respects and uses the laws of natural reason which Aristotle well analyzed.

[40]See J. E. Fenton, *The Concept of Sacred Theology* (Milwaukee: Bruce, 1941), 15-25.

[41]The outstanding example of this is the encyclical *Humani Generis,* in which Pius XII gave instruction not merely on the content but on the proper methods of theological research and teaching.

[42]John of St. Thomas, *Cursus Theologicus* (Solesmne ed.), Tom. 1, Disp. 2, a. 3.

[43]Human faith, on the other hand, may be certain (otherwise the truths of history could never be certain). But it cannot be habit, because although a human witness can be trusted in this or that case, he cannot always be trusted. Hence human faith is to be classed as a disposition, not a habit.

[44]This is the general situation in all sciences, that only the person who has the tools of research is able to solve new and more difficult problems. We should not think, however, as some are inclined to do, that the value of theology consists chiefly in research and the extension of knowledge to new problems. The goal of wisdom is contemplation, the enjoyment of truths already known, in which the mind circles rather than progresses.

[45]This is perhaps the commonest objection to the teaching of theology in college. Often it is given as a reason to omit it altogether or to delay it to the junior or senior years.

[46]Thus Father J. C. Murray, S.J., in the article cited in footnote 36, speaks of two theologies: "Both 'theologies' will be *secundum quid eadem*: each will verify the abstract idea of theology—the science of faith in the service of the Church. But each will be *totaliter diversa* in its concrete mode of realizing; each will verify this idea in quite a different way. Obviously, the total diversity will be of the qualitative order; it is not a question of teaching a different faith" (p. 75). Hence he believes that the college course cannot aim at the same habit of theology as that sought in scientific theology. Similarly, Father Weigel (cf. footnote 36), who thinks that scientific theology is neither for the seminarian nor the college student but only for the graduate student. Is this because both consider that scientific theology consists especially in *positive* theology and in theological *research*, rather than in *speculative* theology and the *contemplation* of known truths? Obviously neither the seminarian nor the college student can be equipped with the auxiliary disciplines required for the details of positive theology, nor are they being equipped to do theological research, but why can they not share in theology as it is a wisdom?

[47]In opposition to Étienne Gilson, Father Klubertanz states: "Another question which can be asked is this: supposing that a distinct Thomistic metaphysics can be developed, should it be? This question can hardly be answered in the abstract, and my interest is only in a concrete answer, namely, as far as concerns an American Catholic liberal arts teacher and student. For, looked at abstractly there is no doubt that an integral Thomistic sacred doctrine has many advantages. But they are not advantages for the American Catholic of the second half of the twientieth century. He lives in a secular civilization. He is constantly challenged by difficulties which purport to be purely rational. He has only a limited time in which to prepare himself to meet these difficulties, and to prepare for his apostolic mission of communicating his goods to his non-believing, non-philosophical fellow citizens. These goals are vital. They can be obtained only by suitable means. A second reason for the development of a distinct discipline of metaphysics inside Thomism is the danger of theological imperialism and nominalism, etc." ("The Teaching of Thomistic Metaphysics," 204; cited in footnote 13).

On this point I agree with Father Klubertanz as against Gilson, but not merely for pedagogical reasons. Gilson's "Christian Philosophy" is, as he himself admits, theology. Students need genuine philosophy for an adequate liberal education, although I will admit (with Gilson) that they need theology even more.

[48]See, for example, the article of Justus George Lawler, "Obedience and Scholarship: An Obsession with Docility," *Commonweal,* LXXI (1959), 15-19. During the recent controversy about why Catholic schools are not producing intellectuals, the reason often suggested was that they lay too much stress on the authority of the teacher. Is not the danger rather that we permit students to accept this authoriy in a merely superficial and passive way, instead of stimulating them to an active co-operation with the teacher in his authoritative role? Docility is an active co-operation, not a merely inert condition.

[49]*Summa,* II-II, q. 49, a. 3 on docility, q. 116 on studiousness; and q. 15 on the sins opposed to the intellectual gifts. Pius XI in *Studiorum Ducem* neatly summarizes: "St. Thomas enumerates the causes that make sacred study fruitless and barren: these are curiosity (which is the disordered lust for knowledge), intellectual sloth, and the cowardly shirking of difficulties; and as remedies against these, he urges a lively eagerness for work which will enkindle the fires of piety and gather strength and force from a holy life."

[50]A well-known historian of philosophy and a patrologist writing of the attitude of the Fathers of the Church on this question says: "The only intellectual activity which, by the standards of the Fathers, ought to be taken fully seriously is theology. It is the primary intellectual business of all educated Catholics, the subject in which they ought to be most interested, which they ought to

want to talk about when they meet, and which should be the basis of any sort of common action. This implies that, as far as we have any choice in the matter, we must subordinate our other studies in philosophy, the liberal arts and the sciences to the one overriding concern of penetrating more deeply into the meaning of Christian revelation. But this does not, I think, necessarily mean that we must be as rigorist as the Fathers in our attitude to these other studies, though there is plenty of room for self-deceit here, and I think we must take their warnings against *curiositas,* the frivolous pursuit of irrelevant information, more seriously than is fashionable." A. H. Armstrong, "Theology and the Liberal Arts," *The Downside Review,* LXXIII (1955), 137.

[51]*In Boethii De Trinitate,* q. 5, a. 1, ad 2.

[52]See my article, "The Role of the Philosophy of Nature in Catholic Liberal Education" (cited in footnote 5), 62-84, for references to the various opinions on this subject, and a refutation of the view as regards natural science.

[53]For the reasons for this classification see my book, *The Arts of Learning and Communication* (Dubuque: The Priory Press, 1958), 283-299.

[54]This is why up to the time of St. Albert the Great, Christian education consisted of two parts: (1) The study of the liberal arts; (2) the study of the Scriptures or theology. This division remained the very foundation of the organization of the medieval university and is reflected today in modern universities by the division between *arts and letters* (humanities) on the one hand, and "*science*" on the other. St. Albert, however (followed by St. Thomas Aquinas), proposed a new division: (1) liberal arts (logic and mathematics), (2) natural science, (3) ethics, (4) metaphysics, (5) the study of the Scriptures or theology.

[55]See *The Liberal Education of a Christian Person* (Chicago: St. Xavier College, 1953), 55 ff.

[56]See Vincent E. Smith, *The General Science of Nature* (Milwaukee: Bruce, 1958), 26-47, and William H. Kane, "The Extent of Natural Philosophy," *New Scholasticism,* XXXI (1957), 85-97. This position has been repeatedly misrepresented in current articles in two ways: (1) Some have accused these writers of saying that *all* of modern science is a single intellectual habit, while in fact they admit *two* habits, that of mathematical physics, and that of natural science (or natural philosophy) strictly so called. (2) Some have accused them of "philosophism," i.e., of trying to absorb the sciences into philosophy, but these authors insist on the distinction between natural science (or natural philosophy) and metaphysics (philosophy in the strict sense), and are only arguing that the philosophy of nature as usually understood is not a distinct habit from that of the modern non-mathematical investigation of nature. They are arguing that modern science needs to deepen its own foundations by a more critical understanding of its basic principles, and that such an analysis of the basic principles of natural science is *interior* to natural science and constitutes its foundational part. They object to assigning this foundational part of natural science either to a distinct "philosophical" habit other than metaphysics (Maritain's view), or to metaphysics itself (Renoirte's view).

[57]See the article of Father Gerald Van Ackeren, S.J., cited in footnote 2.

[58]Father Klubertanz in "The Teaching of Thomistic Metaphysics" (cited in footnote 13) says: "[Some say that] metaphysics essentially needs certain points from the philosophy of nature, for example, act, potency, notion, substance. This thesis is really a very dubious one, and capable of a number of interpretations. It may mean that act and potency are understood in exactly the same way in the philosophy of nature and in metaphysics, and in that meaning it involves placing the two disciplines on the same basis, and making them into the same kind of knowledge—and this is at least un-Aristotelian and un-Thomistic. And since we are considering precisely Thomistic metaphysics this position is not relevant. Again, the thesis may mean that the generalizations of metaphysics are drawn from the more special instances found in the knowledge of

some kind of being; this meaning may be Aristotleian; it is certainly Baconian, and is equally certainly not Thomistic. What St. Thomas' argument says is this: since all human knowledge begins with sensible things, we must first study act and potency, and so on in sensible things. But this study can be carried on metaphysically from the very beginning, for the first philosopher is concerned even with sensible things inasmuch as they are beings" (p. 194).

Father Klubertanz is certainly right in saying that act and potency have a much wider, transcendental meaning in metaphysics than in the philosophy of nature, since this transcendent and analogical meaning is derived from the analogates found in our sensible experience. It is strange, however, that he considers it "certainly un-Thomistic" to hold that the concepts of act and potency are first studied in the philosophy of nature in the restricted instances of form and matter, and thence used by metaphysics in a wider sense, since St. Thomas explicitly says: "Although divine science is by nature the first of all sciences, with respect to us the other sciences come before it. For, as Avicenna says, the order of this science is that it be learned after the natural sciences, which explain many things used by metaphysics, such as generation, corruption, motion, and the like" (*In Boethii De Trinitate,* q. 5, a. 1, ad 9). St. Thomas is explicitly speaking here of "natural sciences" and not of sensible experience as the source of metaphysical notions. This can be clearly seen also if we study the way in which St. Thomas actually develops any one of his metaphysical concepts. It is always by reference to the physical analogate as treated in Aristotle's physical works or to mathematical analogates (e.g., *Summa Theologiae,* I, qq. 2 to 11). Nor could we escape this by saying that St. Thomas in these passages gives the Aristotelian terms a new metaphysical meaning, since we can find this same procedure in St. Thomas' commentary on the *Physics* where (whether he is remaking Aristotle or not) he certainly intends to propose physical doctrine.

[59]For the genuine Thomistic view of psychology see the first lectures to the commentaries on the *De Anima* and the *De Sensu et Sensato,* where problems of "rational psychology" and what we would today call "experimental psychology" (for example, the study of the sense organs, their anatomy, physiology and functions, and the laws of learning) are arranged in a single science. The present division originated with Christian Wolff, and reflects the Cartesian mind-body dualism.

[60]The treatise on the Old Law is unfortunately neglected in many theology courses, but in it is contained St. Thomas' outline of a "theology of history."

[61]The term "Christian philosophy" which has been used in the papal encyclicals creates no difficulty if it is understood to mean a philosophy which is in harmony with the higher truth of the Christian faith, both because it submits to its *negative* control and to its *positive* inspiration and confirmation, provided that this philosophy does not rely on faith for the establishment of its *principles,* i.e., provided that from the logical point of view the light of faith remains *extrinsic* to the philosophical argumentation. If, however, principles borrowed from faith are admitted into an argument it becomes formally theological, and is no longer philosophy in any proper sense. Thus the view of Jacques Maritain that moral philosophy must be *subalternated* to theology, i.e., that it must use principles known by the light of faith, turns ethics into moral theology.

In a more subtle fashion Étienne Gilson considers Christian philosphy to consist in philosophical truth as is used by the theologian under the light of faith. Cf. *Elements of Christian Philosophy* (New York: Doubleday, 1960). This book shows by its order and structure that by "Christian philosophy" Gilson means an exposition of those parts of theology which deal with natural truths that have been revealed by God as an assistance to man. As he quite correctly points out (p. 289, footnote 36), truths of the natural order, when considered in this manner, are not pure philosophical truths, but formally theological truths, and

St. Thomas in considering them in this fashion is a theologian. Hence Gilson's own book is not a philosophical textbook but a theological textbook. As such it has great merits. It is of little value, however, in teaching students philosophy in preparation for theology because it does not use a philosophical method or order. It presupposes from the very outset that the student either accept the existence of God on faith, or that he be convinced of this by the *quinque viae* as presented in the *Summa.* However, if the student is really to grasp the *quinque viae* in a scientific fashion, he must go back and study philosophy in the order and manner so often approved by St. Thomas (at least logic, mathematics, philosophy of nature).

Thus although Gilson is entirely right in his insistence on the fact that philosophy as it is the handmaid of theology is wonderfully ennobled, he has not correctly presented St. Thomas' conception of philosophy, the right manner of studying it in preparation for theology, nor the way in which it is Christianized by theological guidance without losing its own proper value *outside* theology. I do not see how Gilson can escape the just charge of "theologism" which in the past he has leveled against other thinkers, since for him in a Christian context philosophy exists only as it is formally a part of theology. It must be admitted that no important commentator on St. Thomas in the long history of Thomism seems ever before to have found this view in the texts of St. Thomas, but rather they have all stressed that one of St. Thomas' greatest achievements was to vindicate philosophy as a *way* to theology, following its own methods and order. I would humbly suggest that this brilliant Thomist, who has done so much to awaken the shamefully ignorant world of the learned to the value of St. Thomas, has never given them in any of his works an exposition of a Thomistic philosophy which *begins* where all philosophy must begin (with the data of the senses) and works slowly up to *conclude* to God as pure existence. Rather, he always presents a Thomism which *begins* with this truth.

This is undoubtedly because he is convinced that this is where St. Thomas the theologian himself began. I would agree, but I would also insist that as an apologist for the faith St. Thomas saw that it is necessary to begin from the other end. Consequently, Gilson, who now writes as a theologian (since "Christian philosophy" is a part of theology in his view), does not follow the method proper to theological apologetics, which is to present the philosophical arguments that lead to the faith in a philosophical order and by a strictly philosophical method.

[62]The canonical approbation was again reiterated by Pius XII in *Humani Generis:* "If one considers all this well, he will easily see why the Church demands that future priests be instructed in philosophy 'according to the method, doctrine and principles of the Angelic Doctor' (Code of Canon Law, Can. 1366, § 2), since, we all know from the experience of centuries, the method of Aquinas is singularly pre-eminent both for teaching students and for bringing truth to light; his doctrine is in harmony with divine revelation, and is most effective both for safeguarding the foundation of the faith and for reaping, safely and usefully, the fruits of sound progress. How deplorable it is, then, that this philosophy received and honored by the Church is scorned by some who shamelessly call it outmoded in form and rationalistic, as they say, in its method and thought. . . . Our traditional philosophy, then, with its clear exposition and solution of questions, its accurate definition of terms, its clear-cut distinctions, can be, they concede, useful as a preparation for scholastic theology, a preparation quite in accord with medieval mentality; but this philosophy hardly offers a method of philosophizing suited to the needs of our modern culture."

[63]See S. M. Ramírez, O.P., "De philosophia morali christiana," *Divus Thomas* (Freiburg), XIV (1936), 87-141, 181-236.

[64]It is true, of course, that metaphysics defends the principles of the lower sciences but this does not mean it should be studied first. If one were to con-

clude this then it would also be necessary to study metaphysics before logic since metaphysics defends the validity of logic. Furthermore, it would have to precede sense experience which metaphysics also defends. Truths which are immediately evident such as the principles of the sciences are not *proved* by metaphysics, since what is already evidently true is not proved. They are merely defended, i.e., metaphysics shows the fallacies of arguments brought against them. A person who sees these principles to be true is in no doubt about them and can proceed to build a science on them, even though he does not know how to reply to difficulties raised against them, whose solution he leaves to the metaphysician. Thus the natural scientist does not have to answer difficulties raised by idealism before he can be sure of the validity of his own science.

11

COLLEGE THEOLOGY AND THE LITURGY

Christopher Kiesling, O.P.

Now on leave from the faculty of theology at St. Rose Priory, Dubuque, Father Kiesling, who holds the lectorate and licentiate in sacred theology, is pursuing doctoral studies at the Pontifical Faculty of the Immaculate Conception, Washington, D.C. After completion of studies at the Angelicum in Rome, he taught moral theology at St. Rose for several years and has in preparation a volume on the theology of the liturgy.

Today the liturgy is the center of much attention. The encyclical letter of Pope Pius XII, *Mediator Dei*, the Instruction of the Sacred Congregation of Rites on church music and liturgy issued September 3, 1958, and most recently the reforms of the breviary and of the Mass which went into effect on January 1, 1961, have given the highest sanction to the liturgical revival which began in this country in the middle of the 1920's. All the institutions of Christian life are implicated in this liturgical revival—the hierarchy, the family, the schools, including the college. Since the function of the college is to teach, the college must assume the delegated role of teaching the liturgy in this movement.

But to assign the college the task of teaching the liturgy is to assign a rather vague task. Should the college teach the liturgy in the sense of teaching the student how to participate in the liturgy? Or should the college teach the student to know what the liturgy is? Moreover, there are several approaches to this latter task. The college might teach the history of the liturgy, so that the student knows what the liturgy is insofar as it has evolved from the distant past; or it might give the student such knowledge by analyzing the rites, the prayers, the feasts that make up the liturgy, in order to understand the meaning of these signs and symbols; or the college might be content to detail what the Bible or the Fathers of the Church have said about the liturgy. Finally, the college course in liturgy might lead the student beyond the data of Scripture and Tradition, the materials of positive theology, to inquire into the inner nature of that mystery called the liturgy revealed by these sources of faith—an inquiry which would be the work of scholastic or systematic theology.

The purpose of this study is to determine the role of the college in teaching the liturgy. This is truly an essay, because, first of all, it is a "striving" for a solution, for a general program of teaching the liturgy in college; adaptation of it to particular circumstances is beyond our scope. This is an essay also because it is written from a limited point of view, that is, it presumes as true that theology is a truly objective wisdom and science about God; that, like any body of science, theology has an order and integrity that cannot be violated without destroying it; that this theology is a necessary and all important part of the education of every student in the college. As a consequence of these presuppositions (which are, indeed, convictions), teaching the liturgy must be fitted into the college program without any major alteration in the theology course. The reasonableness of this position will be made clear in the course of this paper.

The first consideration to be taken up concerns the role of the college in instructing the student about how to participate in the liturgy; secondly, we will consider the teaching of liturgy by imparting theoretical knowledge of its history, an analysis of liturgical forms, its theology. Since the one wisdom which is theology has many functions, the relative roles of biblical, patristic, symbolic and scholastic theology will be studied. Finally, some practical suggestions for the professor of theology and/or chaplain will be offered with regard to promoting the liturgy in college.

Active Participation in the Liturgy

Instruction in liturgical practice is not, for the most part, proper to the college. The student entering college should long ago have been taught by his parents and by his grammar and high school teachers how to participate actively in the Mass and in other liturgical functions. The college student's liturgical worship must be perfected, made more natural and more meaningful, but it should not have to be initiated when he is in college.

These common sense facts have been embodied in the Instruction of the Sacred Congregation of Rites, September 3, 1958, on sacred music and the sacred liturgy.[1] This instruction notes:

> The Christian family is the natural and first school of Christian education. . . . An effort should be made, therefore, to see to it that the children, according to their age and reason, learn to participate in the pious exercises and liturgical functions, especially in the sacrifice of the Mass, and begin to learn and love popular religious song in the family and in the church.[2]

The September instruction directs that in schools in which the Church has a free hand "provisions should be made for the children to learn popular sacred hymns . . . and to receive, according to their understanding, a more complete instruction on the holy sacrifice of the Mass and the manner of participating in it. They should also begin to sing the more simple Gregorian melodies."[3]

The instruction of the Sacred Congregation reaffirms and reinforces this directive for elementary schools in its directive for secondary schools:

> What has been said about the primary and elementary schools applies with even greater necessity to the intermediate or secondary schools where adolescents must acquire that maturity needed for sound social and religious life.[4]

The universal liturgical know-how envisaged by Rome is apparent from the norms proposed for participation in the Mass, where specific responses, specific parts of the ordinary of the Mass, and specific chants are pointed out with the directive that "every effort must be made that the faithful of the entire world know how to give these responses in chant" and that "care must be taken that the following easier Gregorian themes be learned by all the faithful throughout the world. . . ."[5]

The student entering college should be able to participate actively in the Mass, share devoutly in Benediction of the Blessed Sacrament, and prayerfully witness a baptism. College experiences will increase the understanding and appreciation of these acts of worship and enrich their fruitfulness for the student and the Mystical Body. But college is not the proper place for courses in attending Mass or any other liturgical ceremony.

The September instruction of the Sacred Congregation of Rites speaks of those pursuing higher studies as requiring "a fuller instruction in the complete Christian life,"[6] which implies that the teaching provided on lower levels of education is already in some sense "full," or sufficient for "that maturity needed for sound social and religious life."[7] In college, a student's liturgical practice is to be brought to a perfection beyond "full" and approaching "maturity":

> Therefore, all priests in whose care university students have in any way been entrusted should strive to lead them theoretically and practically to a more complete knowledge and participation in the sacred liturgy, and as circumstances permit should use that form of Mass which is treated of in numbers 26 [Missa cantata] and 31 [dialogue Mass].[8]

Today, of course, college students do not always, or perhaps even frequently, have this background of liturgical practice dictated by common sense and called for by the September directives of the Sacred Congregation. By reason of circumstances, therefore, the college may have to do remedial work with regard to liturgical know-how. It would be a mistake, however, for the college to consider that in the present situation the only or the foremost task of the college is to make up for what the student lacks by inaugurating courses to teach liturgical practice. The college should take as its primary task that of imparting to the student the heritage of Christian civilization in which theology in general and the theology of the liturgy in particular occupy an important position. The liturgical practice of the college student will, with a little assistance, take care of itself.

If the college curriculum presents to the students a dynamic Christian wisdom which necessarily includes an understanding and appreciation of the liturgy, and if the college administration, priests and chaplains provide the opportunities for participation in the liturgy, the students with a minimum of instruction or advice will quickly learn what should have been learned in their previous education. Interestingly, in discussions among those teaching and studying in college about how to encourage and promote participation in the liturgy, the discussion invariably comes around to the quality of the theology course. It is generally recognized that at the college level, if the students can be led to understand the significance of the liturgy and appreciate its importance in their lives in the theology class, the liturgical practice will follow—provided, of course, that chaplains and administration give ample opportunities for the students to share in the liturgy.

Besides academic encouragement, a non-college factor is at work to remedy the college student's lack of practical liturgical ability. The dioceses and parishes throughout the country are, in increasing numbers, inaugurating programs of lay participation in the liturgy. With the training the college student receives at school, he should be able to fall in with the liturgical activity around him and, if he has been taught convincingly of the truth of the liturgy, he will eagerly join in it. Because of these programs in dioceses and parishes, more and more students coming into college will have increased liturgical ability. The more adept at active participation should be able to carry along those less skilled.

Although it would be a mistake to make college teaching of the liturgy an instruction in "how to do it," this is not a recommendation that nothing should be done to instruct college students in liturgical participation, because it is too obvious that today's college student, as a future leader of society and a molder of children, must be skilled in such worship. The September instruction urges those caring for college and university students to have them use those forms of participation in the Mass which are the most advanced and which in fact may rarely be found outside of institutions of higher learning, seminaries and convents.[9] But at the college level, instruction in liturgical practice should be able to be accomplished almost as an aside—an occasional general assembly, a part of a theology class, a sermon before a liturgical function. Because of the present situation, there will be many of these "asides" in college today to compensate for what has been left undone in the past. But with each year there should be less and less need for instruction in liturgical practice at the college level.

Theoretical Teaching of the Liturgy

Teaching the liturgy in the sense of imparting theoretical knowledge of the liturgy is proper to the college. But two points should be noted here. First of all, this theoretical knowledge is not be be understood as exclusively theoretical; it can and should influence the liturgical practice of the student. But this influence can and will be felt only if this knowledge is pursued with zeal, tried in the fire of scientific thinking, and thoroughly assimilated, not by the memory, but by the understanding, so that it shapes the habitual outlook of the student and forms the frame of reference for his value judgments. Because the conscious stress must be on the *theoria* rather than the *praxis* which follows, the knowledge under discussion is referred to as theoretical knowledge.

Secondly, the primary aim of the school as school is the acquisition of truth, the perfection of the mind. The motive that triggers men into establishing schools or entering them is to learn, whatever other motives they may also have. The school also happens to be a community, and as a community, imperfect though it be, it has responsibilities, functions and aims other than knowledge: it is concerned with morals, with the development of Christian character. The teaching of the liturgy in college as school is aimed primarily at theoretical knowledge of the liturgy as one of the great mysteries of the Christian religion and in every Christian's life. The college as community, however, also has an obligation with regard to the liturgy, that is, to make liturgical practice a vital part of the life of the college so that it will help shape the Christian personality of the student.

The first sort of theoretical knowledge of the liturgy which the college should impart as part of its proper task is history of the liturgy. The history of the liturgy offers several advantages. It familiarizes the college student with the liturgy he practices in greater detail. It makes the liturgy more acceptable to him, insofar as it shows him that many elements in the liturgy which seem strange and meaningless to his twentieth century mentality have significance and purpose; he is no longer totally embarassed by, and alienated from his modern milieu by engaging in liturgical participation, because history affords him a bridge of intelligible continuity from the remnants of the past into the present. History of the liturgy also heightens the student's awareness of his place in the flow of mankind's story; he sees his liturgical practice as a part of mankind's strivings, and his youthful yearning to accomplish and to contribute finds satisfaction and stimulus in the liturgy now seen in the light of history.

But on the other hand, the history of the liturgy is concerned with externals more than with the inner mystery of the liturgy; it is concerned more with the past than with the present. A high school teacher once made the observation that if you say "yesterday" before a group of high school students, you have lost their interest immediately; they simply are not interested in the past, today and the future are all important. To a great extent the same is true of college students, at least freshmen and sophomores. The liturgy of today is often not very important in their eyes and the liturgy of the second century even less so. And even though the history of the liturgy shows that the elements of today's liturgy have meaning and that the liturgy is not unreasonable, this does not necessarily make the liturgy meaningful for today or make it not merely acceptable (because explainable) but desired (because pertinent to the present).

History of the liturgy must find a place in the college teaching of the liturgy. That history is part of the Christian heritage the college is meant to pass on to its students. History is an excellent apologetic weapon. A knowledge of the history of the liturgy does, in fact, prepare the way for an understanding of the mystery of the liturgy and for better participation in the liturgy. But for the college student the history of the liturgy has too superficial a value, too little interest, and too little relevancy to be the staple of a course devoted to the liturgy or of part of the theology course devoted to the liturgy. The history of the liturgy can and should be taught to the college student by interweaving it with other courses—history proper, theology, Scripture, etc.—by occasionally lecturing on a phase of liturgical history, by explaining the development of the liturgy before some liturgical ceremony, etc. The market is deluged with excellent books on the history of the liturgy, which provide abundant material for reading assignments. An undergraduate college course dedicated entirely to the history of the liturgy would not seem to warrant the time and effort expended upon it.

Another kind of theoretical knowledge of the liturgy is acquired from the analysis of liturgical forms, the study of the symbols—prayers, actions, festivities, etc.—which form the sensible aspect of the liturgy, enveloping the mystery of faith which is the worship of Christ and his Church. This sort of knowledge of the liturgy is profitable. Like the history of the liturgy, it familiarizes the student with the details of the liturgy he practices, and manifests the reasonableness, the acceptability, of this worship of God. Much more than the history of the liturgy, this approach presents the here-and-now meaning and relevance of the liturgy and necessarily advances toward the inner mystery of this worship by seeking the things signified which lie behind the signs or symbols of the sacred rites. Because of its concern for the present and its approach to the inner reality, the study of the "shape" of the liturgy is more appealing to the college student and more immediately useful for him in his own participation in it than the study of its history. Teaching the student the meaning of the liturgical year by analyzing texts and feasts is more important, more appealing and more useful than teaching him about the influence of the Advent season in the now defunct Gallic practice or the Advent season of the Roman rites during the Middle Ages.

With the growth of the liturgical revival and instruction on the liturgy, this analysis of liturgical forms will be imparted more and more in earlier years of schooling. It seems to be the sort of theoretical teaching of the liturgy most proper to the secondary or high school, where history would have even less appeal than in college, and where theological analysis would be too advanced. Besides, the college student should be able to acquire much of this knowledge through explanatory notes found in missals, current liturgical publications, and sermons and homilies which unfold the meaning of the liturgy.

The college should, however, strive to increase the student's knowledge of liturgical forms. This is an extremely valuable aid to a theological understanding and appreciation of the liturgy and to more attentive and devout participation in the liturgy. But again, as in the case of history, this sort of knowledge can and should be conveyed to the student through means other than a course devoted to analyzing liturgical forms. This approach is excellent for study clubs and discussion groups, because it does not require much research or profound theological ability. Under the moderation of someone who does know theology, the students, using their habitual knowledge of their faith as well as what they are currently learning about their faith and their world, can discuss the meaning of liturgical prayers, actions, ceremonies, etc., and find them meaningful and profitable for themselves in their own terms here and now. This approach to the liturgy, the analysis of liturgical forms, can find a place in other courses: the literature course can analyze psalms or even the Mass;[10] the theology course can use liturgical texts as positive sources (*loci theologici*) for various doctrines to be studied. There is a great advantage to be gained, it is worth noting, from infusing the study of liturgical forms and even liturgical history into a wide variety of courses; it impresses upon the student that the liturgy is not an isolated element in life, but that all phases of life have a bearing upon the liturgy and the liturgy, in turn, upon all aspects of life.

It may be noted here that "theology" courses which attempt to teach sacred doctrine by using the missal as the textbook are teaching, not theology, but liturgy in the sense of analyzing liturgical forms. The result of such courses is a collection of many truths about God and man occasioned by whatever liturgical texts happened to have been used as the text for the course. But the student does not have any objective, reasoned order in his knowledge about God and man; he does not have the wisdom and science of God which is theology; he has the sort of knowledge about his faith that might well be expected at a high school level.

Theological Knowledge

A third kind of theoretical knowledge of the liturgy is theological knowledge, the imparting of which is the most proper task of the college. The importance of teaching theological knowledge of the liturgy in college derives not only from the primary aim of the college as school, an institution devoted to the communication of truth, but also from the very needs of the college student.

Knowledge of the liturgy which consists in memorized responses to questions (the sort of knowledge the catechism fosters) is proper for the child whose powers of reason have not yet awakened and who must, nevertheless, begin to come into possession of the content of his faith. Knowledge of the liturgy which consists in understanding how important the liturgy is for *me,* what worlds of truth it opens to me, what powers of achievement and reform it places in my hands, is proper for the high school student, whose interest in his own developing personality and in his social relationships is at its height. But at the college level students should have stored away the facts which constitute the objects of faith; they should have achieved some integration of their personality and some stability in their social position, and they should have found the place for the liturgy in their personal and social lives. They come to college to seek the truth, to submit themselves to the truth, not the truth to themselves. If they wish to be accountants, they submit themselves to the mathematical sciences and the art of accounting. If they wish to be lawyers, they submit their minds to the body of law. It is now no longer a question of mere memory; it is now no longer a question of personal appeal; it is the objective truth which rules. The same must hold for the college student's approach to the liturgy: he must submit his mind to this truth as it is in itself; he must evaluate it on the basis of its own merits, not on the basis of what he may gain from it.

The future liturgical practice of the college student depends in no little measure upon the college student's acquiring this kind of objective knowledge about the liturgy, one of the great mysteries of his faith and in his life. The grasp of this mysterious truth is through the gift of faith, but that gift of faith is possessed and used by man freely: it may be left dormant or it may be exercised; when exercised, it may flicker like a match or rage like a forest fire. If the truth of the liturgy is presented to the college student as so many facts to be memorized or primarily as a means of tremendous personal advantage, there is little likelihood, from a human point of view, that in future years the college student will be willing to lay down his life for the mystery of the liturgy. If the truth of the liturgy held by faith is not tried in the same scalding fire as the truths of science, if the truth of the liturgy is not objectively analyzed, probed, defended and set in its context of divine truth, the college student will let his faith in the liturgy lie dormant in favor of some science or art of the human order which has been tested. Or if he exercises his faith in the liturgy, it will lead him at most to carry out a dimly recognized duty rather than fire him with zeal for the house of the Lord.

Theological knowledge of the liturgy calls into play the various functions of the wisdom and science of God known as theology. Since the liturgy is a mystery known only by faith, divine revelation must be consulted to learn what God has revealed to man about the liturgy. Revelation is contained in Sacred Scripture and in Tradition, this latter leaving its traces in the writings of the Fathers, in liturgical texts, in ecclesiastical art and elsewhere. How the revelation contained in Scripture and Tradition is to be interpreted and what is to be accepted by faith as divinely revealed is determined by the teaching of the Church in her ordinary and extraordinary *magisterium.*

Theological knowledge of the liturgy requires that the college student be introduced to, and become familiar with at least the principal documents of the Church and the chief portions of the Bible concerning the liturgy. If possible, he should have acquaintance with some of the writings of the Fathers of the Church. Thus the college student should read and become familiar with the encyclical *Mediator Dei* of Pope Pius XII and with the main lines of the worship of the Mosaic Law, together with its successes and failures, and as it finally culminates in Christ's institution of a new worship. He should be familiar with St. Paul's description of baptism in the epistle to the Romans (Chap. 6) and of matrimony in the letter to the Ephesians (Chap. 5). If the student can be introduced to St. Justin Martyr's account of the Mass in mid-second century (*First Apology*, Chap. 65 and 67) and *The Apostolic Tradition* of St. Hippolytus of Rome for the end of the second or the third century, he will uncover valuable and interesting material. The more scriptural, patristic and ecclesiastical texts concerning the liturgy to which the college student is introduced the better, provided study of liturgically relevant texts does not become an obstacle to reaching the heart of the theology of the liturgy.

The knowledge of the sources of revelation concerning the liturgy is only a beginning of this theological knowledge. These sources inform man about what God has said about the liturgy. But one may be able to quote verbatim every biblical and patristic passage and every ecclesiastical pronouncement pertinent to the liturgy and still not understand what the liturgy is in itself. He may not have passed beyond the signs given by God to manifest the liturgy in order to reach the heart of the matter. He would be like the biology student who spent all his time studying the microscope and never did get around to studying the living creatures seen through the microscope.

The Bible, the writings of the Fathers, the Church's teachings are the means *by which* man comes into contact with a mysterious reality, the liturgy, the worship of Christ and his Church. The mystery itself in its objective reality is *that which* theology seeks to know. To teach the college student biblical, patristic and ecclesiastical texts and to describe that as the theology of the liturgy is to mistake a means for the end, a part for the whole.

To teach the theology of the liturgy is to behold the divine mystery manifested by the sources of revelation and to see what relationship the liturgy has to other divine mysteries revealed by God, to discover what likenesses to it may be found in nature which may help us to understand it better, and to decide what importance this mystery has for man, for self, in the search for eternal happiness.[11] This is the heart of the theology of the liturgy. The study of relevant documents in which the college student engages must be measured by the needs of this more demanding and necessary search.

The theology of the liturgy which the college properly imparts to its students must not stop with knowledge of the sources of revelation concerning the liturgy but must proceed under the direction of faith to seek scientific understanding of the reality revealed by those sources. This means the college theology of the liturgy seeks to give reasoned, thought-out answers to certain basic questions about the liturgy. St. Peter urged, "Be ready always with an answer (*apologia*) to everyone who asks a reason (*logos*) for the hope that is in you" (I Pet. 3:15). The college student should be prepared to give answers to basic questions about the liturgy, not only questions proposed by Protestants and atheists attacking the liturgy, but questions proposed by the human intelligence of the college student himself about the truths he accepts on faith. Faith is not an invitation to cease asking questions about the great problems of human existence; it is, on the contrary, an invitation to ask more questions than ever, for it opens up a whole new world transcending the world of human science and demanding to be known by the divine science of theology. Do not Catholic students in secular universities often lose their faith precisely because they cannot give an answer—a reasonable, thought-out answer—to the questions they find in their own minds as a result of the lectures they hear and the books they read? Do they not lose their faith often because their minds need theology as a defense of their faith, and they do not have theology?

The liturgy is an action, the worship of Christ and his Church. The human mind inevitably asks certain fundamental questions about any action, whether it knows about that action through experience or through God's revelation. The answers to these fundamental questions constitute scientific, objective, reasoned knowledge about any particular action. The college student, whose mind is examining in such scientific fashion the action of chemical elements, the action of protons and neutrons, the action of organs of sensation, the action of nations and societies, should and indeed must examine with equal objectivity and rigor of thought the action of Christ and his Church which is the liturgy. This examination by no means excludes the study of Scripture, the Fathers and the teachings of the Church. Quite the contrary, for this scientific examination takes its subject of study from these sources; it draws the answers to its questions from the fonts of revelation; and it finds its term, its rest, in contemplating with deeper understanding the divine truth which faith sees in and through the pages of the Bible and the record of Tradition guarded and interpreted by the teaching of the Church.

Briefly, the questions which should be asked and answered for a reasoned understanding of faith's teaching about the liturgy are as follows. Even though the existence of the liturgy is accepted as a fact of faith, three questions can be asked about the liturgy's existence: 1) Who gave the liturgy its existence (*efficient cause*)? 2) What needs does the liturgy satisfy (*fittingness*)? 3) When did the liturgy's existence begin and how long will it last (*duration*)? With regard to the essence or nature of the liturgy several more questions can be asked: 1) Who performs the liturgy (*agent*)? 2) With what powers does the agent perform the liturgy (*powers of agent*)? 3) What is the liturgical action generically, i.e., into what general category of things is the liturgy to be classified (*genus of definition*)? 4) What is the liturgical action specifically, i.e., what is unique about the liturgy that makes it to be the liturgy and distinct from any other action (*specific difference of definition*)? 5) What effects does the liturgy produce? 6) What is the ultimate purpose of the liturgy?

These questions and answers about the liturgy can find a place in the ordinary, required course of college theology. Following the order of St. Thomas' *Summa Theologiae,* the treatise on the Old and New Laws (which is, in fact, a kind of theology of history) provides an opportunity to consider the duration of the liturgy: to see its prefigurement in the Old Testament, its present reality and its future status after the Parousia.

The treatise on the virtue of faith—in particular, the study of the obligation to confess one's faith—provides an opportunity to consider the needs the liturgy satisfies and the powers with which the liturgy is performed. The liturgy is the normal manner of professing one's faith before men, a natural inclination and an obligation not limited to times of persecution. Faith, moreover, is one of the powers behind liturgical action.

The treatise on the virtue of religion adds to the knowledge of the powers behind the liturgy and gives information about the general category into which the liturgy is classified, worship. In this treatise the student becomes familiar with devotion, prayer, adoration, offering, sacrifice, praise and the use of sacred symbols. Here the interior and exterior aspects of the liturgy can be considered as well as the Divine Office and the liturgical year, the role of churches and art in worship, and many other aspects of the liturgy.

The treatise on Christ provides essential knowledge of the liturgy. The reasons and ultimate purpose for the Incarnation can be extended to explain the existence of the liturgy, which is the prolongation of the Incarnation among men. The study of Christ's priesthood, to be complemented later by a study of the sacramental characters, adds still more information about the powers which cause the liturgical action. The doctrine of Christ as the Head of the Mystical Body leads to knowledge of the agent of the liturgy, the Mystical Christ.

In the treatise on the sacraments, scientific knowledge of the liturgy can be completed. The liturgy is more than simply the sacraments; the teacher, therefore, must not be content to present only sacramental theology, but must apply to the sacraments the previously mentioned dogmatic and moral truths significant for an understanding of the liturgy. But since the sacraments are the heart of the liturgy, they form the focal point for other liturgically relevant truths; and an accurate knowledge of the nature of the sacraments is truly the key to an understanding of the entire liturgy.

The nature of the sacraments as efficacious signs is of extraordinary importance for understanding the liturgy. Here is an opportunity to deepen an understanding about its generic nature, which is, for the most part, the use of sacred signs—sacraments, sacramentals, ceremonies, words—as expressions of religion and living faith.

The study of the institution of the sacraments and their necessity provides information about the existence of the liturgy and the needs it satisfies.

The study of the effect of the sacraments—sacramental grace, Christian grace—is the substance of the knowledge of the effect of the liturgy. It is important in this matter to concentrate less on the mechanics of conferring grace and to attend more closely to the kind of grace which is conferred—grace proportioned to the sacramental signs which confer it, grace likening men to Christ—and to the dispositions of the recipient necessary for a more fruitful reception of the sacraments

Consideration of the effect of certain of the sacraments, namely, the characters imprinted by baptism, confirmation and holy orders, completes the student's knowledge of the liturgy. Here elements from the treatises on faith, religion and the priesthood of Christ are brought together and focused on one activity of the Mystical Body of Christ, its worship, which is the unique worship that it is because through the sacramental characters Christ himself worships in his Church and his Church in and through him. At this point the student can discover what makes the liturgy to be the unique reality it is: the worship of the Mystical Christ.

The Course of Theology

The college student can acquire the theological knowledge of the liturgy which he can, should and must attain in the ordinary, required course of theology or sacred doctrine which is well balanced and which offers the student the full heritage of Christian thought. The teacher, of course, must be alert to the possibilities of the theology he is teaching with regard to the development of the student's understanding of the liturgy. The student cannot be expected to see the relevancy of various truths taught in the sacred doctrine course to the liturgy any more than he is expected to see them in relation to other facets of his life. Referring the contents of the theology course to the liturgical practices in which he actually engages can help to make the theology class more relevant to the student; the theology class in turn can aid him in deepening his own liturgical piety by showing him its value and place in life.

To teach the theology of the liturgy in the ordinary, required course of theology, not by instituting a distinct course in the liturgy, but by relating the matter at hand to the liturgy, seems a far better way to bring these truths to college minds. The other alternative—instituting a course on the liturgy in place of the required course—brings up the question: why a course in the liturgy rather than in some other mystery of the faith? If the liturgy is given a whole semester of treatment, then why not the lay apostolate or the Church or Mariology? Such divisions break down the entire course in theology as a transmission of Christian wisdom.

If it is argued that today the liturgy is very important and one of the foremost interests of the Church, it can be argued also that the college prepares the student, not for today, but for tomorrow, by passing on to him the principles of life according to the Gospel, so that when he steps forth into the world as an educated adult and leader he will be able to meet the problems of that day by the application of the principles he has learned in college. The college as community tends to care for the responsibilities of the student body, not relieving him of responsibilities, but by rules, safeguards, advice and the general atmosphere of the college community. The college functions in this way so that it can be free to operate as a school to implant principles of Christian living in the student's mind so that he will be able to assume responsibility for others as well as for himself in the future.

There is no little danger in emphasizing one facet of the faith out of proportion to others. The history of the Church reveals that most councils of the Church and papal definitions and pronouncements have been occasioned by a well intentioned but distorted emphasis on one element of the Christian truth to the neglect or denial of other elements. Indeed, the encyclical on the liturgy by Pope Pius XII, *Mediator Dei,* was occasioned not only by the lack of enthusiasm and appreciation for the liturgy found in some quarters but also by the excesses and errors indulged in and propagated by those who could see no other reality than the liturgy.[12] The college is surely dedicated to fashioning the man of integrity, the wise and prudent man, who sees reality from God's point of view, so that he can handle the problems of the day in accord with God's will. The theology course must, therefore, give the college student a view of reality as God sees it, not as the men or some men of this day or this decade see it.

Besides the danger involved in teaching an unbalanced view of reality by emphasizing what is currently of "high fashion," there is the futility of such an approach: fashions change very much from decade to decade, and if the college gears its courses only to meet the "fashion," the student's college education is soon out-of-date. If the college abandons teaching the principles of all theology, it forsakes its own goal as transmitter of the Christian heritage and it betrays its students, who expect to be equipped for life, not for a day, by their college education.

The college student must be taught the theology of the liturgy and the college as a school is the proper agency to give that instruction. This can be accomplished better in the ordinary course of theology, for the opportunities are present in the content of the whole theology course, and the resultant view of the liturgy is indeed a balanced one: the student sees that the liturgy does in fact have relevance to other elements of the Christian life but that, like the other elements of the Christian life, it is not the whole.

If this theological training in the liturgy in the required course of sacred doctrine (a function of the college as school) is complemented by opportunities for liturgical practice, and occasional and more or less informal instruction about one or another phase of the liturgy (a function of the school as community), the college student can leave college with that more complete knowledge and participation in the liturgy called for by the instruction of the Sacred Congregation of Rites. As the result of this program the student may not be as ideal a participator and propagandist for the liturgy as some would wish; but, if the college is functioning as it should in other areas, the student will at least be on his way toward being a whole man equipped to live the whole Christian life.

Practical Suggestions

By way of practical suggestions toward increased instruction in the liturgy, both from the speculative and practical points of view, it should be noted that very much responsibility rests with the teacher of theology in the college. This is the *de facto* situation, whether it is right or not. Therefore, the teacher of theology must see to it that he does use the opportunities found in the ordinary course of theology to explain the liturgy. He will also have to promote study groups, projects and actual liturgical functions to insure the student's growth in the theory and practice of liturgical worship. He may not believe this is his responsibility, but as the situation exists today the rest of the college faculty tends to think it is his duty especially. The implementation of the decree of the Congregation of Rites falls, at least by default of others, upon the theology professor. If the theology teacher is chaplain of the school, then he has even more responsibility, especially with regard to providing opportunities for liturgical practice and with regard to instruction which will help the students understand what they are doing.

The theology professor must use tact, of course, in promoting interest in the liturgy and its practice. Minds must be prepared gradually before any unusual practice is advanced. Greater participation in the liturgy is, moreover, more a matter of understanding and devotion than of new and unusual practices. The primary liturgical revival is qualitative rather than quantitative. The theology teacher or chaplain must endeavor tactfully to bring other faculty members to an understanding and appreciation of the liturgy and to see their opportunities and responsibilities toward promoting the liturgy. In this way the whole college, as community and as school, can be educating its students liturgically in theory and in practice in a manner that does justice to the importance and all-pervasiveness of God's worship in the Christian life.

Footnotes to Study 11

[1]*AAS*, L (1958), 630-663; all references will be to the translation provided by the NCWC News Service, 2nd printing, January, 1959.

[2]*Ibid.*, n. 105.

[3]*Ibid.*, n. 106.

[4]*Ibid.*, n. 107.

[5]*Ibid.*, n. 25.

[6]*Ibid.*, n. 108.

[7]*Ibid.*, n. 107.

[8]*Ibid.*, n. 108.

[9]*Loc. cit.*

[10]Cf. Benedict M. Ashley, O.P., *The Arts of Learning and Communication* (Dubuque, Iowa: The Priory Press, 1958), 473-78, for an analysis of the Mass as drama.

[11]Cf. the Vatican Council, Sess. III, *Dogmatic Constitution on the Catholic Faith*, Chap. 4, "Concerning Faith and Reason"; Denz. 1796.

[12]Cf. *AAS*, XXXIX (1947), 524, 532-33, 553, 562-63; NCWC trans., nn. 7-10, 28-31, 88, 113-15. Many other citations could be given indicating that excesses and errors were, in part, responsible for various sections of the encyclical on the liturgy, excesses and errors springing from an unbalanced view.

12

THEOLOGY AND THE MARRIAGE COURSE

Augustine Rock, O.P.

A co-author of Toward Marriage in Christ, *the popular college text for the marriage course, Father Rock (S.T.D. from the University of Fribourg) was for eight years professor of Church history and patrology at St. Rose, Dubuque. Author of the volume,* Unless They Be Sent, *a theology of preaching, he is professor of graduate theology at De Paul University, Chicago, an official of The Priory Press, and editor of the* Dominican Educational Bulletin. *He also collaborated on* Christ, and His Sacraments *of the college theology text series.*

Nearly everyone agrees that some kind of a marriage course is in some degree necessary as a part of a college curriculum. Beyond that point there does not seem to be a great deal of agreement. What such a course would amount to depends on the principles of life, thought and education which govern those preparing and providing such a course. Those who are in basic agreement on principles should be able to reach basic agreement about a marriage course. Based on Christian principles of life, thought and education interpreted Thomistically it is possible to offer some reflections concerning this matter, keeping in mind the great variety of actual circumstances to which these ideas have to be adapted.

The Purpose of a Marriage Course

The purpose of a marriage course in the college curriculum seems to be threefold. Most of the students will some day marry. As educated

Catholics they should have as clear an idea as possible of what they are doing, of the nature of marriage, and of its consequences and implications both for the individuals marrying and for society. This would certainly seem to be a valid purpose for such a course, though it may be questioned as justification for its inclusion in an academic curriculum. In fact, if this were the exclusive purpose of the course there would be just reason for excluding it on academic grounds, though it does not seem that it would be necessary to exclude it altogether.

The second purpose is similar to the first. As parents and in other capacities as well the students will very likely have a role to play in guiding those younger than themselves through the years of marriage preparation and selection of a marriage partner. Some systematic knowledge of the factors involved will prepare them to make a more intelligent approach to this matter than would otherwise be the case. Once again, however, one could question the value of this purpose as a justification for inclusion in the academic program, posing the same difficulties as could be raised about the first purpose, though perhaps with less force.

The third purpose of a marriage course, however, seems to justify beyond question an academic course concerning marriage. Educated people owe society an intelligent contribution to the solution of its problems, the formation of customs, the establishment of values. The family as the unit of society and marriage as the cause of the family are the concern of everyone. Therefore, an educated Catholic should have well formulated ideas about marriage which he should be able to support with intelligent reasons and which he should be able to apply in varying circumstances.

The pastoral mind would be likely to be more concerned with the first two purposes mentioned, the academic mind with the third. Unfortunately, the pastoral mind has often had too much to say about the curriculum of the Catholic college, but it is an oversimplification to say that there is necessarily opposition between the two. This is a significant point, since the form and content of the marriage course will be influenced by whichever of the purposes mentioned is taken as foremost.

The apparent opposition between the pastoral and the academic approach stems more from shortsightedness in the pastoral viewpoint than from a real conflict of interests. In the long run the welfare of souls seems best served by allowing Catholic institutions of learning to determine their programs on academic principles. This may be seen as a facet of the eschatologist-incarnationist problem. Should the Church forget the world and its institutions to concentrate its efforts on the salvation of individual Christians? If men become Christian, institutions will follow as a matter of course. Or should the Church take a vital interest in the Christianizing of society in order to create a climate favorable to the conversion of individuals? Those who espouse the first point of view would be inclined to favor the inclusion of a marriage course and the construction of such a course based principally on the first two purposes mentioned. The pastoral mind which inclines to the second interpretation of the Church's mission would be likely to agree with the academician that the most important purpose of the marriage course is the third, though for reasons more ultimate than those which directly concern the educator.

There seems to be no good reason why the first two purposes need be neglected or excluded if the third purpose is accepted as the guiding norm for the construction of the course and the determination of its place in the curriculum. Naturally we trust that correct thinking on the part of the student will contribute to correct behavior on the part of the man.

It must be kept clearly in mind that a college marriage course is being considered here. Frequently courses are offered in high schools which may proceed from a greater orientation toward behavior. Here there is rather a question of Christian doctrine than of theology, of indoctrination rather than of science. St. Thomas lists the kind of instruction which should be given to youngsters as a kind of preaching.[1] Preaching for him included instruction together with persuasion to a life in accord with what is taught.[2] Obviously such instruction as that offered by pre-Cana conferences, pre-marriage retreats, etc., is ordained essentially and immediately to right behavior on the part of those being instructed. In college the subjects taught should be approached scientifically. There is no need to labor this point here.

The question here is of college courses about marriage. College courses are scientific in their approach; their proper objective is truth rather than goodness. In this perspective the third purpose of a marriage course—the formation of the student's mind concerning the nature of marriage and the family as well as the role of marriage and family in the total life of society—is accepted as normative. The other purposes are not eliminated but they are secondary.

Man can be the subject of many intellectual disciplines depending upon the aspect under which he is studied. The same can be said of marriage. The disciplines chiefly concerned with marriage are sociology and theology. Sociological courses concerning marriage and the family are valuable, and one would expect to find them in any well developed curriculum. But a theological study of marriage is under any circumstances of the utmost importance in the formation of the educated Christian mind. In the circumstances of our own time and nation its already great importance is enhanced by the general disregard for Christian principles and even for the requirements of nature incorporated in the laws and customs under which Catholics must live and which they must strive to reform according to the principles of prudence. Therefore, if a course in marriage is required (whether it should be is a subject for later consideration), the course would be a theology course.

General Value in Christian Formation

A theological study of marriage is one tract in an extensive and unified science. In a properly integrated curriculum in which the study of theology holds the place which belongs to it in the scheme of human knowledge, the theological principles and conclusions concerning matrimony would find their normal place among the sacraments. Thus Chapter XV of *Christ, and His Sacraments* gives the theology of marriage within the same limits and according to the same perspectives as those which govern the treatment of the other sacraments.[3] But since marriage presents special problems to the modern Christian, many colleges rightly consider that the subject deserves a more developed and more detailed treatment. The study of marriage can well be used as a developed example of the relevance of theological principles to everyday life, both the life of the individual and the life of society.

In the study of the theology of marriage very clear instances can be brought before the college student of the tensions which exist between Christianity and the "world," as well as of the manner in which theological principles developing and making clear the truths of revelation can show that nature itself is well served only when men and society submit to the order revealed by God. Society's only salvation is to be found in the restoration of all things in Christ. This is made abundantly clear in a detailed study of the theology of marriage set into a historical and sociological analysis of the abuse of marriage and the consequences of this abuse. The whole meaning of the Incarnation and of the role of Christ and his Church stands out sharply when marriage is presented in this manner.

"Now my just one lives by faith" (Heb. 10:38). The perspective of the Christian is broadened, his mind is released from the confinement of its natural limitations, to range over a wide area closed to the man bound down to what he can discover for himself. Natural truth is not lost nor is it changed except in its relations by the vastly extended horizons of the man of faith. Grace builds upon nature, and faith extends but does not destroy natural knowledge. In few areas is this great truth so amply illustrated as in the study of Christian marriage. Christ himself taught his doctrine concerning marriage precisely in this context. "'What did Moses command you?' They said, 'Moses permitted us to write a notice of dismissal, and to put her away.' But Jesus said to them, 'By reason of the hardness of your heart he wrote you that commandment. But from the beginning of creation God made them male and female. "For this cause a man shall leave his father and mother, and cleave to his wife, and the two shall become one flesh." Therefore now they are no longer two, but one flesh. What therefore God has joined together, let no man put asunder'" (Mark 10: 3-9). On the basis of this divine revelation clarifying the purposes of nature, the Church has taken its stand in support of the good of nature against the world and every religion the world has ever produced.

Among the significant non-Christian religions of the world not one proposes monogamous marriage as the norm. Of course, it must be remembered that the idea that morality, and particularly sexual morality, is the direct concern of religion is by no means universal. One of the most impressive features of Christianity to many in the Roman Empire was its almost unique fusion of religion and ethics. The Judaic religion, of course, offered detailed prescriptions for the guidance of the moral life, but it did not demand monogamous marriage. The religions of Buddha and Hinduism are not noted for high sexual standards. Mahatma Ghandi, the great modern apostle of Hinduism, professed that he loved the temples but recognized and personally abhorred the sexual license that is part of their very atmosphere. Islam specifically allows a man four wives and divorce privileges, and permits concubinage.

It is clear, as Christ points out, that nature expects monogamy. No reasonable man can doubt that the procreation of children and their education is best provided for by the permanent union of one man to one woman for this purpose. Nature always strives for that which is best. Why then has monogamy been so rare even as an ideal? Original sin sufficiently unleashed concupiscence to make monogamy an exceedingly difficult standard to live up to. Concentrating on the difficulties of preserving it, men have been more willing to accept the problems raised by divorce for the formation of children than the problems in adult self-control raised by monogamy. But Christ restored to the human race what its very nature makes best for it. That is the precise reason he made marriage a sacrament; he laid no burdens upon men that he did not provide the means to carry. The unity and indissolubility of marriage were made acceptable by making the contract itself the source of the grace necessary to preserve them.

Heretics have consistently dropped or distorted the ideal proposed by Christ. Robert Neuner of the Yale University law faculty has pointed out that the main characteristics of our modern divorce system were created by Luther, Calvin and the reformers. The Church of

England was born of a divorce. Calvin concluded his argument that marriage is not a sacrament with this statement: "They [the churchmen] appropriated to themselves the cognizance of conjugal causes: as the thing was spiritual, it was not to be intermeddled with by profane judges. Then they enacted laws by which they confirmed their tyranny . . . and enact that a husband who has repudiated an adulteress may not marry again. . . ."[4]

Luther said at first, "As to divorce, it is still a moot question whether it be allowable. For my part I so greatly detest divorce that I should prefer bigamy to it."[5] He did exactly that—both in his judgment on the case of Henry VIII and in the case of Philip of Hesse. This ambiguous position is explained in a letter to the Chancellor of the Duke of Saxe-Weimar where he wrote, "The Scriptures prevent me from permitting anyone to take several wives at the same time. It is a commendable practice but I would not be the first to introduce it among Christians." Yet, first or not, he did introduce it; and eventually he also decided for divorce. In his *Commentary on the Sermon on the Mount* he stated, "We do not order or forbid this divorcing, but we ask the government to act in this matter, and we submit to what the secular authorities ordain in regard to it." And in the same passage he allowed divorce because of adultery and extended the Pauline privilege to any case of desertion.

Only the true Church has preserved, even among the religions calling themselves Christian, the restoration of the fullest natural goodness in marriage, for which Christ provided the necessary grace. Is there any better example than that provided by Christian marriage of the great truth that "in the state of corrupt nature man needs the help of grace to heal his nature"?[6]

Surely a college marriage course is an excellent opportunity to fix this fundamental Christian concept in the minds of young Catholics. This use of the marriage course seems so important in the total process of forming Christian minds that at the risk of seeming to labor a point it should be noted that Christianity is unique in this, that it seeks to sanctify man as man, a creature composed of body and soul, the point at which matter touches spirit. The Oriental religions seem to seek to sanctify man by disembodying him, while Islam (and even Judaism) is excessively materialistic. It is the genius of Christianity to sanctify the natural, and it is the genius of the Christian mind to perceive that grace builds upon nature.[7] The whole sacramental system is based upon this idea; nowhere is it more evident than in the study of the sacrament of matrimony.

General Value for Society

The study of the sacrament of matrimony from a theological orientation has been shown to be of significant value as a study of detail in the vast tapestry which is the Redemption. The formed Christian mind habitually appreciates the revolutionary quality of the Incarnation. "The wolf shall dwell with the lamb, and the leopard shall lie down with the kid . . ." (Isa. 11: 6). The study of the Christian approach to the reproductive process (distinctive in that it conforms to nature, more distinctive still in that it transcends nature) forces the student to face up to the unique quality of the Christian way of life. This cannot be brought home too sharply to young people on the threshold of an adulthood which must be well informed and deeply convinced to muster the courage necessary to walk the narrow and the craggy path, when all the world around them coasts on a path that is wide and flower strewn. But it is not enough that they should walk the right path. *Noblesse oblige.*

"He told them another parable: 'The kingdom of heaven is like a leaven, which a woman took and buried in three measures of flour, until all of it was leavened'" (Matt. 13:33). A Christian cannot wash his hands of the rest of men. The gifts, the talents that have been given to him must be used for the benefit of the society in which he lives—for the benefit of his fellow men. Who makes the laws and customs under which we live? They are not the work of some meaningless abstraction called the state or society. They are not the result of incomprehensible forces beyond the influence of men. In reality they are made by men, either deliberately or by default. They are made by men deliberately to the extent that they are the result of conscious planning and intentional activity. But sometimes the weakness of men allows customs to develop which were not planned or deliberately formed, because those responsible did not plan or act when they should have. The tendency of trousers is to fall and shirt tails to become loosened. It is easy for things to fall apart if they are not watched. If no one is vigilant the innate selfishness of fallen man will replace order with anarchy. If those who are vigilant are ruled by standards opposed to those of Christianity, the laws and customs of society will lead men from, rather than towards true happiness. "If a blind man guide a blind man, both fall into the pit" (Matt. 15:14).

Christians cannot allow men without the faith, men whose principles are opposed to those which Christ charged his followers to spread throughout the world, to have unopposed voice in making the laws and forming the customs which affect all of society. On the other hand, Christians are not fanatics. The principles of toleration will guide the practical approach to civil laws which are contrary to the natural or divine law.

For example, divorce laws are commonplace in our society. In the practical order it is impossible to strike them from the books. The practical Christian does not recognize their validity, since human law cannot negate divine law; so he does not make use of them himself. Moreover, he does what he can to make the natural law known and to persuade others to recognize it and abide by it. But he does not upset society entirely by a fanatical attempt to eliminate the civil law of divorce. Catholic lawyers and judges will make every effort to administer these laws in such a way that their harmful effect upon society will be minimized as much as possible, but their efforts will fall short of violation of the law. Any other course would, in effect, close the legal profession to Catholics. Nor will Catholics presume to stand in judgment on those who make use of such laws in good conscience.

To arrive at practical conclusions concerning the approach and content of a marriage course designed to prepare educated Catholics to take an active role as intelligent citizens in making laws, administering the laws that are made, and in influencing the development of customs helpful to the happiness of all men in this world and the next, consideration must be given to the influence of law and custom on marriage and the family. Then it will become clear to what extent a mature understanding of what is true and good concerning marriage and the family is a necessary part of the aims of Christian education.

It can be argued that it is enough for an uneducated man to know that his Church rejects divorce, and to reject the possibility as far as his own life is concerned. Such Catholics can be said to achieve their role in the leavening of society by force of the example of their lives. But Catholics who have the advantage of a college education should be able to support their position with intelligent reasoning based upon an understanding of the nature of man and of marriage. The teaching of the Catholic Church concerning marriage is reasonable and consistent. All of the Church's teaching is reasonable and consistent, but the reasonableness and consistency of its doctrine concerning marriage is particularly clear and evident and can be strongly supported by experience and by scientific evidence furnished by several purely human sciences.

This is so true that it is possible for Catholics to be misled into thinking that their case is best rested on these purely human sciences. Some Catholic colleges teach marriage as a sociology course, with divine revelation concerning marriage added on by way of an appendix. This method produces two major difficulties: it misses a wonderful opportunity to fix clearly in the student's mind the formal reason for living by the teaching of Christ; it works in the direction of a natural approach confirmed by faith rather than of a supernatural approach confirmed by reason. A further difficulty of this method is the strain it places upon a wobbly reason.

The marriage contract is concerned with the acts which are of their nature ordained to the generation of children. These acts involve the most powerful of man's emotions. As a result of original sin, emotion has more to say than it should in forming all kinds of convictions, but in this area so powerfully influenced by emotion, to make reason seem to be the front line of defense against the decisions which passion so easily dictates can easily prove disastrous. The history of the race, as has already been noted, shows how weak reason is in defending the natural law concerning marriage. Christ's way is, "And I say to you. . . ." What he says to us we often can support by reason, and when we can we should; but the formal reason of adherence is faith, not reason.

The educated Catholic must be prepared to give an intelligent account and defense of his convictions. Such reasoning will not normally lead men to accept the Catholic position, since men are not able to be reasoned out of positions they did not reason themselves into. But in those who possess a minimum of urbanity and right thinking, it can produce a greater appreciation of the Church's position and a somewhat closer approach to it than would otherwise have been the case. At the very least, it can do much to lessen further corruption of the natural law in the civil law. This can be the case in the very making of the laws themselves. But the influence of such intelligent presentation of the Catholic position can be especially vital and significant in the actual administration of the laws.

Often an opportunity to influence interested inquiry into Catholic teaching is lost because a supposedly intelligent and educated Catholic in a group gathered for social or business reasons is not quite sure what the truth is, let alone how to defend it. This sort of thing indicates an accidental result of the quality of Catholic schooling, of its success in forming Catholic minds, but it points to the importance of its achieving just that.

The Determination of the Content

Other things in life are more important than sex. It would be absurd if the primary purpose of man were to reproduce his own kind. To say that such is his primary purpose is to say that he is made for his species—a vicious circle. Lower animals which seem to have no other purpose as individuals than to reproduce are, nevertheless, made to provide food for higher animals, or for some other purpose in achieving the balance of nature. But the higher is not made for the lower. Thus the absurdity of those who would make the use of sex to be man's primary function.

However, sex is important. Its importance is so obvious that it can be exaggerated to the point of overshadowing everything else, a form of exaggeration found in the thinking of some psychiatrists, and in the writings of many novelists. A large segment of the entertainment industry seems to base all of its thinking on an exaggerated distortion of the role of sex. The influence of sex, even when contained within its proper limits, extends to many areas of human living. Since the sexual functions are fittingly employed only in marriage, the institution of marriage, the myriad customs which surround it and preparation for it, the attitudes of society toward it—all deserve the careful consideration of the educated man. Therefore, starting with divine revelation, Christian higher education should include a careful consideration of that which is essential to marriage. But it cannot stop here. It must also carefully investigate the actual conditions of the society in which the Christian education is taking place so that it can measure current customs as well as current laws by the standards of Christianity.

Theological principles are definite. What is right and wrong in the abstract is clear. But in the practical order abstract principles are meaningless. They gain meaning in the last analysis only by application to the particular concrete situation, and this is the work of the virtue of prudence. Yet there is not a void between the principle and its ultimate application. The cloth can be cut in its general lines based upon the average proportions of the kind of subject to which it is to be fitted. Before the suit can be worn the final adjustments must be made to the individual case. The laws, customs and practices of a social group can be studied and compared with the universal norms of virtue clarified by the theologian's study of revelation which proceeds under the guidance of the *magisterium*.

Laws are definite and ascertainable. To the extent that they are, it is possible to determine with accuracy which ones among them are in accord with the true nature of marriage. Yet there are many matters more or less directly connected with marriage which are covered by legislation. Whether such laws are good, bad or questionable often involves judgments based on political prudence. What changes are desirable (keeping tolerance in mind) and what kind of laws would be useful and beneficial concerning marriage and kindred matters is a subject to which the educated Catholic should give some thought.

Law, however, has nothing to say about many of the practices common in society relating to preparation for marriage, marriage itself, and family living. Much is determined in these matters by custom. Customs are vastly more arbitrary and changeable than laws. Nor do they have the same universal validity. As a result of mass communications and mass entertainment media, customs develop and are moderated and changed quickly. Fads come and go. It is especially difficult for adults to keep track of the rapid fluctuation in what is acceptable and what is out of date among the teen-age set. It is often impossible to delineate clearly current practice, except along general lines. Yet an educated Catholic must be prepared to assess these customs in the light of Christian principles. Not only must he be able to do this in order to determine the course of his own behavior and that of his own children, but he must be prepared to do whatever his state in life allows to promote those customs which make for virtue and for stability in family life, as well as to repress those which do not.

What can a college marriage course do? What can it provide to prepare young Catholics to act as a true Christian leaven in society? First, they must be led to an understanding of the true nature of marriage and of its role in the life of the individual and of society. Then they must be led to give careful consideration to actual conditions, to the general secularism of society and to its consequences, especially for the family, for marriage and for courtship. They must be shown the opposition between principles and practice to the point where they are themselves able to discover new evidences of this opposition. Of course, in this process they will also be able to discover accidental accord, which can often lessen the difficulty of practicing Christianity. Finally, a survey of all that has been learned should be crowned with an analysis of the sublime supernatural role of marriage, "a great mystery—I mean in reference to Christ and to the Church" (Eph. 5:32).

Books, pamphlets and articles about marriage are without number. Even if it is recognized that many are worthless, a vast body of useful literature remains, on a subject with almost infinite ramifications. No one could hope to study and assess them all. It would be a herculean task merely to achieve an intelligent awareness of all the aspects of this subject, which covers such an extensive area of human life both individual and social. The educator must be selective. Everything cannot be taught to everyone in school. Idle curiosity concerning sex and marriage knows no limits. Columnists are able to make a handsome living by exploring problems day in and day out from the tragic to the ludicrous which pertain to this element of human life. Before considering in some detail the material suggested in the last paragraph for a college marriage course, some justification of its limitations can rightly be expected.

From the vast body of material concerning marriage, a selection must be made, keeping in mind several factors. Marriage and the family are not an isolated matter, having no connection whatever with anything else in human life and learning. The sociological study of the family presupposes an understanding of general principles of sociological investigation and must fit into a more general knowledge of society. Taken out of context, the sociology of the family becomes meaningless. Much the same thing is true of a theological study of marriage. It is possible to say many true and useful things about marriage, but an understanding of it presupposes acceptance of the authority of the Church, a minimum of Christian doctrine, and a dash of common sense. Such things are said in sermons. In the classroom reasons must be given, facts analysed, connections explored. It would be possible for students completely innocent of chemistry to be taught something of a special tract within the science. It would be unsatisfactory—even if the professor spent much of his time explaining general principles as their employment became necessary—but within limits it would be possible. It is likewise possible to teach a theological course concerning marriage to students innocent of theology; it is unsatisfactory, but a lesser evil than mere pious platitudes. If the student is studying marriage in an integrated theology program, it is not necessary for the professor to linger over a defense of the authority of the Church, the nature of theological reasoning, the role of canon law, general sacramental theology, the definition and division of virtues, and other theological matters pertinent to the study of marriage. If the student is ignorant of theology, some explanation of these things must be offered as they become necessary.

The concern here is a marriage course offered to all, or the vast majority of students, as part of a general liberal education. The purpose of schooling is to provide the orderly knowledge necessary to live an intelligent life. Of course, having the necessary knowledge does not guarantee that an intelligent life will be lived; each man must live his own life. But without the necessary knowledge it is impossible to live a truly Christian life. Many Catholics, invincibly ignorant of the relevance of their faith to those areas of life which transcend the narrowly personal, have seriously scandalized many, though they themselves may well have been guiltless. A man who has had no opportunity for advanced schooling will seldom be faced with problems which require theological knowledge to solve in a Christian manner. Presumably the college educated man will. His work, his reading, the conversation and interests of his friends, all will raise questions which the limited perspectives of the catechism will fail to illuminate with the light of faith. An educated Catholic should be prepared to face questions raised for individuals and for society by marriage and the family within the perspective of the "one thing necessary." That he may do this at the level one can expect of him as a man supposedly disciplined in mind by the various sciences, he must see marriage in its relevance to the total Christian revelation and to the salvation of men and of society. The sociology of the family will not develop this view. Other knowledge of marriage and the family is useful, but for the formation of a Christian mentality theological knowledge is essential. There is neither time nor opportunity to teach everyone everything. That which is essential must find its place in the curriculum; if time remains that which is less important can be taught.

The objection may be raised against the material proposed that, though a supernatural view of marriage is necessary to the Christian, nonetheless he is a man before he is a Christian. Thus he requires natural knowledge of marriage both for himself and because he will have a better chance of defending the good of society in this regard by means of natural knowledge, since he must hold discussion with each man on the level which that man accepts. In response, it can be noted that grace builds upon nature; that, especially in regard to marriage, grace works first to heal nature. The theology of marriage, therefore, makes more clear than any other discipline what the requirements of nature in this matter truly are. Theology provides both the most sublime motivation for the defense of real values in this area of human life, and the arguments (whether natural or supernatural) to provide the strongest possible defense.

The Subjects of the Course

A systematic study of anything demands, in the beginning, a definition of terms. Objections are sometimes raised to the "Catholic scholar's habit" of starting with rigid definitions (which, it is claimed, are arbitrarily made) and then merrily reasoning on from such unexamined premises. There is some justification for this complaint. The theologian is concerned with a unique science, a science with a singular regard for authority. The definitions with which he starts are by no means arbitrary. They are drawn from revelation as proposed by the authority of the teaching Church. There is no point in defending this procedure here. Those who have the faith experience no difficulty in accepting as unquestionable the objective validity of such a method. However, it must be recognized that some theologians (there are bad theologians, just as there are bad chemists) do not distinguish with sufficient clarity between definitions drawn from unquestionable authority and those which they have copied from an earlier theologian's personal cogitations. The validity of the subsequent reasoning of such scholars is obviously lessened in proportion to their laxity in justifying their definitions.

Catholic philosophers sometimes borrow the method of prefabricated definitions from the theologian. They do so illegitimately, if somewhat understandably. Certain positions in philosophy have been so completely justified for so many generations that it is easy to make the error of looking upon them almost as "articles of faith." The philosopher must start with what are at best provisional definitions, and justify them as he proceeds. Since the order of invention is not always or necessarily the best order of proposition, the question here is not so much one of time as it is one of method. But the concern here is with a theological study. It is, therefore, not only legitimate but necessary to accept as a starting point definitions provided by faith.

The definitions with which a theological study of marriage begins must, of course, be explained, and their consequences investigated. Therefore, the first part of a college marriage course should be a study of marriage according to the four causes, then of the properties, and finally of the impediments to marriage.

A study of the intrinsic causes of marriage reveals its essence. The natural essence of marriage can be arrived at by way of revelation, since (as has been shown) Christ did not change the nature of marriage but restored it to its full vigor. However, the study of the natural contract should proceed in such a way that the full power of natural reasoning is employed to make crystal clear the value to human society and to human individuals of the indestructible monogamy insisted upon by Christ.

While this is done especially in considering the properties of marriage, the foundation of the reasoning is laid in the consideration of the essence of marriage, of the matter about which the marriage contract is made. Then the inseparability of the contract from the sacrament for those capable of receiving a sacrament is demonstrated theologically, that is, based upon revelation as proposed by the teaching Church.

The terms used in canon law when treating of marriage must here be explained, and this furnishes an occasion for a digression by the teacher which is sometimes necessary and always useful. If the students have not already had an adequate grounding in fundamental theology, it is necessary to explain and defend the authority of the Church, briefly but systematically, both in general and as exercised in relation to Christian marriage.

Even if they have already been exposed to this explanation and defense, to review it here briefly is valuable because of the temper of the times. In our society respect for authority is at a low ebb. While Catholic boys and girls—to the extent that their faith is strong and well instructed—accept the authority of the Church, they cannot escape the influence of the times. It is more difficult for them to accept habitually and easily this authority (which they would not think of deliberately questioning) than would be the case if the whole force of social pressure were in the direction of respect for legitimate authority. Moreover, they want, and have a right to expect from their Catholic education intelligent arguments, in order to defend before their acquaintances outside the Church the allegiance they freely give to the right of God's Church to order the direction of their lives.

Having exposed and explained the essence of marriage, the extrinsic causes of marriage complete the study of its four causes. The material included in this section is very important. The consent which is the efficient cause of marriage must be true matrimonial consent in order to effect a true marriage. Since the validity of many marriages is challenged on the basis of defective consent, the student's mind must be very clear about two things: what is necessary in order that consent be truly given; and that to which the consent must be given in order to effect a marriage. Those things which impede the true giving of consent must be explained with care, in order that the student will be clear as to what has been legislated in this regard. For what might be true consent in other matters is prevented by positive law from being acceptable as true consent in effecting a marriage.

The natural nobility of monogamy nowhere appears so clearly as in the study of the purposes of marriage—the goals which lead human beings to enter into marriage, and the goods which accrue to those who have entered into this state of life. The supernatural values of this state are expounded here (together with the natural values), as they are founded upon but transcend the natural values. Yet the full appreciation of the supernatural role of matrimony will be the logical culmination of the total study of Christian marriage.

The student has been shown that consent may be given to any kind of a contract or partnership, but it is not consent to marriage unless it involves the *perpetual* and *exclusive* right to those acts which are ordained to the generation of children. The properties of Christian marriage, therefore, are indissolubility and unity.

Divorce is a major factor in the life of our nation. If the question is approached from the point of emotional reaction to the unhappiness of a particular couple in specific circumstances, it is not difficult to see how many are led to overlook the catastrophic results for society (and, of course, for the individuals who make up society) that follow upon the weakening of the marriage bond. Our age has gone far toward losing the sense of sin, of personal responsibility. The criminal is often wept over rather than punished, wept over as an innocent victim of circumstances of psychological conditioning rather than as one who has offended God and man, one who must be suitably punished for his own good and for the good of society. This attitude is easily taken toward those who have rashly entered marriage for immediate purposes and without thought to the future, and toward those who refuse to accept the responsibilities to one another, to their children, and to society which they have taken upon themselves in marriage.

Divorce makes the kind of marriages that end in divorce. Marriage would be entered into less rashly, and, once entered upon, married people would be more inclined to make the effort to achieve the adjustments necessary to make it work if it were realized that society will accept no further marriage until one spouse is dead. Every effort must be made to impress upon young Catholics the social nature of marriage, the fact that it is not a private affair in which society has no valid interest. They must be also led to a practical realization that the Church is a society, like the state a perfect society. The welfare of children is imperiled by divorce (as experience and statistics make clear), other families are scandalized, and the whole order of society is disrupted. The will of God is indeed the good of men.

If a marriage is not ratified or not consummated divorce is possible under certain conditions. This should be made clear, together with the reasons. An educated Catholic should be able to explain to those who are disturbed (or who are merely curious) that it is not money or influence but a well defined position in law which results in the dissolution of such a marriage.

The meaning of annulment must also be stressed. Few have a clear idea of annulment as a mere declaration of the fact that marriage never existed. It is useful to stress the fact that the instant a ratified and consummated marriage exists, its existence is for the life of both spouses. Annulment is a term commonly used, and it cannot be ignored. It should be frequently equated, however, with the better term, "declaration of nullity."

Lest the student miss the forest for the trees, the treatment of impediments and of the form of marriage which concludes the first part of the marriage course is well introduced with the general notion that if what appears to be marriage is actually not a marriage it will be for one of three reasons: (1) defect of consent, which results either from the fact that true consent was not given or it was not given to the perpetual and exclusive giving and receiving of the rights to those acts which are ordained to the generation of children; (2) the existence of a diriment impediment not validly dispensed; or (3) the form was not observed by those bound to the form.

In considering the impediments, the conditions of the times seem to require that two points be stressed. The first of these two points is the evils of a marriage entered with a dispensation from mixed religion or from disparity of worship. Some would say it is even more important to stress the advantage of marriage in which both parties are good practicing Catholics. They are right, but these advantages can be made clear only after showing the disadvantages of mixed marriage. The prohibition of mixed marriage certainly extends to mixed dating, since courtship of its very nature leads to marriage. Of course, there are reasons why the Church dispenses from these two impediments. Such reasons can make mixed dating legitimate, but it must always be noted that the Church *tolerates,* it does not encourage, mixed marriage. It is a lesser of two evils. The dangers of mixed marriage are for the faith and for the marriage. Such dangers cannot be accepted without good reason. Young people often do not realize that marriage is not a series of heart-warming dates from which questions of religion can often be more or less eliminated; it is day in and day out life. In marriage there is no place to hide religion; it must be faced. The advantages in union of heart and mind between two sincere Catholics, both to themselves and to their children, become more clear. The loss to the Catholic party of a sacramental union when disparity of cult is involved will appear even more strongly in the final part of the marriage course.

The other point which deserves stress when treating of the impediments is the difference between those diriment impediments which arise from the divine law and can never be dispensed, and those which arise from the ecclesiastical law. The latter can be, but sometimes in practice are not, dispensed. Here in a special way the jurisdiction of the Church over marriage becomes clear. This seems as good a time as any to explain the workings of the marriage courts.

By this point the student should be aware of marriage as a way of life, an ultimate reality, inseparable from the married person's total or integral goodness or virtue as a human being. He should also be aware of marriage as a supernatural reality, a natural human institution raised by God to a new order of existence and ordained to the very work of salvation of the married people. The student is now ready to consider in relation to the concrete realities of the world in which he lives the factors involved in preparation for the married state.

The whole mode of procedure in this part of the course must, in the nature of things, be different from that which went before. Thus far concern has been with universal and objective truth. This second part is an exercise in Christian observation and judgment. It requires observation and consideration of the mores, customs and practices of society as they now are. It requires that the fullest possible understanding of Christian principles of belief and practice concerning the nature of man and his destiny be drawn upon as the framework within which society's ways should be studied and judged. In other words, what is necessary for a Christian to believe and do must be determined, together with the manner of carrying out what is necessary with the least possible alienation from the society in which Christians must live. Also what is useful and better from a

Christian point of view, and the extent to which what is useful and better can be practiced, must be determined.

The work of this part of the course can well be begun with some general consideration of the tension which, in the nature of things, will always exist between Christianity and the world. Christians have always been called upon to make sacrifices to live up to their ideals. The history of the Church is written in blood. The sacrifices American Catholics are called upon to make do not reach the point of shedding blood. Because the sacrifices necessary are normally relatively small, there is great danger of American Catholics developing an attitude toward any sacrifice as being unnecessary, of considering it quite possible to be a good and faithful Catholic while participating uninhibitedly in all the current ways of American life. A careful investigation of the relationship between American behavior in regard to marriage and courtship as well as Amercan beliefs concerning the place of marriage and the role of courtship and sex on the one hand, and on the other the demands of Christian revelation, is an excellent practical exercise in the formation of a truly Christian mentality toward the world and its ways.

This material gives room for useful, controlled discussion. Indeed discussion is necessary in order that the teacher may become aware of the actual misconceptions and attitudes of his students. However, the method of procedure will necessarily differ depending upon whether the students have had adequate courses in moral theology and in the theology of man or not. In any teaching it is always a mistake to underestimate (as it is to overestimate) the preparation of the students for considering the matter of the course. An outline for a consideration of this material is to be found in the second part of *Toward Marriage in Christ.*[8]

All Christians are called to be saints. To do so they must fulfill the obligations from their state in life and they must do this in the supernatural mode and by means of supernatural graces. Since marriage is intimately and directly concerned in the ultimate purpose of married people, it must be studied precisely under the aspect of morality, of man's way to God. Thus special consideration must be given to the obligations of married people. And the study of marriage will then be crowned by an analysis of the sacramental signification of marriage, which is itself the channel of the divine grace necessary to fulfill consistently and sincerely the obligations arising from Christian marriage.

The morality of marriage includes the obligations of the spouses to one another and their obligations as parents to their children. To each other the fundamental obligation arising from the very nature of the marriage contract is that of the conjugal debt, and this study leads immediately to a consideration of married chastity. In the spirit of Thomistic moral theology, the positive aspects—the virtuousness of the marriage act and the ideal of married chastity—will furnish the best approach to this consideration.

The manner in which this ideal is destroyed by infidelity need no more than be noted. Depending upon time available and upon the extent to which the student is already familiar with principles, the evils of artificial birth prevention should be explained. The subject of the so called "population explosion" should be raised, if at all, only in the terms of the American bishops' pastoral letter, unless the professor has investigated the research and writings of those who have competently studied the question. As in the treatment of other moral questions which touch the sciences, physical or social, more harm than good can often be done by proposing statements which are easily shown to be unreliable or unfounded.

At this point a question arises which is very important to many Catholic married people. Periodic continence does not directly attack the essential goods of the marriage relationship. Therefore, it is not itself an essential moral evil. But it often involves serious dangers for the individuals and for the marriage. As good moralists have always held, and as the late Pope Pius XII made clear, these dangers can be tolerated if there is sufficient reason for doing so. If a danger is present it should be known and provided against as much as possible. Otherwise it may have done its damage before its presence is even realized. Before the spouses fully realize what it is that is creating the strain on their relationship, married love may have already been seriously corroded by the practice of periodic continence justified by circumstances. Often, had they realized the danger involved, they would have preferred to carry the special burdens which in their case were consequent upon the spontaneous use of the marriage relationship, rather than take the chance of its deterioration.

Special care should be taken to make clear the distinction between periodic continence and absolute continence. The conditions which must be present to justify undergoing the dangers attendant upon periodic continence must be emphasized. One of the evils consequent upon periodic continence is the limitation of the principal good of marriage, namely, of children. Circumstances may make the limitation of children a lesser of two evils, and when this is the case the better way is the practice of absolute continence, a heroic course which may be a greater burden than some could bear. (Though, of course, if absolutely necessary, divine help will make it possible.)

The other duties toward one another in the sharing of a common life must then be noted. Here especially should be emphasized the importance of the husband's taking his role as head of the family. With gentleness and determination he should always be ready to take the responsibility for a final decision in those rare cases in which he deems it necessary. This takes the kind of pressure she is not prepared to carry off of the wife, since she knows that the ultimate responsibility is not hers, that she has the security of a man to depend upon. It should also be made clear that the wife's contribution to the home is herself, not the money she might make by working outside the home. In rare cases such work is necessary; the wife of the elder Tobias, the mother of the younger, worked outside the home after her husband became blind and her son was no longer a child (Tobias 2:19). In her case it was necessary.

In treating the duties of parents toward their children, the principal concern of the college marriage course is the basic obligations which arise from nature and from the elevation of the Christian to the order of grace, and indeed as nature and grace are found in the concrete reality of time and place. The professor is not expected to be a child psychologist or a pediatrician, but a basic understanding of human psychology as it applies to family relationships together with some experience can provide helpful observations which can do much to turn the minds of the students in the direction of reality and common sense. The fundamental obligation to rear the child in the love and fear of God must be focused upon.

Finally, to the fullest possible extent the total objective of the course should be summed up in an analysis of the Christian meaning of marriage, its sacramental significance, the bond created by it, the effects of the graces it produces, the gifts of the Holy Spirit as they relate to marriage, and the actual graces that may be expected. This concludes a basic theological course concerning marriage suited to the needs of college students.

Who Should Take the Course?

Instruction in Christian truth belongs in every area of education, and that instruction must be at the same academic level as are the other courses offered. As has been shown, the marriage course offered in college should not be an exercise in preparation for marriage. It should be an introduction to the Christian concept of marriage, of its role in society, both natural and supernatural, and of the relationship between male and female from early youth as they prepare spiritually, mentally and physically for Christian marriage. These things should be known and appreciated by all educated men and women, not only by those who themselves intend marriage.

Local circumstances may limit or extend the time which can be devoted to this study. Where good courses are offered in moral and sacramental theology, an hour a week for a semester seems adequate in a four-year course. There is as good argument for requiring this course of all students as for requiring any other. Thus normally it should be a required course.

Should it be required of non-Catholic students in a Catholic college? The answer to this question, which is just one part of the larger question concerning the general religious instruction of those who are not Catholic but are enrolled in Catholic schools, is well stated by Father Alexander F. Sokolich, who concluded his discussion of this subject by saying:

> To teach the natural law apart from Catholic doctrine to non-Catholics while giving instruction and education in the Catholic religion to Catholic students is to teach two objective standards of morality, one for Catholics and one for non-Catholics. This can only

lead to Indifferentism. There can be no place in the curriculum of an American Catholic university or college for "electives" in some other field of knowledge as a substitute offered to non-Catholic students for courses in the Catholic Religion, even though that field be philosophy or sociology. Much less can there be accorded a "complete academic freedom" to the non-Catholic students with reference to a study of Catholic teaching. Pope Pius XI quoted a layman who wrote: "The school, if not a temple is a den. When literary, social, domestic and religious education do not go hand in hand, man is unhappy and helpless."[9]

Footnotes to Study 12

[1]*Summa,* III, q. 71, a. 4, ad 3.

[2]*Commentaria in Psalmos,* XVII; cf. my study of the theology of preaching, *Unless They Be Sent* (Dubuque: Wm. C. Brown Co., 1953).

[3]Donlan, Cunningham, Rock, "College Texts in Theology," third volume of *Theology: A Basic Synthesis for the College* (Dubuque: The Priory Press, 1959).

[4]*Institutes of the Christian Religion,* Bk. IV, Chap. 19.

[5]*The Babylonian Captivity of the Church.*

[6]Cf. St. Thomas, *Summa,* I-II, q. 109, a. 3.

[7]The teacher of the marriage course would find much inspiration and help in developing this idea in Christopher Dawson's *Progress and Religion,* especially Chapter VII.

[8]Donlan, Cunningham, Rock, 2nd rev. ed. (Dubuque: The Priory Press, 1960).

[9]*Canonical Provisions for Universities and Colleges,* Catholic University of America Canon Law Studies, n. 373 (Washington: Catholic U. Press, 1956), 163.

13

PREPARATION OF THEOLOGY TEACHERS

James M. Egan, O.P.

As Chancellor of the School of Sacred Theology, Saint Mary's College, Notre Dame, Indiana, Father Egan, perhaps more than any other American theologian, has exercised a wide influence upon theology in the Catholic college. A Doctor of Theology from the Angelicum in Rome, Father Egan is editor of Magister, *newsletter of the SCCTSD, and a member of the Board of Directors of that society.*

A reader who has arrived at this chapter certainly needs no lengthy arguments on the necessity of training those who must undertake the challenging task of fulfilling the rather awesome role of a theologian even on the college level.

However, this conviction of the need for training leaves wide open the question of the type of training. Interest in this question is not lacking, especially in America, where, fortunately, we are being awakened to the need of special training for those who staff the college theology department.

This question of the type of training, intensely interesting in itself, becomes more complexly interesting because of two allied questions that are warmly discussed within American academic circles. One, confined principally to Catholics, is concerned with the type of theology that should be taught to college students. While this is probably an oversimplification, two types of approach (if not two kinds of theology) are vigorously defended under the designations, "scientific" and "humanistic."[1] The other question, of more general concern, is the character of the doctorate degree in every field. Again, at the risk of oversimplification, the question can be stated in terms of "research" vs. "teaching." In other words, should the doctorate degree be geared primarily to producing research specialists or liberal teachers?

The solution of both these questions is essential to any answer regarding the training of college teachers of sacred doctrine. There are, however, some questions preliminary to these problems.

The College Theology Department

Before coming to the question of the type of training, it seems sensible to ask: "Who shall be trained?" This is equivalent to asking: "Who shall teach theology in our colleges?" Some thought has been given to this question, some positions have been taken. It is probably fair to say that there is a tendency to favor a full complement of priests as the ideal theological faculty. In recent years more brothers and sisters are receiving graduate training in theology, and naturally they expect to take their place on the theological faculties of their colleges. In a few instances, laymen and laywomen have appeared on the scene with advanced theological training. Are they to be employed only because of a dearth of priests, brothers and sisters?

I should like to suggest that the ideal faculty for the theology department of a Catholic college should consist of priests, brothers or sisters, and laymen or laywomen.

In a college directed by priests, it would be expected that the personnel of the theology department would be predominantly clerical. Yet there is no reason why laymen (or, if the institution is coeducational, laywomen) should not be added to the staff for the advantages to be noted below.

What of the colleges directed by brothers and sisters? Should the administration aim at an all-brother or all-sister theological department? This, I believe, would be a serious mistake. For the sake both of the whole faculty and of the student body, a priest or two should, if at all possible, be members of the department. While the priesthood does not make a man a theologian, theology is still the science of the word of God, and even in the college community the theological task requires the collaboration of the priest.

It is a good thing that brothers and sisters can also join competently in this same task. It is even better if laymen and laywomen can hold their own with priests and religious in the great work of initiating students into the science of sciences. It is especially important from the psychological viewpoint of the students, who will not be tempted to look upon theological teaching as mere "following the line," which would be expected of priests and religious.

Even in a college directed by priests with an adequate supply of priest professors, the addition of the laity would be a stimulus to the faculty and an inspiration to the students.

A "pluralistic faculty" is, I'm sure, the ideal. It will be a more vital faculty, it will present a greater challenge to the students. Finally, it will provide students with a variety of personalities to whom they will feel freer to go with their problems, intellectual, moral or social.

A Degree for Teaching Theology

Let us state briefly: the master's degree is sufficient, but not adequate, for teaching sacred doctrine on the college level. This, of course, admits of exceptions. Some master's degrees may not be sufficient, others more than adequate; some doctor's may not be adequate or even sufficient. It is to be hoped that more attention will be given to teaching sacred doctrine on the high school level, and for this a master's degree should be required. Professors with a master's degree can be employed on the college faculty; yet a determining number should have doctorates, and those having master's should look forward to the opportunity of working for the terminal degree in sacred doctrine.

This is in accord with the academic trend in American colleges. "It is a truism that the Ph.D. is the union card of college teaching. Although only about 25 per cent of the current crop of initiates into college teaching have the doctorate—many of the have-nots work on it while teaching—those without are consigned to a kind of academic lumpenproletariat."[2]

A similar need is felt among Protestants who are engaged in teaching theology in religious-affiliated or non-sectarian institutes of higher learning. "Most of the faculty members are trained through at least the doctorate level, a theological degree marking a kind of midway point, with the doctorate degree, usually in a recognized graduate school, either already in hand or, among the younger staff, still in process."[3]

At this point we might ask: "What should constitute a terminal degree for college teachers of sacred doctrine?" The question was raised recently by Richard Russo, S.J., ". . . why is it that in none of the discussions of teacher training is the notion advanced that the college teacher of theology, just as the college teacher of physics or English, needs to become a professional scholar in his field or sub-field, such as New Testament, ecclesiology, canon law, etc., and acquire a really terminal degree?"[4]

As we shall see later, authorities in the field of education are having serious doubts about the value of training college teachers in any field given in current doctorate programs. While research is necessary for the vitality of college teaching, a training program that concentrates the trainee's attention on a narrow field of research may be hindering his over-all development as an inspiring college teacher.

Furthermore, I can foresee no future college situation which would call for a canon lawyer, a missiologist or an ecclesiologist on the staff. A case might be made for a trained specialist in Sacred Scripture, though not for one in the Old Testament and another for one in the New Testament. Terminal degrees of this type are, of course, required by those who staff graduate schools of sacred doctrine; but they would, I believe, require such specialized training (to the neglect of a more generalized training) as actually to hinder the efficacy of teaching at the college level.

This does not mean that the college teacher may not choose one of these fields for his research; but, as we hope to show, vital research in sacred doctrine may be undertaken without concentrating on minutiae.

Two Misleading Ideas

Clear discussion of the type of training suitable for college teachers of sacred doctrine is hindered by the intrusion of two ideas that have very unfortunate effects on the conclusions reached.

Once again we turn to Father Russo for a discussion of one of these ideas. In the review cited above, he asks: "What is the value of the PhD. degree granted for what looks suspiciously like little more than the routine course given in any seminary . . .?"[5] The presupposition is that the *one* way theology has been taught in the Church is the seminary way. This is a misconception. While the Church has been most careful in regulating the training given in her seminaries, she has been equally careful in setting up a *ratio studiorum* for graduate faculties in the sacred sciences, including theology. Technically, the distinctions are expressed in the terms "academic" (*cursus academicus*) and "seminaristic" (*cursus seminaristicus*). While in the catalogue these two courses seem suspiciously alike, there is, in fact, a vast difference between them—not so much in material content as in method of communication. Anyone acquainted with the theology schools at Catholic University in Washington, the Gregorianum or Angelicum in Rome, the Albertinum at Fribourg, is well aware of the differences between the two courses. It is most important to realize that the academic course is completely ordered to graduate training in theology. Within five years the degrees of bachelor, licentiate and doctorate in theology are conferred upon qualified students. Is there any question but that the Church's official program of studies should serve as a guide for a graduate program devoted to training college teachers of theology?

The strongest objection against this conclusion was raised by John Courtney Murray, S.J., in a magnificently challenging pair of articles on theology for the laymen.[6] His thesis was considerably strengthened by ignoring the distinction made above between the academic and seminaristic approach to theological training. He conveyed the impression that the seminary was the only norm for training priests in theology.[7] The rhetorical persuasiveness of Father Murray's thesis was further enhanced by his avoiding a clear-cut distinction of the twofold finality of theology, the speculative and the practical.

Theology is, primarily and inescapably, a speculative doctrine; it is concerned with the sapiential and the scientific penetration of divine reality, either as it is God himself or the participation of God by creatures. While each student of theology will differ in his grasp and appreciation of its speculative riches, the distinction will certainly not be based on the clerical or lay status of the student. Moreover, it is essential to realize that the study of theology, even in its speculative aspects, should not be divorced from its religious values. To the joy of knowing must be added the joy of loving the object known. To the inquiry of the intellect must be added the worship of the inquirer as his mind stands in the presence of divinity. Given the complex nature of the student, knowing *can exist* without love, *inquiry* without commitment, but it *should not* be so. And adding affection to knowing does not, in any way, draw the knowing outside the bounds of speculation. Love gives the impulse, the final direction; it does not determine the rules of the inquiry. It casts a warm glow over the object of knowledge, it does not blur its intellectual lineaments.[8]

The unitary character of theology is not lost to it in its practical aspects, but these are so vast that a good case can be made for a distinction between the type of theological training given in a seminary and a theology for the laity, including the training of college teachers of theology. Certainly no one would suggest that college theology put an emphasis on moral and pastoral theology such as is to be found in a seminary program.

Yet here again we must avoid postulating distinct theologies. The practical aim of a theology course for laymen should be adapted to the needs of their own spiritual life and their apostolate. Now their spiritual life is the one that is nourished and directed by the pastors trained in the seminaries, and their apostolate is a collaboration with the apostolate of the hierarchy. The aim of the apostolate of the laity is identical with that of the apostolate of the hierarchy, even though the laity operate in their own more specialized field and with methods appropriate to those spheres and to the position of the laity in the Church. This requires considerable diversity in the practical aspects of theology communicated to the clergy and the laity; it falls far short of requiring different theologies.[9]

Scholar vs. Teacher

The preceding remarks, exploratory and preliminary as they are, lead naturally to our second problem. While the dilemma, research vs. teaching, could be discussed within the context of sacred doctrine itself, it should be of interest to all of us that the discussion is being carried out in the broad field of graduate education. It is expressed in the question: "What should the Ph.D. represent?" Perhaps many will deny that there is any tension between research and teaching, will even maintain that without research there can be no great teaching. While it might be difficult to define good teaching (and even more difficult to define "great teacher"), it is relatively easy to detect a good teacher from his effect on his students. There is, on the other hand, a considerable amount of ambiguity in the term "research scholar," of which we must be aware in the following discussion.

The most trenchant discussion of research vs. teaching appeared in the *New York Times Magazine*.[10] The situation is briefly summarized in the statement: "The observant teacher, for example, sees that he is never promoted to more teaching, but always to less."[11]

Personal experience in several institutes of graduate theology supports the following observation: "Faculty preoccupation with research cannot but affect the content and emphasis of teaching, and teaching is the primary purpose of colleges and universities. To begin with, it will tend to select what is taught in the classroom; the research-minded faculty member will be tempted to give his major attention to his research interests and to research methods."[12]

The author is careful to avoid any misunderstanding: "Of the importance and value of research, and the responsibility of centers of higher education to promote it, there can be no doubt. That many members of collegiate faculties should be interested and participate in it must be equally clear."[13]

Yet he has the insight to ask: "Is this research which extends the boundaries of man's knowledge, or is it but a series of projects in the learning processes of those concerned? Is research the discovery by researchers of things they did not know before, or is it an adventure of able minds to open up new areas of man's understanding?"[14]

"John Q. Academesis" is a pseudonym; hence, the extent of his experience and the weight of his authority must be taken on faith. More clearly authoritative is the report of a conference, sponsored by the Committee on College Teaching of the American Council on Education, which was held in Washington, D.C. in 1958.[15] The following are, I believe, the key questions that were discussed by the participants. Is the Ph.D. training now current capable of forming good college teachers? Should the Ph.D. training continue to aim at producing research scholars, and something be done to make the M.A. the normal college teaching degree? Should education training be added to the Ph.D. for those wishing to teach? Should the Ph.D. training be so revised that it will provide the springboard for those who wish to continue as research scholars and also train college teachers who have the ability to do fruitful research? While there was no unanimity in regard to the last question (or to any of them, for that matter), a good number thought that it was the solution. Permit me to quote some of these authorities, since they confirm the position I should prefer to take, especially in regard to theology. (Incidentally, these quotations throw light on the important question of a dissertation requirement for the Ph.D.)

William R. Dennes (Professor of Philosophy, University of California, Berkeley) made a very important point: "Getting command of a field, understanding it, and being able to communicate important things about it—all these are equally important, whether a man is going to devote himself to research or to teaching."[16] Two participants contributed valuable suggestions about the nature of research. J. Peter Elder (Dean of the Graduate School of Arts and Sciences, Harvard University): "Research or original study may be done even if a man never puts a single word down on paper. The good teacher works and studies on his own; he may or may not publish this. There is a great deal of research that is done privately in the study and is contributed only to the classroom."[17] Ralph E. Cleland (Dean of the Graduate School, Indiana University): "The principle should be to insist that the student do a piece of original work and a *significant* piece of work, if that is possible, in his particular field."[18]

R. M. Lumiansky (Dean of the Graduate School, Tulane University) became a bit more specific: "We should like to see dissertations in the field of literature not aimed at a definitive, publishable work. We should like the student and the professor, or his committee, to work out an important topic that they think can be handled adequately in a year's study and writing. And the only way we can effect this is to keep steady discussion going among the professors charged with directing these dissertations about the kinds of topics, about the limits, about what we are after. We want a good, solid, critical and scholarly exercise, which, bear in mind, the student has some years after he receives a Ph.D. to work on in addition."[19]

Mrs. Esther Raushenbush of the Faculty of Literature, Sarah Lawrence College, adds this nuance: "It is the process, it is what happens to the candidate in working on suffixes, or whatever, that really counts. One watches people struggle through the process of writing a dissertation with the notion that something has to come out at the end, not at all concerned with what is being learned in the process. . . . The subject, whether original or not, is less significant."[20]

It seems that the debate between research and teaching would be simplified by distinguishing between graduate and undergraduate teachers. A considerable output of research in the strictest sense of original contributions should be expected of graduate teachers. They were appointed to their posts because they manifested an interest and ability in pure research. This should not excuse them from being good teachers, nor justify them in short-changing students who sign up with them for general content courses. They should be assigned, in addition, special courses in which they can initiate students into the secrets of research by utilizing their own current researches.

The undergraduate teacher should primarily be a good teacher, capable of communicating a broad and profound knowledge of his subject. It is to be expected that he will have his own special interests within that field; it is to be hoped that he will produce research that will deepen his and others' understanding of the field; it is to be welcomed without unnecessary surprise if, on occasion, he contributes something original.

A Doctorate Program

It is quite obvious, from previous chapters, that theology has a very delicate function to perform in all other fields of human knowledge. Not only must it know how to utilize all of their valid results in order to communicate sacred doctrine in as timely and vital a way as possible, it must offer them inspiration and direction which carefully respect their autonomy. Theology can perform these various functions: she is still the Queen of the sciences, but she is a queen without subjects, for she can rule only through her prime ministers, the theologians. Yet theologians will fail to fulfill these functions if they have been trained only in theology. This is why it is absolutely necessary that a rigorous training in the liberal arts, a liberal acquaintance with the natural and social sciences, as well as the fine arts, and a high degree of philosophical understanding be presupposed to the formation of a theologian who is going to be a "universal specialist."

Since such ideal preparation requires the co-operative efforts of all in the academic field, the theological school may have to be content at present with less than the ideal. The minimum prerequisites are: an A.B. or B.S. degree; a solid foundation in philosophy; and a reading knowledge of Latin. A reading knowledge of German, and especially of French, is also of importance. Students who lack this reading knowledge should be encouraged to acquire it by courses specially designed to enable them to read the theological literature in these languages.

There is one temptation that a training program must strenuously resist: the temptation to satisfy all the demands that can be, and will be, made upon it. Any training program that strives to produce a "universal specialist" must aim at what is truly universal, with a realization that the specialties will be determined by future contingencies. So let us recall the words of William R. Dennes: "Getting command of a field, understanding it, and being able to communicate important things about it"—that is the ideal for any training program, but it is especially valid for a theological program.

Theology, as it exists today as a body of knowledge to be communicated, has been developing for at least four thousand years; much of this development has been under the special inspiration of the Holy Spirit, all of it has been under the watchful guidance of the living *magisterium*. Theology is the only science that has, in essence, developed in a straight line (*in eodem sensu*), and any further development, the fruit of research, must preserve intact the unchangeable truths already acquired. We want to produce audacious theologians, especially for our colleges, but not foolhardy ones. And the only way to do that is to train them in the traditional thought of the Church in all of its manifestations.

As an example of such a theology program for teachers, one suited to brothers, sisters and the laity, one may cite that designed for the graduate school of theology at St. Mary's College, Notre Dame, Indiana.[21] Following the listing of courses, the rationale of this program will be explained in some detail.

First Summer

Sacred Doctrine and Its Sources	1 hr.
The Origins of Christian Belief	2 hrs.
The Word of God: Synoptic Gospels	2 hrs.

First Semester, First Year		*Second Semester, First Year*	
God, One and Three	5 hrs.	God, Creator and Ruler	5 hrs.
Beatitude and Human Acts	5 hrs.	Principles of Human Acts	5 hrs.
Greek	2 hrs.	Greek	2 hrs.
Introduction to *Summa*	1 hr.	Reading Seminar	1 hr.
Elective	2 hrs.	Elective	2 hrs.

Second Summer

Old Testament (The historical, prophetic and sapiential books in cycle)	2 hrs.
New Testament (The Johannine writings, Acts and epistles in cycle)	2 hrs.
Biblical Theology	2 hrs.

First Semester, Second Year		*Second Semester, Second Year*	
Incarnation and Redemption	5 hrs.	The Sacraments and the Four Last Things	5 hrs.
The Virtues of the Christian Life	5 hrs.	The Virtues of the Christian Life	5 hrs.
Spiritual Theology	1 hr.	Spiritual Theology	1 hr.
Church History	3 hrs.	Church History	3 hrs.
Reading Seminar	1 hr.	Reading Seminar	1 hr.

Third Summer

Same as above for Second Summer

First Semester, Third Year		*Second Semester, Third Year*	
Elective	2 hrs.	Elective	2 hrs.
Reading Seminar	1 hr.	Concentration on Research	
Concentration on Research			

The major emphasis is on Sacred Scripture and theology, both dogmatic and moral. The texts are the Bible, the documents of the *magisterium* and the *Summa Theologiae.*

The Scripture Course*

While college teachers of sacred doctrine are becoming increasingly aware of the need of technical training in Scripture, and energetically meeting this challenge, at the moment many of those who come to graduate schools of sacred theology have had very little background in Bible study. They have received very few principles to guide them in reading the Bible as, e.g., types of history writing in the Old and New Testaments, the nature of prophetic preaching. Neither do they have a clear understanding of biblical history, especially of Old Testament history. From teaching "lives of Christ" and Church history, the facts of New Testament times are much more familiar to them than Old Testament events. Only too often, however, their knowledge of the New Testament reduces itself to a chronological "life of Christ" or to a defense of the Church, a system which smooths out the differences between the various New Testament writers; to that extent these approaches leave them unacquainted with the actual text of the New Testament. This situation is quickly changing, since

*This section has been contributed by Rev. Carroll Stuhlmueller, C.P., who is Professor of the Old Testament and of Biblical Theology at St. Mary's School of Theology.

Scripture courses are being introduced in many novitiates and juniorates for brothers and sisters and also in colleges and universities for lay students. A similar interest in Scripture is stirring in grade and high schools. A Scripture professor, therefore, assigned to teach in a graduate school of theology, should wisely determine the background of the class and then adapt himself to the prevailing situation.

A clear statement is in order about the use of modern English translations of the Bible. The Confraternity of Christian Doctrine version provides the finest of translations of the Old Testament and should be used; very soon three volumes will be available: Vol. I, Genesis to Ruth; Vol. III, the Sapiential Books; Vol. IV, the Prophetical Books. The present Confraternity version of the New Testament translates the Latin Vulgate and is quite unsatisfactory. The Catholic Biblical Association of America is sponsoring a new translation of the New Testament. Till it is published, perhaps the Kleist-Lilly version is to be recommended. Freedom to use the Chicago Bible (*The Complete Bible,* edited by Smith-Goodspeed and published by the University of Chicago Press) and the *Revised Standard Version* should be brought to the attention of teachers. Anyone engaged in formal study of the Bible needs no further permission to read or consult these two editions of the Bible (cf. canon 1400).

The number of hours to be devoted to the various departments of Scripture study will naturally depend upon the total number of hours allotted to Scripture. The following ratio would be recommended: for one-half credit hour given to General Introduction, allot three hours to Old Testament exegesis and two or three hours to New Testament exegesis. This arrangement is *not* recommending only three hours to the Old Testament and only two or three to the New Testament, but is presented solely on a ratio basis.

Biblical theology should be restricted to advanced students, already well acquainted with the text of the Bible. Subsidiary courses, like archaeology, history or geography, should never substitute for basic, exegetical studies.

The course in General Introduction should include explanations of the following items:

1. External form of the Bible:
   1) number of books in the Old and New Testament;
   2) methods of dividing the books, based upon the Massoretic text and the Greek Septuagint;
   3) texts and translations, with special emphasis on the history of Latin and English translations;
   4) position of the Vulgate in the Roman Catholic Church, its "official authenticity."
2. Internal form of the Bible: "inspiration," with special emphasis upon instrumental causality. Because of the transmission of the Bible in oral tradition and under liturgical auspices, mention should be made of "later" inspired additions and of modifications of earlier inspired texts.
3. Senses of Sacred Scripture: literal (proper and improper), typical, accommodated, *sensus plenior*.
4. Laws of interpretation:
   1) literary laws;
   2) divine laws: *magisterium*, Fathers, Biblical Commission.

It would be best to reserve any detailed study of literary laws to exegesis. Before beginning the Pentateuch, some lectures can be offered on the nature of history writing in the Bible and on the Pentateuch as *Torah* or "Law"; before Ezechiel, something should be given on apocalpytic writing; before Jonah, something on Midrashim writing.

If the course on General Introduction is pared down to absolute essentials, it is presumed that later on the students will constantly be questioned on such items as literal sense, inerrancy, texts and versions, etc. For instance, when explaining the first three chapters of Genesis, application of the meaning of proper and improper literal sense should be demanded. If Chapter 12 of Isaias is presented as a later addition to the Book of Emmanuel, the students should be drilled on inspiration.

The purpose of the courses in exegesis is to acquaint the students with the actual text of the Bible, so that the students will be enabled to use and read their entire Bible, intelligently and prayerfully. Exegesis should not be talk about the Bible, nor should it center on difficulties arising from the Bible, and least of all should it become polemics against rationalistic scholars. The professor should consider his primary task the explanation of the positive, doctrinal content of the word of God.[22]

If the student body has had no previous courses on the Bible, then a general survey reading-course seems demanded. Those students who have already covered such a course should be separated, if this is at all possible, and to them should be offered either a course in biblical theology (see below) or a more intensive exegesis of select passages in the Old and New Testaments.

Methodology in teaching exegesis courses will naturally vary with different teachers. The following is but one way among many others:

1. *Quickly* summarize the historical background and psychological factors before beginning any book of the Bible. A handy booklet for these details is: *Foreword to the Books of the Old Testament* by F. L. Moriarty, S.J. (Weston, Mass.: 1954).
2. Select key chapters in the book to be covered. These chapters should represent the major doctrinal and historical developments in the book.
3. The professor should point out important verses from the key chapters, and then comment upon the verses, linking the verses with the background of the times and with the character of the prophet, pointing out the doctrinal involvements in the word of God, both for the Israelites and for us today. He should also clarify any geographical details or historical data which occur.
4. In the meantime, the students are expected to jot down in their notebook the essentials of the class lecture. They can do it conveniently under chapter and verses. Gradually the students will acquire their own commentary upon Scripture.
5. At the end of each biblical book of the Bible the important matter should be quickly summarized under the following headings:

   Who was Josue; Isaias; etc.? *Who* was the author(s) of Josue? Isaias?

What is the outline or general contents of the book of Josue? Isaias?

When did Josue live? Isaias? *When* was the book written? (Here the history of the book's transmission through early oral tradition to its final written form should be traced.)

Where did Josue live? Isaias? *Where* was the book written?

How or *In what manner,*

1) can the *text* be described? the important translations?
2) can the *style* of the author be described?
3) can the *doctrinal content* be described?
   a) about God?
   b) about God's demands on man?
   c) about Messianism?

It is advisable to handle these details *after* the exegesis of a particular book. If these problems are taken up at the beginning, before the students are immediately aware of the contents of the book, the presentation is much more difficult and the students' grasp more problematical.

A prerequisite for the courses in biblical theology must be at least two or three courses in the exegesis of the Old and New Testament. Biblical theology organizes the doctrine of the Bible into a logical sequence according to the concepts and thought-patterns of biblical writers. Just as scholastic theology demands a thorough acquaintance both with philosophy and with Christian religious truths, so biblical theology must presume some notion of biblical thought-patterns and a general knowledge of the contents of the Bible.

These courses in biblical theology are invaluable for teachers of sacred doctrine, because they alert them to the development of doctrine from the Old and New Testament and ensure an adequate handling of biblical texts.

The Sources of Sacred Doctrine

In his encyclical letter *Humani Generis* (August 12, 1950), Pope Pius XII laid down a norm that should guide every theological enterprise, whether research or teaching:

> It is also true that theologians must always return to the sources of divine revelation; for it belongs to them to point out how the doctrine of the living teaching authority is to be found either explicitly or implicitly in the Scriptures and tradition.
>
> Besides, each source of divinely revealed truth contains so many rich treasures of truth that they can never really be exhausted.
>
> Hence it is that theology through study of its sacred sources remains ever fresh; on the other hand, speculation which neglects a deeper search into the deposit of faith proves sterile, as we know from experience.

It is of capital importance that Catholic college students be made keenly aware of the Church as a living teacher, as the living voice of Christ, which sounds out today as clearly as it has done throughout the ages. Such an awareness can be communicated only by teachers who are equally aware of this voice and have an intimate acquaintance with the witnesses to it through the centuries.

We cannot doubt that Christ intended the apostles and their successors to carry on his work, proclaiming to all men the truth he had come to reveal and providing them with the powerful means of grace to follow that truth which he had won for them by his redemptive death. The Church is Christ in the world yesterday, today and tomorrow.

It would be misleading to overemphasize the conserving role of the Church in regard to truth and doctrine. Her primary function is to proclaim the word of God to men, but since this entails a serious obligation on men to accept her teaching, she must be certain that it is the word of *God*, which was communicated to the apostles by Christ and the Holy Spirit. The Church lays claim to no new revelation of truth after the death of the last apostle, St. John. The deposit of divine truth was completed then; the task of the successors of the apostles is to present *this truth* to the men of each age. This explains her intense interest in her traditional teaching. It is a fact that there are witnesses still intact that attest to the living teaching of the Church throughout the ages.

Of these the New Testament holds a place of special privilege for two reasons: first of all, it was written by men who were firsthand witnesses of the teaching of Jesus Christ and of the early Church (or, in the case of Mark and Luke, by their disciples and friends); secondly, it is a divinely inspired account, which means that it is God's own account, written through the instrumentality of human authors. The professors of theology in a training program for Catholic college teachers of sacred doctrine can warmly second the program outlined above for acquainting students with the text of the Bible, both the Old and the New Testament.

The next witness to the teaching of the Church, also enjoying a privileged position, is the official record of the acts of general councils held in conjunction with the Bishop of Rome (and even acts of provincial councils, approved by Rome) and the records of the official teaching of the Roman see, of the Roman pontiffs themselves and of the Roman Curia.

In the third place are the Fathers and Doctors of the Church: their authority as witnesses depends on the approval that the Church herself has bestowed upon them.

There is also the liturgy, both in its present form and in its historical development. The liturgy, which is the public worship of the Church, has always been carefully supervised by ecclesiastical authority, and hence it is presumed to be a faithful witness to the teaching of the Church.

Lastly, there are the theologians and ecclesiastical writers (canon lawyers, Scripture scholars, historians, etc.) who have received the approval of the Church.

Of the documents that witness to the living teaching of the Church, special emphasis should be placed in the training of Catholic college teachers on the encyclicals and other statements of the present Holy Father, of his predecessors, especially Pius XII, and of the Roman Congregations. The material contained in these documents should be utilized, not only in the theology courses themselves, but should be called to the attention of teachers in every department of the college by the members of the theology department, so that they in turn may acquaint themselves and their students with the thought of the Church on questions of the natural sciences, history, the social sciences and the liberal and fine arts.

The following is a summary of what the Catholic teacher may expect to find in these documents:

1. An infallible doctrine defined by the Holy Father (never a congregation) exercising his solemn *magisterium.*

2. Many statements of infallible doctrine according to his ordinary *magisterium,* truths that are universally accepted in the Church as revealed by God.

3. Many statements that are guaranteed by his prudential authority concerning truths that are not of faith, yet must be held as certain by Catholics.

4. Many condemnations of errors in various fields of human thought, to which the faithful must give real internal assent.

5. Many truths of a philosophical character, which enjoy a special authority, since they are truths established by the philosophy of St. Thomas, who enjoys special authority in the Church.

6. Many statements concerning human sciences and arts that do not engage the pontifical authority in any way, but bear witness to the breadth of the pontiff's knowledge and the careful patience of his research. These statements, moreover, are always made in the light of traditional Catholic thought both theological and philosophical.

Dogmatic and Moral Theology

No apology is needed for using the *Summa Theologiae* of St. Thomas in both dogmatic and moral theology courses. It is important, however, to stress for the students just what the *Summa* is and is not.

Mastery of the *Summa* is not a substitute for the beatific vision; we must always be reminded that our knowledge of God, scientific or mystical, is not a univocal knowledge of God. Yet the knowledge communicated in the *Summa* and the love of divine reality inspired by the knowledge will find its culmination in the vision of God. The *Summa* is not the faith. Theoretically, the assent of faith is the minimum requirement for theological inquiry; in fact, no one can fully possess the wisdom of the *Summa* without a lively faith, an ardent hope and a deep love. On the surface, the *Summa* is a work of continual analysis, of pulling apart and carefully scrutinizing all the elements of divine revelation; essentially it is a work of synthesis, the analysis being only a necessary preliminary. The synthetic character of the *Summa* is lost unless one follows the order which is St. Thomas' greatest achievement, and this can be found only in the text of the *Summa* itself. Ultimately, however, the synthesis must be accomplished by strictly supernatural means, an exercise of the theological virtues, if the *Summa* is not to remain a purely abstract pattern, a prestidigious exercise in logic and metaphysics.

Moreover, the *Summa* is not theology; otherwise, the Fathers and Doctors of the Church, St. Bonaventure, St. Albert, Scotus and Suarez, would not be theologians. The *Summa* is, in fact, and in the reiterated judgment of the Church, the supreme achievement of the human mind in the realm of theology. It is the culmination of the process begun under the inspiration of the Holy Spirit in some of the final books of the Old Testament, and notably in the writings of St. Paul and St. John in the New Testament. It is the fruit of the infallibly directed efforts of the Fathers and Doctors of the Church to penetrate the intelligibility of divine revelation.[23]

Finally, we must note that the *Summa* is not finished. This is true not only of the part that was not written, but also of the part that was. Intimate acquaintance with the work of St. Thomas makes the student realize that he constantly strove to establish his thought on the strong foundations of the living teaching of the Church, the inspired words of Sacred Scripture, and the traditional teaching of the *magisterium* and the fathers. We are in a much more advantageous position than St. Thomas with regard to all these sources of sacred doctrine. The Church has continued to teach in a more explicit way many of the truths contained in divine revelation; we are witnessing tremendous progress in biblical studies; the texts of the Fathers are more available and more accurately edited than ever before.

Granted the tremendous contribution made by the developing doctrinal teaching of the *magisterium,* the renewal of interest in the word of God, the many studies being done in patristics and the liturgy, it remains true that the basic insights, the overall order and the theological formulations of the great truths of divine revelation as found in the *Summa* retain all their validity and timeliness and are as necessary today for the formation of a theologian or a teacher of theology according to the mind of the Church as they have been since St. Thomas first produced his magnificient synthesis.

That this is as true in moral theology as in dogma is born out by the following observations.*

Regardless of how one attempts to teach theology—and this will be determined ultimately by the character, temperament, dispositions and preparation of the students—the teacher ought to possess theology as an intellectual habit acquired by the use of scientific methods as traditionally understood. In moral theology as in dogmatic, the teaching of the Church is of first concern. This is the doctrine to be defended, explained, drawn out and applied. For the doctrine to be possessed in a rational way, there is no possible substitute for the study of moral theology through the *Summa* of St. Thomas. It is difficult, but rewarding. The orderly application of the most basic practical principles to constantly new problems gradually brings order out of what would otherwise be chaos. Experience shows that time after time, religious and laywomen grow more and more reverent by this study in their attitude to the Church's teaching and to the mastery of St. Thomas; most of the students become more and more prayerful and even contemplative. If this is genuine, it comes indispensably and primarily from God; yet at the same time this way of studying moral theology is an occasion of meditation and self-examination that is also called for on man's side.

St. Thomas never loses sight of the first great practical truth: the good to be supremely sought above all things, in everything we do, towards which our whole lives must be uncompromisingly aimed, the infinite Good which is the Divine Beatitude that beatifies us also. Our supernatural intention to have this good is charity, and it pervades all that St. Thomas has to say in the entire second part of the *Summa*. The resources of Holy Scripture (and, to a lesser extent, the teaching of the Fathers) must be brought as prominently as possible into the theological exercise. The importance of using the mind to understand or conclude to the variously graduated principles of the

*These were contributed by the Rev. Leo A. Arnoult, O.P., who has been Professor of Moral and Spiritual Theology at St. Mary's School of Theology since its inception some fifteen years ago.

natural law; the necessity of using our reason as well as we can in order to discover what is good and what is to be done concretely—all of which comes under the head of motivating virtuous conduct—is something that has been largely neglected in even some Catholic presentations of morals, and has been neglected or despised in other circles. The Thomistic presentation of the doctrine on the gifts, beatitudes and fruits will surely in the end protect us from the notion that Christian moral doctrine, as found in St. Thomas, is ultimately Aristotelian ethics.

No matter what decision is taken about the way the courses of moral theology should be shaped, content wise, for the college—that is, just how much should we hope to communicate, whether it should be taught scientifically or humanistically—the main concern should be to try to get the people who are to teach college theology to possess the doctrine in a broad, well-rounded and sure-handed fashion. Until a person has gotten a firm hold on all the great roots of moral theology, he should not be trusted in a college classroom. This cannot be assured by giving them theology solely or principally in a humanistic mode.

* * *

These words written by Fr. Arnoult have received confirmation from the highest authority in the Church. In an address to the Fifth International Thomistic Congress held at Rome, Pope John XXIII presented his thoughts on St. Thomas' moral teaching and explicitly desired that it be communicated to the laity as well as seminarians. The following are two excerpts from the address:

> The first remark We are led to make is this: Aquinas' moral teaching, while it seems to strive for only one proximately determined end (namely, an investigation of the nature of things), whenever its higher purpose is traced, always aims at disposing men for the sure and perfect attainment of their supreme supernatural end—their eternal happiness.
>
> Wherefore, We strongly desire a daily increase in the number of those who draw light and instruction for themselves from the works of the Angelic Doctor; moreover, these should be, not only priests and learned scholars, but also students of all the arts and sciences; especially, We wish to see more young graduates who are enrolled

in the various ranks of Catholic Action. Finally, we earnestly desire that the treasure, as it were, of St. Thomas' precepts be unearthed ever more abundantly, to the great profit of Christendom, that his writings be published more widely among the people, in such a way that method of procedure and choice of language should in no way be at odds with the temper and character of our day.[24]

Subsidiary Courses and Electives

A training program for teachers of sacred doctrine can be inspired by the *ratio studiorum* of the Church without necessarily reproducing all of its features. It is especially in the subsidiary courses and the electives that greater liberty of emphasis should be adopted. Nevertheless, two courses that find place in the *ratio* are also invaluable for the prospective college teacher. A course in spiritual theology, embracing both ascetical and mystical theology, should be a fitting climax to the course in Thomistic moral theology.

A strong course in Church history is also advisable. It should aid the student to trace the march of the people of God through the ages since their manifestation to the world as a Church on Pentecost, emphasizing not so much dates and details, but the broad outline of the relations between the Church and the world. Above all, it should not be undertaken in an apologetic spirit, concerned to give historical evidence against the false accusations of outsiders, but should, without glossing over the weaknesses, bring a proud conviction and joy in the achievements of the Church under the guidance of the Holy Spirit.

Two other subsidiary courses might be explicitly included, canon law and liturgy. Since it would be out of the question to attempt anything like a complete course in canon law, it is better to omit it. The professor of moral theology will have an opportunity to explain the nature of ecclesiastical law in connection with the treatise on law in the *Summa*. Perhaps he could also consider the Code at this time, and an explanation of its format could be included. The legislation of the Church on the sacrements is best considered in connection with the sacraments themselves. Such referals to the Code can be made in a manner of treatises to give the students a sufficient acquaintance with the work itself.

A special course in the liturgy is also not a necessity. The theology of the liturgy can be investigated in connection with the virtue of religion. A further penetration of the liturgy can be given in the course on the sacraments. In fact, every course should draw on the liturgy as a witness to the faith and life of the Church in a particular mystery under consideration.

Elective courses should be planned with the greatest freedom; in these it should be possible to face the more immediate problems of the teacher of sacred doctrine in the Catholic college. Courses in contemporary Protestant thought and in the theology of the lay apostolate, for example, would be helpful. From the viewpoint of a deeper penetration of the thought of St. Thomas, some electives could be devoted to the great questions of philosophy that have been integrated into his theological system. Questions of logic and natural philosophy are of more help in following the *Summa* than those of metaphysics cut loose from its moorings in the humbler fields of philosophical speculation.

Reading Seminar and Research Project

These are the final instruments for the preparation of the teacher. Here again freedom is the norm. It has been found helpful to devote the reading seminar to the great classics of the theological tradition. Here the student can be brought into immediate contact with the Fathers of the Church, theologians of the schools, important modern contributions to theological thought. Of course, it need not be a *reading* seminar. The professor may wish to use it to initiate students into theological research by concentrating on a field in which he himself is working.

The research project is preferable to a dissertation. The copious quotations given in a previous section express the position of the author on this question. The student who is preparing to undertake the broad and liberalizing task of communicating divine wisdom to college students should be granted great freedom to develop a fairly broad problem in theology through much reading and critical thought, without the compulsion of producing in writing something that is completely original.

Environment

We have already pointed out that the thorough training of a theology teacher depends to a great extent on the vitality of his supernatural life. While the study of theology, as outlined above, does contribute to the deepening of one's spiritual life, it is study, and there is always the danger that the supernatural element will be neglected under the strain of simply getting the matter.

A theology program should provide students with safeguards against falling into this temptation. While we may have seemed to neglect the liturgy as a subject of study, it should be lived by the students in their daily lives. Opportunities for participating in the Holy Sacrifice, the formation of a liturgical choir from their number, homilies and conferences by the same professors who teach them should be added to the program. Provision for monthly days of recollection should also be made. Ample opportunity for confession and spiritual direction should be provided.

Despite the pressure of studies, in all probability the years devoted to theology will be a precious respite from the busy round of activities the students have had before they came to school or that they will be engaged in after they obtain their degree. Most students appreciate the opportunity as a precious gift from God.

Conclusion

In concluding, let us return to the set of distinctions that were cited at the beginning of this chapter, the distinction between subjective integration and objective integration, on the one hand; and the distinction between the humanistic and scientific approaches to theology on the other.

The first distinction is useful and valid, if properly understood. I take subjective integration to mean the integral effort in a subject responsive to the demands of divine revelation. These demands, however, are not dictated by the irrational will of God to be fulfilled by a blind obedience on the part of the subject: "No longer do I call you servants, because the servant does not know what his master does. But I have called you friends, because all things that I have heard from my Father, I have made known to you" (John 15:15).

This means that in connection with the demands on the subject God has revealed in an intelligible way (objectively) the reasons for these demands, which are in fact a vast realm of supernatural truth about God himself and the relation of all things to God.

In the final analysis, subjective integration is the most important thing in this life. "It is better to love God here below than to know him," is the way St. Thomas puts it.

Subjective integration is the work of a lifetime. It depends upon the unique character of each man, the environment in which he is placed, and, above all, on the training he receives in the life of virtue. It begins from his earliest childhood, during which most of the emphasis is on subjective integration. Yet even the First Communion catechism is an initial and initiating attempt at objective integration.

Perfect subjective integration is in this life an unattainable ideal except through an extraordinary grace of God. Yet it is an ideal for which every Christian must strive. In effect, perfect subjective integration means that the individual responds with an act that is both naturally and supernaturally virtuous in every situation in which he finds himself.

If a student arrives in college without the degree of subjective integration that might be expected of him, he needs to be converted, he needs spiritual direction. A course in theology will not suffice. The subjective integration of each student is unique; one cannot plan a theology course on that basis.

If there is an objective integration within the faith (and who can doubt it), the college is the place to present it in all its force to the Catholic student. A mature insight into the objective validity and coherence of the teachings of the Church is precisely the thing that will inspire the students to continue working for subjective integration.

On the supposition that the majority of students entering a Catholic college have attained a certain degree of subjective integration, the college certainly cannot overlook its obligation to foster further development. Yet this is not the special task of the theology department as such, nor is it the primary task of the college as an academic community. Yet as a Catholic college, it is, for all practical purposes, the home and the parish of its students for four years, and the whole atmosphere and intellectual activity of the place must conduce to growth in virtuous living, to subjective integration.

The second distinction, between the "humanistic" and the "scientific" approach to theology is, I fear, not a very happy one. It certainly does not coincide with the distinction between subjective and objective integration, as we understand it. Moreover, it is misleading because of the ambiguity of the term humanistic. Certainly, those who use it do not wish to employ it in its strict (and only really useful) meaning, as indicating a relation to the humanists of the Renaissance—their outlook, their education philosophy, their bookishness, and so forth. In this sense, it can be truly distinguished from "scientific."

According to Fr. Mooney, quoted above, the "humanistic" approach communicates "an abiding vision of human life and work."[25] If, now, this is distinct from the scientific approach, are we not led to the conclusion that Plato's is a human achievement and Aristotle's is not, that St. Augustine is human, the *Summa* is not, that Dante's *Divina Commedia* is human, Einstein's theory is not? Are we not contributing to the unfortunate tendency to deny humanizing value to science in both its traditional and contemporary meanings? We are denying to students, at any rate, in the most important area of human thought—faith seeking understanding in every possible mode—one of the greatest of human and humanizing achievements, which is enshrined in a work called the *Summa Theologiae*.

Footnotes to Study 13

[1]"[The Church] injects into the educational process itself a totally new approach to reality in the order of knowledge, an approach of which she alone is custodian. This is her theology. . . . In keeping with the objectives of the American college she will not present this intellectual discipline to the student as she herself has elaborated it, in the scholastic and speculative framework so heavily freighted with metaphysics. . . . Such an approach, moreover, cannot orientate the student toward his function in the Church, nor is it capable of satisfying his deepest spiritual needs. For what the undergraduate needs and seeks is some ultimate frame of reference for the countless intellectual and emotional stimuli involved in the maturing process called college, some

subjective integration of all those vital forces which the development of his natural powers has suddenly released within him. . . . Hence on the college level the Church will present her intellectual discipline humanistically, as an abiding vision of human life and work, so that the student will have a rational basis for reacting in a Christian fashion to the society in which he finds himself." Christopher Mooney, "College Theology and Education," in *Thought,* XXXIV (1959), 328-329.

[2]David Baroff, "American Fetish: The College Degree," *New York Times Magazine,* Jan. 14, 1960, 61.

[3]J. Edward Dirks, "Trends in Teaching Religion in Independent and Church-related Colleges and Universities," in *Religious Education,* LIV (1959), 168. In reply to a query, the author kindly responded: "On the matter of the terminology employed in the sentence you quote, I will try to clarify. The overwhelming number of permanently appointed professors of religion in these colleges and universities are persons who hold doctoral degrees, most of them Ph.D. and some Th.D. In addition, almost all of them hold degrees in theological studies, normally the kind of degrees also held by parish ministers, the B.D. or the Th.B., the kind of degrees awarded by theological seminaries. There are, of course, among the younger teachers a number of persons who hold the B.D. degree from a seminary, and an M.A. in religion from a graduate school of theology or, if not an actual M.A. degree, are finishing requirements for a Ph.D. or a Th.D. degree in some similar institution. . . . Very few, and a decreasing number, terminate with a degree that is prior to the doctorate."

[4]Review of *Proceedings of The Society of Catholic College Teachers of Sacred Doctrine,* 1959, in *Catholic Biblical Quarterly,* XXI (1959), 385.

[5]Cf. footnote 3.

[6]"Towards a Theology for Laymen," *Theological Studies,* V (1944) 43 ff., 340 ff.

[7]Father Murray's articles were, quite unintentionally, a critique of the way theology has been taught in seminaries. They are an early and important contribution to the debate on the lack of intellectual achievement among American Catholics.

[8]Father Edwin G. Kaiser, C.PP.S., has pointed out that such an integral concept of theology stems from St. Augustine. Cf. *Sacred Doctrine* (Westminster, Md.: Newman, 1958), 6.

[9]Anyone concerned with the finalities of sacred doctrine in Catholic colleges would profit by being mindful of the careful distinctions and useful conclusions proposed by Martin Hopkins, O.P., in "The Lay Apostolate vs. the Lay Vocation," which appeared in *Anima* (Catholic Action Office, Notre Dame, Ind.): "1. *The lay vocation*: This consists in the fulfillment of the duties of one's state in life. . . . This is the layman's vocation, his inalienable task, in which he alone is competent. But it is not the lay apostolate in the strict sense. 2. *The lay aposolate in the broad sense*: This is the contribution of those model Christians who fulfill the duties of their state in life so perfectly that their good example overflows into their environment. . . . The Pope [Pius XII] called this the 'apostolate of prayer and personal example,' and concluded that it 'should be referred to as an apostolate only in the wide sense of the term.' 3. *The lay apostolate in the strict sense*: This is the official collaboration of the laity in the apostolate of the hierarchy. . . . Pius XII has made it abundantly clear that this apostolate is not binding on all Christians: 'The vocation to be an apostle is therefore not addressed to all alike,' and 'not all Christians are called to engage in the lay apostolate in the strict sense.'"

[10]Feb. 21, 1960, 14: "Too Many College Teachers Don't Teach," by John Q. Academesis. The author is concerned with a special manifestation of the research mania, as is clear from the following: "Research is one of the magic words in our vocabulary. It is the modern form of pioneering, the competitive

weapon in a rapidly changing society. To it management looks for increased profits; for labor it opens up vistas of greater ease and more leisure; to consumers it means even more refinements of living. It unlocks vaults of large foundations, and increasingly it emerges as the basis of national survival." Yet many of his observations have wider application.

[11]*Art. cit.*, 72.

[12]*Loc cit.*

[13]*Art cit.*, 76.

[14]*Loc. cit.*

[15]*Graduate Study for Future College Teachers*, ed. by Joseph Axelrod (Washington: American Council on Education, 1955).

[16]*Op. cit.*, 12.

[17]*Loc. cit.*

[18]*Op. cit.*, 13. Author's italics.

[19]*Op. cit.*, 15.

[20]*Op. cit.*, 19.

[21]For many reasons, the requirement at St. Mary's has been set at three years and three summer sessions. This arrangement has proven satisfactory to both the professors and the *students*. One eminent value should be noted: it has enabled St. Mary's to engage outstanding scholars as professors of Sacred Scripture, for all the courses in Sacred Scripture and biblical theology are given during the summer sessions.

[22]Cf., "An Instruction of the Biblical Commission: the Proper Way to Teach Sacred Scripture in Seminaries and Religious Houses," *Rome and the Study of Scripture* (St. Meinrad, Ind.: 1958), 152 ff.

[23]"We would risk, with Albright and others, one last statement which will doubtlessly seem to many enthusiasts for thinking along Hebraic lines to verge on heresy, but which seems to us inevitable and which the Fathers of the Church emphasized in the first place. The new stage of Western mankind attained by the Greeks with the discovery of being, of the abstract and necessary concept of the universality of reason, seems to present one of the last 'conditions' required on the part of man for the Incarnation. Without it, the human foundation for the universally valid proclamation of the Gospel would have been defective. There would have been lacking not only the appropriate means of expression, but also certain human experiences, certain structures of thought needed for grasping the meaning and import of the Christian universal." Hans Urs von Baltasar, "God Has Spoken in Human Language," in *The Liturgy and the Word of God* (Collegeville, Minn.: The Liturgical Press, 1959).

[24]Translated from the Latin text as printed in *L'Osservatore Romano*, September 18, 1960.

[25]Cf. footnote 1.